A READER'S GUIDE TO
THE NINETEENTH CENTURY BRITISH NOVEL

by Frederick R. Karl

A Reader's Guide to Joseph Conrad

*A Reader's Guide to Great Twentieth Century
English Novels (with Marvin Magalaner)*

The Quest (a novel)

The Contemporary English Novel

*An Age of Fiction: The Nineteenth
Century British Novel*

The Noonday Press A DIVISION OF
Farrar, Straus and Giroux, New York

Frederick R. Karl

A READER'S GUIDE TO
The Nineteenth Century British Novel
REVISED EDITION

originally published as AN AGE OF FICTION:
THE NINETEENTH CENTURY BRITISH NOVEL

ACKNOWLEDGMENTS

The author gratefully acknowledges use of copyrighted material from the following publications:
From "The Mayor of Casterbridge: *A New Fiction Defined," reprinted from* Modern Fiction Studies, *VI, No. 3, to the Purdue Research Foundation.*
From "Beauchamp's Career: *An English Ordeal," reprinted from* Nineteenth-Century Fiction, *XVI, No. 2, to the University of California Press.*
The author wishes to express his special gratitude to Professor John D. Rosenberg of Columbia University for his helpful comments on the manuscript. Any errors of fact or judgment are, of course, the author's.

For my Mother and Father,
Dot and Sid

Contents

A READER'S GUIDE TO
THE NINETEENTH CENTURY BRITISH NOVEL

ONE *An Age of Fiction*

The determined opposition to the Victorian novel within the last few decades has so diminished that we may now foresee an exaggerated swing of the critical pendulum. Critics and general readers who once embraced the contemporary novelist at the artistic expense of his Victorian counterpart have come to qualify both their praise and their disdain, although the discriminating reader never deserted Dickens, Thackeray, George Eliot, and Meredith for the equally rewarding Conrad, Lawrence, and Joyce. The more temperate and flexible readers of the English novel have always recognized that every major writer offers particular truths and that to argue that the novel with time and changing conditions "improves" is to destroy with pseudoscientific reasoning what should be supported with literary taste.

This is not of course to claim that "advances" do not occur: the work of any major novelist can, in one way, be measured by his difference from his predecessors and contemporaries. The quality of each writer, whether Jane Austen or James Joyce, is determined by what the writer is intrinsically and by what he adds to the novel, by the way the novel is refined to say something unique. Thus, certain novels of Dickens and Hardy were as unique in their day as was *Ulysses* in the 1920's and 30's. Nevertheless, preoccupied almost solely with what the novelist adds to the genre, several critics have tended to ignore the broader implications of the work of the nineteenth-century novelists; while, conversely, apologists for the Victorian novelist have often refused to grant deficiencies in their hero. Both groups by exaggerating their views have undermined their positions, one through obsession with form and symbol, the other through the need to counteract the first overstatement with another. As a social document, a moral structure, and a work of art, the novel from Defoe, Fielding, and Richardson through Jane Austen and Hardy generates the kind of realism that both creates the world it reflects and mirrors the world it creates. The novel is in the peculiar position of defining reality as no other art form does, and yet paradoxically it has, somehow, to avoid a direct representation of reality. The moral focus of the novel does not justify a course of action, but brings it under scrutiny and demonstrates the extent of human variety. Music, poetry, art do not address the same problem as the novel, for no matter how realistic they become, they still contain elements of artificiality. When we listen arbitrarily to sounds, we do not hear music; when we speak, we do not talk in poetry; when we observe phenomena, we do not see in the shape of paintings. When we approach these art forms, we encounter them as elements that recreate or distort reality; they are never the thing itself. When we read a novel, however, whether it be *Don Quixote* or *Ulysses,* we face real situations involving real people and real language. Distortions and originality there may be, but nevertheless a novel occurs at a certain time, in a certain place, with a certain cast of characters. These elements of the real, the substantial, and the solid are ever-present. Yet while the novelist must never lose sight of them, he still must disguise them. If they prevail, his work becomes realistic in the wrong sense; it is journalistic, ephemeral, superficial, not artistic.

In encountering the crucial issue of what is real and what is illusory, *Don Quixote* is in essence the first novel. Through the Don, Cervantes asks which is more real, the world of practicality and daily events, or the conceptual world, the world of fantasy and illusions, the world of imagination and art. Cervantes carries us back to the medieval mind which saw everything as symbol and emblem. The Don indeed sees real things, but chooses to ignore them in favor of his conception of them. Since, to him, the earthly object derives from the ideal heavenly or imaginative object, man's mind must vault phenomena to get at the real thing, to move behind the physical to the spiritual. Consequently, the Don's so-called madness is the madness of every artist who tells the reader or observer that *his* insights or metaphors are the stuff of reality rather than what the reader senses his own reality to be.

As an artist, the Don recreates the world in his own image, making his adventures into poetic metaphors that seem untruthful, even mad, upon analysis. The Don illustrates that he is concerned with more than social justice, although to seek justice is surely part of his quest. His true vocation, however, is to create a way of seeing, just as every novelist must transform reality into something both more and less than the original object. In his quest for this different kind of reality, the Don convinces nearly everyone, including the reader, that his vision is preferable to what he encounters, and that individual interpretations can never be dissociated from the real.

Like a poet, a revolutionary, a "sane madman," the Don forces a re-evaluation of one's assumptions, for his image-making mind is constantly reforming events. Even if we assert that his vision is mad, we cannot embrace what he denies. No matter how mad he is, his motives are altruistic, just, good; while those around him, neither all good nor bad, have the voice of the real, semi-corrupt world. Under his tutelage, we remember, Sancho progresses from a pleasant but greedy hanger-on to a just and shrewd governor.

Yet such is Cervantes' realistic insight into the ambiguous world he created that he knows that the Don and his metaphors must not prevail. No matter how superior his imagination is to reality, reality must triumph. The norm for Cervantes is a God-driven universe in which man must make a final choice between illusion and reality, as the Don himself does. And when man makes his choice, he sorrowfully rejects poetry and imagination, and then dies. Since Cervantes' is not a romantic view of things, man is not immortal; he must be reduced. Such is the tragic nature of the world, such is Unamuno's tragic sense of life. Man may heroically assume that he is more than he is, but inevitably he must return to body and substance and forgo his dreams.

What Cervantes says about the Don becomes a paradigm for the novel itself. No matter what metaphors the writer establishes— whether those of Earwicker's imaginative dreams in *Finnegans Wake* or Robinson Crusoe's more tepid premonitions on his island —the ultimate effect heightens reality without rejecting it. In *Don*

Quixote, the scene in the Cave of Montesinos (Chapter 23, Part II) is so significant because there the Don has to maintain his role as artist (novelist) at the same time he is aware of the illusory nature of his experience below ground. As he later tells Sancho, he will protect Sancho's illusions if Sancho will protect his. So the novelist makes a pact with the reader, who must suspend both his belief and disbelief and allow himself to be transported into a world he knows, logically, is untrue.

To effect this condition, every eighteenth-century novelist, no matter how conservative, attempted to mask the real nature of his material, or, conversely, to reveal the real nature of his material. From Defoe's reliance on "true history" and Richardson's on the epistolary method to Fielding's emphasis on the episodic narrative and Sterne's on the breakup of plot, the novelist, like the Don, imposed a particular kind of vision upon daily events. Jane Austen herself, with her essentially classical approach to fiction, employed irony to take the edge off a directly moralistic treatment of man's imperfections.

The eighteenth-century English novel, to which Jane Austen, Dickens, and Thackeray were much indebted—a debt that extended also to Meredith (through Dickens) and to George Eliot (through Jane Austen)—provided the principal form and substance of what we now know as the novel. Our use of the term "novel," as Ian Watt has remarked, did not arise until near the end of the eighteenth century, although the content itself was formed earlier in the century by Defoe, Richardson, Fielding, and Smollett. The dominant form of the novel was realism, defined not only by the kind of life it represented (individualized people, everyday affairs, material concerns) but by the way it presented it (denotative prose, use of clock and calendar time, solidity of setting, details of dress). In Defoe, early in the century, we see an emphasis upon particularity and individuality of situation, detail, language, a reliance upon real time. In Richardson, we see even more clearly the stress upon a single person in a trying situation, the analysis of which becomes the plot of the novel. In part contrary to Richardson's practice, we find in *Tom Jones* a prose comic epic that assumes the importance of plot over character and of normal life over heroic action. But while Fielding appears to have influenced novels as diverse as *Pickwick Papers* and *Vanity Fair,* it is really Richardson who became the chief literary influence on the nineteenth-century novel.

Although Defoe had particularized man in his physical setting and had also used language realistically, Richardson—that bourgeois author of conduct-books—evolved the novel of character, morals, and sentiment. The conflict of social behavior in every nineteenth-century author from Jane Austen through George Meredith is suggested in Pamela's reward for virtuous behavior in the face of temptation. Furthermore, the strong moralism implicit in Pamela's defense, a mixture of exemplum and embonpoint, was especially to appeal to nineteenth-century writers restricted by a middle-class reading public. Although Pamela lacks Elizabeth Bennet's penetrating wit, her independence and self-sufficiency under trial identify her as possessing the mettle of a Jane Austen heroine. Jane Austen, who began writing seriously less than four decades after Richardson's death, also found in Sir Charles Grandison, the virtuous hero of Richardson's last novel, a model for several of her male characters—Knightley, Edmund Bertram, Captain Wentworth. In Darcy himself, once his pride has been defeated, we see a less athletic Mr. B. (*Pamela*), a less egoistic and sadistic Lovelace (*Clarissa*).

But if Richardson's mise en scène seems restricted, then it is in Fielding that we find a greater range of situation and a more flexible morality. Jane Austen found in Fielding's novels the irony so congenial to her own nature, although his unconventionality did not suit her temperament. Close to Richardson on moral issues and on norms of behavior, Jane Austen and her successors were to make Fielding's sense of mockery and parody into a dangerous social weapon. The fact that Richardson's epistolary style does not reappear in the major nineteenth-century novels indicates that while his ideas and attitudes had been absorbed into the mainstream of fiction his methods were uncongenial. Fielding's use of dialogue to reveal character was more suitable, reaching its most effective usage in Dickens' novels, wherein conversational idiom is character. In Jane Austen, who, in many ways, provides that elusive creature, the transitional figure, the main characters also reveal themselves in their talk. Like Henry James later, Jane Austen early recognized that emotional significance can replace dramatic violence, and incisiveness of character and situation the discursiveness of the romantic novelist. Through the dramatization of short scenes, she intermixed Fielding's reliance on plot with Richardson's realistic analysis of character. This became, with varying revisions, the dominant mode of nineteenth-century realism.

The main influences on the later novel came predominantly from the first half of the eighteenth century; Defoe was dead in 1731, Fielding in 1754, Richardson in 1761, and Smollett ten years later. In the latter half of the century, the novel faltered and sprayed its energies in a series of minor efforts: the novel of sensibility, the Gothic romance, the novel of sentiment (an extension of Richardson and Sterne), all of which Jane Austen satirized directly in *Sense and Sensibility* and *Northanger Abbey* and indirectly in her other works. At this time, from about 1760 through 1795, the novel was a relatively unstable commodity. Since it did not have the standing of either poetry or drama, the novelist himself was considered slightly disreputable, an opportunist of a sort. It is not surprising that few novelists took their work seriously or deemed themselves professionals. In her close study of the popular novel in England (1770-1800), Dr. J. M. S. Tompkins asserts that during the years "that follow the death of Smollett [1771], last of the four great novelists of the mid-eighteenth century, the two chief facts about the novel are its popularity as a form of entertainment and its inferiority as a form of art." Later she comments that "the business of the novel was to teach those who by nature and upbringing were unqualified for serious study."

The novel, in brief, had become more a means to something else than a unified narrative with developed characters and an "artistic" intent. The composition of the reading public was itself undergoing several shifts, and this fact had a great deal to do with the changing tastes in fiction. In the second half of the eighteenth century, the reading public became a modern one, that is, one no longer united in common tastes or assumptions, or rooted in a common tradition, as the public once fixed in Augustan principles of order and objectivity or an earlier one based on the recognition of religious revelation. The relative success of *Pamela* in the 1740's already signalled the change in tastes, with its popular theme of the successful servant girl and its reliance upon sentiment rather than classical impersonality. After his *Shamela* failed to stem the popularity of *Pamela,* Fielding tried to retain the classical virtues by stressing the epic theme, but his style (plot over character) was not to be influential until the following century. The new reading public was not sophisticated, but, in part, a semi-literate one— particularly servants—who demanded what *Pamela* provided. On the other hand, the growing merchant class demanded *its* kind of fiction, one based on practical virtue, not metaphysical truths, and the several circulating libraries near the end of the century catered to these tastes.

Both groups found their desires satisfied in the so-called novel of sensibility, which, like Methodism and Romantic poetry, elicited compassion and suffering. As Walter Allen remarked, this attitude, one in which the reader is easily moved by the pathetic, leads to morbidity, which becomes an end in itself; and reality "is sought only as a stimulus to the exercise of sensibility." Sensibility in itself is not of course to be decried, especially when, as in Fielding, Smollett, and Sterne, it is underlaid by strong doses of humor: Jane Austen was concerned not with sensibility alone but with the wrong kind which led to immoderate and ludicrous decisions— thus her fun at Marianne Dashwood's expense in *Sense and Sensibility.* Novelists like Henry Brooke (*The Fool of Quality*), Henry Mackenzie (*The Man of Feeling*), and Oliver Goldsmith (*The Vicar of Wakefield*) were to cultivate sensibility for itself, often to the exclusion of reason.

This preoccupation with single modes of behavior had its counterpart in the Gothic novel and its emphasis upon a terror-filled past. Walpole's *Castle of Otranto* in 1764, with its synthetic emotions, its unintentionally funny morbidity, its stress upon omens and outlandish horrors, set the style for novelists like Clara Reeve, Mrs. Radcliffe, and "Monk" Lewis. Their excesses are parodied in Jane Austen's *Northanger Abbey,* and the Gothic novel as such seemed to disappear in the early nineteenth century, except perhaps for Maturin's *Melmoth the Wanderer* in 1820.* In Mary

---

* The Gothic novel did not of course spring ready-made from Walpole, nor did it always manifest uniform qualities. Prior to and contemporaneous with *The Castle of Otranto* was a considerable body of literature which we can

Shelley's *Frankenstein* (1818) and Emily Brontë's *Wuthering Heights* (1847), the mode was considerably qualified. With its stress upon the ghostliness of a supernatural past, the Gothic novel was absorbed into Romantic poetry and the Romantic novel, becoming

identify as Gothic in tone: the supernatural elements of the ballad, the eerie quality of the epic, the extravagance and violence of Elizabethan drama (now being revived), the wildness of pagan Europe caught in Ossian (1760-63) and slightly later in Percy's *Reliques* (1765), the exoticism of Oriental and Near Eastern tales, the excesses of the chivalric romance, the death-orientation of Graveyard Poetry (Young's *Night Thoughts*, 1742; Blair's *The Grave*, 1743; Gray's *Elegy*, 1751), the Rousseauistic admiration for frenzied and disordered nature (manifest in the planned irregularity of English gardens). All these forces and interests operated as emotional counters to the realism of the main tradition of the novel in Fielding, Richardson, and Smollett, although the latter in *Ferdinand Count Fathom* (1753) provided a link between realism and Gothic; and Richardson himself in *Clarissa* suggested the darknesses and terrors peculiar to the later form. Clarissa dreams of being stabbed (raped) by Lovelace in a churchyard and then tumbled into a deep grave and trampled beneath his feet.

As Gothic developed, it gained in excesses and horrors, so that Mrs. Radcliffe (in *A Sicilian Romance*, 1790; *The Romance of the Forest*, 1792; *The Mysteries of Udolpho*, 1794; *The Italian*, 1797) is no more like Matthew Lewis (*The Monk*, 1795; *The Bravo of Venice*, 1804) or Charles Maturin than Jane Austen seems like Thomas Hardy. Mrs. Radcliffe's genteel scenes of eeriness contrast sharply with Lewis's and Maturin's masochistic-sadistic images of torture and brutality in which pain and pleasure blend imperceptibly into each other in one long blood-bath. Calculated to thrill and excite, popular fiction of the early nineteenth century continued the macabre tradition. (See E. S. Turner's *Boys Will Be Boys*).

In the later nineteenth century, Gothic reappeared directly not only in Dickens' unfinished *The Mystery of Edwin Drood* (1870), but in the work of the man who influenced that and earlier Dickens novels, Wilkie Collins. In *Basil* (1852), *The Woman in White* (1860), *Armadale* (1866), and *The Moonstone* (1868), Collins demonstrated that he was heir to the atmospheric devices of Mrs. Radcliffe, the sensationalism of the Newgate novels of Bulwer-Lytton and Ainsworth, and the melodramatic tensions of Poe. Like the afore-mentioned Gothic writers—and here unlike Dickens—Collins stressed story-telling at the expense of characterization, comment, humor, even cogent psychology. The thread of mystery is all. As he wrote in the Preface to *The Woman in White*:

> I have always held the old-fashioned opinion that the primary object of a work of fiction should be to tell a story; and I have never believed that the novelist who properly performed this first condition of his art

re-evident in Scott's evocation of a historical past and in Dickens's obsessive emphases upon prisons and criminals.

By the time Jane Austen began to write in the mid-1790's, she had been nurtured on the Gothic romance and the novel of sensibility, although amidst their extravagance the novels of Fanny Burney and William Godwin (*Caleb Williams*, 1794) explored new areas. Fanny Burney in particular was trying to write a novel without excesses; in the Preface to *Evelina* (1778), she stated her intentions, which while obvious now did help clear the way for several major novelists who followed. (One need only compare her statement with George Eliot's in *Adam Bede* [Chapter XVII, "In Which the Story Pauses a Little"]):

Let me, therefore, prepare for disappointment those who, in the perusal of these sheets, entertain the gentle expectation of being transported to the fantastic regions of Romance, where Fiction is coloured by all the gay tints of luxurious Imagination, where Reason is an outcast, and where the sublimity of the Marvellous, rejects all aid from sober Probability. The heroine of these memoirs, young, artless, and inexperienced, is

No faultless Monster, that the world ne'er saw, but the offspring of Nature, and of Nature in her simplest attire.

We find here Richardson's ideas reappearing, and it comes as no surprise that Fanny Burney cast her novel in epistolary form backed by a conscious moralizing attitude. Her subject, like that of *Pamela*, is the triumph of a virtuous young woman in the face of temptation, however superficial Evelina's temptation may seem compared with Pamela's (and Clarissa's). Although Fanny Burney retained elements of sentimentality from the novel of sensibility, especially in the emotion-filled letters of the Reverend Mr. Villars

---

was in danger, on that account, of neglecting the delineation of character—for this plain reason, that the effect produced by any narrative of events is essentially dependent, not on the events themselves, but on the human interest which is directly connected with them.

From Collins' work to the modern detective story is not distant, although a writer like Graham Greene—and Dostoyevsky and Conrad before him—further transformed the Gothic-and-mystery elements into narratives bearing a philosophical, even a doctrinal, weight.

to his ward, nevertheless she was able to objectify her subject and create some memorable minor characters.

The kind of sensibility demonstrated in Fanny Burney's novels was to carry over into the nineteenth century, and her type of heroine—sweet, amiable, sensible, somewhat naive, yet vain enough to know her worth—was to reappear throughout the following century as often as Jane Austen's independent and knowledgeable heroines. By the turn of the nineteenth century, despite the excesses indicated above, the outlines of the genre were becoming firmer: Jane Austen was to indicate one direction and Scott the other. The latter's romances absorbed the Gothic elements and excesses of sensibility; Jane Austen carried on the classical tradition while redirecting the novel of sentiment into the mainstream of Victorian realism. Her classical awareness of form, however, was less important in the Romantic Age than her use of reason and wit in writing about romantic topics. Jane Austen's views prevailed in the nineteenth century in a permanent way denied Scott's, although his immediate influence, unlike hers, was immense. Her reasonableness and comic awareness, rather than his historical imaginative, became the norm, and the kind of moralizing implicit in her plots fitted the views of the rapidly growing middle class audience of later years.

One of the curiosities of literature is that at the very time Rousseauistic sentimental humanism was so strongly evident in the English Romantic poets, Jane Austen was working the opposing stream of realism. Only with Dickens's major fiction did the two streams become absorbed into each other to form the prevailing tone of romantic realism that then predominated in the nineteenth-century English novel until Hardy.

While the novels of the eighteenth and nineteenth centuries do have several important similarities, the emphasis on a common tradition should not destroy the real differences between them. One tends to group novelists for the sake of labeling them and moving them around, although their divergences are obviously greater than their similarities. One of the chief differences lies in the responsibilities each century places upon its writers. The nineteenth-century novelist not only faced a more severely changing world, but—along with the prophets and poets—found himself in a greater position of importance.

The serious novelist was becoming increasingly aware of his "role" in society, and the novel itself was becoming socially conscious in a way rarely attained previously. Taking on the qualities of a sermon and an entertainment, the novel reflected the main issues of the day: rapid industrial and commercial growth, passage of democratic legislation and the establishment of democratic institutions, migration to the cities, Benthamite legislation, Evangelical piety and philanthropy, the Oxford Movement, the "new science," the social consequences of evolution, the conflict between faith and doubt. A list of issues always sounds dry, yet such was the economic and social barbarism of the age—in a professedly Christian society—that many responses were shrieks of outrage and abuse.

Although most nineteenth-century novelists were not, categorically, social critics, nevertheless to read the novel from Jane Austen to Thomas Hardy is to gain the flavor and substance of nineteenth-century social, political, and cultural life in a way no other literary mode can provide. Curiously enough, most of these issues—whether modified or not—remain significant in the twentieth century, although the contemporary novelist can no longer deal with specific issues in the same fashion as his predecessors. To find out what people really thought about their pressing problems, the reader must turn from the metaphysical concerns of the present-day writer to the particularities of the Victorian author.

In full bloom, the Victorian novel carried the genre through to its development: the modern novel becomes a modification and reassessment of what already existed, even when one allows for the broader range of subject matter and the greater technical facility of the contemporary novelist. If we find elements of Fielding and Smollett in Dickens, then we discover Dickens in Conrad and Lawrence. If Richardson reappears in Jane Austen, then the latter recurs in George Eliot, whose pastoral settings, along with Hardy's, are evident, once again, in Lawrence. And at the end of the major tradition is Joyce, taking bits and pieces from continental as well as English novelists, not the least of whom is Sterne and Dickens.

The crucial time for the English novel was clearly the nineteenth century, when it might have either flowered or degenerated into a minor and stunted form.

A large and voracious audience was now a ready market for the novelist who could meet its moral and cultural demands. W. P. Trent estimates that by the end of the eighteenth century there were perhaps 100,000 habitual readers upon whom the book-sellers and circulating libraries could count. In the nineteenth century itself, literacy outdistanced population growth by more than five to one. The Christmas annuals, the hundreds of sentimental novels, the "yellow backs" sold on railway stalls, the shilling number of a novel and then the shilling magazine, the rapid growth of circulating libraries, the prevalence of the three-decker novel —all of these resulted from catering to an audience that desired in fiction an "entertaining morality." There was also, even by mid-century, a basic optimism; if society were not progressing in a linear fashion, at least there was still the possibility of perfection, as the vast Crystal Palace of 1851 indicated. Faith was a positive attitude and not simply a defense against the unknowable, al-though Tennyson's *In Memoriam* heralded the new note of doubt. The novel responded, and at its worst, as in some of Bulwer-Lytton and Scott, it catered directly to the waiting audience. Even in the major novelists the spirit of compromise was evident, and Dickens, Thackeray, and Meredith, to name only three, worked artistically within what the century allowed: a Christian morality and a Christian view of sex.

At its best the novel demonstrated categorically the triumph of good over evil; and after mid-century only Hardy fully sensed the bleakness that would prevail once faith became an empty phrase and despair a commonplace of everyday life. George Eliot and Meredith still retained a belief, if not in progress and perfectibility, then in the ability of the individual to resurrect himself through self-knowledge. Thackeray maintained a basically sentimental view of life beneath his surface worldliness, and Dickens qualified his tragic view with happy endings. Only Hardy remained true to a world in which the ceremony of innocence is mocked and smashed. From the self-possessed and confident Jane Austen at the beginning of the century, we pass to Hardy, who recognized that life itself is destructive whether man is basically good or evil.

Perhaps nowhere more than in the development of the "hero" does the nineteenth-century novelist reveal his basic assumptions. In the previous century, Defoe had placed his main characters in a recognizable social setting, although he had paid only lip service to human psychology; much more interested in people's houses than in people, he created characters in his own image: rugged individualists with a Puritan (not puritanical) morality. Fielding gave his protagonists a different morality, but while emphasizing plot over character he was not so concerned with underlying motives as with surface wit and clarity. Unlike Robinson Crusoe, Tom Jones—the "new hero"—can enjoy his appetites as long as he remains basically decent, and can repent without severe suffering. Richardson, moving the emphasis from plot to character, made the heroine's success—indeed her survival—dependent upon her virtue. In contrast, Smollett stressed the undomesticated hero, the picaresque character whose bumptiousness or rascality masks a basically warm and realistic individual. In his hands, the narrative became full of "on the road" episodes, the kind of novel appropriate to rural settings unaffected by industrialization. Sterne himself wrote the first novel without a hero, the first novel without a plot. Like Thomas Amory's *Life and Opinions of John Buncle* (1756, 1766), Henry Brooke's *The Fool of Quality* (1766), and Henry Mackenzie's *The Man of Feeling* (1771), Sterne's *The Life and Opinions of Tristram Shandy* (1760-67) reduced all life to whimsy and all people to lovable, frail creatures. The hero is laughed out of existence. When he is five, a window almost destroys his manhood.

By the time Jane Austen began to write near the turn of the century, English traditions had weakened and the eighteenth-century gentleman—the redeemed Tom Jones, Squire Allworthy, Matthew Bramble, Walter Shandy, Mr. B., Lovelace—no longer held his undisputed position. The new moneyed classes and increased literacy created a new type of gentleman: the genteel man of attainments. The stress is now upon what a person is, not solely upon what he has been born into. The gentleman of attainments, further, becomes the sole person capable of holding back the encroaching vulgarity of the industrialized and commercialized middle class, which has no uniform standard of conduct.

It is on this frontier of change that Jane Austen places her batteries of wit and irony. Birth, income, and family tradition, while still important, nevertheless become of secondary significance: the man must still prove himself, for his reputation is not sufficient to make him palatable to a Jane Austen heroine. Like Evelina with Lord Orville, Elizabeth Bennet is not prepared to accept a proud (somewhat vulgar) Darcy, no less a Mr. B., whom she would mock for his pretensions to supremacy. Jane Austen's heroines themselves desire the kind of equality denied to the eighteenth-century woman, and they demand romantic love as well. Marriage must be prudent, dignified, and romantic. In brief, these clear-eyed girls stand as virtuous individuals with assertive rights. The male can be no undisputed conqueror; he must be civilized and domesticated, brought to heel *before* he offers his name and fortune. The picaresque hero now attends church on Sunday, sips tea in the afternoon, and spends long evenings at home looking through the latest books.

Jane Austen celebrates the rites of happy monogamy, and her standard was to prevail for nearly half a century, with the possible exception of *Wuthering Heights*. Furthermore, her break with the episodic eighteenth-century novel heralded a similar break throughout the century, although Dickens in *Pickwick* followed the form he knew best from his early reading; Thackeray also worked in a semi-episodic form in several of his novels, supplying recurring themes, however, to offset episodic stringiness.

In his sometimes valuable book, *The Hero in Eclipse in Victorian Fiction* (1956), Mario Praz develops the point that the Victorian stress on realism made the typical novelist similar to the seventeenth-century Dutch genre painters, who "domesticated" painting by reducing its size and heroism and making it suitable for middle class consumption. The novelist becomes a *Biedermeier,* or solid citizen, interested in goodness, pathos, morality, someone anxious to strike down aberrations and to mute dissonance. Since the novelist is socially democratic, the traditional hero—with his supremacy based on superior birth and position—is incongruous. The typical Victorian "hero," accordingly, reflects his times.

Less grand than his predecessors, he gains virtue from his common sense and compassion. He must be aware of a norm of behavior, as Jane Austen shows us, and if he departs he must be punished before being again accepted. If he departs too far, then he is incorrigible, and he must go into permanent exile or die. If, however, the hero honors social norms—that is, if he lacks ego and vanity—he can gain all, even though his birth and income may be relatively low.

The comic play of the Victorian novel becomes evident as a device for questioning existing standards and for creating social equality. In his essay on Comedy, Meredith remarked that the Comic Spirit would create equality between the sexes; but it does far more. It reveals, and in many cases, purges all anomalies of behavior—whether for good or ill. By exposing the egoistic, the vainglorious, and the snobbish, the Comic Spirit in a burst of ridicule discloses frailties and unmans the offender. As a side effect, unfortunately, it also discourages originality and imagination. In its pursuit of the personally gauche and the socially unacceptable, it tries to reduce all people to the level of social consistency. It leaves little room for the rebel or revolutionary. What Meredith calls the Comic Spirit, Jane Austen incorporated as irony, and the practice extends, in one form or another, through Dickens, Thackeray, and George Eliot, only to fade out and become meaningless in Hardy, who turned the Comic Spirit which mocks foolishness into the Universal Will that condemns all.

As we shall see, social comedy provided both the great strengths and apparent weaknesses of the novel in nineteenth-century England, indeed of the English novel (with few exceptions) virtually from its beginnings through Joyce Cary and Henry Green. It is a somewhat melancholy thought that until the work of Hardy and Conrad, almost the sole mode of tragedy in the English novel was Gothic. A good deal of the blandness—as well as the positive sense of life as lived—that we find in the novel is the result of its comic conventions. Tradition, history, customs, a past—all those elements that work only in time—are ever-present, and they are the substances that make comedy possible.

Unlike the American novel, the English novel principally takes place in time, not space. Obviously, the temporal novel is most often representative of an old and established culture. It is often a love story, for love is possible when time is plentiful. As soon as time becomes precious, however, love turns to lust. Further, temporal fiction is usually far more realistic than spatial fiction, which is frequently based on the assumption that moving on will bring something better. When the novelist works in a given locale and is aware of the weight of time, he can bring to bear a kind of comic social criticism that all must accept to survive. As soon as characters are given great mobility—as they are in many American novels—there are few common assumptions, and there is accordingly little room for comedy, or for tragedy either. Comedy, like tragedy, then, works on the sharing of suppositions which derive from common traditions. And both depend on time as a factor, for, as the past unfolds, these common assumptions gain the semblance of universal truths.

The major novel of space, on the other hand, is neither comic nor tragic. It conveys an altogether different mode of experience. It may indicate violence, the chase, lust, lurid adventures, chance affairs. It rarely contains solid marriages, mature love, normalizing behavior. It depends on rebellion, dissatisfaction, a sense of drift. The novel of time, conversely, makes possible the cohesion of people within commonly accepted institutions, and when we define comedy and tragedy we almost always do so within the realm of time considerations. As the English novel developed and heroism (tragedy) as a credible idea declined, comedy became entrenched as a major mode: a comedy played out in time.

Going further, one may well speculate that the lack of extremism in the English novel—the lack of violence which so clearly differentiates it from American, Russian, and (some) French fiction—results from its stress upon comedy. The converse may be equally true: that the stress upon comedy precludes extremism. If, as we have already seen, comedy works to bring deviates back to social norms, then extremism itself can be contained, or else discredited as a viable way of existence. The extremist, when he does exist, usually drifts away or dies of a broken heart; even Emily Brontë—hardly a comic novelist—follows this tradition with Heathcliff. Working in time as he does, the comic novelist allows little flexibility in his major characters. Only in his minor figures, where being "outside" does not seem to matter significantly, can he countenance controlled deviation and extremism. Thus we have the insipidity of so many male protagonists and their sweet ladies in the nineteenth-century novel, while the peripheral, minor figures generate excitement, interest, and humor.

The bourgeois novelist, like many Elizabethan dramatists, developed a double plot with a double standard. While the nineteenth-century audience required certain norms in its "heroes" and "heroines," it tolerantly relaxed these standards (rarely, however, in sexual matters) when the lower classes were concerned. For comic purposes, Dickens often exploited this double standard: gaining raucous fun from the economically deprived, but requiring respectability from his central characters. That he could deploy two such attitudes with both dignity and compassion is a mark of his genius. Similarly, George Eliot gained dramatic tensions from her upper-class characters while she exploited the humor of her peasants.

The comic writer obviously cannot tolerate traditional heroism; the hero depends for sustenance upon his ego, and ego is fair target for the darts of the Comic Spirit. Ego and its twin, Vanity, are the basis for the false gentleman, who loses his status when stringent standards of conduct are applied. Thus, Joe Gargery is more of a gentleman than Bentley Drummle, and Adam Bede more than Arthur Donnithorne. Money having become the great equalizer in a commercialized society, standards of excellence came to be based on intrinsic qualities, although a prudent heroine opted for both the true gentleman and a fortune. As Jane Austen demonstrated, prudence and romance are not necessarily alien to each other.

With the reduction of the romantic hero to smaller size, there followed a stress upon the details of everyday life. As the genre painters placed man in his setting, so too the nineteenth-century novelist identified his characters through an explicit and detailed background. Jane Austen's provincials—as later George Eliot's— are recognizable people whose lives fit their surroundings: a novel like *Mansfield Park* conveys the flavor of boredom on a respectable country estate, and *Pride and Prejudice* shows that marriage is the sole ritual of maturity when society provides little else for a girl to do. As closely as Jane Austen's characters are identified with their provincial background, so too Dickens's and Thackeray's characters act like city people. The spirit of place is very much a part of Victorian fiction, understandably so once the novel has lost its episodic nature and the action becomes rooted to a particular spot.

Language itself changed to suit the realistic presentation of characters and situations, the movement reaching its culmination in the unselfconscious dialect of George Eliot's and Thomas Hardy's provincials. As the hero becomes a commonplace character, his language loses the rhetorical flourishes and affectations common in the eighteenth century. Declamation turned to slang (Sam Weller), and speechifying to realistic dialogue (Adam Bede). Communication was established with a large public unaware of "pretty speech," one attuned to the colloquial language of a relatively urbanized existence.

Characters came to reveal themselves by their talk. Lacking a suitable psychological method and yet aware of the "inner man," the nineteenth-century novelist relied on conversation to disclose the unconscious. This is one reason perhaps why the Victorian novel is full of personalities and the Victorian character seems a person rather than an artificial or fictitious creation. Dickens's characters, for example, are close to the reader because their language reveals submerged details of their personality; they are, as it were, speaking directly to the reader. Although not all nineteenth-century novelists were as aware of their audience as was Dickens, most created intimacy of character and situation through the same personal device of realistic conversation. How different the twentieth-century novelist with his objectivity and impersonality, with his removal of his characters from daily life through symbol and suggestion!

The nineteenth-century novelist was interested in conveying the very feel of life in its details, and when taboos disallowed overt statement, he could suggest aberrations. Dickens, after all, created "Dostoyevskian" characters like Steerforth, Dolge Orlick, and Bradley Headstone; sometimes the Thames seemed to signify to him not commerce but death. Even sexual taboos became fixed only in the 1860's, probably the result of the increase in a middle-class reading public and Victoria's own moral stringency. The 1840's and 1850's were not tightly bound by such strictures, although popular authors like Dickens and Thackeray were careful not to offend public taste directly. The Victorian novelist knew that his books were intended for family reading, and therefore he translated sex and passion into sentiment, the sexual act itself into fainting and weeping and shuddering. The careful reader, however, recognizes that beneath the currents of sentiment there lies a great deal of disguised passion and beneath the layers of respectability there rests, particularly in Dickens, a demonic vision of an aberrant world. Even Meredith, whom we generally (mis)interpret as an eternal optimist, presented through his romantic heroes savagely brought to heel a cruel world in which unthinking idealism can lead to personal tragedy. We forget that suggestion is often as effective as detailed analysis.

Comedy, then, gave the novelist a weapon, and he used it to expose the worst of the very middle class which imposed strictures upon him and then read his work. He reviled vulgarity and coarseness, mocked vanity, and ridiculed the affectations of the nouveaux riches. In a way, comedy provided a type of revenge on those who would restrict him to soap opera. The major nineteenth-century novelist was a figure of common sense, redirecting the vulgar and the eccentric into acceptable behavior and burlesquing them if they remained obtuse and selfish. By the time of George Eliot and Thomas Hardy, however, laughter is insufficient in a world in which the innocent as well as the guilty can be destroyed not through their own foibles but through life itself. With Hardy, as with Butler in *The Way of All Flesh,* the Victorian novel had run its course; the beliefs the world had about itself were being modified, and the novel, although fixed in some of its basic forms, was sufficiently flexible to meet change. Hardy's bleak outlook becomes the norm: the novelist no longer suggested darkness in a world of light, but now occasional light in a world of darkness, and frequently the light revealed the path to self-destruction.

Clearly, the Victorian writer was sensitive to the major political, social and intellectual movements of his day, more so than either the eighteenth- or twentieth-century novelist. It is commonplace now to speak of the novel's response to the manners and morals of the age; but it is not unusual that the novel should be rooted in contemporary values, for its very length requires the solidity of a particular society. Often, the nineteenth-century novelist became a political spokesman, although the novels in which political and social ideas dominate *directly* are weak and unconvincing, as George Gissing's sincere but monotonous books demonstrate. Dickens himself responded to labor unrest (the aftereffects of Chartism) and following the injunctions of Carlyle wrote a "social novel" in *Hard Times,* which exposes the frustrations and evils of the economic system. Of course, virtually all of Dickens's major fiction is concerned with contemporary English life, with only formal religion excluded as a serious topic. Meredith, in *Beauchamp's Career,* dealt directly with the political situation by creating an idealistic young man who wished to change England, and who found instead that good will and idealism are insufficient values to counter entrenched interests. George Eliot was of course immersed in the social (*Middlemarch*), religious (*Adam Bede*), and political (*Felix Holt*) developments of the century. Jane Austen and Thackeray were alike in not responding directly to definite movements, but their works reflect two of the major strains of the day, the growth of democracy and the development of industrial and commercial enterprises. Hardy, writing in the latter third of the century, was strongly affected by Darwin's publications; in *The Mayor of Casterbridge* and *Jude the Obscure,* as well as in several earlier novels, he reflected a Darwinian world in which man gains heroic stature through his struggle against inexplicable forces that will ultimately destroy him. For still later novelists, Darwin was the English Nietzsche.

An army of minor novelists further mirrored various aspects of the economic and political situation and prepared the way for ameliorating legislation that made for shorter hours, better working conditions, and more equitable pay (Disraeli, in his "Young England" novels; Charles Reade, in *Hard Cash, It Is Never Too Late to Mend;* Mrs. Gaskell, in *Mary Barton, North and South;* Harriet Martineau, in nine volumes of *Illustrations of Political Economy*). Under the pressure of several prophets (like Carlyle and Ruskin) and political events themselves (Chartism, Poor Laws, Corn Laws,

Reform Bills)—as well as from a sense of moral outrage—the novel became "serious," and the gap between fiction with a message and the novel of sheer entertainment began to widen, until by the end of the century the novel appealed in different ways to two separate reading publics.

Several novels also dealt directly with the Oxford Movement and the significance of Anglo-Catholicism, *Robert Elsmere* by Mrs. Humphry Ward being perhaps the most popular and successful. Moreover, by mid-century many Victorian novelists began to deal less with the whole range of society than with significant aspects of it, often restricting their efforts to one segment. With Charles Kingsley, among others, we start to get specialized fiction, a story, for example, about a tailor (*Alton Locke*, 1850) who attempts to raise himself socially and economically. Nevertheless, despite their fierce opposition to abuses in the economic system, both the major and minor writers believed in England herself and assumed that hard work and perseverance—their heritage from the seventeenth century— were sufficient for success. With the exceptions of Gissing and Hardy, most accepted the Horatio Alger-like views of Samuel Smiles (*Self-Help*, 1859; *Character*, 1871; *Thrift*, 1875), who equated diligence with virtue. Dickens, for instance, rejuvenates Pip when the latter realizes, first, that he must work for a living and, second, that snobbery and parasitism are inter-related sins.

In a pre-existential, democratic age, it was perhaps inevitable that virtue should be defined as a man's ability to develop himself to his full potential regardless of his bad beginnings. The need to transcend oneself becomes, then, the religion of a period in which commercial values were generally accepted despite sporadic defiance. Earlier, in Defoe and his successors, the values of a commercial society were the normal, expected ones. In the next century, these values, although attacked fiercely and brilliantly in the vast body of anti-Victorian literature, were still acceptable once outrages were removed. Only in the twentieth century were the values and all their ramifications viewed as villainous. One need only compare the all-consuming silver mine in Conrad's *Nostromo* with the commercial outfit that "saves" Pip after his great expectations have been smashed. Conrad is concerned with showing how commerce can corrupt; while Dickens presents a similar condition as a means of salvation. Even his savage Coketown might have been redeemed if Bounderby and Gradgrind could be transformed. The Victorian novelist believed that a change of heart would improve conditions that were themselves basically sound, even though malpractice created disturbing circumstances. Not until the end of the century did the novelist find conditions themselves corrupting and turn inward, to the soul of the individual, to try to redeem him in a world that was beyond visible hope.

The secularization of the novel that began with Defoe was never more apparent than among the Victorians, depending as the form does on a public interested not in metaphysics but in daily events: money, wills, bills to meet, credits, debits, marriage contracts, real estate arrangements, wages, working conditions. Despite the presence of strong religious standards under Victoria, the major novelists were secular in their works, reflecting an age that paid only lip service to the religious prophets. Thackeray, George Eliot, and Hardy were free thinkers; Meredith was a Wordsworthian nature-lover who replaced an orthodox God with the vague trinity of blood, brain, and spirit; Dickens was more concerned with a Christian morality than with the details of orthodoxy, and his characters are graded according to their gentle hearts rather than to their religious declarations. Throughout the century, the clergyman appears as a Chadband (*Bleak House*) or (particularly often) as a High Churchman like Mr. Collins of *Pride and Prejudice,* hardly as a devoted man of God. Trollope's secular clergymen are representative of a period in which competitive commercial values left little room for the spirit to flower. Nineteenth-century novelists, Ian Watt points out, "would continue Defoe's serious concern with man's worldly doings without placing them in a religious framework." The dignity of labor became itself the justification of the individual's secularity.

The economic and social nature of the Victorian novel was set, then, in the work of Defoe and Richardson a hundred years earlier. The economic individualism of Robinson Crusoe was readily translated into the ennobling nature of work. Furthermore, work was a means of closing the gap between social classes. A diligent merchant could rise to all but the top of the aristocracy by making a fortune, buying an estate and a town house, bringing his sons up as gentlemen, and marrying his daughters to titled but impecunious men about town. In its various aspects and developments, this world became the stuff of the nineteenth-century novelists. It became the source of much humor and much spite, although its essential nature went unquestioned if the people involved were decent and demonstrated benevolence and compassion.

Lest, however, social and political content seem to dominate at the expense of art, we should remember that the Victorian novelist was concerned with art, although not so consciously as were Flaubert, James, Conrad, and Joyce. While it is true that the novelist often remained an unhappy slave to his reading public, he did recognize that the novel was capable of doing many things. Dickens, while obeying the dictates of a public he tried to cultivate, peppered his letters with references to his craft, and in his later novels was fully conscious of the need for artistic form. *Great Expectations,* whose original ending he changed only at the insistence of Bulwer-Lytton, is itself one of his most carefully wrought works, balanced, unified, and almost completely lacking the episodic stringiness of his earlier fiction. George Eliot, through the advice of George Henry Lewes as well as through her own experience, recognized the limitations of strict realism, and in *Middlemarch* tried to fuse art with social reality. The same may be said of nearly all the major novelists, including even Hardy, despite his open disavowal of the novelist's craft.

The Victorian novelist brought to his work a concern with form that for the first time gave weight and depth to longer fiction. Those who do not blindly restrict the criteria of the novel will see that it has changed only in several emphases, not in essentials, from the previous century. David Copperfield, Pip, Pendennis, and Richard Feverel have become Ernest Pontifex, Paul Morel, Leonard Bast, Lord Jim, and Stephen Dedalus; Dorothy Casaubon has changed into Mrs. Dalloway and Mrs. Ramsay; Becky Sharp has been transformed into one of Aldous Huxley's vampire women, or perhaps into Lady Chatterley herself; Heathcliff is now Lawrence's Gerald Crich. Only Joyce's Leopold Bloom finds no exact counterpart in the nineteenth century, but Bloom is all men who have failed; and the nineteenth-century novelist, culminating in Hardy, knew a great deal about failure in an age of far-reaching success.

TWO *Jane Austen: The Necessity of Wit*

hose who claim that Jane Austen's restrictions deny profundity and breadth to her works ignore the fact that her world includes courtship and marriage, among several other aspects of social behavior, like vulgarity, gentility, and correctness—and all is judged by her ironic sense that expands the immediate moment into a general truth; restrictions that, in truth, allow her a good deal of the world to explore. Simplicity, limitation, provincialism of any kind are the butt of her humor. Her detachment and her seeming coldness mask the virtue of ironic understatement; her comedy is not vicious or contemptuous but a moral force that cuts through nonsense and insensitivity. An economically sound marriage is not, for her, made at the expense of love; her heroines never marry for convenience or mercenary purposes, although considerations of fortune are of course present once love has been attained. What has been considered her inability to create male characters is belied by her depiction of Henry Crawford and Edmund Bertram (in *Mansfield Park*), of Henry Tilney (in *Northanger Abbey*), among others. Her female figures are not always simple, that is, either good or bending, or both—witness Mary Crawford (in *Mansfield Park*), Catherine Morland (in *Northanger Abbey*), Marianne Dashwood (in *Sense and Sensibility*). Her restraint is not the result of her lack of force but a consequence of her desire to understate, to find humorous what another might prejudicially indict. And her emphasis on breeding is a stress upon the mind and the senses, upon attitudes toward life, not upon birth or fortune.

Her attack on sentimentality and all forms of excessive feeling is her attempt, in reaction to the eighteenth-century sentimentalists, to return the novel to a stable course. Her heroines display both good sense and wit as a way of returning an "immoderate" society to normal behavior. We can see how close the function of her irony is to the general purposes of Molière's satire, despite the great differences between the two writers. In both, wit and irony provide stability because they regulate conduct; and they are necessary precisely because there are divergences from common sense which provide pockets of social anarchy.

Later, in Meredith's use, comedy serves as a moral force, exciting something akin to the fear and pity of tragedy. In this sense, comedy and tragedy meet in a common purpose—to reveal abnormality and to return man (or society) to the values of the normal and moderate. Thus, in *Pride and Prejudice,* even Elizabeth Bennet, one of Jane Austen's most attractive heroines, must be chastened into the realization that her judgments are erroneous and her insights weakened by human frailty; and Emma in her novel becomes acceptable only after she understands her general fallibility.

Jane Austen's practices clearly suggest what Meredith later claimed for comedy: its freeing power, its ability to force judgments and to create distinctions. Comedy, in brief, separates the fools from the wits; it divides the simple from the complex, the vulgar from the well-mannered, the snob from the real gentleman, the unfeeling from the feeling, those who feel lust from those who understand love. In the hands of Jane Austen and other nineteenth-century novelists, therefore, comedy becomes a method by which the middle-class gentleman replaces the classical hero.

The concept of the gentleman was one that Jane Austen played with, refined, and further redefined. In an age caught between "tradition-directed" and "inner-directed" values (to use Riesman's convenient terms), an age in which the social structure had undergone relatively large changes, the only norm left to the genteel was a mode of behavior. As money superseded rank, and the virtues of business overcame the virtues of birth, personal gentility became the last barrier to social anarchy. As the work of Henry James later emphasized, only in a society that has a strongly stressed class structure can class be an issue, with its concomitant stress on manners, tradition, pride of birth, courtship behavior, and "noblesse oblige." If, like Jane Austen, the novelist deploys the forces of pride, vanity, vulgarity, or dignity, then the gentleman, who is the only possible transitional figure in a society that rejects breeding in favor of business, must be clearly defined in the novelist's mind. Furthermore, in a moneyed society, the picaresque hero or romantic protagonist can no longer function: as money lines close, he cannot wander, but must work or enjoy the privileges of an unearned income while acting civilized and human. Thus, the eighteenth-century picaresque hero becomes the gentleman of the Victorian era who, through exemplary conduct, resists the temptation to be as vulgar as his surroundings.

Accordingly, the gentleman in Jane Austen's novels is often more an idea than a person, more an ideal than a reality. Each of her heroines has her own idea of *the* gentleman, and then accepts the man who best most closely fits her image. The gentleman *may* be poor (although he usually has sufficient income to prevent money itself from becoming obtrusive), but not ignoble in behavior; aristocratic in ideals, but not proud; forthright in his attitudes, but not righteous or priggish; witty and entertaining, but not inconsiderate or frivolous. In *Persuasion,* her last complete novel, Jane Austen's description of Mr. Elliot suggests what a gentleman should be, although he in reality lacks the virtues listed, subservient as they are to a well masked basic vulgarity:

As Mr. Elliot became known to her [Lady Russell], she grew more charitable, or more indifferent, towards the others. His manners were an immediate recommendation; and on conversing with him she found the solid so fully supporting the superficial, that she was at first, as she told Anne, almost ready to exclaim: "Can this be Mr. Elliot?" and could not seriously picture to herself a more agreeable or estimable man. Everything united in him; good understanding, correct opinions, knowledge of the world, and a warm heart. He had strong feelings of family attachment and family honour, without pride or weakness; he lived with the liberality of a man of fortune, without display; he judged for himself in everything essential, without defying public opinion in any point of world decorum. He was steady, observant, moderate, candid; never run away with by spirits or by selfishness, which fancied itself strong feeling; and yet, with a sensibility to what was amiable and lovely, and a value for all the felicities of domestic life, which characters of fancied enthusiasm and violent agitation seldom really possess (1297).*

At all times a moderating force, the true gentleman obviously plays a central role in Jane Austen's society. If ever he temporarily drifts, he must return to what society expects of him, and this, naturally, without ostensible effort. He must not be rebellious, but conventional. The strong convictions which he should possess must be tempered by good sense and correct behavior. If he happens to be rather too dry or somewhat wooden, the heroine engages to give him more style by working on his native wit. Thus, the gentleman through accomplishment replaces the aristocrat by birth and becomes, in effect, the representative of a new middle-class elite.

Most significant, the gentleman eases over the transition to a society rooted in material things which determine all aspects of family and community life. Courtship itself, which is Jane Austen's chief narrative theme, becomes under these conditions a kind of civilized ritual. Yet a question arises: When a character must be regulative and proves relatively inflexible, how can he also be individualistic, civilized, gentlemanly?

The one area in which the character can be both regulative and individualistic is in his choice of a mate. In the early nineteenth century, as the novel reflects it, marriage was the sole means of initiating the female into adult life; before marriage, she was a kind of dumb ornament, perhaps pretty but useless. If she was not marriageable—that is, if she lacked sparkle or possessed no dowry—like Miss Bates in *Emma*—then she could expect to be treated as a child and a burden.

In Jane Austen's hands, as befitting her understanding of the eighteenth-century conduct-books, courtship becomes metaphysical in scope.† Part of the involved ritual is designed to hide or disguise feeling; yet each partner must say and do enough to convince the other that feeling is indeed there. In her novels, the her-

---

* All page references are to the Modern Library Giant edition of the novels of Jane Austen.
† The ritualistic details of middle-class courtship are described by Thomas Gisborne in *An Enquiry into the Duties of the Female Sex* (1797).

oines' high spirits, their playfulness, and their energy are indicative of the range of their emotional lives; and her "heroes" suggest their romantic tendencies through refined manners which overlay a submerged current of passionate feeling. Since the suitor rarely, if ever, saw his intended alone before the actual engagement, the courtship has to be a subtle affair in which she understands what he is and what he intends, without their interest being noted by the several onlookers. Contact between them must therefore be made through the glance of an eye or the nuance of a word. There is of course no surety until a certain kind of "unverbalized response" is evoked, and even after it is, one proceeds by intuition. To be hasty or overbearing is to be vulgar; to be eager in courtship, like Mr. Collins in *Pride and Prejudice* or Mr. Elton in *Emma,* is to show an unpleasant sexuality equivalent in our terms to direct physical offense. Furthermore, this ritual of banter, this dance of jousting affections is another way of testing a person's manner. With money as the great equalizer, society had to raise ritualistic barriers to equality, and one evidences his breeding in his style of courtship.

In this connection, however, feeling is not quite enough; the hero must also possess property. A strictly "love" marriage, like Lydia's with Wickham, is vulgar and unadvised, while a marriage solely for economic reasons, like Charlotte Lucas's with Collins, also elicits disdain. Feeling and property must be allied for a successful marriage, and every one of Jane Austen's heroines knows an eligible suitor both by the feelings he attracts and by his income. In the union, there is the merging of a civilized romantic convention with an economic primitiveness. One without the other is unfortunate, vulgar, or degrading: therefore, Elizabeth Bennet's disdain for Charlotte when the latter marries solely for security.

Charlotte's marriage raises several important issues in the world that Jane Austen represents, issues whose implications echo beyond the immediate situation in *Pride and Prejudice.* If we recognize that for Jane Austen moral judgment is *not* easy, that one must choose among several tempting possibilities, then we realize that awareness of choice is of primary importance to her major characters. Only a complex character, however, can have this moral sense which overrides pride, prejudice, arrogance, excessive sensibility, sensuality, and selfishness. Awareness is also an antidote for vulgarity. Elizabeth Bennet's great quality is her growing awareness of *all* possibilities; her rejection of a simple view of life is an indication of her breeding and manner. To her credit, she understands nearly everything but a few aspects of her own motivation; and it is to point up her occasional moments of self-deception that Jane Austen's irony is directed. So, in *Pride and Prejudice,* dramatic conflict lies not in violence but in the emotional significance of a word, a gesture, a confrontation. And although choice in a regulative society rests within severe restrictions, one can still manifest self by correct and meaningful decisions.

With this in mind, we can better understand Elizabeth's inability to accept Charlotte's marriage with Collins. Further—and more important—we see how Jane Austen plays with her heroine's lack of perception and ironically mocks this limitation. Charlotte is older than Elizabeth; she is 27, plain, and relatively spiritless, although with a pleasant manner and not lacking in common sense. She cannot wait for a Darcy or his equivalent, but must seize the first opportunity to escape impending spinsterhood. Accordingly, she takes immediate advantage of her sole chance to replace economic anxiety with security. She fully recognizes what Collins is, and precisely because she feels no love for him she can tolerate him by ignoring his foolishness. Unlike Elizabeth, Charlotte realizes that in an "acquisitive society" when a girl is plain, it is often impossible for her to fulfill her romantic wishes; love must be sacrificed to long-range security.

Yet Elizabeth nobly disdains Charlotte's marriage because it lacks love. Had Charlotte fallen in love with Collins, then Elizabeth could have dismissed the situation as ludicrous. But precisely because Charlotte knows her own feelings, Elizabeth cannot understand her actions. If *she* could not marry a Collins, how could her friend? Elizabeth is blinded by her own situation, as later she is blinded in her judgment of Wickham, unable to understand that Charlotte must be "acquisitive" if she is to avoid a spinsterish fate.

Elizabeth believes that a complex person possesses complete free will to choose her own fate, and that Charlotte because of her inexplicable choice cannot aspire to be complex. Such, however, is Jane Austen's irony that Elizabeth is at her weakest when she chides her friend, failing to recognize that both are tied to a society which often forces simple decisions on complex people.* Elizabeth's own choices are not as free as she would believe, for choice is rarely unalloyed. The simple and the complex, as the English critic R. A. Brower has pointed out, are not far apart. Consequently, Jane Austen's irony works best when Elizabeth believes that she has herself chosen freely. Once again, irony becomes a way of regulating an excess of individuality, a means of restricting too free and unenlightened a spirit. Elizabeth, finally, does make her choice, but how wrong she has been in her previous judgments: Wickham, her favorite, turns out to be an amiable villain, and Darcy, whom she detested, is transformed into an unsmiling romantic hero. And while Elizabeth makes a marriage both prudent and romantic, it seems that she has been playing much the same game as Charlotte.

Even though the base of Jane Austen's novels is economic— her vocabulary abounds in contemporary commercial terminology —her heroes or heroines are not permitted to mention money as such. With rank and inheritances now falling to middle-class businessmen with earned incomes, the standard of gentility forbade discussion of how money was gained. In *Emma,* for example, Mrs. Elton reveals herself as a "petite bourgeoise" because she parades family connections, especially the wealth of her sister. Although Emma herself often verges on the vulgar, Mrs. Elton sets a standard of vulgarity compared with which Emma appears genteel.

With her heavy reliance upon irony to ridicule vulgarity, Jane Austen's detractors—as, later, Henry James's—have sometimes accused her of carrying detachment to the point of evading personality altogether. She loses, they claim, sympathy, pathos, tenderness, even passion, through objectifying all emotion into rational channels. This view, however, entails a severe misunderstanding of Jane Austen's intentions and art. First of all, emotion is certainly present in her characters, but not always overtly, just as sexual feeling is also present, but disguised in rhetoric: consider the oily effusiveness of Collins, who in his sweaty, sensual way suggests a somewhat panting attitude toward sex, a Lovelace in a clerical

* For "simplicity" and "complexity" in the works of Jane Austen, see Marvin Mudrick's *Jane Austen: Irony as Defense and Discovery.*

collar. Further, Jane Austen's marriageable characters are by no means ascetics. Those critics who judge her as lacking in feeling often seem to suggest that her women are ready to enter convents, her men monasteries. On the contrary, her young people are anxious to marry, and a pleasant face, a good complexion, and a graceful figure are as important as a solid income or good breeding. In addition, a character's conversation is indicative of his sexual desires: the ritual of genteel conversation cannot completely disguise the energy and force of a strong sexual personality. Darcy is attracted to Elizabeth because of her person, despite her birth; Mr. Knightley desires Emma for her personal attractions, despite her immature opinions and seeming vulgarity. In *Mansfield Park*, Edmund Bertram is drawn to the attractive Mary Crawford although her trenchant wit outrages his genteel sensibilities. The attraction remains despite other serious disadvantages. And while physical appeal alone can never effectively disguise a vulgar manner, the physical cannot be ignored as though non-existent.

Thus, if sexual feeling is present, however disguised or partially minimized, so too are sympathy, tenderness, even pathos, although carefully regulated and muted by common sense. We remember that Jane Austen's juvenilia and early novels (*Northanger Abbey* and *Sense and Sensibility*) burlesqued respectively the extremes of the Gothic novel and the novel of sentiment. She felt that her contemporaries demanded emotional responses far in excess of what their fiction required, that they distorted human behavior to suit literary conventions, and that the only way to free the novel from its exaggerations was through burlesque. So, in her early work, she parodied the novel of sentiment with its ever-present sermonizing and affectation, burlesquing as well the Gothic novel with its instruments of terror and the picaresque novel with its episodic, meandering development. Rather than demanding tears or horror from her readers, she elicited laughter; rather than drawing sentimental characters seriously, she tried to purge all nonsense through wit; and rather than making her audience suffer through a series of false events, she tried to entertain through a set of realistic conventions. Jane Austen's great contribution to the English novel was her ability to create a set of plausible circumstances and to make the novel less strictly an entertainment or a homily and more a way of looking at the world.

From this point of vantage, we can argue that Jane Austen's method was perfectly suited to the realistic novel. As one critic has remarked, her detached method may have been the ideal way to penetrate the cold veneer of the middle class to its material base, the only way to strike at its false hopes and righteous complacency. Detached irony removed Jane Austen from the supercharged arena in which girls must wait hopefully for husbands, mothers must desperately try to arrange marriages, fathers must give dowries to the point of hardship, in which middle-class values mock old aristocratic names and the coming democracy isolates the well-bred gentleman, a society in which manners remain as the only way of determining worth, and good manners *may* mask an essentially unaware and unfeeling person. As Molière long ago discovered, what more fruitful themes for detached comedy!

Pride and Prejudice, known in its initial form as *First Impressions* (begun October 1796, completed August 1797), shows the marks of an extremely youthful novel when compared with *Mansfield Park* and *Emma* written more than fifteen years later. As contrasted with the latter's more complex development and sense of pace, the movement of *Pride and Prejudice* is direct and straightforward, more artless than not; as contrasted with the more varied situations of *Mansfield Park,* the episodes of *Pride and Prejudice* have the quality of fixed tableaux that might have appeared in a dozen novels of the day; and again, as contrasted with the rich, ambiguous texture of *Mansfield Park,* the narrative of *Pride and Prejudice* offers a gay, witty, clean line with a singleness of purpose. Yet this novel has rightly remained the favorite of Jane Austen's novels perhaps because it raises fewer serious problems than either of the other two and its heroine has just the right amount of sophistication, wit, and immaturity to be charming.

Since attachments in Jane Austen's novels must be based on the right kind of love, it is not surprising that *Pride and Prejudice* should have as its basis the conflict between "real love" and "simple love." Real love is felt only by aware persons, while simple love ensnares unthinking people unaware of alternative possibilities. Thus, a young woman's choice of partner determines what she is capable of. Further, since the choice of mate is about the sole choice a girl in her time could make for herself, Jane Austen treats this decision as a moral judgment, based as it is on the girl's complexity or simplicity of mind, on her ability or inability to feel, and on her positive or negative reaction to life. If she has moral awareness—as do Elizabeth Bennet, Emma (at the end of her novel), Anne Elliot (*Persuasion*), Elinor Dashwood (*Sense and Sensibility*), and Fanny Price (*Mansfield Park*)—then, obviously, she is attractive, substantial, and lacking any trace of vulgarity. Awareness overrides pride, prejudice, arrogance, sensuality, lack of consideration; it even overrides an excess of energy and spirit. Awareness in a Jane Austen heroine complements the comic spirit, for both work toward a norm of behavior and strip away excesses, even those of wit. Thus, Emma must be chastened, for her high spirits border on the vulgarly playful.

Elizabeth Bennet is almost fully aware; her sense brings a note of moderation into a foolish world. If we recognize that in Jane Austen's novels dramatic conflict lies not in violence but in its emotional significance for the characters, then we grant that Elizabeth's awareness of choice is of a kind that can sustain a major novel. Whenever she temporarily loses her power to distinguish, she becomes the butt of Jane Austen's irony. Without any real experience of the world, Elizabeth tends to judge hastily and form quick impressions, but she has sufficient sense to recognize her mistakes. Like all of Jane Austen's heroines, she grows when the situation calls for maturity; and this she does because basically she is aware, has feeling, and can be judicious.

With this theme of the free individual who acts from choice, Jane Austen was foreshadowing one of the major motifs of the nineteenth-century novel. With society radically shifting into new alignments, the element of choice was paramount: a "hero" or "heroine" could no longer accept a given role. What kind of person was he or she to be? How should he or she react? What are the decisions involved? All these questions had once been answered in terms of tradition and convention, but now Pip, Becky Sharp, and Dorothea Brooke, like Elizabeth, Emma, Mary Crawford, and Fanny Price, must answer them for themselves. The individual is now free in a new way to destroy his fortunes and himself by his own unthinking decisions.

The theme of real and simple love is reflected in the relationships between Mr. and Mrs. Bennet, Elizabeth and Darcy, Charlotte and Collins, Lydia and Wickham, and Jane and Bingley. Of this group, only Elizabeth and Darcy can be said to have found real love, although Jane and Bingley are not quite simple. The contrast between these two romances is underscored in the differences between Darcy and Bingley and between Elizabeth and Jane. Because Bingley is controlled so easily by his friend, his feelings, sincere though they may be, cannot be too deep or too serious; honesty in him is not to be confused with real passion. Likewise, Jane must be bound by her feelings for Bingley, who is *her* type: uncomplicated, well-made, finely bred, attractive, and untroubled by any excessive emotions. They will, perhaps, be happy in a way denied to Elizabeth and Darcy, although, by its very nature, their relationship will be less intense. Lydia's affair with Wickham, on the other hand, is as simple as Mr. Bennet's courtship was with his wife. In fact, in Wickham's expediency, Mr. Bennet recognizes the wiles of his own wife; each traded on a pleasant face and figure in lieu of real feeling or sense. And because of this realization, he is unable to feel actual disdain for Wickham; for the latter's presence curiously brings home all his own mistakes. Similarly, the marriage between Charlotte and Collins is for both partners one of expediency: Charlotte, to gain security; Collins, to soothe his vanity after Elizabeth's refusal.

Bingley would be unsuitable for Elizabeth, for he is too singular in his reactions. Darcy himself temporarily seems to lack depth, and it is this failing, as much as his rudeness, which turns Elizabeth against him. When she discovers in him a stratum of complexity and even the agony of indecision, then she is increasingly attracted. Once she sees Wickham as fixed and simple, she rejects him, despite his charming manner. In her ability to distinguish character, Elizabeth frees herself, just as later George Eliot's Dorothea Brooke, a much weightier and more substantial Elizabeth, finally sees Casaubon for what he is and by so doing partially frees herself. In Jane Austen's provincial society this was a girl's only freedom; and in this sense Fanny Price (*Mansfield Park*), despite her insipid personality, attains a heroine's stature by rejecting Henry Crawford.

The choice, admittedly, is often fine. When Fanny rejects Henry Crawford, he is eligible, sincere, really in love; yet she senses an underlying frivolity, reversing Elizabeth's early rejection of Darcy for his *lack* of playfulness and humor. Precisely as Henry's high spirits mask a nature that might have grown serious under the tutelage of true love, so Darcy's sobriety disguises a soul that can be touched by energy and wit. Elizabeth attracts him, we remember, because of her high spirits, not despite them. His gravity becomes a foil for her wit exactly as Fanny's staidness is a contrast to Henry's levity. Both novels are obviously structured on just these alternating acceptances and rejections.

The comic play of the novels gains direction from the very choices the heroines must make. From the famous first sentence of *Pride and Prejudice*—"It is a truth universally acknowledged that a single man in possession of a good fortune must be in want of a wife"—it is obvious that Jane Austen retains irony or wit as a classic device; that, granting large and significant differences, she is in the line of Aristophanes and Molière, and foreshadows the play of manners in the novels of Thackeray, George Eliot, and George Meredith. The irony is implicit in Elizabeth Bennet herself: as a complex person, she can judge others, but as a middle-class heroine with bourgeois tendencies, she can herself be pleasantly fallible. While Elizabeth can laugh at Darcy, her parents, and her sisters, we can laugh at her.

The decline of the hero or heroine as an infallible creature really began with Jane Austen. Except for Anne Elliot and perhaps Elinor Dashwood, her female characters are faulty, and their errors almost bring them permanent grief. Elizabeth and Emma make repeated errors in judgment; Fanny Price is backward and insipid—her lack of sparkle is almost vulgar; Catherine Morland is a farcical heroine in a mock-Gothic romance; Marianne Dashwood is too carried away by her emotions to be stable; Mary Crawford, with energy for two, allows boredom to destroy her sense of propriety. Elizabeth Bennet's own imperfections make correct judgment that much more difficult, and her complexity arises specifically because she is not an unalloyed heroine. By making gentility or civility of conduct her norm, Jane Austen could direct irony toward both her characters and situations. When she said of *Emma:* "I am going to take a heroine whom no one but myself will much like," she recognized that her heroine would be sailing into the teeth of a storm. Her conception of Emma indeed almost succeeds in fulfilling her threat: Emma will finally do, but she is not really likable even after her penance and absolution.

Jane Austen saw the world as fundamentally silly and, therefore, populated by silly people. She had, nevertheless, no animosity for these people—even her fools, like Mr. Collins, are not the product of hatred or persecution once she has fixed their characters. At the same time, she has been accused of providing little or no affection for her characters, what H. W. Garrod meant when he accused her of being interested only in the manners of men but not in their hearts. If we see, however, that manner is connected to a fundamentally decent attitude toward life, then we also perceive that manner and heart are interdependent. Mr. Elliott of *Persuasion* has mere manner, in Garrod's deprecatory sense, but for Jane Austen he fails precisely because he lacks a feeling heart. He has, for her, a vulgar manner. In *Pride and Prejudice,* Elizabeth will not accept Darcy until she is sure of his heart; his manner is bad enough, surely no indication of how he really feels. It is clear that Jane Austen, despite her concern with silly, mannered people, is also much concerned with heart, attached as it is to right feeling, good conduct, sane motives, and general amiability.

A seeming lack of affection for her characters means to Jane Austen not a want of interest but an opportunity for detachment, the method that Henry James later modified and called "the post of observation." Striving for the absolutely first-rate, Jane Austen was able to maintain a yardstick for civil behavior at a time when such values were threatened. Interested in the real, she disdains the realistic; working with particulars, she allows room for generalities; rejecting the weak of heart and manner, she likes only the consciously strong; and setting up strict standards of behavior, she can almost compromise her own heroines. In her ability to remain detached and objective, she is a moralist in the best sense of the word.

Pursuing the ironic method in her novels—the method that makes possible the successful resolution of the above qualities—one can see that even as early as *Pride and Prejudice,* her irony worked between characters, not between author and characters. Only in her *juvenilia* do we find the author's irony directed toward her characters; later, by juxtaposing the constituted character with a situation, she gains irony when the character's actions are in excess of what the situation demands. Thus, Elizabeth, believing that she has few restrictions, *plans* to act freely; yet every situation shows her tied to a system that controls her as much as it does Charlotte Lucas, her sisters, the Bingleys, and her father. She prides herself on her judgment, only to find Wickham a genteel villain and Darcy an amiable hero. Similarly, Charlotte, a girl of good breeding and sense—as level-headed as the heroine—must in the nature of things marry a Collins. Then Darcy, who disdains Elizabeth's connections, especially her mother, is himself tied to his aunt, Lady Catherine, whose snobbishness and contempt neutralize Mrs. Bennet's vulgarity. Further, Mr. Bennet, whose one mistake was to allow feeling to overrule sense when he courted Mrs. Bennet, sees the pattern repeated in the elopement of Lydia and Wickham. To top all these reversals, Lydia is happy and triumphant upon returning married to Wickham, while the Bennets, who see more deeply, have suffered from their realization of her hasty action.

The irony is particularly effective in those scenes in which an innocent Elizabeth begins to gain experience of the world. In this sense, *Pride and Prejudice* is a kind of apprenticeship novel in which the heroine, at first naive and callow, is introduced to a world infinitely more complex and varied than she formerly had believed. Such a book becomes the forerunner of George Eliot's *Middlemarch* and the Gwendolen Harleth part of *Daniel Deronda,* Henry James's *The Portrait of a Lady,* and Conrad's *Chance,* with marginal affinities to the novels of Charlotte Brontë, particularly *Jane Eyre* and *Shirley,* and to Hardy's *Tess of the D'Urbervilles.*

Elizabeth herself foreshadows, among others, Clara Middleton of Meredith's *The Egoist,* as well as his Diana (*Diana of the Cross-ways*), and Dorothea Brooke of *Middlemarch.* In her wit and sense of personal liberty, she is a genteel, subdued forerunner of Thackeray's Becky Sharp.

Within her restricted world, Elizabeth can of course react only in fine shades of difference. Because Jane Austen replaced violence with slight vibrations of sentiment, her heroine had to develop almost solely through psychological conflict, principally the one involving the choice of a husband. In this area, Jane Austen suggested change and nuances of feeling, and tested hearts and minds as well. Elizabeth's recognition of Darcy's true quality has the dramatic force of a revelation, as does Emma's growing awareness that she loves Mr. Knightley. With Elizabeth, furthermore, her reaction to Darcy means a rejection of that very freedom of choice in which she had reveled. Thus, Jane Austen writes of her change of heart:

She began now to comprehend that he was exactly the man who, in disposition and talents, would most suit her. His understanding and temper, though unlike her own, would have answered all her wishes. It was an union that must have been to the advantage of both: by her ease and liveliness, his mind might have been softened, his manners improved; and from his judgment, information, and knowledge of the world, she must have received benefit of greater importance (417).

Despite the early date of *Pride and Prejudice,* it illuminates Jane Austen's most mature point: that Elizabeth is wrong when she sharply divides the simple from the complex people, when, in fact, in areas of day-to-day living they are similar in motivation and reaction. As Elizabeth calculates what her fortunes are to be, she finds Darcy appropriate for what she wants within the range of what she can have, in the same way that Charlotte Lucas has measured what her range of choice is and has decided the best she can hope for is Collins. Jane Austen's irony works precisely on this degree of difference.

In another area, Mr. Bennet is a gentleman by birth—the side of the family that is considered to have breeding—and yet his attitude toward his wife and family, witty as it is, is tainted by chagrin for his own mistake in marrying a fool, a woman "whose weak understanding and illiberal mind had very early in their marriage put an end to all real affection for her. Respect, esteem, and confidence had vanished for ever; and all his views of domestic happiness were overthrown." His attitude is not lost on Elizabeth, who, while appreciating his affectionate treatment of her, sees clearly that he has exposed his wife to the contempt of her children. She judges her father to be wrong, and he undoubtedly is, but she fails to recognize how debilitating it is to live with six women when male issue had been necessary to secure the estate to his own family. The irony is two-fold: Mr. Bennet in feeling disdain for his family is not a gentleman; but Elizabeth arrives at an over-simple verdict when she finds him remiss. He has feelings which Elizabeth does not understand, and she has reactions of which he is unaware. Yet they consider themselves close to each other.

Unlike Emma, Elizabeth is an ironic spectator, not a manipulator. She judges without participating and classifies without regard for failings in her own standards. Both heroines are fallible, both are egoists of a sort. Elizabeth leans on her sense of comedy as much as Emma on Harriet Smith. Both need other people as playthings—in order to shine, they must do so *against* someone else.

Rarely does a Jane Austen heroine show her qualities in isolation, that is, apart from the society which makes her what she is. What probably gives Jane Austen's novels their unique quality is the solidity of her given society in which each member must ultimately find himself by finding his rightful place. The great shifts in English social classes had already begun by the turn of the nineteenth century, but the mobile units which we find in Dickens's novels were not too apparent forty years earlier. Therefore, one's *allegiance* to society, including family and neighbors, served the same function then that one's *divergence* from these groups serves in the major twentieth-century novels. Since Jane Austen's society did not permit deviations, the whole notion of personal eccentricity could not be tolerated. Irony, which in one aspect measures the distance between the social norm and one's deviations from it, becomes a social weapon of the novelist who predicates a stable world. The family unit is still the basic element of stability in Jane Austen's novels, although her family groups are by no means idyllically content or even, necessarily, happy. The parents in fact are frequently an unpleasant lot: when both are living, one is usually a fool (Mrs. Bennet), the other fully aware of it (Mr. Bennet); or, as in *Mansfield Park,* one is too harried to give necessary attention (Mrs. Price), the other a wastrel (Mr. Price); or else, in the same novel, one is too stern (Mr. Bertram), the other a jelly-like mound of flesh (Mrs. Bertram); further, when only one is living, he is a nagging old half-man, half-woman (Mr. Woodhouse), or flighty and undependable (Mrs. Dashwood in *Sense and Sensibility*).

Nevertheless, the family unit must be honored despite its faults, foolishness, over-protectiveness, vulgarity. Emma honors her very trying father, and this fact, which perhaps in our day would condemn her for lacking independence, is in Jane Austen's eyes one of her virtues. Since the family unit becomes the limit and extent of a girl's world, her sense of responsibility must be tested there. Further, in an author devoted to gentility as the sole mark of distinction, whatever one's family does reflects on the individual. When Lydia, for example, runs away with Wickham, Elizabeth herself feels stained, and so much is she a part of her family that she expects Darcy to disdain her. But he too has his family burden, Lady Catherine, whose vulgarity surpasses that of Elizabeth's mother and sister. And even though Darcy possesses an independent fortune, he is still responsible for his aunt. Similarly, the deference that all of Jane Austen's heroines pay their elders, despite the latter's evident lack of good sense, is a significant mark of their gentility. Notwithstanding Elizabeth's full awareness of her parents' insufficiency, she withholds her disdain for them. To do otherwise is to forfeit the very quality that Darcy admires: the moral earnestness that he knows exists beneath her witty exterior. To keep her bubbling spirits within bounds, a Jane Austen heroine honors those very people whom good sense might tell her to scorn.

The family unit acts, then, as a regulative force within a society that might otherwise become unstable. On one side, Jane Austen's irony forces norms upon a potential eccentric, and, on the other, the family shelters him from further deviation. Connected with the family of course is the entire ritual of courtship and marriage. The family imposes the ritual as a means of retaining control over the girl or man until the marriage; then the cycle starts again. In this way, power is transmitted in small quantities, and the chance of eccentricity or marginal conduct is minor. Regulated, restricted, and hemmed in by custom, the individual has to react within a given range of emotions and actions, and this fact forces the author to project a world in which nuances and small touches must determine a character or scene. The reader accustomed to large and open passions finds Jane Austen restrictive, when actually her protean wit could not exist in a passive temperament.

Precisely because in Jane Austen's most successful work the small touch controls scene and character, *Pride and Prejudice* begins to deteriorate as soon as Lydia's elopement is revealed. Previous to this change of fortune, Jane Austen was able to unfold her characters through a series of inter-related scenes that avoided the stringiness of the episodic narrative. The complexity of Elizabeth Bennet's development is gained through an increasing revelation of character, each step small but significant. After Lydia's elopement, all complexity is lost in the episodic nature of the chase, which becomes a cliché of its type—the errant daughter, the distraught parent, the outrage of respectable people, the handy uncle, the unknown benefactor, the happy conclusion for both the guilty and the righteous.

The novel diminishes here simply because the working out of the details of the chase precludes adequate development of character along the earlier lines, the forward thrust of the novel ending in a long dénouement. The revelations of narrative replace the revelations of character, and the latter was clearly Jane Austen's forte. One indication of how the novel forsakes its power is in the flattening out of the irony, which now becomes secondary to details of the story line. With the loss of irony, Jane Austen lost her chief weapon for gaining complexity. Darcy himself, we suddenly realize, is not nearly so richly complex as Elizabeth thinks, for he reacts as a stock hero: the man of solid intentions, the unknown benefactor, the stoical creature with the bleeding heart who disguises his wounds beneath pride and shyness, the potentially stable husband who softens and becomes malleable with the right touch. Darcy is the picaresque hero tamed to domesticity; the racy, mysterious "rogue" of the first part dissolves into the middle-class gentleman of the second. Elizabeth wanted a benevolent knight who lived somewhat dangerously, but through her own example reduced him to a bourgeois hero, solid and enduring, a story-book lover. Instead of Heathcliff, she gains John Tanner.

While the events in the latter third of the narrative become dreary, the characters themselves lose their playfulness and become righteous and shrill. Mr. Bennet, whose witty, sarcastic retorts have previously been a pleasure, reveals his inadequacies as he retreats into ruefulness and disdain. He *is* a man of awareness, but, unlike his daughter, he is also susceptible of vulgarity. Elizabeth herself becomes somewhat shrill when she cannot allay her horror at Lydia's elopement and triumphant return; perhaps an abject Lydia would have commanded her pity or reduced her fears for the loss of the family's reputation.

The question does indeed arise whether or not we should side with Lydia in her rebellion; she is, after all, willing to sacrifice all for love, and heroines have often gained immortality for less. Within the terms of the novel, however, Lydia's actions are deplorable because she acts thoughtlessly from passion rather than from love. Guided solely by her own pleasure, she reveals herself as one of the simple people who inadvertently hurt others. Unaware that she is dependent upon a family which is connected with her fortunes, she victimizes her sisters by pursuing a singular course of action, and with this behavior she proves herself frivolous and irresponsible. Jane Austen's disdain is obvious:

Their [Lydia's and Wickham's] reception from Mr. Bennet, to whom they then turned, was not quite so cordial. His countenance rather gained an austerity, and he scarcely opened his lips. The easy assurance of the young couple, indeed, was enough to provoke him. Elizabeth was disgusted, and even Miss Bennet was shocked. Lydia was Lydia still—untamed, unabashed, wild, noisy, and fearless. She turned from sister to sister, demanding their congratulations; and when at length they all sat down, looked eagerly round the room, took notice of some little alteration in it, and observed, with a laugh, that it was a great while since she had been there (419).

Mrs. Bennet's reaction, the very opposite of Elizabeth's, discloses her vulgarity, for she is exicted, not appalled, by the marriage. She fails to see that Wickham's charm dissembles a desperate expediency and that Lydia's manner reflects not real feeling but flightiness and frivolity. Elizabeth's recognition of the real situation indicates that in the future she will not repeat the mistake she made about Wickham: once she has learned about the world, she can distinguish manner from character.

A charming manner in Jane Austen's males usually hides the irresponsible rogue beneath. The amiable Wickham is later transformed into the quasi-acceptable Frank Churchill of *Emma,* the treacherous Mr. Elliot of *Persuasion,* and, in a different form, the flighty Henry Crawford of *Mansfield Park;* in Jane Austen's early fiction, he also appears as the villainous Willoughby of *Sense and Sensibility.* All except Frank Churchill contain a streak of vulgarity which forbids them real feeling; all go outside the bounds of propriety when their egoism, rather than family or group feeling, dictates their pleasures; all make people uncomfortable without knowing it; and all force others to protect them against themselves.

Meredith later was to develop this very point in *The Egoist,* that the people of real feeling and propriety must protect the egoist from recognizing what everyone already knows. This protection they afford is indeed one mark of their civility. The egoist should himself come to see he is being rejected, but since egoism often precludes such realization, the situation is ready made for the author's irony. Jane Austen herself indicts her self-seeking males by contrasting their egoism and expedience with the restraints and sense of propriety that an aware man should possess. Thus, as Meredith was later to describe brilliantly, the impish furies of the comic spirit follow eternally in the train of egoism.

Philosophically, egoism is co-equal to individuality, and we have seen how Jane Austen recognized that excessive individuality (or self-gratifying egoism) must be restricted through laughter and brought back to a norm. In *Pride and Prejudice,* Elizabeth judges Darcy's pride to be evidence of egoism, and her object is to break down his rigidity so that he can laugh. She wants to transform his self-importance into comic realization, and by so doing infuse high spirits into one now wooden and stiff. Once she has ascertained that Darcy is capable of change, to make him unbend will be Elizabeth's mission after marriage. Thus, Darcy's excessive pride (or pomposity and egoism) must be restored to normal by the comic play of one who refuses to honor his high seriousness. To draw Darcy out is to bring to light the qualities his shyness has masked. Elizabeth has a perfect mate. In time, he will even enjoy frivolity.*

As the above remarks have suggested, Jane Austen is interested more in character than in personality. By character we mean the essential trait of the person which makes him what he is, while personality involves the attitudes and qualities of a person rather than his essence. Thus, for Jane Austen, personality has to be regulated, and it can be controlled in a figure whose character is essentially decent. Darcy is solid in character, although his personality is deficient in certain qualities that Elizabeth at first confused with character. Personality can be changed, but not character—in that sense, Jane Austen is not a social writer. Mr. Collins, the sweaty, foolish clergyman, has a character that is detestable, and his personality reflects the greed and pomposity of the man. Similarly, Wickham and Mrs. Bennet are weak and frivolous characters; Wickham's pleasant manner and Mrs. Bennet's former beauty are merely façades behind which lie characters that cannot be altered.

Once Jane Austen fixes the character of her figures—usually through their conversation—there is little chance of change. Later, in *Vanity Fair,* Thackeray was to follow this method, wherein the characters of his main figures are fixed. Dickens (in part) and George Eliot worked differently: their characters have the potential, and often the actuality, of change. As the rudimentary psychological novel was devoloped by George Eliot, character became more subject to modification. With Thomas Hardy, the change itself—as in Henchard (*The Mayor of Casterbridge*)—becomes the substance of the novel.

This distinction between character and personality is particularly important in *Emma.* As every critic has noted, Emma is a

* His type of London gentleman turned somewhat foppish reappears later in several novels of the Silver Fork School, which flourished from about 1825 up to the publication of *Vanity Fair.* Robert Plumer Ward, for example, in *Tremaine* (1825), created his main character as a kind of dandiacal, "exclusive" Darcy. In this connection, Jane Austen's novels were known to the fashionable set who primped and pranced during the Regency, and the Regent himself is said to have been fond of her work. (See also p. 179n.).

quite imperfect person—but basically a decent character—and the novel proceeds along the lines of her chastening until she becomes worthy of Mr. Knightley, who is the measure of a civilized and genteel society. Jane Austen's daring here is obvious: the novel depends on her success in making her heroine good enough for a somewhat stodgy hero; at the same time she must convince the reader that her heroine has only a faulty personality and not a disagreeable character.

That Jane Austen could attempt so much is an indication of her own maturing powers between the two novels. In his depreciating treatment of her, Garrod claimed that she showed no development between the ages of twenty and forty, that her range never widens, her tone never deepens, her plots—always a husband-hunt—never change. Yet, it should be obvious, *Emma* is different from her earlier novels, different in content as well as in technique. In its use of the heroine's growing awareness, of increasing recognition, of developing self-knowledge, *Emma* retains the classical virtues. Almost alone, Jane Austen resisted the romantic novel of her day, with its affectations and sentimentality, its loose construction.

Accordingly, the novel raises several crucial questions about character: does Emma have a "good" heart, or is she selfish? can she control her high spirits within the limitations society demands, or is she vulgar? has long association with her soft, indulgent father blunted her perceptions, or is she capable of discernment? is Harriet Smith merely a casual prop, or is she more? is she quite vulgar in her behavior to Miss Bates and to Frank Churchill, or are her actions simply the result of high spirits that must find an outlet? are her snobbery and sense of superiority merely personality traits, or are they unalterably embedded in her character? Jane Austen's answer to these questions defines the difference between character and personality.

As Elizabeth Bennet awakens, so too Emma must become aware. She must satisfy society (Mr. Knightley is its representative) that she is compassionate. As long as her personality does not fit into the standards of a genteel society, she is marginal to good sense and taste and cannot gain union with a decent man. In the steps toward acceptance, she must recognize her false judg-

ment, temper her high spirits with common sense, and admit that
her witty sallies bordered on the vulgar. Then, the former "outcast" enters into what she has perhaps subconsciously tried to
avoid: the world of middle-class values, from which, incidentally,
she had never been too far.

Part of Jane Austen's chastisement of her heroine derives from
her ridicule of the romantic novel. Against romanticism, with its
careless notions of unregulated behavior, she placed a no-nonsense,
non-illusionary world of reason and good sense. Her *juvenilia*
reveals her impatience with the romantic conventions of the late
eighteenth century, and her parodies foreshadow the realism of
her major work. By 1814-15, the years in which she wrote *Emma,*
her penultimate (complete) novel, she had firmly established that
a romantic heroine must also have common sense. Pure romanticism may lead to chaos, but tempered by good sense, it leads to
a happy state regulated within the demands of a civil society. Conversely, pure realism, unqualified by romanticism, derives from
expediency, and this too is condemned. In her mixture of modes,
Jane Austen found stability: her protagonists could enjoy the bene-
fits of both love and an unearned income.

In her injunction to Emma to be good rather than clever Jane
Austen was repeating her warning from *Mansfield Park,* published the same year she began *Emma* (1814). In that novel,
Fanny Price is good, and Mary Crawford clever; the latter is
effaced, while the former prevails. The question immediately
arises whether or not Jane Austen destroyed her really interesting
figures for the sake of propriety; whether, in short, gentility stultifies high spirits, and dull virtue triumphs over interesting vice.
Given her intentions, we can see that a stable society in which
civility is honored exists by virtue of its regulative powers; further,
that those capable of right action and speech *must* obey society's
dictates, for *they* have awareness and are themselves responsible
for social stability. In self-interest, they must regulate themselves.
Because Mary Crawford, Marianne Dashwood (*Sense and Sensibility*), the early Emma, and others border on the "chaotic," they
have to be limited, and that through loss of what they want, or
through great suffering, or chastisement.

Jane Austen asserted that the best of character remains after high spirits have been partially allayed, although spirit itself must also remain. As a counter to Fanny Price's dullness and physical weariness is her improvement in looks as the novel progresses: her "high spirits" are manifest in her appearance and manner. In brief, Jane Austen compensated for the kind of regulated mediocrity she imposed on her characters: Fanny gains physical attraction; Elizabeth Bennet gains in judgment and maturity; Emma loses the streak of vulgarity and presumption which underlies her wit.

An undeniable tastelessness clings to several of Jane Austen's heroines, however, despite her attempts to compensate for them. Although Fanny Price's desire to protect others' feelings shows a certain style, she is listless and colorless. A Christian heroine, she is too self-sacrificial, too little touched by conflicting desires and mixed motives to come completely alive. Anne Elliot (*Persuasion*) is perfection itself, able to judge for herself in nearly all matters. Emma says and does many things which mark her as a snob, although a complicated one. Catherine Morland (*Northanger Abbey*) is too silly to compete with the later heroines, herself being the butt of Jane Austen's parody of romantic heroines. Only Elizabeth Bennet, perhaps together with Elinor Dashwood (*Sense and Sensibility*), is able to withstand the debilitating darts of the Comic Spirit without becoming mediocre, tasteless, dull, or exasperating.

Measured in terms of what Jane Austen was trying to do in her later novels, *Emma* is considerably more mature than *Pride and Prejudice*. The plan of the book not only requires a classical unfolding in reverse—instead of the fall of a hero, we have the rise of a heroine—but also provides an involvement of narrative and a density of texture that mark it as an original effort. Since the irony operates deceptively, the novel upon careless reading may seem as unpleasant as the heroine. The narrative itself is one of the double take; that is, unknown to Emma, but apparent to the reader, something is always occurring below the surface. The reader sees her expose her spirit—perhaps more than any other of Jane Austen's heroines—and the degree to which the girl is deceived is a measure of the irony. Emma is not fixed, not constant; she unfolds in complexity, even though the outcome is evident.

The Comic Spirit comes to Jane Austen's aid, as later it was to work for Meredith in *Beauchamp's Career* and *The Egoist*. The comic imps mocking Emma's judgments bring common sense, fresh insights, and balance to an egoist. Like Sir Willoughby Patterne, Meredith's egoist, Emma has an inflated style which only the comic spirit can puncture. As an egoist, Emma is proud, vain about her intellectual accomplishments, snobbish, possessive, almost vulgar, and as immature in judgment as she thinks herself mature—all qualities that foreshadow Meredith's character. Emma, however, is a very young girl, while Sir Willoughby is thirty-two. She *can* lack judgment and survive; at his age, lack of self-knowledge is suicidal.

In another way, Emma's reliance on Harriet Smith, the sweet girl of little mind and fewer accomplishments, parallels Sir Willoughby's dependence on Laetitia Dale, who serves as a prop for his ego. Whenever Emma looks at Harriet, she sees herself reflected; whenever she speaks, she is honored and heard seriously. Part of Emma's attachment to Harriet results from her own deficient background in which no critical spirit was developed. Doted upon by a foolish father and deferred to by a genial governess, Emma faced none of the personal setbacks that would have matured her judgment. Even her sister is inferior in attainments to her, and therefore Emma's ego was allowed complete freedom. She judges everyone by the same standards she had judged her father and Mrs. Weston, and thinking herself loved by all, she considers herself infallible. At this point, the comic imps roll in glee.

Jane Austen suggests that there is more here than merely an indiscreet girl being put through her paces until she satisfies society's norms. Emma is more than high-spirited; she has tendencies which deny tenderness and real feeling to her, attitudes in which she seems basically deficient, including an inability to see beyond her own needs that could, under certain circumstances, injure her substantially. That she stops short of harm is an indication of how far she is stabbed by the shafts of the comic imps, which, like the furies of old, force awareness.

Jane Austen establishes Emma's position on the first page: "The real evils, indeed, of Emma's situation were the power of having rather too much her own way, and a disposition to think a little too well of herself. . . ." Isolated from most of society by virtue of her position, separated from her father by a great disparity of age and temperament, and from her sister and her former governess by distance, Emma has become accustomed to turning inward rather than outward. In Harriet, she finds a sweet, docile girl considerably beneath her in station and intelligence; that Emma, with her snobbery, would accept a friend of illegitimate birth is an indication both of how desperately she needs support and of her basic decency. Friendship with Harriet would not in itself have weakened Emma's understanding had she not conceived of the girl as more than she really was. In judging Harriet to be superior to Robert Martin, a respectable farmer, Emma brings temporary unhappiness to both parties. She, of course, fails to see that Martin is superior to Harriet, and in sense and innate judgment superior to Emma herself.

Through Harriet, Emma is able to try on courtship and marriage "for size" without committing herself to either. Harriet is the guinea pig, the laboratory for Emma's hitherto untried ideas. Harriet is also a buffer between Emma and the world, like Sir Willoughby who uses Laetitia both to "protect" him and to receive his witticisms. With Harriet, Emma can never be wrong, for the former's strength is her amiability, not her powers of understanding. The relationships in which Emma encourages Harriet—first with Mr. Elton, then with Frank Churchill, and finally with Mr. Knightley—furnish diversion for a girl essentially bored and without suitable companions. English provincial life, even when one lived only fourteen miles from London, permitted small amusement outside the rounds of social calls the daughter of the first family was expected to make. When we recognize the empty, social nature of these calls, we can see that the desire for entertainment may well override good sense.

Harriet, then, is sport for Emma. A superior person may trifle with an inferior; Darcy controls Bingley's feelings in *Pride and Prejudice*. Give Harriet substance of her own, and she would no longer serve Emma's purpose. To give Emma her due, however, we must recognize that she means well for her friend and honestly overrates the girl's qualities. For Emma to realize precisely how presumptuous she has been is part of the comic pattern of the novel, part of the "double-take" implicit in the texture of the narrative.

Emma seems the most rhythmic and the most mobile of Jane Austen's novels, perhaps because as soon as we become fixed, something occurs to upset us. Further enriching the texture of the novel is our implicit recognition that we are to accept Emma despite her flaws. Here, unlike *Pride and Prejudice,* there is no misunderstanding between completely stabilized characters; character, not events, unfolds. Thus, our own sympathies are in flux, as they are not in *Pride and Prejudice, Mansfield Park,* and *Persuasion,* in which the protagonists are relatively stabilized. Darcy does not change; Elizabeth merely comes to see him as he really is; similarly, he comes to see her as she is. In *Persuasion,* Anne Elliot and Captain Wentworth come together after certain obstacles have been removed, but these two remain unaltered. In *Mansfield Park,* Fanny Price and Edmund Bertram do not change; they are suitably joined after certain impediments are removed. Only in *Emma* does the development of characters become the spine of the novel, and only in Emma does the heroine have to come through the fires of chastisement and become purified before she rightfully assumes the role she has marked out for herself. So far has Jane Austen come from the platitudinous novel of romance!

Such is Jane Austen's ability to create a complex of attitudes that Emma's flippancy to Miss Bates (Chapter 43), which horrifies Mr. Knightley for its disrespect, both attracts and repels the reader. Miss Bates is a pleasant, garrulous, tiresome, good-hearted, well-meaning fool of a spinster, a burden despite her desire to please. Nevertheless, compassion should evoke a certain tolerance of Miss Bates; one must mask one's distaste behind decorum. The maiden lady in English provincial society was either a burden (because of lack of funds), a pest (because of lack of sense), a gossip (because of nothing to encourage self-interest), or a stoic resigned to a fate that is, at best, cold; or, more likely, a combination of all. The old maid is somewhat childish, the result of having lived alone or with a widowed mother in straitened circumstances. She is very often dependent on charity because there is nothing at which she is able to work. An object of pity, she is also the butt of derision. She is, in short, a test for the truly genteel person, whose conduct is measured by how he or she behaves to a spinster. Therefore it is not surprising that Emma's flippant remark to Miss Bates is a key to her character and to the direction the novel will take.

In that important scene, Emma and her party had been spending a dispirited day at Box Hill, with the group rarely mixing or harmonizing. Even Frank, whom Emma expected to be lively, was silent and dull. She desires attention, and risks a subtle flirtation to revive her spirits. The talk turns to games, a way of relieving boredom. With her usual self-effacement, Miss Bates admits her own dullness, and Emma, caught in the grip of a whim, suggests that Miss Bates is too modest: she really is duller than she gives herself credit for. After a moment, the remark reaches Miss Bates, but only she and Mr. Knightley seem aware of its vulgarity, and the matter passes.

When, later, Mr. Knightley strongly chastens Emma, he touches upon the superiority of the young girl in fortune, birth, and situation to the unfortunate woman she has attacked with such a lack of sensitivity. Emma rightly feels mortification and deep concern. Her education begins at this point: she questions her propriety and decides to make amends by a contrite appearance before Miss Bates. Only then can she "re-enter" society, which is governed by Knightley.

The latter provides a measure of social morality for which there is no exact equivalent in *Pride and Prejudice*. A kind of elder statesman, Mr. Knightley becomes a father-friend to Emma, who lacks real family guidance. In this capacity, Mr. Knightley seems somewhat righteous and pedagogical, although not so much as the wooden Colonel Brandon of *Sense and Sensibility*. Mr. Knightley is, however, the "good man," a kind of mellowed Darcy. He is, perhaps, more flexible than Darcy, and he definitely is not perfect, his momentary display of jealousy revealing the flaws in a seemingly impassive personality. Withal, we measure the conduct of all the other characters by Mr. Knightley's example: they must satisfy him to achieve acceptance. Against his example, the Eltons, and even Frank Churchill, show up as vulgar, and only by following his mature advice is Emma herself able to become discreet.

The entire interplay between Emma and Frank, and their relationship to Jane Fairfax, is one of the most interesting in a Jane Austen novel, showing as it does a large advance in complexity of conception, and revealing the several sides of Emma: her flirtatious spirits and her realization of personal defects; her vanity and her awareness of wrong; her sense of superiority and her feelings of insecurity. Emma's attitude toward Frank, as toward Harriet, retains a freedom of movement which more serious feeling would preclude. She flirts easily with Frank precisely because she can be admired, as Harriet respects and admires her, while still remaining uncommitted. With neither, however, is her true mettle tested—only with Mr. Knightley must she be on guard. Both Frank and Harriet—neither of whom she *fully* respects—in varying degrees give to her the attention and admiration she had received from her father and governess, the type of pleasant deference which puts no restrictions on her energies; the type of obeisance, indeed, that allows her imagination to run free. It is just this element of freedom—closer to license than freedom in Jane Austen's terms —that must be curbed, for it disallows genteel behavior and spurs vulgar outbursts.

In her "pseudo-affair" with Frank Churchill, Emma provokes a style of banter in which wit indicates a lack of feeling and gossip a lack of propriety. Talking about Jane Fairfax with Frank, whose secret engagement she is of course unaware of, Emma is able to indulge in a subtle denigration of the girl who has, she recognizes, attainments superior to her own. The delicate "play" between Emma and Frank—somewhat akin to the "forbidden play" that the bored Bertrams and Crawfords prepare in *Mansfield Park*—becomes a try-out of feelings in which nothing serious has to take place. Yet, at the same time, the issues are serious: attachments, possible love, hurt sensibilities, reputations are at stake. As a result of their intimate conversations, Emma can imagine that Frank loves her, while she in turn rejects romance in favor of friendship. Jane Austen's satiric prose catches each turn of Emma's mind:

But, on the other hand, she could not admit herself to be unhappy, nor, after the first morning, to be less disposed for employment than usual; she was still busy and cheerful; and, pleasing as he was, she could yet imagine him to have faults; and further, though thinking of him so much, and, as she sat drawing or working, forming a thousand interesting dialogues, and inventing elegant letters; the conclusion of every imaginary declaration on his side was that she *refused him*. Their affection was always to subside into friendship. Everything tender and charming was to mark their parting, but still they were to part (923).

Emma's behavior comes under satiric condemnation because she plays with what should be serious feelings. We saw from *Pride and Prejudice* and *Mansfield Park* that energy or high spirits must never crowd out right feeling: that charm is usually an inadequate substitute for a cold heart. Energy must be tempered by reason, wit by balance, and fun by civility. Mary Crawford traduces these commandments while Fanny Price honors them, and therefore the latter's dullness triumphs over the former's sparkle. Perhaps personality is sacrificed to morality, but Jane Austen believed that people must have both form and matter.

Emma, of course, recognizes that she has gone too far when, in her bleakness of soul, she resolves that, "however inferior in spirit and gaiety might be the following and every future winter of her life to the past, it would yet find her more rational, more acquainted with herself, and leave her less to regret when it were gone" (1022). This realization is, in effect, the triumph of sense over sensibility, the victory of stability over chaos. As long as Emma "plays" with feelings, she is bound to hurt people—as she does Jane Fairfax and Harriet; as long as she is frivolous, she mocks the forces which someone of her "ruling" class should protect. If she is the best that society can produce, she must attain this ideal through purification. The suffering entailed in gaining self-knowledge is the penitential road, short though it is, that she must travel.

Two questions immediately suggest themselves: if Emma is so weak throughout most of the novel, so obviously fallible in her judgments, why is not Jane Fairfax the heroine? Similarly, if Emma is occasionally tasteless and vulgar, how can she judge Mrs.

Elton, who, like Mrs. Bennet in *Pride and Prejudice,* is the personification of vulgarity?

Each question throws light on Jane Austen's methods and on the qualities of her characters. With her bad health, her grayish complexion, her air of long suffering, her lack of sparkle, Jane Fairfax lacks gaiety and energy. Like Fanny Price of *Mansfield Park,* she is somewhat debilitated by physical ailments which restrict her energy. Clearly, a Jane Austen heroine must have health —Mr. Woodhouse tirelessly makes the point; in his words, health must supersede wisdom. Even Fanny blooms when she is ready to stalk Edmund Bertram. Unlike Jane, Emma has health, sparkle, and vivacity, a combination that only Mary Crawford, among Jane Austen's leading characters, shares without assuming a heroine's role. Jane, then, becomes a contrast, although she does win her way through good manners and breeding—qualities of character rather than of personality. She is, however, too faded in manner to be more than secondary; her fortunes work out, but rarely forcefully enough to be of central interest.

Furthermore, Jane Fairfax's secret engagement indicates that somehow her bad health and secret feelings complement each other, the first acting as a kind of physical punishment for the latter. In addition, her mental anguish, another aspect of her suffering, results from the deceit which any secret entails. Moreover, Jane's offering of herself as a governess, unknown to Frank, is clearly another way in which she is tortured by deception. At this point, when Frank learns of her intentions, he too recognizes the dangerous consequences of a secret engagement and discloses his plans to his uncle. Jane Austen would not countenance secret affairs, engagements, or marriages. Whenever she wishes to display a character to the reader's outrage or distaste, she forces an elopement or a secret attachment that will do no one much good: Lydia Bennet and Wickham in *Pride and Prejudice,* Henry Crawford and Maria Bertram in *Mansfield Park,* among others. Emma herself is punished for having devised secret relationships involving Harriet, Frank, and Mr. Elton. Perhaps part of Jane Austen's intention was a literary attempt to destroy the romantic connotations of suddenly revealed secret engagements or elopements that begin in rebellion and end in domesticity. Her ideal was an above-board courtship and marriage in which prudence and love mutually forbade deception.

One consequence of the secret affair is that Frank Churchill, although misunderstood, never quite removes from himself the taint of vulgarity. His tastelessness somehow, inexplicably, rubs off on Jane. His secret gift of the piano to Jane compromises her position considerably, since the source of the gift obviously cannot be divulged. Also, on his part, it is a vain display of material power, surely generous in intention but crude in execution. The gift is a showpiece; it trumpets a kind of money value. As later in Henry James's work, money itself or what it can do must never be mentioned because it, in turn, is attached to sharp practices, crude business devices, perhaps to corruption. Money debases, although, Jane Austen readily admits, it is needed for a successful marriage.

This kind of lavish gift, then, traduces the standard of propriety that Jane Austen's society imposed specifically to ward off the uncouth encroachments of an industrialized age. Although Mr. Knightley is to some extent touched by jealousy, he does perceive rightly that Frank's spiritedness causes pain, and he correctly cautions Emma about him. Frank, of course, is rarely vulgar like Mr. Elton. His indiscretions are the result of whim rather than basic character traits. He can be salvaged through lessons of caution, as Mr. Knightley himself admits, and his end is somewhat similar to Emma's: both repent after suitable chastisement and admit the errors of their ways, Emma to Mr. Knightley, Frank in his long letter to Mrs. Weston.

The second question raised above concerned Emma's seeming vulgarity as contrasted with Mrs. Elton's actual vulgarity: how the young girl could judge the clergyman's wife rightly when both might be cut from similar fabric? If the gentlemanly ideal is the standard of Jane Austen's society, then the chief evil is vulgarity based on materialism. At the core of materialism, as Dickens was to reveal more extensively a few decades later, is a mean and cold heart. It is precisely because Emma (and Frank Churchill, also) is capable of communicating real feeling that she avoids vulgarity, although she never completely loses her initial leaning toward tastelessness. We suspect, further, that she will have to go to school to Mr. Knightley for some time before his example will succeed in edifying her. Nevertheless, despite her shortcomings, Emma means well even by those whom she plans to use. Her attachment to Harriet does seem honestly felt, although the reader may well question her original intentions in forming the relationship.

In addition, while Emma is playing with Frank Churchill and imagining him her captive, he is playing with her in order to conceal his engagement to Jane. The quality of the relationship between the two is consistent, although again the motivations of each differ. Nevertheless, in her feeling for her father, Emma shows true devotion, a point in her favor in a period when family stability was, fictionally at least, honored more in the observance than in the breach. Of course, devotion to a father who worships her is relatively simple, but Emma never takes advantage of the relationship. Her assiduous interest in his comfort illustrates a side that Jane Austen was very anxious to illuminate.

Only in those areas where extreme snobbishness and vanity have wed to spawn vulgarity is Emma culpable, and only here does she bear comparison with the tasteless Mrs. Elton, a typical nineteenth-century nouveau riche. In comparing and contrasting the two, Jane Austen has placed the old against the new, the traditionally bred against the daughter of the manufacturing classes, and claimed that the old with all its flaws is as preferable to the new as Goldsmith's Vicar of Wakefield is to the modern clergyman, Mr. Elton. It is a matter of manner and style, and Mrs. Elton reveals hers in one of her first speeches when she cites Maple Grove, her sister's residence, as her referent for everything she values. In her anxiety to display her wealthy connections, she reveals herself through language, with its stress upon size, goods, money, good society—all the elements that must be assumed but never mentioned. After these outbursts, she cannot possibly be considered genteel, and Jane Austen need not comment further. In an age without depth psychology, the individual is indicted by his own admissions.

Obviously, if Mrs. Elton is the norm of vulgarity and tastelessness, Emma is not vulgar and tasteless. In comparison, Emma, we recognize, is merely young, immature, high-spirited—capable of development once she must serve as well as reign. She is not cold and unfeeling, falsely amenable, or grasping. She is to be among the saved; Mrs. Elton is not.

The same distinctions are apparent when we attempt to evaluate Mr. Elton. His charm masks a grasping nature, and his affability an expedience that is at variance with his religious calling. A less oily descendant of Mr. Collins, Mr. Elton becomes one of a long line of worldly clergymen in Charlotte Brontë, Dickens, Trollope, George Eliot, and Meredith. In her presentation of Mr. Collins and Mr. Elton, Jane Austen comes closest in her work to satire and the didacticism upon which it rests. Her portrayal of these characters, however, satirically indicts them for the disparity between their worldly natures and their spiritual calling. Since Chaucer, this kind of pseudo-pious character has been the source of fun as well as animosity, and Jane Austen, like Fielding before her, rarely misses an opportunity to puncture egos.

In direct contrast, there are Edmund Bertram (*Mansfield Park*) and Edward Ferrars (*Sense and Sensibility*), both of whom are more interested in souls than in wallets. There are also the several minor clerical characters who come off well so long as their concern for their livings does not stultify their spirit. Mr. Elton, however, is not of this class; his manner of affected elegance and amiability hides a calculating and cold nature, a worldliness that is not even pleasant. To force the point, Jane Austen's "bad" clerics are presented as *more* venial than their worldly counterparts, more closely tied to the success of a materialistic business world than are the manufacturers and shopkeepers themselves. As a young man, Mr. Elton wishes to rise, but his lack of piety and his falsity of manner indicate he will rise at the expense of the necessary amenities. Emma does not fully recognize Mr. Elton's vulgarity as long as she sees him as Harriet's husband, but when he pays attention to herself, she repulses him with disdain and begins to understand him as he is.

Emma's condescension toward Harriet is never more apparent than in her willingness to see her friend joined to men she herself does not desire. As always, Emma's wish is to let Harriet live directly for her, especially since her home provides a warm, incubated existence which nothing can seriously disturb. With all her vanity and pretentiousness, Emma is merely a very young girl, who, lacking real adult support, wishes to remain in a perpetual cocoon, admired from a distance but untouched, as yet lacking the real juices of sexuality. Her moments of witless energy, her playfulness, her hasty judgments, her complacency and superiority are all asexual traits that will eventually disappear under Mr. Knightley's firm guidance.

Fortunately she is dimly aware of the dangers of resisting the comic spirit: egoism may be channeled into spite, vanity and pride into narcissism, and pomposity into vulgarity. Unlike Meredith's Sir Willoughby, Emma is embued with comic resiliency and with the youthful flexibility which allows development and eventual growth. In her situation, the comic spirit brings relief and clears the air when she admits that she has been a presumptuous fool. "How to understand [she realizes] the deceptions she had been thus practicing on herself and living under! The blunders, the blindness of her own head and heart!" Or again, "With insufferable vanity had she believed herself in the secret of everybody's destiny. She was proved to have been universally mistaken; and she had not quite done nothing—for she had done much mischief." Emma's temporary suffering—and it is indeed slight, for her "crimes" and schemes are indeed less than venial—allows the comic spirit to triumph: it only demands her penance. While the imps may continue to hover near her, their role in the future will be diminished.

The comic spirit has brought balance to Emma, precisely as irony restored the temporary lapses of judgment of Elizabeth Bennet. The society at the end of both *Emma* and *Pride and Prejudice* is more stable and therefore more sane than at the beginning. Through the mating of young people after they have been purified of their excesses, society perpetuates itself on the basis of its best members. The mating season ends, balance is restored, and normality returns. The stability of English provincial life is assured, for the comic spirit has brought fresh air to a hitherto dense atmosphere. Dullness, complacency, and false manner have all fallen victim to its painful darts. Civilized behavior, polish, and a kind of wisdom reign in their stead. Generosity has replaced self-love, and warm judgment the idiosyncracies of unreasoned likes and dislikes. Those with basically honest hearts gain happiness, while the expedient and the crass, if not unhappy, at least stand revealed for what they are.

Gentility, civility, and stability are the keys to Jane Austen's world. While she was not the last major British novelist to value these qualities, she was the last, Meredith perhaps excepted, to conceive of this world almost entirely in terms of the relationship between the sexes and to seek cosmic order in courtship and marriage. England was changing too much for her successors to tread upon her ground, and therefore Jane Austen's work remains unique in English fiction as an example of revelation through restriction.

THREE

Sir Walter Scott: The Moral Dilemma

With Scott's literary reputation now at such a relatively low point, it takes a broad imagination to understand his popularity in his own day. Then, in the 1820's and 30's, he rode the wave of interest in the exotic, the romantic, the far-off, the bizarre, the regional and provincial. And it is indeed true that Scott's novels are praiseworthy in nearly every respect except their literary merit. Clearly, to discuss him in serious literary terms is to uncover all his obvious faults, and yet if he is to be considered in the company of major English novelists both before and after him, he must stand or fall according to his literary merit.

Scott at his best is represented by four or five novels: the perennial *Heart of Midlothian, Old Mortality, Rob Roy, Redgauntlet,* and *The Antiquary.* His lesser novels—one like *Ivanhoe,* for example—are poor in the worst possible sense; that is, they are not poor because they are the preparatory attempts of a great writer, like some of early Thackeray or Hardy; they are poor for being presumptuous, for retaining the grand trappings without the seriousness that would make them palatable, poor for making a mockery of dialogue, action, and general behavior. At their most dismal, they fall into stereotypes of pure romance while trying to establish realistic points about society. At his worst, Scott is caught uncertainly between demands of realism and romanticism, while when he is at his best, we tend to forget, momentarily, that his ideas are often meaningless when placed within a romantic context.

There seems to be a basic realism within the work of novelists who endure. When we trace the major line of the novel in English from the seventeenth-century novels influenced by *Don Quixote* through *Ulysses,* we see that each novelist attempts to exercise firm control over what is real and what is illusory, unreal, imaginative, intangible. Even at his most illusory, Cervantes brings the Don back to his place in a real world, and even at his most imaginative, Joyce rarely departs completely from naturalistic detail. We might except *Tristram Shandy,* but this work is a sport, a prose piece which we label a novel for lack of another name. And even that fiction might have been more realistic if Sterne had lived to realize his original intention: to write an apprenticeship novel in which Tristram grows up and faces life.

It is here that Scott fails us, and fails us in a big, important way that permanently affects our reaction to his novels. Despite their vitality, their knowledgeability, and their earnestness, his novels fail to generate either meaningful ideas or emotions. Within a romantic context, he creates what appear to be realistic characters; yet when these characters must act, they do so unrealistically, creating an evidently stilted situation. Further, even within realistic scenes his characters do not act according to any inner logic, but rather to the needs of the plot or the predisposition of the author: to preserve the old order and protect property. Faced by a complex present, he tried to recall the past. And whenever he confronted the past, it satisfied him personally while often it betrayed him artistically.

That Scott wrote too much and too fast is obvious. Lockhart remarks several times that Scott never revised: "It is, I suppose, superfluous to add, that in no instance did Scott rewrite his prose before sending it to the press. Whatever may have been the case with his poetry, the world uniformly received the *prima cura* of the novelist" (pp. 367-8, Everyman ed.). Between first draft and proofs, there was only the editor who removed discrepancies. With such a system of composition there was no going back for Scott; once a character had been established, he had to remain as he was. Like some Calvinist locked within a preordained system, the character performs according to predetermined behavior. As such, only external conflicts have significance; the character does not often generate his problems and conflicts, but only reacts to them.

It is questionable, however, whether even extensive revision of each novel *before* it went to the printer would have seriously affected this weakness. The faults of the novels are basic to Scott's view of men and behavior. He seems to have had only a limited sense of humankind; in its way it was more bounded than Jane Austen's, despite her avoidance of violence, death, and many social and political issues. While Jane Austen through her irony was able to convey the feel of a larger world, Scott with his relatively straightforward presentation could not create another dimension of potential existence.

His style, for example, makes *his* world seem to be the complete universe. There is nothing left over, virtually nothing to discuss in terms of ideas or intellectual patterns. Lockhart reveals that Scott had little time indeed to think about his work. He quotes him as saying: " 'I lie *simmering* over things for an hour or so before I get up—and there's the time I am dressing to overhaul my half-sleeping, half-waking *project de chapitre*—and when I get the paper before me, it commonly runs off pretty easily. Besides, I often take a dose in the plantations, and while Tom harks out a dyke or a drain as I have directed, one's fancy may be running its ain riggs in some other world' " (p. 338, Everyman ed.). Lockhart reveals further that Scott was always doing something: ". . . but the grand secret was his perpetual practice of his grand maxim, *never to be doing nothing.*" That this activity was perpetual is obvious if we note the publication dates of his works: from 1815 to 1830, for example, he published two or three, perhaps four, books a year, for a total of some fifty books in that period, many comprising several volumes, and some of them demanding extensive background reading, annotation, and collation of texts. Trollope's remark on his own productivity, that he wrote by his watch, is often cited, but compared with Scott, Trollope was an amateur sprinter.

Such haste is obviously not conducive to consistent quality. Even Dickens at his busiest was rarely so prolific as Scott at his most leisurely. Also, he entertained far more extensively than Dickens and moved in social circles that remained relatively closed to Dickens. Scott's vast establishment at Abbotsford was a veritable tourist attraction; there was an aura surrounding him like that surrounding Tolstoy after the latter became identified as a saint, and Abbotsford became a Scottish Yasnaya Polyana. However, one may ask whether Scott had the imagination to see further into life even if conditions for work had been more promising. After all, he chose these conditions, he restricted his working time, he decided to be a world figure, all at the expense of the peace and quiet that might have led to more time and more thought. At any rate, the result of this deliberately chosen haste is that Scott's views remained superficial, and despite his amazingly wide knowledge he never came to know more than relatively little about human beings.

It is, perhaps, unfair to gauge a man's thought by his political opinions; but certainly we gain some knowledge of how a person thinks by the way he formulates his political ideas and how he approaches problems that concern his fellow men. In this respect, Scott's Toryism shows virtually no perception of changing conditions, little realization that what he was arguing against—certain aspects of the 1832 Reform Bill—had already been effectively answered. "Correct" or enlightened political opinions do not of course lead to first-rate fiction; curiously, the greatest writers are often political mavericks or hopelessly inconsistent. But Scott never seems to have doubted his views: once established, they remained stable, even innocent and naive. It was this very point that Hazlitt had in mind when he wrote that ". . . if you take the universe, and divide it into two parts, he [Scott] knows all that it *has been;* all that it *is to be* is nothing to him. His is a mind brooding over antiquity—scorning the 'present ignorant time.' He is 'laudator temporis acti'—a *'prophesier* of things past.' The old world is to him a crowded map; the new one a dull, hateful blank. He dotes on all well-authenticated superstitions; he shudders at the shadow of innovation."

As an ineluctable result of Scott's political romanticism is his presentation of realistic characters within romantic trappings, and then ultimately his intertwining of the two so that the characters come to seem unrealistic and the atmosphere unromantic. Coleridge recognized Scott's inability to blend the natural and the supernatural, Coleridge's terms for the realistic and the romantic.

In failing to find a middle way—what Fielding discussed so knowingly in the Preface to Book IV of *Tom Jones,* and in which he claimed that what we now call the novel must steer a middle course between romance and history—Scott created incredible heroes and heroines and spotty narratives. As Coleridge remarked, even in Scott's most successful works, the tale is the worst part.

Scott's energetic young protagonists are all of a kind suitable for a past age that can be idealized for its integrity, staunchness, courage, and sincerity. Whether the hero is Frank Osbaldistone (*Rob Roy,* 1817), Henry Morton (*Old Mortality,* 1817), Alan Fairford (*Redgauntlet,* 1824), or Lovel (*The Antiquary,* 1816), the values remain the same: one hero merges into all, one protagonist into several. Thus, the main thrust of virtually every Scott novel is vitiated by the predictability of the main characters, and to find life and substance one must move among the minor characters. Even here—and we are now dealing with figures held sacred even by Scott's many detractors—there is a simplicity of conception that appears to derive directly from the theory of humours: that is, the character once defined by a leading trait, or personality affliction, remains fixed by what he is. Within this theory, change of personality was virtually impossible since one's humour was determined by one's physical makeup, the conjunction of the stars at his birth, the elements of destiny operating to make him what he is. To break out of this complex sequence of events is, in effect, to remake what has already been fixed. Humours, clearly, do not allow for character development as such and are more suitable to allegory than to realistic presentation. Accordingly, we see that Chaucer, a realist among allegorists, relied upon the theory of humours for very few of his characters and even then not restrictively. Scott, however, retained the principle of a characteristic trait: thus, Rashleigh Osbaldistone (*Rob Roy*) pursues without relief a career of conspiracy and villainy; Rob Roy himself remains rigidly true to his principles at the expense of human traits like vacillation and self-doubt; even Diana (Die) Vernon of the same novel—so often held up for admiration —is seen from a distance and is motivated, not by any self-interest, but by rightness of principle. Scott's *unquestioned* political views penetrated into all aspects of his fiction—everyone by conviction is conservative, fixed within his character, dependent upon a predominant humour. Consequently, he circumscribed his minor as well as major figures, allowing them little life of their own beyond his interests and emotions, what Coleridge meant when he commented that Scott's intellect replaced all intellect in his characters. Coleridge brought the further charge that Scott failed in his attempt at imaginative characters, and this point is attached, surely, to the intellectual and emotional monotony of his figures, their inability to act positively in ways that Scott disapproved of or felt were inadequate as modes of behavior. As a contrast, one immediately thinks of Maria Edgeworth, whose work so strongly influenced Scott's regionalism, and of her ability to limn those she ultimately found inadequate without making them villains or even distasteful.

With his major characters, Scott failed to allow heroes or heroines to diverge from their training: thus, the famous case of Jeanie Deans, whose Cameronian background will not permit a lie even to save her innocent sister. Jeanie is simply one of several who are molded by background and atmosphere and therefore remain incapable of independent action. Scott applauds their staunchness even when it leads to righteousness, presumption, and fatuousness; worse, he supports staunchness even when it destroys characters and creates, instead, tin gods. In *Old Mortality,* for example, Scott is fascinated by Claverhouse, a professional soldier and a man of honor who has committed terrible acts in order to defend the monarch. Scott evidently respects a Claverhouse—a man who responds to his principles and does not shrink from the slaughter of innocent people—at the same time that he is somewhat appalled by the brutality that a man of principle may perpetrate. Nevertheless, Scott presents him favorably as a man providing the type of guidance and direction which must come from above; Scott assumes—how wrongly history bears out—that the man of principle even when wrong is gallant and admirable. Claverhouse's speech to the sensitive Morton displays all the things Scott admired in a man of action. We remember, incidentally, how much a man of action Scott himself was and how only his lameness prevented him from entering more fully into the defense against Napoleon's invasion.

"You would hardly believe," said Claverhouse in reply, "that, in the beginning of my military career, I had as much aversion to seeing blood spilt as ever man felt; it seemed to me to be wrung from my own heart; and yet, if you trust one of those whig fellows, he will tell you I drink a warm cup of it every morning before I breakfast. But in truth, Mr. Morton, why should we care so much for death, light upon us or around us whenever it may? Men die daily—not a bell tolls the hour but it is the death-note of some one or other; and why hesitate to shorten the span of others, or take overanxious care to prolong our own? It is all a lottery—when the hour of midnight came, you were to die—it has struck, you are alive and safe, and the lot has fallen on those fellows who were to murder you. It is not the expiring pang that is worth thinking of in an event that must happen one day, and may befall us on any given moment—it is the memory which the soldier leaves behind him, like the long train of light that follows the sunken sun—that is all which is worth caring for, which distinguishes the death of the brave or the ignoble. When I think of death, Mr. Morton, as a thing worth thinking of, it is in the hope of pressing one day some well-fought and hard-won field of battle, and dying with the shout of victory in my ear—*that* would be worth dying for, and more, it would be worth having lived for!" (XXXIV).

As rhetoric, this is magnificent; one sees bloody sunsets, sharp salutes, Gunga Din, perhaps Errol Flynn. It is noble, gallant, manly; it bespeaks a fair mind that is willing to accept as well as to give. For Scott, Claverhouse is the gentleman: the man who remains unperturbed at the most severe incidents and who reacts with suitable style and tone. Yet, under examination, Claverhouse gradually seems a pompous fool; his imperturbability is ridiculous, his style a disguise for a murderous, unfeeling disposition, despite Scott's attention to his sense of principle and his occasional acts of humanitarianism. To define his man better, Scott contrasts Claverhouse with General Dalzell, a butcher lacking all humanitarian impulses, although he is always a brave soldier. Nevertheless, even in juxtaposition, Claverhouse will not do. He is a little boy's dream of a soldier: fierce, but fair; disenchanted, but solidly principled; slight in stature, but strong as Hercules.

In a different sense, Morton also will not do. He leads a charmed life; while hundreds around him are killed, he survives, a romantic creature in a realistic setting. When he does run, it is because of principle, not from cowardice. Morton's gentlemanly birth carries weight with Scott, and yet how can the latter believe in the dignity of the individual while he still accepts the doctrine that guidance must come from a higher source than the individual himself? Can a man be dignified and yet be incapable of arranging his own life? Are not natural virtues sufficient without being wedded to birth and position?

It is unfortunate that one has to read Scott in this way, for he obviously should not be exposed to doubting minds. He is fine sport if one stops thinking seriously and relaxes to gain immediate pleasure. Scott's narrative descriptions are exciting and suspenseful; his dialogue—Coleridge thought it undramatic—is nevertheless witty and pungent; his sense of panorama is virtually unmatched in British fiction. These are all real virtues, but they are qualities we are prone to ignore at the present. We tend to ask the embarrassing questions, and to dismiss rather easily novelists without adequate answers. In the long run, however, Scott must come to terms with these concerns, for they involve moral issues of the greatest moment, and complex moral issues are so closely connected to the entire range of fiction that no single novel can successfully avoid them. Yet Scott's presentation of moral issues is inadequate, not so much because unresolved as because they are introduced without his sufficient awareness of their ambiguity. In brief, Scott saw moral issues clearly, perhaps more clearly than any other British novelist of stature, and this very clarity reduced his sense of conflict, externalized what should perhaps remain naggingly internal and irresolvable.

In a final sense, Scott forced upon his readers a world in which happiness was not only desirable but also possible of attainment. The serious contemporary reader, however, has turned away from that hope toward the more tangible ones of identity and survival. With the internalization of the problem, the modern novelist has lost sight of happiness as a potential goal for all people, and assumes, unlike Scott, that happiness is relative, that it may be defined by the absence of as much pain as one can avoid, but that as an actual thing, it cannot be conceived. Scott assumed that happiness was the reward for pain and struggle, that all events and life itself were purposeful. This belief, of course, was also held by other eighteenth- and nineteenth-century novelists, but their views are somewhat more qualified. Even Jane Austen—that great believer in happiness as an attainable goal—was able to present unhappy marriages, disagreeable personal relations, acts of vulgarity which create pain. All these elements are part of her quiet, unobtrusive realism. In Scott, we find little of this sense: every ending is not simply a relaxation into a happy marriage, but a fairytale conclusion in which heroes and heroines inevitably find each other, faultless creatures who have always acted from principle, rarely from other human needs.

Several critics begin their discussion of Scott by comparing his characters with those of Jane Austen, now seen to be his most distinguished contemporary, although then relatively unknown. Such a comparison is inevitable, for Jane Austen, and Dickens directly after her, indicate the main line of the novel in English and leave little room for Scott. His exploration of "realistic romance" was to become a minor genre, often merely a convention, demonstrating an outgrowth of eighteenth-century Gothic traditions before relapsing into nineteenth-century regionalism. When Scott employed melodrama, it became his major mode; when Dickens used melodrama, it was to heighten his tragic intention, so much had he broken with the main body of the Gothic tradition. As various factors forced the novel away from romance, Scott's type of novel became increasingly a backwater, the region for historical novelists in which panorama supplanted character, setting superseded psychological insight, ornamentation replaced mature social relationships.

Connected with Scott's weak sense of social relationships is his weak and disorganized novel structure. One need not be an intolerant structuralist to find dissatisfaction with Scott's techniques. One need not even be particularly concerned with form to find Scott's devices an evasion of the most elementary narrative principles in a long novel. Repeatedly, one finds Scott's technical apparatus sufficient for the novella, the short narrative burst, but unequal to the task of sustaining fiction of four hundred or more pages. Even in a relatively late novel like *Redgauntlet* (1824)— by which time one would have expected a sure hand—we become aware of serious flaws. The novel begins in the epistolary style, with a correspondence between Darsie Latimer, a young adventurer, and his close friend, Alan Fairford, whom Lockhart identifies as a portrait of Scott himself. Both are typical Scott young men, both capable of great deeds of courage and acts of integrity—men for all seasons. Suddenly, one-third through the novel, Scott reached a narrative impasse that could not be overcome through reliance on correspondence. With two paragraphs of explanation, he shifts uncomfortably to a third-person narrative with an attack upon the epistolary style itself:

The advantage of laying before the reader, in the words of the actors themselves, the adventures which we must otherwise have narrated in our own, has given great popularity to the publication of epistolary correspondence as practised by various great authors, and by ourselves in the preceding chapters. Nevertheless, a genuine correspondence of this kind (and Heaven forbid it should be in any respect sophisticated by interpolations of our own!) can seldom be found to contain all in which it is necessary to instruct the reader for his full comprehension of the story. Also it must often happen that various prolixities and redundancies occur in the course of an interchange of letters, which must hang as a dead weight on the progress of the narrative. To avoid this dilemma, some biographers have used the letters of the personages concerned, or liberal extracts from them, to describe particular incidents or express the sentiments which they entertained; while they connect them occasionally with such portions of narrative, as may serve to carry on the thread of the story (I).

With a further explanation that his shift in technique is comparable to mountain climbers who jump across chasms after inching their way along precipices, Scott plunges into a more familiar method of narration. By rejecting the Richardsonian epistolary method, Scott revealed his narrative strength, but at the expense of the psychological depth which correspondence unquestionably provides. By avoiding the redundancy of the method, Scott also avoided the slow manner of character-building, the way of seeing an object from several aspects, the methodical reliance on detail, the sense of structure and architectonic provided by the epistolary style. His explanation, moreover, seems to fit the impasse in the novel rather than to suit any natural development: the reader comes to question the very beginning of the novel and wonders why Scott did not revise the entire book to fit a third-person narrative. Once again, Scott's fiction suffered from lack of time, lack of thought, lack of care except about immediate publication and sales, all part of his need to meet expenses at Abbotsford or to pay off his obligations.

In *Redgauntlet,* the reader can see that once Scott became involved in the epistolary method and tried to fit it to uncongenial material, he had to excuse his failure to be consistent. On several occasions, before the shift to the third-person narrative, he explained that important letters had not arrived, that time had passed —all the problems that must be considered if the letter style is to fit the content. Scott, however, was unable to go back, even though his need to sketch in the Jacobite rebellion had indeed little to do with the personal revelations that correspondence calls for. The faults in the technique, here as elsewhere, are the faults in the content. The novel seems a series of starts and stops; the forward thrust of one part ends, a second part begins, and the characters— despite their loyalty and integrity, or perhaps because of it— rarely gain substance.

The reader inevitably falls back upon *The Heart of Midlothian* as Scott's best novel, but somewhat reluctantly because this is such an imperfect work. Scott's inability to see human nature in its ambiguity virtually defeated him in every area except those involving large masses of people who operate in line with a mob psychology rather than according to individual wishes and desires. It is not unexpected, therefore, that the Porteous Riot scene should demonstrate Scott at his best, for his sense of historical panorama could not here be frustrated by his relatively simple view of individual psychology. In this respect, there have been several critical attempts to remove the burden of history from Scott's work, to demonstrate that he was not a historical novelist; and yet in novel after novel, the things he does best are connected with his ability to recreate the past and to work with historical details. He has little to say to nineteenth-century England, but he has a great deal to say about the past, a point that Hazlitt early recognized.

Without necessarily becoming involved in the never-ending controversy over Jeanie Deans' refusal to tell a lie, one can see that Scott revealed here a good many of his assumptions. If *The Heart of Midlothian* is his best novel, then Jeanie's conflict in several ways is an epitome of his entire work. Its very strength unfortunately is the chief source of its weakness, for obviously Jeanie's stand upon principle derived from her Covenanter father creates a rigidity of character that can be sustained only if Scott finds another way to save Effie Deans. Since he does find such a way, the original honesty is somewhat compromised, for Jeanie in the final assessment can be honest and still her sister will be saved. This is not to say that Effie must die to guarantee Jeanie's inflexibility, but it does indicate that Scott was working within the framework of didacticism: a life based on a lie, and the guilt ensuing from it, he would claim, cannot bring happiness. By making happiness conceivable only within a context of rigid honesty, Scott compromised realistic behavior and approved an action that may save one person's soul at the expense of another's life. All this is to say that honesty of Jeanie's kind should have severe repercussions if honesty is really to mean anything; it is too easy for Jeanie to be honest and for Effie to be saved through other devices.

In the final analysis, Scott is a moralist who was unable to question his moral vision sufficiently to be creative. He suffered, paradoxically, from an inability to doubt himself and his vision, from a failure to achieve "negative capability." Every great novelist—every great creator—is able to dramatize his doubts and fears and can, against the grain, allow alternatives to poke through. Scott seemingly was unable to recognize that the kind of perfection one may hope for cannot be carried unqualified into fiction without an attendant penalty. His simplistic view of people and social relationships, the very sense of integrity that made him assume the enormous debts of Ballantyne and Constable, operated against him in his fiction. Conceived too easily, written too hastily, and published too rapidly, Scott's fiction remains in a minor genre, even while we recognize that his influence as a critic, indeed as a moral force, was immense.

FOUR

The Brontës: The Outsider as Protagonist

erhaps because *Wuthering Heights* (1847) is so far outside the mainstream of early Victorian fiction, readers have tended until recently to be fascinated less by the novel itself than by Heathcliff, its melodramatic protagonist. *Wuthering Heights,* however, is *more* than Heathcliff, for here we have, probably for the first time in British fiction, a view of society from a completely individual point of view, foreshadowing in its way the novels of George Eliot (in part), Conrad, Lawrence, and Joyce. In this area, Emily Brontë's departure from Jane Austen is obvious. The latter accepted her society as given and through irony strove to maintain its stability. Emily Brontë has moved to the periphery of society to delineate people who survive by passion alone, tempestuous and disordered figures who live marginal existences in which reason is subservient to violent feelings.

Heathcliff himself is symbolic of this world of anarchy, his very appearance setting him aside from the mainstream of humanity: dark-skinned like a gypsy, morose, brutish, diabolical, sullen, a kind of Byronic misanthrope with a great capacity both to love and to hate. He exists on the edge of humanity, a marginal or underground figure who becomes a personification of energy, the spirit of the moors, an antagonist of civilization. His often larger-than-life qualities partake of the elements that usually go into a legendary character: unknown birth, the suggestion of demonic origin, a veritable prince of darkness in his embodiment of antisocial forces. The novel becomes an operatic fable of light and dark, in which Heathcliff's dark is opposed by Catherine's light;

and from this personal tension, the novel spreads into several areas of conflict from which emerges a new vision of society.

One of the difficulties with *Wuthering Heights* is that Heathcliff provides a center for the novel without becoming a "hero," in this way somewhat like Richardson's Lovelace. He is *not* admirable or sympathetic. Neither is he realistic; rather he is a figure from an unsentimental melodrama, illustrative of the author's break from both eighteenth-century realism and Scott's romanticism. The title itself refers to the atmospheric tumult that a weathering station is exposed to in stormy weather, and we recognize that passion and torment rather than rationality or rational relationships are the substance of the novel. In *Jane Eyre,* by contrast, Rochester, although similar to Heathcliff in several superficial ways, is caught in a situation that fits a more reasonable pattern, and his behavior—even his intended bigamy—is realistic within this situation. Moreover, Jane Eyre herself, while suffering torment and pain, reacts within the terms of her society, according to a realistic expectation of behavior. Heathcliff never fits; indeed, the point is that he cannot fit, that he is, like Panurge, an immaterial substance, outside the terms we usually apply to fictional characters.

Both Charlotte and Emily Brontë were obviously influenced by late eighteenth-century and Romantic poetry, and particularly by Byron's work, influences which are most apparent in their *juvenilia,* Charlotte's Angria stories and Emily's Gondal novels. Certain of the latter's themes, as well as the characters and incidents, are carried into the Yorkshire locale of *Wuthering Heights,* although the destruction of most of the Gondal Chronicles makes more definite proof impossible. Gondal (the work of both Emily and Anne) contained a moral atmosphere not unlike that of *Wuthering Heights.* As Fannie Ratchford, the long-time student of Brontë *juvenilia,* writes: ". . . in Emily's Gondal sin was real, paid for with Old Testament certainty in fixed wages of suffering—real suffering—and death. And Emily admitted no arbitrary force for good or evil; her Gondals were free moral agents following their own wills in accordance with circumstances." When we add a reading of Emily Brontë's poetry to even a sketchy knowledge of her early work, we see that *Wuthering Heights* was no sudden miracle, nor need it have been written in collaboration with her brother Branwell, as some have strongly suggested.

Working as a parallel force in *Wuthering Heights,* as in early Browning and Meredith, are the same or similar forces that came to the surface in the so-called Spasmodic poets, especially in the feverish romanticism of Philip James Bailey, whose *Festus* (1839) —a kind of Byronic *Faust*—was perhaps known by the Brontës. The Spasmodics, among them Sydney Dobell (later, a personal friend of Charlotte Brontë), Alexander Smith, and Richard Horne (Meredith's friend), were more concerned with violent emotions reminiscent of Elizabethan tumult than with realistic romance of the Scott variety. Their Byronic "gods" swoop through life in sublime flights of imagination, carrying all before them in their great bursts of energy and search for power. Incorporeal, unrealistic, of doubtful origin and even more doubtful direction, they parallel Heathcliff and, to some extent, Rochester. Although only *Festus* was written early enough to influence the Brontës' major work, the resemblances are plain.

Wuthering Heights, truly a novel without a hero or heroine, is episodic and loose, held together solely by the doubling of structure and character as well as by the counterpointing of themes. The structure of the inner novel—that apart from the Lockwood-Nelly Dean frame—consists of three sets of lovers: the "mythological" lovers, Heathcliff and Catherine Earnshaw; the childish lovers, young Cathy and young Linton; the healthy lovers, young Cathy and Hareton Earnshaw. This world is then counterpointed to the "normal" and loveless world of Lockwood and Nelly Dean, a ferocious, acquisitive, passionate group contrasted with the middle-class society of the narrators.

In addition to these obvious contrasts, there are the thematic conflicts implicit in the differences among the lovers themselves. Thus, on several levels, as Richard Chase has pointed out, we find schisms between Other World and This World, Savagery and Civilization, Devil and God, Matter and Spirit, Stasis and Motion; as well as those between middle-class values and the impulse to destruction, between Experience and Innocence, and, finally, between the Tale and the Frame. The novel evidently works its way out in conflict, and to trace the limits of each is to see how Emily

Brontë tried to give structure to what would otherwise be an altogether rambling and loose narrative.

The Lockwood-Nelly Dean frame obviously provides a norm
for the behavior of the interior characters. Without such a standard
that allows judgment, Heathcliff would seem the measure of all
things, rather than appearing as the spirit of male rebellion which
he is. Through this relationship, Emily Brontë also secured a
solid anchor in reality, so that Heathcliff, in contrast, acts unrealistically, again on the level of disobedience and freedom that the
role demands. Like Richardson's Lovelace and Byron's Manfred,
for example, Heathcliff is outside the world of sin and guilt; his
actions, while seemingly real, become in point of fact heightened
realism, a kind of surrealistic expressionism. Heathcliff strides
rather than walks, fasts rather than eats, keeps vigil rather than
sleeps. Just as his physical needs are obviously different from those
of other men, so his life is motivated by desires other than those of
normal men. His physical deprivations are, as it were, manifestations of his unconscious, obsessed as it is with the smell of revenge
and the sweat of passion; to judge him within the terms of the realistic novel would be both inappropriate and misleading.

His pursuit of Catherine Earnshaw, consequently, is on a level
of pure passion; lacking matter, their affair is pure spirit, pure motion. It clearly moves the two beyond the confines of this world
into another one known only to them. Thus, Linton can never successfully see into Catherine's heart, for he searches with the eyes of
this world, and Catherine has already been transported out of it.
Furthermore, he is fixed, while she and Heathcliff are in flight.
Like Milton's Satan, the latter is part of the spirit of motion. Heathcliff has flown up from the underworld into a potentially blissful
union with a Catherine inexplicably denied to him by a material
world which judges him unsuitable.

In working out further contrasts, Emily Brontë introduced
Gothic elements to demonstrate how far removed the interior story
is from the frame world of reality. Whenever Lockwood enters
Heathcliff's world, he enters a domain whose substance consists of
pain, melodrama, horror, and terror. From the title itself to a description of the interior of the Heights, the atmosphere is reminiscent of the Gothic novels which Jane Austen had parodied in

Northanger Abbey fifty years before. The oft-quoted scene in which Lockwood, asleep in his coffin-like oak closet, dreams of an ice-cold hand which grasps his and which he rubs back and forth on the broken pane, is full of the sadism and bizarre effects implicit in the Gothic tale. Moreover, Heathcliff himself is as melodramatic and gloomy as the typical Gothic protagonist. Nelly Dean in fitting terms describes his actions when he hears of Catherine's death:

> He dashed his head against the knotted trunk; and, lifting up his eyes, howled, not like a man, but like a savage beast being goaded to death with knives and spears. I observed several splashes of blood about the bark of the tree, and his hand and forehead were both stained; . . . (p. 176, Chapter XVI).*

Nelly asks herself on occasion: " 'Is he a ghoul or a vampire?' " She wonders where he came from, this male witch, and she reveals her terror, her sense of shock at this goblin who loves like neither man nor beast.

Once we note these similarities to the Gothic novel, however, we must recognize that *Wuthering Heights* looks ahead to the late works of Dickens, and to Dostoyevsky and Hardy more than it looks back to Walpole, Mrs. Radcliffe, "Monk" Lewis, or Charles Maturin. Its excesses contain a potential of realism, and its protagonist brought down by forces he cannot understand or control has become a commonplace of existential literature.

The love between Heathcliff and Catherine Earnshaw is far removed indeed from earthly considerations, for they travel in spheres unrecognized by the mortals in the novel. Like D. H. Lawrence's "sacred lovers"—Birkin and Ursula Brangwen, for example—they climb to spiritual heights, while the love of others remains merely physical. To recognize this point is to begin to understand the kind of language Emily Brontë uses when they come together. At first, seemingly melodramatic, excessively mannered and affected, it becomes a clear attempt to move beyond normal, everyday conversation. Both lovers speak from a well of passion which calls for a language different from the ordinary; and thus,

* All references are to the Heather Edition of the Brontës' works (London: Allan Wingate, 1949).

as Mark Schorer has remarked, the preponderance of violent verbs, tempestuous adjectives, and charged epithets, all attempting to exalt the power of human feeling. Through language, Lockwood and Nelly as well as the reader are instructed in the nature of a grand passion.

As part of their unique love, Heathcliff and Catherine become one body and one soul: they are inseparable both in life and death. Early in the novel, Catherine tells Nelly she loves Heathcliff not because of his handsomeness but because " 'He's more myself than I am. Whatever our souls are made of, his and mine are the same; and Linton's is as different as a moonbeam from lightning, or frost from fire' " (p. 92, Chapter IX). Since Catherine and Heathcliff are one, to separate them is to kill them: both literally waste away from love-longing. Having Linton's child mortally weakens Catherine, for union with anyone but Heathcliff destroys her, just as he, too, weary of a now meaningless life, dies of anguish. As lovers of medieval intensity, they live only for love. Heathcliff compares his love with Edgar Linton's: " 'If he loved with all the powers of his puny being, he couldn't love as much in eighty years as I could in a day. . . . It is not in him to be loved like me: how can she love in him what he has not?' " (pp. 158-159, Chapter XIV). Heathcliff claims supernatural qualities, as if comparing himself to a god, a being in whom love is so fierce that it explodes into altogether new dimensions.

After Catherine's death, Heathcliff goes to her grave and uncovers her coffin, planning to embrace her and to die, if he must, in her arms. Through his over-ruling passion, Heathcliff has clear affinities with the medieval lover who "dies" for his love. In this tradition, the love is both earthly and unearthly—a real woman becomes the object of a spiritual passion; actual consummation, at least theoretically, could destroy the relationship. Characteristic of the man's feeling is a love-longing that weakens and enervates him, destroying his health and his initiative in the public world. His love occupies the whole of his time, leaving no room for other activities, for he devotes his entire life, as would a slave, to his mistress. Heathcliff's love fits into this tradition: possessed and obsessed by his attachment to Catherine Earnshaw, he becomes a slave to a grand, destructive passion.

Although Heathcliff's towering figure undoubtedly dominates the novel, neither he nor his relationship with Catherine is the whole of *Wuthering Heights*. After Catherine's death, the narrative shifts to young Cathy and young Linton, the childish lovers who are each the issue of a "bad" marriage, one that went against the laws of love. Linton is, of course, the opposite of Heathcliff: weak, effeminate, and sensitive, and, as such, the butt of his father's derision and sadism. Cathy, on the other hand, has characteristics of Heathcliff: she is untamed, tempestuous, frenetic. She is Heathcliff's daughter by temperament, as if her mother in conceiving her had imprinted Heathcliff's love upon the child. Linton is Heathcliff's burden both for having married Isabella Linton and for Catherine Earnshaw's failure to marry him. Young Linton, then, is a mockery of Heathcliff's own obsessions. More clearly than ever, we can see that the novel works on character contrasts: Heathcliff has a son approximating Edgar Linton, and Catherine has a daughter resembling Heathcliff. The roles are completely reversed: Heathcliff's sadism is now practiced by young Cathy, and Edgar Linton's compliance by young Linton.

As Richard Chase has remarked, children dominate *Wuthering Heights;* only Heathcliff and Linton become mature. Isabella is a childbride, fitting into the pattern of women who after marrying for romantic notions never grow up; Dora Spenlow of *David Copperfield* and Amelia Sedley of *Vanity Fair* are contemporary examples. Hindley is an inebriate who regresses into helpless childhood after his wife's death; then later, his son Hareton has the emotional reactions of a sullen boy, not those of a grown man. Similarly, Catherine Earnshaw dies almost a child (herself giving birth to another child), not having developed into womanhood, her love for Heathcliff retaining the fierceness and blindness of a young girl's. Then the two childish lovers themselves, young Cathy and young Linton, fit into the cycle, to be completed by the union between young Cathy and Hareton, also two very youthful and immature lovers. Their wooing, in turn, is that of two children, filled as it is with the taunts of young Cathy and the sullen affection and morose sympathy of Hareton. The latter's awkwardness and social gracelessness are an obvious throwback to young Heathcliff, although Cathy, despite her condescending manner, is capable of both compassion and decency. Once she is satisfied that she has impressed Hareton, the union can take place on an equal basis. The foundation for a healthy marriage has been laid, and Heathcliff, now lacking all energy and direction, acquiesces; for the world of children's love can no longer engage even his wrath. As Heathcliff dies, the Heights are purged, and normality returns, in the form of an acceptable love union. The novel that began with Heathcliff clawing and biting amidst the Earnshaws, and then defying Fate and Fortune in a quest to attain love, ends with a typically "healthy" Victorian dénouement: a happy marriage between two childish people who nevertheless have the right instincts to bring mutual completion. The novel concludes on a note of domesticity and peaceful balance, with the children in firm control.

Except for Edgar Linton, who is peripheral to the main thrust of the narrative, Heathcliff is, then, the sole adult in a children's world, a kind of devil amidst angels. Furthermore, he is the sole active personality in the novel; everyone else is acted upon. His position as mover gives him the flexibility and mobility that make him seem a devilish giant—a huge figure from the world of injustice, of which he in turn had been a victim—moving among pygmies. Similarly, Heathcliff seems blacker than black, for his darkness (he is a Prince of Darkness) is exaggerated when contrasted with the whiteness of others. As in several Gothic novels, the deployment of images of dark and light emphasizes the theme of innocence (child) versus experience (adult), with Heathcliff's dark tones indicating him as a figure of repression. His scowl and sullenness seem to have originated in areas into which others cannot reach, a backwash of diabolism, a swamp of mental illness and physical wretchedness. Heathcliff hovers physically over the entire novel: everyone acts to please or displease him, while he acts as *he* pleases.

Emily Brontë built into the novel a "moral conscience" for Heathcliff in the form of the "frame" narrators, Lockwood and Nelly Dean, both of whom become the norm by which Heathcliff can be measured. Without the stability of the narrators, the world of *Wuthering Heights* would hardly differ from that in the youthful tales of Gondal and Angria, lacking as many of these stories did any organized sense of morality, sin, or conscience. Heathcliff would stride through the novel much as the heroes and villains of the *juvenilia,* with nothing to impede them but their own mistakes. The narrators, however, provide a society, or at least an alternative to life at the Heights.

Next to Heathcliff, Lockwood rightly seems fair and slight, a representative from the civilized world coming to grips with an undomesticated and untamed animal. His reasonableness constantly clashes with Heathcliff's tempestuousness, as much as earlier Nelly Dean's Christian precepts had clashed with the headlong paganism of Catherine Earnshaw. While both narrators are instructed in the forms of intense love, in comparison their own feelings appear ineffective and impotent. Against the violence of the tale, they provide order; against hate and sadism, they offer Christian love; against the storm, they suggest calm. Nelly Dean, in particular— her prosaic name is itself an index to her character—tries to explain the ways of God to the Devil, and is tolerated only because Heathcliff recognizes that her advice is harmless and insignificant. Her feelings and Lockwood's are transcended by the unearthly power of Heathcliff, as the latter also transcends the power to love of a typical male, Edgar Linton or Jane Austen's Darcy, for example. As a transcendent power, Heathcliff has the vigor and stature of a god (father) and a devil (father and lover); in both roles, for good or ill he sweeps all before him. Nevertheless, he has to pay the penalty for losing Catherine to Edgar Linton: he must remain wild; unlike Lovelace, he is not to be tamed by love.

Emily Brontë speculates that Heathcliff's attitudes are the result of his unsympathetic treatment in childhood. Unattractive in appearance and uncouth in temperament, he becomes the butt of the other children, particularly of Hindley Earnshaw. As a foundling, Heathcliff is an intruder upon the Earnshaw's hospitality, and he is made to suffer because of his strangeness. Unable to enter into the family, especially after the death of old Mr. Earnshaw, he chooses defiance over acquiescence. With a will toward power, he stays outside and plots revenge without regard for personal welfare or comfort. He extends his hate to all except Catherine, who reaches out her sympathy to this strange boy. Even Heathcliff's name—he is christened after a son who had died in childhood— is that of someone who partakes of another world, into which he is forced back by circumstances. Already established in his childhood is one of the basic contrasts that run through the entire novel, that between the Other World and This World.

However, can a Heathcliff be explained simply by means of a struggling, unhappy childhood? Is he not in reality closer to Hardy's Mayor of Casterbridge, Henchard—whose character is his fate— than to a naturalistic protagonist whose environment determines his nature? Like a Greek tragic figure, Heathcliff is what he is: the elements of his greatness (his will to power) contain as well as his flaw (his overweening passion), and he is unable to escape himself. What keeps Heathcliff from becoming a tragic hero is of course his ignobleness and disagreeableness; he is not sympathetic, unless we confuse his strength with virtue. Closer to a melodramatic hero than a tragic protagonist, Heathcliff nevertheless contains the immoderation and excesses of the Greek hero and gains our temporary, grudging admiration for his defiance of what will eventually doom him.

Nonetheless, the contrast between Childhood and Adulthood once established swells throughout the narrative, beginning with Heathcliff's own childhood among the Earnshaws and then extending into the second generation, in which he imposes the same harshness on young Linton, Cathy, and Hareton that was practiced on him. Particularly in his treatment of Hareton Earnshaw, Heathcliff attempts to strike back at Hindley, but here the motivation is somewhat weak, for after Catherine Linton's death, Heathcliff's virulence is not convincing. True, he rightly hates the Lintons, but his intense persecution of Hindley and then Hareton is excessive. His reduction of Hindley to a penniless and shapeless heap is part of a revenge *outside* his love for Catherine. His treatment of Hindley and Hindley's son is part of a motivation Emily Brontë cannot explain simply by his childhood; for it partakes of the self-destructive, accumulated hatred that makes Heathcliff seem a devil, or a savage from another world.

In Hareton, Heathcliff has a boy whom he systematically enslaves and whose spirit he tries to break, and yet Hareton is at least one part Heathcliff: an outcast, unwanted, sullen, uneducated, revengeful, socially inept, and in love with someone who seems unattainable. The pattern has come full circle; Heathcliff's persecution of Hareton is like the persecution of his alter ego. So strong is his spirit of destruction that he has no sympathy even for himself.

In trying to crush Hareton—for whom he retains a spark of sympathy and understanding—Heathcliff displays attitudes that find no motivation in rational thought. Therefore, to treat *Wuthering Heights* as a realistic novel is to court difficulties. Too much is uncharted and too much unaccounted for in the novel. The motivation moves upon different planes, either deep in the unconscious or else on some transcendental level which analysis cannot reach because reason is no longer a factor.

In several ways, then, *Wuthering Heights* is less a novel than a dramatic poem in which flights of imagination replace analysis, and transcendental language supplants the prose of the realistic novel. The vocabulary is an index not only to the content but to the genre itself. The language is that of the elements—Heathcliff is described as a storm, living as he does in the tumult of a tempest. The language also evokes wild animals, fire, everything that would transcend normal human relationships and raise (or lower) them to a huge abstract conflict in which Heaven and Hell themselves seem at war. Like the dramatic poem which it approximates, *Wuthering Heights* is intensely dramatic, perhaps at times melodramatic. Similarly, like a dramatic poem, *Wuthering Heights* depends less on a realistically conceived chain of events than on a certain atmosphere in which intense conflicts transpire.

If we compare (say) *Pride and Prejudice* with *Wuthering Heights,* we can readily see the differences between the "realistic" novel and the novel conceived like a dramatic or epic poem. As we have seen, Jane Austen's characters are concerned with dignity, breeding, and gentility—all the components of what we call manner; her irony is directed at those who wander ever so little from the expectations of society. Even her heroines must be redirected toward balance and judgment. Furthermore, her males—like Mr. Knightley, Colonel Brandon, even Darcy and Edmund Bertram —have the aspect and manner more of fathers than of passionate lovers, or at least of older men who are fatherly and understanding. They take the heroine into tow; they do not probe the depth of her passions.

Only thirty-five years after the publication of *Pride and Preju-*

dice, the picture has been radically altered. To live like Heathcliff in a perpetual heat of passion and revenge would be physically and psychologically impossible for a character who requires normal amounts of food, rest, and peace of mind. Furthermore, Heathcliff is the opposite of genteel, well-bred, and dignified. Rather than letting his reason command while his passions obey, he is obsessed by passion while his reason lags. Moreover, he hardly provides a fatherly figure—as a father, he is sadistically hateful—and he recognizes few social norms as necessary for his own or others' behavior. In the inner story of *Wuthering Heights,* there is no clear sense of a real world. Few of the daily events which make up life are apparent; none of the daily amenities are recognized. People live within different dimensions, in more heroic terms than the novel rooted in realism usually allows for. Thus the sense of swirl, of violence, of the passions of tragic drama. Up to *Wuthering Heights*—and for half a century after—the serious novel had been muted, dealing more with tones and colors than with the full breadth of emotion. Only Richardson had touched on this ground, but compared with Heathcliff, his Lovelace and Mr. B. are effeminate dwarfs beside an epical figure. Not until Hardy's Henchard was there to be a major protagonist of Heathcliff's intensity and headlong drive for self-destruction.

Not only Heathcliff but also the women—Catherine Earnshaw, young Cathy, Isabella Linton—fall almost completely outside the terms of realism, for they exhibit passions which go beyond those society deems "normal." Clearly, the idea of the conventional heroine, as developed by the eighteenth-century novelists as well as by Jane Austen and Dickens, was no longer acceptable to Emily Brontë. When she wanted a conventional woman, she created Nelly Dean, who provides distance and calm from the *outside* and has little effect indeed upon her charges either as children or adults. No more than fixed and static matter herself, she has no control over the spirit and motion which characterize the other members of the Heights. Moreover, compared to their experience (their involvement in passionate life), her innocence makes her a spectator in an emotional world and precludes her chances of understanding them. She can only report and judge, and remain safely within her own world, which does not recognize the intensity of a Heathcliff or a Catherine Earnshaw.

In the story itself, she has her counterpart in Edgar Linton, and his unfortunate and unhappy life is that of a man who tries to be average in a world that defies normality. His is the measure of correct conduct, and yet rather than becoming a romantic hero, he is stripped of all strength, made to seem effeminate and emotionally ineffective. A virtual cripple among giants, Edgar Linton is part of a group from which only Nelly Dean is able to extricate herself. She can judge while Edgar must act, and therein lies her opportunity to save herself. Even Lockwood, despite a certain worldliness that distinguishes him from Nelly, would be smashed had he been a participant in this turbulent world. He is able to survive this world simply because he receives it in fragments; were he to have received it all at once, like Edgar, he would be staggered and crushed by forces outside his powers of understanding. As part of the frame, Lockwood and Nelly Dean, like Conrad's Marlow in *Lord Jim,* are at a safe remove from events that are enervating and destructive.

In *Wuthering Heights,* everybody shouts. The very winds which whip around the Heights are partially generated by its inhabitants; and the violence of the tumult is the fury of their expression. Gothic terror is now manifest not in ghostly figures who suffer from hallucinatory visions but in passionate people whose lives contain chaotic desires. In this respect, Heathcliff embodies Emily Brontë's vision of the male principle—a composite perhaps of her dominating father, her dissolute brother Branwell, and also of the violent Gondal and Angria characters. More a force or the naked unconscious of a man than a real being, Heathcliff is outside sin and guilt, as are the other characters in contact with him. They live as if they were original man and woman making their own terms without the dictates of a god. The world of *Wuthering Heights,* then, can be seen as a kind of anti-Paradise in which unhappiness rather than happiness is the by-product of human relationships. The arrangement of this anti-Paradise is the working of the Devil; Eve's temptation has indeed infected her progeny, and love is more an agony than a sacred feeling. By the fact that nature itself is cold and bleak life is already partially defined. The demons clash with the fair and innocent, and both are destroyed in a world that gives way completely to the anarchy and chaos of savage passion.

A Prince of Darkness, a powerful principle of blackness, a vision of maleness as it appeared to a virtually isolated authoress, Heathcliff sweeps all before him in his amoral quest for position and love in a world that has made him an outcast. Not for several years was this kind of character on a major scale to turn up in English fiction. While certain of his "underground" qualities appear in minor Dickens characters—Dolge Orlick, Steerforth, and Bradley Headstone, for example—not until the end of the century, with Hardy's Henchard, was a man to defy the universe and destroy himself by virtue of his uncontrollable passions. When a figure like Heathcliff re-enters fiction in the twentieth century, in D. H. Lawrence's novels, he smolders rather than burns; toned down, he appears as a groom or a gamekeeper or even as an animal. He still stalks passionate women, but his greatest attraction is silence instead of violence. Nevertheless, the successors of Heathcliff remain dark, either in appearance or spirit. Mysterious men, they too reject the rewards of a mechanistic world in order to enjoy the rites of passionate love.

Wuthering Heights, which was published in 1847 as having been written by an "Ellis Bell," the pseudonym Emily had already used for the publication of some of her poetry, was not well or sympathetically received. Critics accustomed to Jane Austen's realism, Scott's romanticism, and the early work of Dickens misunderstood and misinterpreted a novel that diverged so far from early Victorian conventions. Even *Vanity Fair,* which was being published at this time, was judged harsh and cynical, the work of a pessimist and a misanthrope, and *Vanity Fair* is certainly less of an anomaly than *Wuthering Heights.* We remember that even *Pickwick Papers* (1837) found many admirers who thought it unfit for family reading, and that *The Ordeal of Richard Feverel* (1859) was considered the work of a wicked man. Sexuality aside, the wildness and violence of *Wuthering Heights* put off the reader, and the novel, carefully wrought as it has been discovered to be, was deemed chaotic and confused.

At the time Emily Brontë was writing *Wuthering Heights,* her sister Anne was about to begin *The Tenant of Wildfell Hall,* and her sister Charlotte, having completed a short novel, *The Professor,* was working on *Jane Eyre.* Although *Jane Eyre* contains several of the unconventional elements of *Wuthering Heights,* it was a great success shortly after publication; and Charlotte Brontë, as "Currer Bell," gained the fame denied to both Emily and Anne. In all Charlotte wrote four novels—*The Professor* (published posthumously in 1857), *Jane Eyre* (1847), *Shirley* (1849), and *Villette* (1853)—but *Jane Eyre* was by far the most popular. On the surface, it is easy to see why *Jane Eyre* succeeded while *Wuthering Heights* failed. Like Emily, she was working with explosive material, but unlike her sister, she presented a temporized Heathcliff in the figure of Rochester and a toned-down Catherine Linton in the person of Jane. Further, while Jane is freer with her passions than the age could fully approve, nevertheless her love domesticates Rochester and leads to happiness, not to destruction.

In the Preface to her first novel, *The Professor,* Charlotte declared, like George Eliot later, that she was interested in a certain kind of "democratic realism." She talks about "real living men" and asserts that her hero "should share Adam's doom, and drain throughout life a mixed and moderate cup of enjoyment." She then admits that publishers were not interested in this kind of realism but instead would have liked "something more imaginative and poetical—something more consonant with a highly-wrought fancy, with a taste for pathos, with sentiments more tender, elevated, unworldly." She then wonders: "Men in business are usually thought to prefer the real; on trial the idea will be often found fallacious: a passionate preference for the wild, wonderful, and thrilling—the strange, startling, and harrowing—agitates divers souls that show a calm and sober surface." Accordingly, once she could not find a publisher for *The Professor,* she turned to another kind of novel in which the "imaginative" and the "poetical" were intermixed with the realistic.

It was precisely these poetical effects in *Jane Eyre* that George

Henry Lewes, the critic and biographer, labeled melodramatic and objectionable.* In her answer, Charlotte Brontë repeated her remarks from the Preface to *The Professor,* claiming that Nature and Truth—her sole guides—were insufficient, that she "restrained imagination, eschewed romance, repressed excitement; over-bright colouring, too . . . [she] avoided and sought to produce something which should be soft, grave, and true." In another exchange of letters, she rejected Lewes' suggestion that Jane Austen should provide a model of restraint for her. She repeated that restraint and shrewdness are not enough; one must follow one's own inspiration:

When writers write best, or, at least, when they write most fluently, an influence seems to awaken in them, which becomes their master— which will have its own way—putting out of view all behests but its own, dictating certain words, and insisting on their being used whether vehement or measured in their nature; new-moulding characters, giving unthought-of turns to incidents, rejecting carefully elaborated old ideas, and suddenly creating and adopting new ones.

Jane Austen, she finds, has created an "accurate daguerrotyped portrait of a commonplace face; a carefully fenced, highly cultivated garden with neat borders and delicate flowers; but no glance of a bright, vivid physiognomy, no open country, no fresh air, no blue hill, no bonny beck."

We should not expect *Jane Eyre* to hark back to Jane Austen's novels any more than *Wuthering Heights* did; rather, it looks ahead in 1847 to the next great woman novelist George Eliot, who was not to publish her first novel for another twelve years. Charlotte Brontë, in her realization that man's hopes must first be chastened by ill success, was foreshadowing George Eliot's own treatment of fortune tempered by adversity. Both authors agreed that the individual worthy of consideration would mature under adversity and that misfortune was a test of his worth. Thus, Jane Eyre does not buckle under ill treatment, but instead grows in stature as she defies persecution. Similarly, Dorothea Brooke (*Middlemarch*) ma-

---

* In his own novel, *Ranthorpe,* published in the same year as *Jane Eyre,* Lewes eschewed "poetical effects" for stereotyped characterization, homespun philosophizing, and a personal brand of melodrama.

tures after her first marriage and gains in sympathy and human understanding. If the "soul has strength," Charlotte Brontë was to say later in *Shirley,* "it conquers and rules thereafter."

Furthermore, her heroines determine their fortunes less by the dictates of society than by their own wishes. Their choice of mate, as well as their choice of circumstances, is based on personal feeling, regardless of what society expects. Jane Austen's heroines, we saw, had far less freedom of movement, and when they attempted to stretch their wings the author's irony brought them back. Restricted mobility, together with certain constrictions in matters of love, binds every Jane Austen heroine to an acceptable social standard. Unlike Charlotte Brontë's heroines and, later, George Eliot's, they do not pursue their husbands; instead, they wait for the man to come who recognizes their innate worth despite their superficial flaws: Elizabeth's prejudice and hasty judgment, Emma's vanity and immaturity, Fanny Price's insipidity, and Catherine Morland's foolishness. Although their passions on occasion are almost uncontrollable, Charlotte Brontë's chief heroines contain few, if any, flaws: Jane Eyre, for instance, is a model young woman, sympathetic, capable of great love and devotion, full of common sense and understanding, and loyal to those who have befriended her. Even her appearance, like Fanny Price's, improves through love.

Similarly, as Jane flowers under the influence of Rochester's passion, so is he purified by the love of a good woman. In *Wuthering Heights,* it is clear that Heathcliff could have been tamed by Catherine's love had she united herself with him, for much of his violence results from her failure to defy society and marry him. The one person who could have domesticated this feral creature is unable to rise to his level of love, and by rejecting him, Catherine leaves his love free to turn into hate and revenge. Jane, on the other hand, by "taming" Rochester prevents the potential violence in him from turning into bitterness, and by providing in her steady love a prop for his passion, draws off the excess onto herself and thus neutralizes him.

Love in both novels provides a meeting ground where personal flaws can, therefore, be minimized and passions given some outlet. Heathcliff recognizes that love transcends all difficulties, including the deficiencies of his birth, but his recognition of the transcendental power of love is not sufficient to carry Catherine outside the demands of social conformity and propriety. Jane Eyre, however, is willing to sacrifice everything for love; her unwillingness to compromise herself in an affair with Rochester is more a matter of personal prudence than a submission to social demands. With this combination of daring and prudence, Jane is able to divide and conquer: Rochester is freed from his mad wife and enabled to marry her.

Clearly, then, Jane's passion is powerful and compelling, not at all the kind of controlled feeling found in a Jane Austen heroine, whose good sense forced moderation even upon her ability to love. The conflict is indeed real in Jane Eyre, for she is almost ready to succumb when Rochester pleads with her to come away:

. . . while he spoke my very conscience and reason turned traitors against me, and charged me with crime in resisting him. They spoke almost as loud as Feeling: and that clamoured wildly. 'Oh, comply!' it said. 'Think of his misery; think of his danger—look at his state when left alone; remember his headlong nature; consider the recklessness following on despair—soothe him; save him; love him; tell him you love him and will be his. Who in the world cares for *you?* or who will be injured by what you do?' (pp. 369-70).

Rochester seizes her, devouring her "with his flaming glances," but sanity, not this temporary madness, dominates Jane's decision. Rochester, however, is fully aware of her true feeling. On that topic, she is not reticent.

In a letter of 1839 to her friend Ellen Nussey, Charlotte revealed that Jane's tenacity extended to the author herself, who had turned down the marriage proposal of her friend's brother: "I felt that though I esteemed, though I had a kindly leaning towards him, because he is an amiable and well-disposed man, yet I had not, and could not have, that intense attachment which would make me willing to die for him; and, if ever I marry, it must be in that light of adoration that I will regard my husband." And in a poem, "Passion," dated December 12, 1841, she wrote: "Some have won a wild delight, / By daring wilder sorrow; / Could I gain thy love tonight, / I'd hazard death tomorrow." In a later stanza, she wrote: "No—my will shall yet control / Thy will, so high and free. / And love shall tame the haughty soul— / yes—tenderest love for me."

The various elements of *Jane Eyre* extend back into the very substance of Charlotte Brontë's life, and, in point of fact, the novel was realized in several essential parts by 1839 or 1840, the time of the above letter and poem. In addition, *Jane Eyre,* more than any other of Charlotte's novels, finds its roots in her *juvenilia,* in the windings and unwindings of her Angria tales, as well as in her early reading. The Byronic Rochester is derived, in large part, from Arthur Augustus Adrian Wellesley, Duke of Zamorna (not Wellington) and Emperor of Angria, around whom the young Charlotte had embroidered the heroic actions of a muscular Childe Harold. She may have come across the situation concerning the bigamous intentions of a basically good man in a story by Sheridan Le Fanu published in 1839. Rochester's mad wife derives from Lady Zenobia Ellrington, who appears in Charlotte's first love story, and who also appears, a composite of nobility and shrieking wildness, in the Angrian cycle. As Fannie Ratchford has pointed out, Bertha Mason Rochester is only partially derived from Zenobia, however; she is also found in "The Green Dwarf," Charlotte's adaptation in 1833 of Scott's *Ivanhoe.**

The idea of a hidden mad wife may also have come from Mrs. Radcliffe's Gothic novel, *A Sicilian Romance* (1790).

Other Angrian figures reappear in *Jane Eyre* in one guise or another, including Rochester's ward Adèle and her mother, Céline Varens, Rochester's former mistress. Outside the Angria stories, even Helen Burns, Jane's sympathetic friend who dies of consumption, is modeled on Charlotte's sister Maria, who, also tubercular,

---

* Scott, we recognize, was for good or ill, of special significance to Charlotte. She exhorted her friend to ". . . read Scott alone; all novels after his are worthless." And, ". . . Scott exhibits a wonderful knowledge of human nature, as well as surprising skill in embodying his perceptions so as to enable others to become participators in that knowledge." Possibly, under Scott's influence, Charlotte was tempted to write Romances rather than Novels, for his presence can be felt throughout the melodramatic and intense love affair in the middle section of *Jane Eyre,* fraught as the affair is with frenzy and danger. However, even without Scott, Charlotte would probably have reached her own conclusions, influenced as she was by late-eighteenth- and early nineteenth-century Romantic poets and by Byron in particular.

died young and unfulfilled. The affair between Rochester and Jane follows the Angria pattern set by Zamorna and becomes a test of Jane's moral values. Unprotected by family or friends, Jane, supported only by her untried principles, must face the temptation of Rochester, just as Mina Laury in the Angrian cycle must confront a tempestuous Zamorna. But while Mina could not resist the forceful Zamorna and succumbs to his attraction, Jane honors her principles despite temporary pain.

While the love affair is obviously the most compelling section of the book, it is by no means the whole of the long novel. Not unlike the opening scenes of *David Copperfield* (to appear in two years), the early sequences of *Jane Eyre* show, among other things, the injustice of the adult world toward children. *Jane Eyre* fits loosely into the group of apprenticeship novels represented by *David Copperfield, Pendennis, Great Expectations, The Ordeal of Richard Feverel,* and in the present century by *Sons and Lovers* and *A Portrait of the Artists as a Young Man,* "loosely" because Jane herself lacks the mobility and flexibility of the typical apprenticeship hero or heroine. As a woman in a restrictive society, she can develop only within severe limitations. Her decisions must, perforce, be few, and they must also be conclusive, for within such restrictions there are few chances for her to resolve a bad choice. Like Flora in Conrad's *Chance,* Jane must make one basic decision, and this will either give her happiness or completely ruin her life. In making this choice, however, she has no other standard than the principles gained in her early apprenticeship to life. When Flora, in *Chance,* chooses Captain Anthony over her father, she makes the sole decision that leads not only to happiness but also to sanity. When Jane Eyre refuses the temptation of an elopement with Rochester—a temptation made particularly attractive by her strong love and alien position—she enters the central part of her ordeal, which must be successfully overcome before she gains her reward, a severely chastened and humbled Rochester.

Within the terms of her limited apprenticeship, Jane Eyre suffers all the indignities of her "low" position, in terms of both class and money. As in Dickens' novels of this kind, injustice consists of the stultification of one's natural feelings in the face of superior authority, be it David Copperfield with Mr. Murdstone or Sissy Jupe with Mr. Gradgrind or Pip with Miss Havisham. Although more civilized than Heathcliff, Jane appears to Mrs. Reed as Heathcliff must have appeared to the Earnshaws: undesirable, a burden, sullen, and socially backward. Clearly, she can gain self-respect and dignity only by entering a world in which she must prove herself.

The scenes with Mrs. Reed in the early pages have the same texture of sadistic cruelty that characterizes many nineteenth-century apprenticeship novels. Jane's experience in the red-room, with its overtones of Gothic terror, is indicative of her entire existence with Mrs. Reed and her spoiled, degenerate children. Charlotte Brontë helped develop the now familiar theme of the basically healthy outcast girl who is persecuted by the warped, depraved children born to privilege. Jane's hysteria in the room is a manifestation of her frustration, her only way of protest against a life that on every side restricts her development. These boundaries placed around the growing spirit—to be repeated by Dickens in Gradgrind's principles of utilitarian education and by Meredith in Sir Austin Feverel's system—are also manifest in Mr. Brocklehurst's Lowood Institution. There, every girl is an outcast, and Jane's alienation from the cruel "norm," no longer singular, does not prevent her coming to terms with herself. And although the sadism and cruelty of Mrs. Reed's are continued in the school, Jane, under the tender influence of Helen Burns, is able to achieve the mental freedom necessary for moral judgment.

Nevertheless, the repressive atmosphere of Lowood is particularly manifest in the treatment accorded Helen Burns. These scenes, as realistic as Jane's later ones with Rochester are melodramatic and wildly romantic, illustrate that non-conformity to nature leads to spiritual, and even actual, death. Mr. Brocklehurst states with all his authority: " 'Yes, but we are not to conform to nature: I wish these girls to be the children of Grace. . . .' " Jane is chastened, even by Helen Burns, for thinking too much of human love. Her friend tells her that a person has other resources which derive from God and which give strength under adversity. But Jane, while calmed by her friend's ability to rise above her immediate circumstances, must follow her heart, which leads her to seek human love and understanding, while rejecting authority and repression.

Central to the apprenticeship novel is a strong character around whom the entire narrative can be structured. This character must be of sufficient substance to sustain the weight of what is usually a lengthy narrative and also to make coherent what would otherwise be merely a string of loose episodes. In *Great Expectations,* Dickens faced this problem and successfully resolved it by severely testing Pip, who significantly changes as the novel proceeds. At all times, he has human shape and human responses. The fault in Charlotte Brontë's presentation of Jane Eyre is clearly her failure to allow change. Jane grows only chronologically, not emotionally or mentally. She is inflexibly right from the beginning; the world she defies at Mrs. Reed's is an unjust world, which she also defies at Mr. Brocklehurst's school. Later, she rejects St. John Rivers' offer of marriage, as before she rejected bondage and suppression. Her oneness of character, then, is both her strength and her fault. As a support, her singleness of purpose and knowledge of self give her moral force as well as social judgment; as a weakness, her singularity forbids the flexibility, the human flaws, and the moral confusion which are part of a truly created character. Charlotte Brontë talks a great deal about the self—especially its demands upon reason—but only rarely allows Jane to face honestly *all* aspects of it.

Jane's common sense, awareness of justice, and equity of temperament make her seem a rationalist in a world of madmen and madwomen. And it is precisely this reasonableness which defines her, despite the currents of great passion which run beneath the surface. Unlike Heathcliff, who lives only fleetingly in the reasonable world and chooses to dwell in an underground hell of passion, Jane lives by her wits without ever forgoing her deeper feelings. She is proper, relatively careful, and temperate even when her heart tells her to be abandoned. These qualities see her through a world which punishes the chaotic and chastens the disordered. Reason, qualified by a strong acceptance of Earth, marks Jane's major decisions, as later it was to mark Dorothea Brooke's choice of Will Ladislaw in *Middlemarch* and Clara Middleton's preference for Vernon Whitford in *The Egoist*. In a letter written late in his life (March 6, 1888), George Meredith revealed certain assumptions which also seem to have been those accepted by Charlotte Brontë forty years earlier. Meredith wrote:

I have written always with the perception that there is no life but of the spirit; that the concrete is really the shadowy; yet that the way to spiritual life lies in the complete unfolding of the creature, not in the nipping of his passions. An outrage to Nature helps to extinguish his light. To the flourishing of the spirit, then, through the healthy exercise of the senses (to Mrs. J. B. Gilman, *Letters*, II, 409).

The novel becomes, in point of fact, the unfolding of Jane Eyre's spirit, from Lowood Institution, to Thornfield, to the conflict with St. John Rivers (who restricts Jane as much as had Mrs. Reed and Mr. Brocklehurst), to Jane's final reward for a sensible choice, her marriage with Rochester. The novel gains its unity more from this thematic element—the conflict between the character's quest for the life of the spirit and the forces which would thwart her—then it does from the presence of Jane herself. In this way it is unlike the typical apprenticeship novel which is usually built on episodes loosely held together by the hero's activities. Thus, *Tom Jones*, the prototype of this kind of novel, consists of a series of chapters which cohere obviously because the activities of Tom hold them together. *Jane Eyre* contains elements similar to those in *Tom Jones* and its successors, but it also rests on a more restrictive philosophical basis, the unfolding of Jane's spirit as she rebels against the repressions that society and personal relationships impose upon her.

In her quest for personal salvation, Jane communes with God and Nature; with the latter particularly she acquires strength. In episode after episode, she returns to Earth, which, as the Romantic poets had indicated, was a source of strength, a personal way to resurrection of the spirit. As Meredith was later to show in *Richard Feverel*, the rain of the storm is a form of baptism and the Earth a life-giver. As Jane wanders lost and isolated, Charlotte Brontë comments: "Nature seemed to me benign and good; I thought she loved me, outcast as I was; and I, who from man could anticipate only mistrust, rejection, insult, clung to her with filial fondness. Tonight, at least, I would be her guest—as I was her child: my mother would lodge me without money and without price" (p. 377). Even in the recurrent reference to the great chestnut-tree, riven and black at the upper trunk but firm and strong at the base and roots, there is the intertwining connection between man and Nature: the tree is a simplified image of Jane and Rochester, seemingly split, with the sap no longer running between them, but nevertheless joined in feeling and memory, their roots also, so to speak, intermixed and inseparable.

Jane Eyre's quest for joy in a world which tries to deny her her rights derives from Charlotte Brontë's pro-feminist attitude, a continuing theme in *Shirley* (1849) and *Villette* (1853). *Shirley* is a plea for equality, justice, and status for the woman, while *Villette* in its love passages demonstrates that the woman's lack of subservience can create admiration and respect. In *Jane Eyre,* the heroine's outrage at Mrs. Reed's injustice becomes transformed into an outraged refusal to be made chattel by either Rochester, whom she loves, or St. John Rivers, whom she does not. She demands the right of choice: to choose her surroundings, occupation, friends, and mate, and to be able to reject those who would deny her this right. When these beliefs come under test, Charlotte Brontë becomes steely, and to this degree her Jane Eyre, with her deep feelings and passionate emotions, is not cousin-german to Elizabeth Bennet of *Pride and Prejudice*. It was perhaps this manifestation of masculine toughness that George Henry Lewes found disturbing in *Jane Eyre* and *Shirley,* for Charlotte Brontë answered him with some indignation:

You will, I know, keep measuring me by some standard of what you deem becoming to my sex; where I am not what you consider graceful you will condemn me. All mouths will be open against that first chapter [of *Shirley*], and that first chapter is as true as the Bible, nor is it exceptionable. Come what will, I cannot, when I write, think always of myself and of what is elegant and charming in femininity; it is not on those terms, or with such ideas, I ever took pen in hand: and if it is only on such terms my writing will be tolerated, I shall pass away from the public and trouble it no more (November 1, 1849).

The chief area in which Jane Eyre has choice involves Rochester and St. John Rivers, both men of strong temperament who are capable of mental cruelty when their desires are thwarted. The throwback to Richardson's *Clarissa* is evident, although Clarissa's need to choose between the dissolute Lovelace and the sexually repugnant Solmes leaves her no room for maneuver. In each relationship, Jane must pass through a dark night of the soul before she can decide what to do, and in each relationship her choice involves bringing to bear a strong personal will upon an almost equally strong will. In each instance, the temptation is to give herself up to a stronger force, to Rochester's love, to St. John's sense of duty and devotion. However, like Lucy Snowe in *Villette,* Jane must return from the nadir of despair and indecision in order to assert the need for personal happiness.

The relationship that St. John Rivers offers Jane is of a completely different kind, providing a marked contrast with Rochester's. As his name implies, St. John wants to be a saint, although he forgets that most saints preserve their celibacy. However, the marriage tie he offers is almost a celibate union, based as it is on duty, sacrifice, discipline, eventual martyrdom. St. John wants a business partner, not a wife, while Jane, who has continually sought love, wants a husband, hence her offer to accompany him as a sister, a relationship which would not involve love. Jane, it is made clear, does not resist duty or sacrifice; she resists a cold union which would carry her back to the episodes with Mrs. Reed or Mr. Brocklehurst. " 'He [St. John] prizes me as a soldier would a good weapon; and that is all.' "

St. John, nevertheless, retains a strong hold on her until she receives the mysterious call from Rochester, his painful voice eerily calling out for help from the hills beyond Marsh Glen. The miracle of love, as mysterious as witchcraft or superstition, is apparent, and Jane is no longer tormented by her decision. She flees to Rochester's aid, both because she loves him and because he needs help. "I [Jane] broke from St. John, who had followed, and would have detained me. It was *my* time to assume ascendancy. *My* powers were in play, and in force. I told him to forbear question or remark; I desired him to leave me: I must, and would be alone. He obeyed at once" (p. 490). Love gives her power, will, and strength. Her energies are now focused upon her own salvation as well as upon Rochester's. Unlike Catherine Earnshaw, Jane domesticates her male and makes him human.

Rochester's cruelty is a composite of frustration and desire, his previous attempt at love now mocked by a mad wife in the eaves of Thornfield and his present desires overruled by a residual propriety and gentlemanliness. His actions, accordingly, are more passionate and tempestuous than reason would dictate, and he becomes a "terrible" man when his will is circumscribed. Rochester needs the love of a good woman to cleanse him, for in marrying Bertha he had fallen through ambition and lust into a loveless union. Although he has had several mistresses—his ward, Adèle, perhaps is his child by a French mistress—yet Jane, the first "good" woman in his life, seemingly is not to be his. The result is a volcanic passion which contrasts with the repressed but equally deep passion that corrodes St. John. A figure of storm, Rochester, like Heathcliff in this respect, has been foiled in love. And all the elements of storm that would ordinarily be dissipated in a happy union remain dammed within.

Rochester's penance for sensuality and pride is his frustration, precisely as Jane Eyre's ordeal is alienation from all societal props. But since Rochester has sinned against virtually the entire order of the universe, his penance must be substantial: his loss of sight and a hand are the measure of his debt. Once it is paid, he is a free man, free to enjoy the fruits of a normal life, purified by his relationship with Jane. In risking his life to save the servants and in trying to help his mad wife in the fire at Thornfield Hall, he becomes a Christian gentleman, coming through an ordeal that physically debilitates him while spiritually strengthening him. Rochester repents, and, unlike Heathcliff, becomes humble:

> "Divine justice pursued its course; disasters came thick on me: I was forced to pass through the valley of the shadow of death. *His* chastisements are mighty; and one smote on me which has humbled me for ever. . . . I began [of late] to experience remorse, repentance; the wish for reconcilement to my Maker" (p. 521).

Adversity has strengthened both Rochester and Jane; and their love, the author indicates, will be the stronger for the barriers it had to overcome. Like her contemporaries, her sister Emily partially excepted, Charlotte Brontë believed that the divine order of the universe would somehow convey happiness after it had exacted its ordeal of pain. This romantic view of love was to hold for more than twenty-five years, until late-Victorian pessimism, in Hardy and others, demonstrated that there is no guarantee of happiness and that pain is the lot of the good as well as the evil man. At this point, courtship and marriage themselves no longer held the center of the novel, and someone like Rochester becomes a Henchard struggling to regain his identity before dying.

By the time of the second edition of *Jane Eyre,* Charlotte Brontë saw that her novel had been misunderstood by a small but influential body of readers, and that some answer was necessary to defend her original intentions. Dedicating the second edition of *Jane Eyre* to Thackeray, she attacked sham and pretense in society. "Conventionality is not morality. Self-righteousness is not religion. To attack the first is not to assail the last. To pluck the mask from the face of the Pharisee, is not to lift an impious hand to the Crown of Thorns." The sentiment is curiously not unlike D. H. Lawrence's seventy-five years later. She goes on to praise Thackeray as a man who has scrutinized and exposed imposture, as "the first social regenerator of the day . . . who would restore to rectitude the warped system of things." Beneath the melodrama, then, Charlotte Brontë reveals herself as a strong moralist, and her decision to attack sham by giving women their rightful place in society was to lead, later, into the novels of Meredith and George Eliot and to the plays of Shaw, several of whose themes are well within the terms set by *Jane Eyre, Shirley,* and *Villette.*

FIVE

Charles Dickens:
The Victorian Quixote

o move from Jane Austen to Charles Dickens is to leave behind one kind of society in favor of another. In the twenty years between the publication of Jane Austen's last novel and the appearance of Dickens's first, English society had passed into the form recognizable now, for her tradition-directed and "inner-directed" social groups were gradually becoming "other-directed" under the impact of industrialization and its social consequences. Even the word *Victorian* itself was not coined until 1851, the year of the Crystal Palace. Birth, breeding, and delicate manner came to be of less importance than a gentle heart, a natural response, an innate gentility of spirit. To possess the latter qualities was to have an acceptable style. "Inner-direction," in its relentlessness, was equivalent to selfishness and/ or egoism, qualities that destroy personal joy and pleasure and frustrate the rights of others.

The differences between the two writers, of course, go deeper for Jane Austen was herself a close part of the society she wrote about, while Dickens, the son of a clerk and a servant, was foreign to nearly all social groups. His failure in his early fiction to achieve an ironic vision derives from his alienation from organized society; irony, as we see in Jane Austen and George Meredith, must come from the writer who is inside—he must know the forms and substance of society before he can mock its vagaries. Dickens's humor differs from that of Jane Austen and Meredith, then, both because he is a different kind of person and because his relation to the society into which he was born is different.

Furthermore, Dickens's world—like Thackeray's—is essentially a male one (although at times not very masculine). These two, in fact, are the sole major nineteenth-century novelists concerned exclusively with a male world. In *Pickwick Papers* especially, woman is an intruder and looms as the enemy. She exists to trap men into marriage—as Mrs. Bardell tries to trap Pickwick and to take away the freedom which his maleness permits him. Women appear as absurdities, chiefly because they are social pawns, expedient chattel waiting to be auctioned off. Later, when they become saviors, they are still remote, other-worldly creatures.

Clearly, Dickens's first novel is almost a direct rebuttal to Jane Austen's female world in which man is himself a mysterious, somewhat absurd outer-world figure. In Jane Austen, the trapping of the sinister, partially undomesticated male, or the events leading up to the ensnarement, comes from the point of view of triumphant women; in *Pickwick,* however Dickens stresses the prevailing innocence of the male, who in most cases becomes untrappable because he is asexual. He is childish, innocent, seemingly unable to carry on marriage functions. His is a pre-female world in which Adam, in this best of all Edens, was not lonely.

While Jane Austen's characters reveal themselves through a type of socially acceptable repartee that defines them, Dickens's creatures, as fitting asexual men, reveal themselves through artificial speech that exaggerates their personalities. If a character can be delineated by his normal speech, then he can also be defined by his verbal excesses. Accordingly, Dickens replaces irony with the language and gestures of the music hall, appropriately toned down for a Victorian audience. His interesting characters—Sam Weller, for example—are given an original turn of phrase, while, conversely, his less commanding characters—like Esther Summerson and John Jarndyce (in *Bleak House*)—have no marked eccentricities of speech. The forensic tradition is very strong in Dickens —we remember that he was a court stenographer and a parliamentary reporter, both situations in which the word must be caught exactly. Also, Dickens was early interested in the theater, and his later public readings which consumed so much of his energy were obsessive extensions of his acting and directing days. Dickens's sense of theater is everpresent: the redundancy of talk, the seizure of every situation as an occasion for speech, the conception of several novels as stage works, the tear-jerking death scenes, the melodramatic turns of the narrative, the double and triple plot levels, the individuality of the minor characters. Consequently, Dickens has been called, by Edmund Wilson, the greatest dramatic writer since Shakespeare!

Why do Dickens's people talk so much? Why do they convey such a sense of effervescence and turbulence? Lacking modern depth psychology or the tools to probe analytically, the nineteenth-century novelist revealed character through conversation. A character is revealed by his speech, not by the author's comments about him; once again, the conventions of the theater, which generally had been absorbed or replaced by the novel, provided an important device. Furthermore, through conversation, Dickens could evoke a wide range of English life, whose many-sidedness had caught his interest as early as *Sketches by Boz* (1835), some of which were written when he was barely out of his teens. The conversational idiom attracted large audiences, many of them illiterate, and for almost the first time in fiction, they heard their own accents. Moreover, the talk, though artificial in itself, implicitly gave them credit for more literacy than they generally showed in reality.

The entire question of a reading public is significant when one discusses a novelist who found his way into numerous homes where fiction had hitherto been unknown. Dickens's use of the conversational format is merely one example of his intuitive grasp of what his readers wanted. The audience had broadened greatly from the eighteenth-century reading public, which itself had taken to the novel in strong numbers. The burgeoning middle classes of course enlarged the audience, while the increase in literacy among household servants also affected the numbers. The steady growth of circulating libraries enabled potential readers to obtain books who could not afford to buy them at half a guinea a volume, a sum representing perhaps $10.00 now. As long as a bulky three-volume novel cost more than the average worker's weekly wage, fiction was only for the few. Lending libraries, however, brought reading to the many by giving the reader books for a set fee totaling perhaps a guinea per year.

Moreover, the rise of a semi-literate reading public that made possible the success of libraries also had much to do with the kind of novel which would circulate. The very fact that the nineteenth century was an age of the novel indicates that the public had reading tastes quite different from those which enriched Alexander Pope for translating Homer into heroic couplets. In addition, the in crease in women's leisure through time-saving devices added a new element to the reading public: the novel became a family affair and had to be appropriate for women and children. At one time or another, Dickens appealed to the servant class, the middle class, and the upper class; obviously, he found readers everywhere who recognized their own accents in the volubility and vivacity of his characters.

Surprisingly, Dickens did not overly emphasize the sure-fire popular themes of his day: he rarely used the formula of the lowly girl who marries rich, and he has not one purely romantic hero or heroine. He did not write romances in the Scott tradition, nor did he play on nationalistic ideas or racist prejudices.* Also, as George

* Throughout his thirty-five-year writing career, Dickens avoided the very popular form of the empire novel, which increasingly furnished escape literature for the Victorian tired of social criticism. Just as the Gothic novel in the latter eighteenth century provided relief from predominantly realistic fiction, so did the novel glorifying imperialism divert a large public anxious for romance. The empire novel—with its exotic settings in Africa and India —enabled the average Victorian to escape temporarily from commercialism, industrialization, Darwinism, the uncertainties of religious belief, Reform Bills, Chartism, the franchise; it led him into areas where men were forced to react as men, with honor, integrity, and heroism. In their way, the novels of empire supplied a virgin frontier, a kind of untrammeled land where a lost Eden might be found through diligence and hard work, much like the image cast by the American Western novels for the average Easterner. Further, in these novels, dangers and potential evils were simplified and could be overcome; there was relatively little of the frustration involved in solving the complex problems of civilized life. As a politician, Disraeli recognized the need for just this diversion and held power through the 1870's by giving the Englishman new empires to contemplate and control.

In one of those curious ironies that only literary traditions can provide, "Angry" writers in the 1950's have created protagonists who sigh after just this kind of uncomplicated life. Being liberals, these anti-heroes cannot of course look to the empire in which to work off their frustrations, and even if they wished to, the empire no longer exists. What was once empire is now as complicated as the home country. In their need, the "Angries" had

Orwell perceived, he was not a radical or serious reformer in any concrete way. Like the equally indignant Ruskin, he offered no program. He had, in short, no simple formula for catching any one part of his huge audience. Each time he sat down to write, he had, as it were, to attract his readers anew. Each novel had to catch on as if the previous one had not existed, and this circumstance perhaps explains the diversity of subjects in his early books: from *Pickwick* to *Oliver Twist,* to *Nicholas Nickleby,* to *The Old Curiosity Shop,* to *Barnaby Rudge,* all published within five years. Without an established formula, Dickens had to *create,* and therefore we return again to the importance of the word in his novels. Only through a certain verbal idiom could he continuously recapture a somewhat vague audience that could easily have drifted away to any one of his popular contemporaries, who catered specifically to the tastes of their readers.

One way to escape the stereotypes of one's contemporaries, as all great writers have discovered, is to talk oneself out of it. From the telegraphic stutterings of Jingle to the fluent verbosity of Sam Weller, Dickens indicated *his* kind of world. In his concern with naming things—his animism is Wordsworthian—he gives a child's force and energy to all objects. His is a world packed with things; there is a density of facts and nouns, a concreteness of background objects packed into the sentences, as if they could talk in their own right. People themselves become turned into the objects they represent, and objects into animated cartoons. This stress on language, at times almost the incessant babble of the child learning how to call things and in the act naming anything that comes into his mind, is connected to the persistent theme of childhood and innocence which recurs in Dickens's work, and which, with various modifications, becomes the thematic motif of *The Pickwick Papers.** The oral nature of Dickens's first novel, the torrents of words, the burlesque of character and situation, the practical-

---

to create new kinds of Edens: plenty of beer, easy jobs, promiscuity, dreams of grandeur, and funny masks for the self. The Victorians found "empire" less degrading.

* *The Posthumous Papers of the Pickwick Club* was the original title.

jokey atmosphere, the verve, enthusiasm, and buoyancy of the Pickwickians, as well as the asexuality of their appetites—all these point to an artist interested in the visionary gleam of a child. We recognize that even Sam Weller, his practicality notwithstanding, is closer to Rousseau's child of nature than to an adult. In his loyalty and desire for fun, he comes from another age, one in which peasant wit is shrewder than urban deception.

Pickwick himself is obviously an innocent in a world of experience. Dickens would somehow have us believe that Pickwick made a fortune without being contaminated, his reactions remaining those of a child in a world of infinite wonder and discovery. This theme of innocence contrasted with experience, so immediately reminiscent of Blake and Wordsworth, is one that would reappear in various forms in Dickens's novels: Sissy Jupe versus industrialism and utilitarianism (*Hard Times*), Pip versus materialism (*Great Expectations*), Little Dorrit versus the Marshalsea (*Little Dorrit*), Lizzie Hexam versus the contaminated Thames (*Our Mutual Friend*), Pickwick versus lawyers. In a world of experience, the "untrammeled soul" has certain expectations; but in rubbing against those who would stultify or change him, he is challenged and finds that his simplicity, according to the ways of the world, must remain partially unrecognized. Thus, while Pickwick seeks goodness in every heart, he cannot impose honest intentions on all whom he meets. Nevertheless, in his dignity, innocence, and firm mettle, he becomes a "hero" by challenging injustice and deceit. Like the knights of old—to whom he is firmly linked in his purity —he goes through a trial of innocence and attains "heroic stature" in his defiance of an experienced world which rejects his ideals.

The theme of great expectations come to nought, or to partial frustration, tied as it is to innocence and childhood, was not Dickens's personal domain. The process of decline of heroes and heroines had already begun with several late eighteenth-century novelists and was accelerated by Dickens's major contemporaries, particularly Thackeray, and later George Eliot and Meredith. A circle might be drawn around Pip of *Great Expectations* and George Osborne of *Vanity Fair,* encompassing as well Richard Feverel, Sir Willoughby Patterne (*The Egoist*), and Lydgate (*Middlemarch*): all potential heroes in romantic fiction, but treated by their respective authors as anti-heroes who must be chastened, frustrated, and then reduced to normal size.

In dealing unromantically with the frustration of childhood hopes and expectations, Dickens was already indicating a major nineteenth- and twentieth-century theme. As George Orwell pointed out: if, like Dickens, a person hates violence and politics, he turns from trying to reform adult society to the education of children. Thus, Dickens started *Oliver Twist* as he was finishing *Pickwick*. In Dickens's hands, education can become a many-sided thing: it can preserve innocence without appreciably harming the child, as with Oliver Twist and Sissy Jupe, or it can transform innocence into something else, as with the ingenuous hopes of David Copperfield and Pip. On the other hand, a Dickens "villain" is not and has never been innocent; he is the voice of the corrupt adult world that deceives and lies and forces children to work in blacking factories or to define a horse as a graminivorous quadruped.

In his life-long concern with education, Dickens believed that the school of learning and the school of life must somehow contrive to keep the child innocent, as Pickwick himself has remained despite his excursions into the great world to secure his fortune. Dickens felt that the school of learning should become a moralized version of the practical world and teach the things close to the heart: naturalness, civility of conduct, warmth of feeling and expression. It should encourage right feeling, cheerfulness, and generosity, and discourage artificiality, deceitfulness, affectation, meanness, and vanity or snobbery. The school should aim at reforming the hearts of men, not at changing institutions, or, at least, it should try to lead men into the right direction despite the corruption of institutions. The school's target should be the preservation of human goodness; if one is rightly educated, then one can preserve his innocence in a world of temptation.

More moral critic than social or political commentator, Dickens tried to reform man's Christian beliefs into practical norms of behavior. As an example of Dickens's ideal in several ways, Pickwick, therefore, seems a fool; for in a society paying only lip service to Christian ideals, the Christian hero—like Don Quixote, Leopold Bloom, and the roles Chaplin created—is a fool. In an age that preaches Christianity but does not practice it, Pickwick seems indeed an absurd child of fortune.

Since work itself disrupts pleasure, indeed spoils the better part of man, and as well besmirches character, Pickwick, like a Henry James character, is mysteriously given money and, accordingly, is free to act as his tastes lead him. Can a man work and still remain innocent? Dickens asks, and answers, with Jaggers of *Great Expectations,* that certain work is dirty business which must be scrubbed off before one leaves the office. Business denotes institutions and involves greed as well as labor, and Dickens wanted his characters to remain pure and generous. Dickens's world, then, is one in which coziness and comfort figure large, a world in which charity comes from the heart, amiability is a norm of conduct, and the joys of innocence predominate.

The metaphysical limitations of Dickens's point of view are obvious and probably account for the arguments of those critics like F. R. Leavis who claim that Dickens cannot engage the adult mind. It is, however, necessary to draw a sharp distinction between the ideas simplified for the sake of discussion and the ideas as dramatized in a particular situation with concrete characters. The humor, the dramatic energy, the vitality of the creation are all lost in the simplification, perhaps more so in Dickens than in any other English novelist. Nevertheless, even after one recognizes that he should not wrench Dickens's ideas from their context, it does become apparent that Dickens's thought lacked consistency. To believe in the power of education, as Dickens did, is admirable, but to believe that the educator can himself throw off the values of his society and return to innocence is to distort the workings of a complex world. For the sake of personal doctrine, Dickens often did simplify: for example, *Hard Times*—with Sissy's vitality opposed to Gradgrind's academicism, and the natural healthiness of Sleary's Circus opposed to Bounderby's hypocrisy and hard-heartedness—provides an obvious example of a homiletic view of society.

Dickens failed to recognize that the institutions he opposed were simply the efforts of people to protect their minority interests. Institutions, Dickens felt, could be tolerated as long as they were benevolent—the servant-master relationship, for example, was viable as long as both believed in *noblesse oblige*—but once an institution began to encroach on the rights of people—Bounderby's form of capitalism, for instance—then it must be exposed as inhuman. Institutions, whether social, political, or economic, were acceptable as long as they were perpetuated by kind and humane people. When we perceive this point, we see how futile it is for Marxist critics to claim Dickens as one of their party, or how presumptuous it is to define him as a serious reformer.

Dickens actually shows little insight into public life as a whole. He sees the queen's subjects in their daily lives, but he rarely sees them as working subjects: in their jobs, professions, and related activities. Orwell comments that Dickens had no ideal of work; and this point gains in significance when one thinks of the ideals of his typical characters. Pip wants to live as a gentleman, David Copperfield to retire to a comfortable life with an easily-earned income, Pickwick to lead the life of a country gentleman, John Jarndyce (*Bleak House*) to be philanthropic on an income that has, mysteriously, never become involved in the Jarndyce court case, and so on through *Our Mutual Friend*. The ideal for a Dickens protagonist remains a good income, preferably unearned, an attractive and cozy house, a loving family with an able wife and handsome children, an idyl in which work itself does not figure.

When this kind of world becomes the reward for a virtuous life, one has passed beyond the realistic novel into what Edgar Johnson has called a fairy tale in which realistic events occur. This is essentially the atmosphere of *Pickwick Papers*. Pickwick is never in real danger, for his economic situation is secure, even though he may *seem* to be in trouble; precisely as in the fairy tale, the *seeming* danger forms the substance of the narrative even while one recognizes that a miracle will occur to save the hero. Pickwick's "miracle" is that he was able to make and retain a fortune to insure a dignified life. Pickwick accordingly is safe, for a man with sufficient money is secure from the trials of life, and therefore one's obvious aim in life is to obtain money or attach oneself to a person who has money or can leave it after death. Money, for Dickens, is not necessarily corrupt. It can indeed bring happiness provided one remains innocent while possessing it, just as money in Jane Austen's novels is necessary for a good life, although to flaunt it is to demonstrate ill breeding.

Edmund Wilson connects this vision of the world to Dickens's own insecure childhood, and especially to the humiliation he suffered when he worked in the public window of a blacking factory while his father was in debtor's prison. According to Wilson, much of Dickens's desire for stability—a loving, practical wife, a warm family life, the security of an income unaffected by fluctuations—is the result of a childhood he never forgot and which he relived intensely in his fiction. This ideal of stability became increasingly attractive when Dickens found his own personal life falling apart as his relations with his wife worsened and a warm home life became a distant ideal. Also, as Dickens threw himself into writing, acting, and reading, all the while maintaining a large correspondence during his several editorships and moving among a wide circle of friends, the ideal of a quiet existence faded further from reality. Not unusually, he found it, in fact, more attractive as it receded from his own life. This ideal indeed became part of Victorian mythology, and its illusions are still very much part of every anxiety-ridden society.

Pickwick's economic security, recognizably, removes all anxiety from his trials. He becomes a bourgeois Don Quixote, with Sam Weller his Sancho, and the road they travel is the road of injustice, which they will not forsake until justice prevails. The resemblance to the Don is not fortuitous, for Dickens was proceeding on the form of the episodic picaresque novel which derived from Cervantes. *Pickwick,* we remember, was begun as an accompaniment to sketches by Seymour, and after the latter's suicide, Dickens, suddenly left with a serial that was attracting little attention, first thought of a parody of the eighteenth-century novel, with each installment a complete story in itself. Then, with the introduction of Sam Weller into the fifth number, the sales jumped from a languid 300 to a phenomenal 40,000, and both Dickens and Pickwick were famous. However, even after Dickens had found the formula that insured fame for Pickwick and Sam Weller, the novel retained its episodic structure through the twenty-four installments, with the picaresque hero turning up as an asexual gentleman. Recognizably, Pickwick starts as something of a weak fool, with at least a lame intelligence and a pronounced complacency, and then like his antecedent Don, gains common sense from Sam Weller, as the Don did from Sancho Panza.

II

The quality of Samuel Pickwick as a pre-Victorian "innocent" reveals a great deal about the assumptions of the young author who became famous the year Victoria ascended to the throne. As a morality in defense of innocence, the novel attempts to recover a world untroubled by conniving lawyers, undirtied by industrial waste, and unconfused by complicated urban living. Its dominant tone is nostalgia. The "merrie England" that Dickens presents—replete with its open and "merrie" Pickwick—is an England of the imaginary Golden Age, a time that shines with splendor in a distant past.

The idea of the Golden Age was particularly attractive in the nineteenth century, almost paradoxically when one recognizes the general prosperity of Victorian England. For the Dickens of 1836-37, perhaps under the influence of the Romantic poets, the Golden Age was to be found in the "purity" of the previous century, as for Browning in the vivid Renaissance, for Southey in medieval times, for Ruskin in the period of Gothic, for Morris and Rossetti in the years preceding Raphael, for Carlyle in the late twelfth century. The Golden Age was a time when anxieties and ugliness were held to a minimum, or, possibly, did not exist at all: thus Pickwick's world has no villains, except the lawyers Dodson and Fogg, who are ultimately harmless if, like Pickwick, one has funds. The norm of this society is good food and drink, cheerful companions, comfortable clothing, well-heated accommodations, pleasant and plentiful holiday celebrations; in short, an existence that protects innocence and returns one to the joys of a secure childhood.

In his ideal of "merrie England," Dickens moved his novel and his hero to the childhood of the country (as Wordsworth understood it), a childhood which meant picturesque open roads, amiable villages uncontaminated by smoke, rocking coaches not yet in competition with railroads, congenial characters who remained genteel and civil despite monetary success.* The nostalgia—again like Wordsworth's, particularly that set forth in the Intimations Ode—is for a lost childhood: to recover, in Dickens's case, what never had been; and in Pickwick's, to exhibit the kind of person who was becoming increasingly rare—the man of substance who remains innocent.

Of equal importance, the novel demonstrates that coziness and comfort were, for Dickens, protection against a cold and indifferent society which had sent him at an early age to work in a blacking factory and which had cut him off from a happy childhood, a world in which sufficient money might have made the difference between misery and happiness. However, Dickens was obviously not writing solely about his own childhood, but the age's. We remember that Dickens grew up at virtually the same time as Victoria, being only seven years older, and came to the literary throne the same year his Queen came to England's throne, and that the age perpetuated in the image of Victoria was an age that Dickens himself helped to create. Its dark side was the substance of his later novels; its "innocence" a basic element of his own attitude; and its great energy and verve the qualities that Dickens more than any of his contemporaries was able to convey. The early Victorian Age was also the Dickensian Age, and the Queen's superiority was challenged, perhaps, only by this son of a servant and clerk trying fervently to turn back the clock to an innocent Golden Age.

Within a materialistic nineteenth-century world, Pickwick would obviously be something of an anachronism, although his asexuality, not to be confused with that of a saint, mirrors one of the public ideals of his age. His sexlessness, however, is more than an individual peculiarity; in Dickens's treatment, it becomes a cultural idea. In a society whose norm is conviviality, people live like

---

* Innocence, open roads, cozy characters, nostalgia, sentimentality, warm feelings, gentle humor—all these qualities are in Mrs. Gaskell's *Cranford*, which Dickens—perhaps as a way of reaching back to the world of *Pickwick*—published in his *Household Words* (1851-53), while he himself was entering his final dark phase with *Bleak House* and *Hard Times*.

happy children. Sex is an intruder or at least creates circumstances that would take the edge off good fellowship, especially if one honors child-like fun above any other kind of gratification. And this kind of fun can be obtained only in a male society; here woman is a perpetual Eve who will lead man into disrupting actions and upset his sentimental, childish atmosphere. Pickwick's world is a pre-Eve Paradise in which women are pleasant but absurd and unreal creatures.

If *Pickwick* lacks experienced lovers—all the men seem much older than they actually are—it is, nevertheless, full of father figures. Pickwick himself is the "little father of the world" and Sam Weller has, figuratively, two fathers, while virtually no mothers exist in the book: Mrs. Weller, we remember, is not Sam's mother. In a world in which woman is like a divine intruder, a being who has no function except to seduce man with tears, soft eyes, or other forms of deception, courtship and marriage themselves become mythical and miraculous. And, further, in a world in which the chief character is a Christian fool, a middle-class humanitarian, sex itself comes to signify an alien world. Therefore the humor Dickens is able to derive from Pickwick in his innocent sexual involvements. All romantic attachments involving Pickwick must of necessity be ludicrous, for he is a sexless Lothario. The joke occurs when he is accused of being a real Don Juan, and is thought of as a picaresque villain instead of the innocent and neuter gentleman that he is.

A great deal of the humor in *Pickwick* works on what may be called the disparity principle: the disparity between what Pickwick is—sexless, convivial, and childish—and the eighteenth-century "roguish" episodes in which Dickens places him. If his innocence of the world's villainy is Pickwick's chief attraction, then what could be funnier than surrounding him with people who suspect that beneath the child lies the potential rapist? The humor of the trial scene rests on the assumption that Pickwick is an innocent accused of Don Juanism. The evidence that Dodson and Fogg bring against him—consisting of a note like " 'Dear Mrs. B., I shall not be home till to-morrow. Slow coach. Don't trouble yourself about the warming pan.' "—is itself a reductio ad absurdam of Pickwick's intentions toward Mrs. Bardell and toward any woman at all. To this might be added Winkle's inadvertent remark that Pickwick was found in a lady's sleeping apartment at midnight; or Pickwick's adventure at the women's boarding-house where he denies being a robber and roars out: " 'I want the lady of the house.' " The humor obviously turns on Pickwick's removal from a world in which relationships between the sexes do really occur. Furthermore, Pickwick seems, as it were, to infect his cronies with a similar sexlessness, so that they appear older and more out of competition than they really are.

In this sense, *The Pickwick Papers* is, like *Huckleberry Finn,* an anti-sexual book, devoted as both are to the retention of childhood and innocence. Moreover, childhood in both novels entails more than the cataloguing of the adventures of children or childish adults—childhood becomes a kind of cultural norm against which all other life is measured. In *Huckleberry Finn,* the river cleanses impurities and allows a nearly full life—it signifies vitality and humanity—whereas the shore denotes corruption, evil, disease. On the river, one has adventures to seek, on the shore only restrictions and frustrations to struggle against. So in *Pickwick,* the open road is like the river, the pre-industrial and pre-railroad England of the eighteenth century, while London and particularly its systems (judicial and penological, among others) are the equivalent of the shore in the American novel. To touch any of these shore systems is to be contaminated, even though they may be important, even necessary. Both Twain and Dickens place faith in people, not in systems or institutions, and therefore Pickwick takes to the road when people fail him, precisely as Huck later was to look for new frontiers where he could retain his innocence.

The key word is *innocence,* the chief ingredient in any work concerned with childhood or injustice. Innocence here, as in much of Dickens's later work, becomes, like childhood itself, a cultural concept. Innocence is connected to the kind of England that Dickens is evoking, one in which love, respect, dignity, and fair play are paramount. This England, we saw, is pre-industrial, pre-merchant, pre-complicated, an England that never existed except as a Golden Age, an earthly paradise, a rosy past. In this England, Father will take financial care of the Sam Wellers. Experience can be partially avoided in such a world, and even when it does clash with the innocence of the characters, it fails to conquer simply because it is culturally unacceptable.

The theme of innocence, in which Dickens returned to a former "merrie England," as if regressing to a transformed childhood of his own, is explicit in several details beyond those mentioned above. *Pickwick,* we remember, contains no really wicked person—the pseudo-villains like Dodson and Fogg are closer to fools than to devils. There is, in Dickens, as we have seen, a great need to acquire sufficient funds not only to maintain one's comfort but also to protect oneself against sudden attacks by evil forces. Pickwick's stay in debtor's prison becomes, accordingly, a continental tour of the underworld, for what can happen, we ask, to a man with funds and respectability? Pickwick is himself safe, but one of the interpolated stories—that of the "Queer Client"—demonstrates what happens to a man who is trapped in debtor's prison and loses all, including his sanity, before getting out into what becomes still another kind of prison. Thus, Dickens's obsession with the idea of "man trapped," allied as it is to the theme of innocence, is revealed as early as his second book. *Pickwick* itself remains jovial and gay because its "hero" is safe from traps, not because there are no traps. However, as Dickens began to probe society in which prison is a primary silhouette, then his characters must become aware of traps in order to survive.

The lack of "experience" in *Pickwick,* outside of that in the interpolated tales, results, obviously, from Pickwick's own outlook, unmarked as it is by suspicion or doubt. Seeing everything through child-like eyes, while Dickens, accordingly, scales the world to suitable miniature proportions, Pickwick has no insight into evil and displays no caution with wicked people. He feels, as every child does, that the world operates from *his* point of view, and that his honesty, freshness, and candor are its also. As there is nothing to trouble him, he sets out, like Cervantes' Don, to see the world only in his own image. Alone, however, he could not long survive, and a child of (relatively greater) experience must accompany him, not so much to protect him against harm as to shield him from harsh facts which would destroy his innocence. When Pickwick asks with incredulity, " 'Why should anyone hurt *me?'* " Sam Weller must guard him against a realistic answer: Pickwick must remain innocent, for he is the last outpost against encroaching evil. With a fairy-tale guardian ever-present as protector, Pickwick can preserve his freshness and naïveté, both qualities that sustain a world racked by ever-growing institutions and systems.

As Dickens was finishing *Pickwick Papers,* he was already starting *Oliver Twist,* a rough treatment of the childhood theme already foreshadowed in the innocence of Pickwick and one that would extend into virtually all of his later novels. Once Dickens realized that the world of Pickwick was irrecoverable, he immersed himself in the world of the child, although later he recognized that there was little chance for the child to escape into a safe past which shuts out with jests and dinner parties a mean and enduring present. Therefore, for the child to remain human in a devitalized, mechanical world, the benevolent godfather or good uncle had to make a miraculous and artificially contrived appearance, a figure not of reality but of the fairy story, created not from life but by an author still trying to recover what is past recovery. Like Rousseau and the Romantic poets who preceded him, and Meredith and D. H. Lawrence after, Dickens turned to the child of nature to deny Original Sin.

In *Pickwick,* however, Dickens as yet had no distinct vision of evil. He felt, instead, the premonition of a world closing in, and through the Pickwickians and their antics tried to hold it in abeyance. Therefore, *Pickwick* contains little of the weightier Dickens which attracted, among others, Dostoyevsky, Shaw, and Lawrence. The only instances of Dickens's presentation of the criminal mind, for example, occur in the interpolated tales, although they may be, as Edmund Wilson has suggested, personal fears revealed and personal events dramatized rather than any attempt to come to terms with the criminal type. Even when Dickens did attain his full powers, he rarely treated the detective story as a reality, as Dostoyevsky was to do, but, rather, as a morality play in which miracles occur to save the protagonist from the criminality of the world. *Pickwick* remains, in this sense, a naïve book in which the criminal indeed lurks, but remains peripheral, slightly unreal, the villain of a fairy tale rather than a condition of society. He is, here, part of a social fable, not of social reality, and he haunts only children's dreams, not their daytime lives. These elements of course remove Dickens from the line of realistic writers like Balzac, Dostoyevsky, and Tolstoy, and place him in a special genre, of which *Pickwick* is a prime example.

III

This type of novel generates its own faults as well as virtues, and the wealth of the latter should not totally blind us to the liabilities. Pickwick himself survives as a partially unrealized character, more important for what he is and what he stands for than substantial as a rounded person, although he gains in stature through contact with Sam Weller. Somewhat the most eccentric of the Pickwickians—what with his gaiters, his little trot, his stout figure, his "greatness"—Pickwick is closer to caricature than to reality, especially when the plot pushes him into real situations and away from fairy-tale life in which he does fit.

Sam Weller, of course, dominates all the scenes in which he appears. As George Gissing describes him, ". . . he is the grown-up *gamin,* retaining his boyhood's impudence, shrewdness, vivacity, and adding to it the caustic philosophy resulting from such rough experience." Trailing streams of honesty and candor, he is a limited comic spirit that exorcises nonsense, a scornful avenger of humbuggery and hypocrisy. He demonstrates an honesty principle with which every view and argument must be squared before being found acceptable. In a formal situation, like the court scene, he shows the foolishness implicit in pretension, and by displaying humor in grim situations, he demonstrates that common sense is the best policy and goodness the most effective principle. He attempts to impose a child-like world of candor and integrity over everything, and when taunted reacts with a wise, childlike reasoning that forms the basis of his humor. Obviously, his range is limited: his humor is restricted to exposing humbug, and rarely does he function as a full comic spirit who makes forays against all of society. As an idealized servant figure, he stands for loyalty, forthrightness, and honesty; and his talk, far in excess of what an illiterate servant would say, indicates that Dickens intended him as a picaresque hero in his own right.

Dickens's mastery of Sam Weller's characterization should not, however, blind us to the shortcomings of the other characters, none of whom is of course so important as are Pickwick and Sam. As they are all more or less eccentrics, it is probably through this novel that Dickens gained his reputation as a caricaturist who seized upon one revealing note—Sam Weller's dialectical quirk, for example—and then built a character around it. This attitude, obviously overstated when applied to the entire Dickens canon, can, however, be substantiated in the relatively minor characters of *Pickwick*. Jingle, the swindler, is established through his stutter, an extraordinary kind of stutter in which whole phrases rather than individual syllables are broken into semi-coherent statements. The language itself is coherent, but the effect is similar to telegraphic prose (the kind of language, also, that a stenographer would be aware of—we are reminded of Dickens's experience as a court reporter). Jingle speaks all in nouns and verbs, suppressing connectives, throwing words together like a child imitating language, with unpracticed starts and stops.

The Pickwickians themselves are each identified with one particular trait: Mr. Tracy Tupman, with his susceptibility to female charms; Winkle, with his sporting appearance which belies the timorous, comfort-seeking soul beneath; Mr. Snodgrass, with poetic and romantic attitudes. En masse, they are delightful men with a keen enjoyment of life, but individually they retain few characteristics beyond their identifying feature. The women also, appearing somewhat absurd as creatures from another world, are just what women would appear to be to sporting gentlemen more interested in good brandy and a toasty fire than the flames of romance. Woman is venerated, sentimentalized, idealized as the very fount of good feeling. How far from here to Rosa Dartle of *David Copperfield,* hardly a companion for a Pickwickian!

The shortcomings of casting a long novel as a fable appear most obvious when the content verges on the realistic, for then the novelist must fall back on miracles to save the situation, and miracles work, obviously, at counter purposes to realism. Thus, when Dickens places Pickwick in debtor's prison, the force of realistic detail is somewhat lost, for Pickwick, because of his miraculous money-making past, is able to buy his way free. In a fairy tale, this factor of relief is always present, and as a comic novel, *Pickwick* should not create many serious anxieties. Nevertheless, the realistic elements are too "raw" for them to be transformed so easily into fairy-tale incidents. Furthermore, Sam Weller's role as a character is weakened because once under Pickwick's care he cannot be injured. Pickwick's benevolence, like God's (Samuel means "his name is God"), is all-encompassing, and nothing will happen to anyone under his care. Paradoxically, the very qualities of protection and insulation which generate the narrative weaken the realistic sections. This factor perhaps explains why *Pickwick* appears uneven—the last great scene is in the courtroom, and that is entirely within the fairy-tale world. Afterwards, the narrative plunges into the depths of prison, which, while it foreshadows one of Dickens's later obsessions, breaks the tone of the earlier parts of the novel, even when we are sure that nothing serious can happen to Pickwick.

The interpolated tales, nine in all, help to foreshadow the scenes in debtor's prison and serve to counterpoint the joviality of the main theme. Opposed to Pickwick as the "little father of the world," the tales present fathers who, like Abraham, would sacrifice their Isaac, although not for love of God. Opposed to the benevolence and gentleness of the Pickwickians, the tales present a world of evil—people ruined by drink, ill treatment, madness, revenge, and bad temper, some of which Dickens had already caught in a limited way in *Sketches by Boz.* Opposed to the safe and innocent life of "merrie England," the tales reveal a world of violence and unease, the opposite of eighteenth-century provincial life. In them, life suddenly gains in complication, although these entr'actes should not be unduly emphasized; most were inserted merely as fillers. Nevertheless, the kind of filler, not the fact of its existence, is of interest. From their world to that of later Dickens is not far, and one is struck by the unity of Dickens's vision: even as early as *Pickwick,* the emotions of his unhappy youth kept roaring to the surface, and the end of *Pickwick* turns into a harbinger of his more profound novels in which innocence crashes jarringly against reality. The settings of the stories here become transformed later into the Thames waterfront, the filth and muck of London streets, the desolate Tom-all-Alone's, the mechanical Coketown, the swamps that contain evil spirits and escaped criminals.

The tales themselves are uneven, and only Numbers One, Two, Three, and Six, called respectively "The Stroller's Tale," "The Convict's Return," "A Madman's Manuscript," and "The Old Man's Tale About the Queer Client" are of interest. The reader is immediately struck by the difference in style between the tales—related from various sources—and the novel itself. Their prose is ordinary and their content commonplace, often the stuff of melodrama or the now degenerating Gothic narrative. There is no attempt at strong characterization, for the whole point seems to lie in the tone of general depression and melancholy that the narrative conveys. Nevertheless, although these tales are of little intrinsic consequence, they are significant for their presence in this kind of work. One could not imagine them as entr'actes in a book like Surtee's *Jorrocks,* on which *Pickwick* and the Pickwickians were modelled, or any other sporting novels of the same kind.*

The first, "The Stroller's Tale," tells of an unsuccessful actor, now old and dying from excessive drinking, who finishes a tale of how he mistreated his wife and child and then drops back dead. The second tale, "The Convict's Return," follows a somewhat similar theme: ill treatment of the wife by the drunken husband leads to her death. The son of the marriage turns bad and is transported; upon his return to his village, he sees his father, goes to kill him, but stops, and the old man falls dead while cursing and striking the son. The third tale, "A Madman's Manuscript," which Pickwick reads late at night, relates how a lunatic is able to exist in respectable society because he has money. The madman buys his

---

* Typical of the raucous sporting fiction of the day was Pierce Egan's *Tom and Jerry: Life in London, or the Day and Night Scenes of Jerry Hawthorn, Esq. and his Elegant Friend, Corinthian Tom, Accompanied by Bob Logic, the Oxonian, in their Rambles and Sprees through the Metropolis* (1821-24). Pierce Egan (1772-1849) presented the "other side" of life from that depicted in the fashionable novels that caught on in the Twenties. Also popular in the sporting vein was "Nimrod" (the pseudonym of C. J. Apperley, a journalist), "picaresque" chronicles of sporting gentlemen who were forerunners of the Pickwickians.

way into a poor family, the girl being sacrificed to him while loving another man. During the marriage, she wastes away, while the madman, caught between pity and hate, plots to kill her by fire, drowning, poison, or a sharp razor which he daily strops. One night while she sleeps, he approaches her bed, razor in hand; she awakes, sees him, and falls into brain fever. After her death, the lunatic further declines and angers the girl's brothers, who feel that he is insulting her memory and showing disrespect for the family, whom he has however continued to support. The madman becomes enraged at one brother in particular and succeeds in almost strangling him when help arrives; he tries to escape and is caught. The sixth tale, "The Old Man's Tale About the Queer Client," tells of a young man who sees his wife and child die because of his imprisonment in debtor's prison at the instigation of his father-in-law. Maddened by their death, he vows revenge. After his release from prison, he looks on as his enemy's son drowns, and then he ruins the old man by buying up at huge prices the negotiable papers the latter had on loan. Hounded by his son-in-law, the old man runs from the law, is hunted down, and dies before himself being consigned to debtor's prison.

These four tales—like many of Poe's—are stripped bare to the passions motivating them. Unrelieved by humor or any show of decent feeling, they present people caught in the horror of situations from which the only escape is death. The main themes are madness, drunkenness, and revenge, the predominant motif being a kind of bedeviled obsession which takes hold of the person and releases him only upon his death. The Abraham and Isaac theme is already apparent in the first, second, and sixth tales— the child becomes a sacrifice to a greedy and/or dissipated parent, a victim of his own helplessness in a world that willingly sacrifices him. Furthermore, the tales reveal a kind of depression that counters the hilarity of the novel itself, two elements that were to run side by side through all of Dickens's fiction. As Dickens matured, these bleak elements grew in importance, until in some novels, *Our Mutual Friend* and *Little Dorrit,* for example, they dominate the narrative. Inartistic as these interpolated tales are, they become the basis for Dickens's growing awareness of underground life and foreshadow his theme of the "wronged man."

To go from these stories to the latter part of *Pickwick,* in which the hero, like Ulysses, descends into the Underworld of debtor's prison, seems a natural progression. Debtor's prison forms a world completely different from the one in which Pickwick is accustomed to move, but he is largely unaffected by it, except to become saddened at what society has done to innocent men. They are the living-dead of a material world which somehow shuts them out; they are the losers in an industrial society. The scenes there last for nearly a hundred pages and strengthen the theme of injustice suggested in the interpolated tales and other parts of the novel. Pickwick is a wronged man amidst the debris of wronged men. Curiously, debtor's prison is arranged like Dante's circles of hell; as one descends, conditions worsen, the situation of the men becoming increasingly hopeless. The tobacco smoke which almost suffocates Pickwick is, as it were, the intolerable smoke of the Inferno which abuts on the prison. The misery and suffering on all sides, especially among the women and children, are more than Pickwick's generous heart can bear; he retreats before it in confusion.

Later, Pickwick makes a general tour of the Fleet, where he sees the debtors sauntering or sitting in "every possible attitude of listless idleness. . . . Some were shabby, some were smart, many dirty, a few clean; but there they all lounged, and loitered, and slunk about, with as little spirit or purpose as the beasts in a menagerie." Like the denizens in Dante's Inferno or in Conrad's Africa, the debtors have given up all hope; their spirits crushed, their bodies useless, they contrast sharply with the well-being and health of Pickwick and Sam Weller. The former can say: " 'I have seen enough . . . my head aches with these scenes, and my heart, too. Henceforth I will be a prisoner in my own room.' " Unlike the others, Pickwick can retreat, both from the scene and from the prison, if he wishes; but innocent as he is, he must go through this ordeal, which forces him to come face to face with suffering and tragedy. Pickwick's retreat into his refuge after having been exposed to the horrors of the real world becomes, in one way, a basic theme of Dickens's fiction: he rewards all his heroes with the comforts of a middle-class life once they have been made aware of threats and dangers.

Lest, however, these grim scenes—about one-eighth of the novel—appear dominant, one must return to the humor which pervades nearly every other aspect of the novel and which depends, in many ways, upon the innocence of the figures involved. Thus, Mrs. Bardell, an inverted middle-aged Venus, now worn out and homely, counterpoints Pickwick's inverted Don Juanism: the relationship between the two must be the source of comedy, even had they terminated the union successfully. Much of the other humor derives from the servant being wiser than the master, the classic comic situation from Molière's farces to Shaw's *Man and Superman*. Sam's shrewdness and Pickwick's benevolence reach a happy medium: Sam, too, has an impulse to benevolence. For this kind of humor to work, both master and servant must be basically kind and decent, although the immediate care of the servant is usually for his own welfare. The pair literally becomes "two against the world," generally impervious to strong attack, although frequently involved in frivolous incidents. The terms of this relationship fit the first part of *Don Quixote,* and most of *Pickwick,* and extend through the democratization of the novel in which the servant gradually rises through society until, still later, he becomes one of its leaders.

The relationship of master and servant provides the unbeatable combination, as we see, of financial security and common sense, the very qualities that in the Christian world secure the safety of the principals. When the reader is sure that the principals are safe, the fiction must be a comedy—it entails a happy ending for the protagonist, who, after a not too difficult struggle, achieves his goal. So Pickwick attains his modest end: to preserve his independence from society's traps so that his innocence can remain untrammeled. Pickwick must remain innocent, or else both the potential and the realized humor are weakened or lost. The loss of innocence is a tragic theme, the preservation of it a comic one. The loss of innocence involves a heroic figure, one who has tragic dimensions; the preservation of innocence involves the mock-heroic. Pickwick's defiance of injustice and "evil" in the world, for all its seriousness, cannot of course be taken as real defiance. For Pickwick, it is merely a whim, not a cosmic defiance—it leads to no change, without which defiance is comic, not tragic. We remember that *Pick-*

wick began as a clownish parody of the eighteenth-century novels of Fielding and Smollett, and we see, therefore, that the mock-heroic convention is already suggested in the intention.

Everything, then, is scaled down to mock-epic size, and the theme of injustice itself must unfold, as it does in the trial scene, as a mockery of justice and also as a defiance of justice. These terms reduce everything to ridiculousness; the trial literally becomes a farce, and that was Dickens's purpose. There is little real satire upon the organization of the courts or upon the judiciary as an institution; the farcical nature of the attack precludes that kind of seriousness. The injustice is, rather, on a small, personal scale, marked down to suit the proportions of the mock-heroic.

The trial scene is squarely within the comic tradition, from Aristophanes to Molière, through Restoration Comedy, continuing in the twentieth century in Chaplin's early silent films. It involves the exaggeration of words and actions, and it must demonstrate the idiocy of people obsessed with a single point of view. Thus, the trial scene develops along the lines of misunderstanding: of words, of intentions, of attitudes. It pulls together the earlier situations and particularly parodies the areas in which Pickwick's innocent sexlessness has rendered him the butt of the suggestive joke. Here we see the Christian hero as fool in the midst of his mockers, his every word and action misunderstood or misinterpreted by those who would persecute him. As an innocent man surrounded by evil, Pickwick is the eternal child in a threatening world. Only the Pickwickians and their friends can momentarily stem the tide of malevolence, and this they do less by defiance than by retreating into a distant, sentimentalized past where wickedness seems negligible.

IV

At this time, irony was not a workable mode for Dickens, and not until *Great Expectations* (1860-61) do we find a novel generated by an ironic vision. In the 1830's, Dickens was as yet too young, too inexperienced, and also too unsure of himself socially. The ironist must himself have some fixed status in society before he can direct his darts against his compatriots. At the time of *Pickwick,* Dickens was too far outside middle-class society to perceive its organizing principles; the relatively uneducated son of a clerk and a servant, then a court stenographer, a journalist, and later author of a novel based on sporting sketches, Dickens was not, in the eyes of his contemporaries, a "solid citizen." A man of this sort may seem to be not far removed from a confidence man, and hardly in a position to indict an entire age.

Certain values, barely suggested in *Pickwick,* are progressively revealed in Dickens's work which followed at almost yearly intervals. *Oliver Twist* (1838), *Nicholas Nickleby* (1839), and *The Old Curiosity Shop* (1841) continue the childhood theme in which the child is first "tortured" before he miraculously gains a kind of bourgeois happiness. This theme is picked up again in *David Copperfield* (1850) after three novels not so easily classified: *Barnaby Rudge* (1841), *Martin Chuzzlewit* (1844), and *Dombey and Son* (1848). All of these books, however, contain elements that are variously represented in *Bleak House* (1853) and *Hard Times* (1854). Nevertheless, for the reader who goes directly from *The Pickwick Papers* to *Bleak House,* the change in structure and content between the two novels seems overwhelming, much more so than they actually are when we consider how Dickens had led, novel by novel, into his later work. The wandering sense of the "road" in the early novels had already been displaced by the intensive examination of London business in *Dombey and Son;* the picaresqueness of Pickwick was replaced by the anti-heroic qualities of the later protagonists; the vagueness of the early narratives gave way to the unity of the later, with their leitmotifs and large social groupings; the first-person narrative of *David Copperfield* was discarded for the objectivity of the third in *Bleak House, Great Expectations,* and *Our Mutual Friend;* the sentimentality and mawkishness of *Nicholas Nickleby, The Old Curiosity Shop,* and *Dombey and Son* became diluted, replaced as they were by an evident stiffening of spirit and toughening of vision.

The theme of injustice is no longer a subject of fun, as in *Pickwick,* or the instigator of a miraculous savior, as in *Oliver Twist* and *Nicholas Nickleby.* It persists now as a leitmotif intensified into a condition of life. Injustice in *Bleak House* and *Hard Times,* as well as in *Great Expectations* and *Our Mutual Friend,* pervades every aspect of life; it is in the great fogs of London, the swamps of Pip's boyhood, the Thames backwash of Lizzie Hexam's daily existence, and the Marshalsea of Little Dorrit's funereal childhood. Injustice enters into nearly every social relationship; it breaks up friendships, and it prevents what would be love-marriages. With injustice ever-present, greed replaces lofty principles, and hypocrisy noble ideas. The later titles themselves suggest the point of view: *Bleak House,* the ironic *Great Expectations,* and *Hard Times.* Dickens's argument has altered, has shifted from the ridicule of institutions and the reliance on individuals, from the parody of law and the emphasis on joviality, from this vague program to the view that if a nation's laws are themselves unjust, then we cannot expect people to have any sense of personal justice.

Dickens realized that order and progress can be maintained only through the discipline and continuity that great institutions provide. Indeed, they enable a society to survive and remain sane. Since all civilized men must perceive this important fact, Dickens felt, then all civilized men must see the importance of institutions that operate effectively. The mark, obviously, of a successful and developing society is successful institutions that work for man and not against him. A malfunctioning institution, Dickens recognized, is an intolerable contradiction in terms, for institutions exist solely for man's benefit. A malfunctioning institution is an indication, then, that part of man is corrupt, for man himself creates his institutions. Taken with Dickens's fear of political anarchy and his desire for security and stability, the corruption of society's institutions becomes doubly meaningful: corrupted institutions mean that man is no longer innocent and that neither he nor the institution can be trusted. Chaos and anarchy are ready to be loosed upon the world.*

* While Dickens deplored violence, he sympathized with the basic Chartist program, the famous "Six Points" (established in 1838) that called for universal male suffrage, elimination of property qualifications for members of Parliament, payment of members, annual general elections (which would have made the government directly responsible to the people), equally divided electoral districts (instead of the unequal county and borough sec-

For Dickens, the one great institution is law. As a member of the rapidly growing middle class that was to smother England with prosperity and cultural smugness, he was fully aware that his class could survive only if the law protected its rights while it was displacing a more traditional and solidly entrenched group. The law was obviously necessary to make the change orderly and to keep it within the social framework. The test, then, of an effectively and smoothly running society is the efficacy and justice of its laws. Since law is a measure of all things, when it fails, all society fails.

Bleak House is as much about order and anarchy as Shaw's play which echoed its title, *Heartbreak House;* and Dickens's attack on law is here so strong that he suggests the entire bleak house of England may fall unless it is bolstered by love and generosity. The law in *Bleak House* is a vast underground force which sanctions greed and makes injustice respectable. The law becomes an inviolable power behind which the supporters of public policy can hide, and it is they, more than the criminal element, that England has to fear. By the time of *Bleak House,* Dickens had arrived at his penetrating insights into the workings of society: that the self-righteous pillars of society support no more than self-interest; that while greed is perhaps a characteristic of all, it is hardly socially harmful when limited only to the indigent; and that the so-

---

tioning), and the secret ballot. The Chartist movement itself agitated for political and economic relief, in particular for a new Reform Bill which would supersede the inadequate voting provisions of the one in 1832. The movement gained in violence and eventually failed completely in 1848 with the fiasco of its attempt to present its giant petition on the redress of wrongs to Parliament.

Mrs. Gaskell's first novel, *Mary Barton* (1848), is cast against a background of labor strife in Manchester in the days of the Chartists. Although she was sympathetic to labor's aims, like Dickens she feared the potential, and actual, violence implicit in union agitation. Her point—still naively optimistic at midcentury—is that labor and management can peacefully resolve their differences and embrace each other, as do John Barton and Mr. Carson, with each realizing that continued struggle will bring only death and heartache. Variations on this theme remained popular during the entire century, entering even into the drama in Galsworthy's *Strife* (1909).

called protectors of society, with their rights of legislation and judgment, can destroy a given society in ways never threatened by the criminal. Dickens writes (*Bleak House,* XXXV):

I [Esther Summerson, the narrator] said it was not the custom in England to confer titles on men distinguished by peaceful services, however good and great; unless occasionally, when they consisted of the accumulation of some very large amount of money.

"Why, good gracious," said Miss Flite, "how can you say that? Surely you know, my dear, that all the greatest ornaments of England in knowledge, imagination, active humanity, and improvement of every sort, are added to its nobility! Look around you, my dear, and consider. *You* must be rambling a little now, I think, if you don't know that this is the great reason why titles will always last in the land!"

I am afraid she believed what she said; for there were moments when she was very mad indeed.

The mature novels, then, like Ibsen's plays later in the century, are about *power* and what it means in a society which professes democracy and justice and which practices the reverse. What are people like in this situation? Who are the governed and who are the rulers? How do people act; how do they live and work? What do they eat and wear? How is one distinguished from the other? And, particularly, how do they speak in everyday situations? under duress? at work, at play, in love?

By the 1850's, Dickens had found a way of grouping his social ideas: the law becomes a presence which, like the fog, pervades every recess of English life. Each character is touched by the foggy law, and his appearance, like that of Wagner's creatures in *Der Ring des Nibelungen,* is heralded by a leitmotif that forces us back to the central theme. The structure of the novel lends itself to a closely-worked and dense pattern, for its double plot, not unlike that of the Elizabethan drama, presents a series of contrasts between one social level and another. As it replaced the drama, the Victorian novel, not surprisingly, took over many of the conventions of the older form, among others, the double plot. Dickens structured *Bleak House* around several basic conflicts: Tom-all-Alone's (Lower Classes) versus Chesney Wold (Upper Classes), Love (Life) versus Moneyed Society (Greed), Honesty and Truth versus the Courts, the forces which will save against those which will destroy. These classifications are general enough to include most of the major characters and forces in the book. And brooding over all is Lady Dedlock, whose rejection of love in favor of a financially and socially advantageous marriage is symptomatic of the evils of the society which Dickens is chastising.

By favoring money and position over love, Lady Dedlock has stultified the only living part of her; she has exchanged her natural feelings for the destructive, false values of a society which rewards vanity and snobbery. Failing as a human being, she fails as a mother and, in several ways, as a wife. Living with falsehoods, she is cursed by her past and must shrink in constant fear of being discovered. Like D. H. Lawrence, Dickens pursued relentlessly those who by suppressing their true feelings followed the path to self-destruction. Dickens describes Lady Dedlock (LV):

> But so long accustomed to suppress emotions, and keep down reality; so long schooled for her own purposes, in that destructive school which shuts up the natural feelings of the heart, like flies in amber, and spreads one uniform and dreary gloss over the good and bad, the feeling and the unfeeling, the sensible and the senseless; she had subdued even her wonder until now.

Lady Dedlock's destruction of life and love represents the decay of noble principles and ideas into hypocrisy, cant, snobbery, vanity, and frivolity. Her first name, ironically, is Honoria, and yet her entire adult life has been a lie for the sake of ambition and social status. She is made impotent by her denial of her lover and by her acceptance of a false code of ethics. Part of her punishment, as Dickens envisions it, is the loss of her infant daughter, which becomes to her, alternately, both a blessing and a sorrow, both a means to life and a denial of life. Yet beneath Lady Dedlock's carefully armored exterior is a loyal heart, a potentially decent human being; she is never one of Dickens's foolish, irrelevant aristocrats. She has sufficient mettle to attract and hold the heart of Sir Leicester, and she rarely hurts anyone but herself by her false game. She is, for Dickens, a type of tragic figure, destroyed by the very society which she desires to emulate. Her destruction is the result of peculiarly false values which lurk in the body of society, ready to infect everyone who is susceptible to their artificial attractions. At one end of the scale is Lady Dedlock, who has sacrificed all for ambition and subsequently is destroyed; at the other is Pip (*Great Expectations*), who is also ready to sacrifice all for snobbery but is eventually saved. Pip can be redeemed because he is young and can be re-educated, while Lady Dedlock as part of the society that Pip aspires to cannot be saved from herself.

Nearly every character in *Bleak House,* and particularly Lady Dedlock, must expect the denial of their great expectations, which are either nullified or partially frustrated: from Jo of Tom-all-Alone's to Sir Leicester and Lady Dedlock, from Caddy Jellyby to Richard Carstone, from Esther Summerson to the Smallweeds, from Miss Flite and Mr. George to Vholes. Jo and Richard Carstone are the most obvious victims: Jo's great expectation is simply to survive in a world which, obviously, has no room for his kind. He has only a peripheral existence—little to eat, no warm place to sleep, no work to do; lacking almost the power of speech and all other means of communication, Jo should be the recipient of English missionary efforts. His existence is worse than that of any African savage whom Mrs. Jellyby wishes to save, and his life, evidently, cannot be helped by the kind of Christian salvation that Mrs. Pardiggle wishes to foist upon his class.*

Dickens mocks particularly this kind of "charity," based as Mrs. Jellyby's is on English exploitation, misery, and destitution. Mrs. Pardiggle's missionary work, founded on religious conversion,

---

* Jo and his type are all to be found in Henry Mayhew's great study, *London Labour and the London Poor* (1851-62). Mayhew was concerned with the marginal existence of 50,000 or more Londoners who lived in the streets, ate garbage, and died anonymously, in most ways more like subterranean creatures than even Kafka's burrowing animal or Dostoyevsky's Underground Man or Hesse's Steppenwolf. Ironically, much of their scavenging for rotting food took place near the Crystal Palace, London's glass beacon of progress and prosperity.

Asa Briggs, in *Victorian People,* demonstrates that hundreds of thousands —perhaps millions—of Englishmen at midcentury were outside the touch of both Church and State. In fact, in most large cities there was not even room for them in church had they wished to attend. Briggs indicates that there was space for only 28.7% of the population in London churches. The Victorian assumption, acted out in detail, seemed to be that England and its institutions existed only for the middle and upper classes.

is, if anything, even more meaningless than Mrs. Jellyby's to bring clothes and spiritual light to Africans, for Mrs. Pardiggle, in the name of religious fervor, will repress those she supposedly is to help. She makes faith the common denominator of progress, never perceiving that faith, as Dickens points out, works well only when one is warm, well-fed, and socially useful. One is reminded of Bertolt Brecht's cry of outrage, "First comes food, then morality."

Mrs. Pardiggle's "salvation" is merely another way of insuring these people's subservience. With religion, they are safe, even if hopeless; they will not interfere with her life, and at the same time they will not become a source of rebellion or dissatisfaction. This kind of missionary work, then, is intended to maintain the status quo; and by attacking it with such virulence Dickens became a forerunner of the Fabians, who saw "missionary" work in terms not of religious instruction but of housing, employment, and food. By rejecting Mrs. Pardiggle and by ridiculing Mrs. Jellyby, Dickens rejected the hypocrisy that passed for charity, without, of course, rejecting help and charity themselves.

If Jo is victimized by a system which has no place for him, Richard Carstone is a victim, in another way, of the same system. Attractive, charming, self-assured and confident, Richard Carstone could well have been the romantic hero of most popular Victorian novels. Like several of his counterparts, he is the young man without money or position who would, through diligent effort, secure both for himself, as well as acquire a loyal wife, bonny children (a boy and a girl), and a cheerful home. At the end of the novel, he would not be unlike David Copperfield by the side of Agnes, an author of books which prove popular and successful, a devoted father, with many years of love and security to look forward to. Or he might be a Pip, less innocent than formerly, much chastened after having been led astray, but still ready for a life which rewards hard work and right feeling.

Richard Carstone is to fit into none of these worlds. Caught by the devil of greed, he is mesmerized by the power of monetary rewards, and, like Faust, makes his fatal bargain. He becomes dedicated to the only kind of hell that a materialistic society can provide. Caught by the wrong kind of success, Richard Carstone loses all sense of perspective. Like the obsessed Miss Flite, he sees the court case as a means of attaining balance in a society which, he should have realized, gives nothing freely. By now, Dickens fully knew that pursuit of materialism debilitates spirit unless one is Pickwick, John Jarndyce, or a Cheeryble Brother (*Nicholas Nickleby*) and can make money without changing a basically charitable disposition. If one is, conversely, a Richard Carstone or a Pip, one must proceed carefully, for money and the resultant rise in one's class become the sole justification for life. One then loses all sense of proportion and creates an imbalance which in itself is self-destructive.

Like the classical tragedians, whom he barely, if at all, knew, Dickens recognized that immoderation led to the smashing of all goals, and that lack of proportion meant a pact with the devil. As mentally upset by the court case as Esther Summerson is physically defaced by the pox, Richard sees his friends as enemies and his enemies as friends. By preferring the greediness of Vholes, who lives off others' misfortunes, to the generosity and kindness of Jarndyce, who lives to help others, Richard rejects the civilized way in favor of the predatory. Like Lady Dedlock, Richard is brought down by the very society he wishes to enter, although his demise just misses tragic proportions, lacking as it does self-realization. Jo and Richard Carstone join with Lady Dedlock as the unhappy denizens of a society that destroys more than it creates.

Still another essential part of this rapacious society is the Smallweeds, whose name and miniature size indicate their low moral stature. Grasping and greedy individuals, sucking capitalists, they represent the rotten core of an era. Their values—both attractive and repulsive to the weak—frustrate all attempts at a natural, wholesome existence, and one can only escape the Smallweeds by rejecting the entire way of life which makes them possible.

Caught between a society that is bad and a childhood that has been lost, Harold Skimpole tries to make the best of both worlds. An adult-juvenile, he refuses to grow up, for then rather than inhabiting the world of the child, he must live in the world of the Smallweeds. Like Peter Pan, he lives with calculated childishness in an adult world, although married and the father of several children. Skimpole's refusal to grow up is both a desire to return to the merriness and untroubled joviality of an earlier time and an attempt to escape a world dominated by Chancery. The reality principle is too strong for him—he has a whiff of Eden—and so he attempts to avoid it by denying adulthood and becoming a parasite. In his flightiness, he is unattractive but believable, a person befuddled by the complexities of life from which it is preferable to retire into dreams.

Unlike Pickwick, Skimpole has never made his fortune, has never contributed in any way to the general welfare or economy. His social contract has always enabled him to draw out and never to put in: he contributes nothing, for he has nothing to give except a dubious gratitude, which he quickly forgets when a new need arises. Precisely because he is parasitical Dickens does not allow him to remain innocent, so far has Dickens's vision deepened since the days of the Pickwickians. Skimpole turns villainous toward the end of the novel, an ending that Chesterton claimed spoiled the "ironical daintiness of the original notion." Chesterton felt that Dickens vulgarized the character simply to achieve a consistent end: an attack upon idleness.

Skimpole's refusal to work or to live as an adult, however, goes deeper than Chesterton grants. Skimpole's attitude recalls the assumptions of all those who come to grief because they feel Chancery will decide in their favor. These people are also parasites, hoping as they do to live off society without any industry. Like several of his later contemporaries—William Morris and the Fabians, for example—Dickens believed in the saving power of work, although the work may not be difficult or even particularly time-consuming. It was sufficient for the Protestant Dickens that a person at least thought in terms of work, any work; idleness brought him to the devil. Paradoxically, Dickens did not seem to know exactly *how* people worked—he describes very few jobs intimately—but work they should. Once they decide to apply themselves, good fortune is their reward, or, at least, the promise of good fortune: thus, David Copperfield, Pip, and Eugene Wrayburn (*Our Mutual Friend*).

Richard Carstone comes to grief precisely because he expects a fortune to fall on him; he too is like a child living in a world of agreeable and generous adults who demand nothing from him. From here to the Smallweeds is not a great distance; for if society is to tolerate idlers, then it must as well bear with money-lenders, usurers, and blood-sucking capitalists like the Small-weeds, themselves direct descendants of Ralph Nickleby, Mr. Dombey, and Murdstone. All operate on the same principle: to put in less of themselves than they take out. Skimpole therefore becomes for Dickens a villain whose hypocrisy and cant must be revealed. His type of childishness—not to be confused with the real thing—must be exposed as reprehensible and mocked as subversive. By the time of *Bleak House,* with England divided—as Disraeli had pointed out—into two houses, one rich, one poor, the social scene was too rotten and the political core too corrupt for Dickens to let Skimpole, or even Pickwick, survive as an adult-juvenile.

Similarly, Sir Leicester Dedlock must be partially destroyed, for he too represents a kind of socially injurious idleness. Sir Leicester, however, must not be seen as a stereotyped aristocrat toward whom Dickens expectedly displays a lower-class virulence. He does achieve stature as a man of principle, and his devotion to his wife after he learns of her unfortunate past indicates his true temper. While not particularly knowing in social and political affairs, Sir Leicester is able to prove himself. Dickens evidently meant him to be an "old school" upright Tory who would defend to the death principle and tradition against reason and social progress. Dickens is careful to show that this aristocrat has true style, and that Skimpole does not. For Dickens as for Thackeray, style meant a basic generosity of heart, a sense of right feeling, an awareness of human sympathy; it was a quality that could exist in any person, whether Sir Leicester Dedlock, or Sam Weller, or Joe Gargery (*Great Expectations*). The standard of style became a way of leveling people, for it failed to recognize birth or achievement. Either a person had style or he did not: only style can determine the gentleman. One could not acquire or buy style, as one bought a seat in Parliament or as one purchased a title or a chair at a lord's dinner table. The crippled, the mentally unbalanced, the illiterate, and the weak could all have style if theirs was a basic generosity. If they could *feel,* they would inherit the earth.

Under these conditions, Esther Summerson should inherit more than the average person, for she is surely generous and charitable. Nevertheless, she is less a real person than a puppet, the kind of Dickens heroine who, like Agnes (*David Copperfield*), Rachel (*Hard Times*), and Biddy (*Great Expectations*), exists only to attach herself to a good man. Like her predecessors and successors, she has saintly qualities, is self-sacrificial, and infinitely sweet, far in excess of what she need be. Esther, however, differs in one significant respect: her personal appearance is marred by pockmarks before she finds happiness with Allan Woodcourt, a romantically-conceived young surgeon. In a novel in which virtually all great expectations are smashed, Esther finds hers also crushed, with the loss of her physical beauty. All that remains to her is her innocence and saintliness, and these, Dickens would have us believe, make her desirable. Her very disfigurement, we remember, is the result of her generosity in helping others. Esther, then, sums up the best in Victorian woman, although she—as well as her friend, Ada Clare—seems singularly unconvincing to us. She is not nearly so appealing as the whimpering Bella Wilfer (*Our Mutual Friend*) or the sadistic, tortured Estella (*Great Expectations*). She looks ahead to the somewhat insipid Little Dorrit and Lizzie Hexam, girls who fail as literary creations because they seem the stuff of sermons rather than life. In fitting them into the convention of the compliant Victorian female, Dickens forsook the opportunity to give them distinction.

Caddy Jellyby, Chesterton feels, is the greatest of Dickens's heroines. She passes from one blight, her "philanthropic" mother, to another, her father-in-law, a self-indulgent Regency gentleman. As a counterpart to Richard Carstone, a man who crumbles because of avarice, Caddy is a woman who endures through strong will and devotion. She tries to find happiness in a world dominated by foolish parents, who, while rarely consciously cruel, forget the responsibilities of their office in indulging self-love. As much as Richard is impelled forward by destructive motives, Caddy is motivated by the kindest of qualities, although she vows to find personal happiness at any price. Hers is a strong quest for life in a world that tries to suffocate it, while Richard, in the same kind of world, pursues a living death.

Only those characters who remain outside the orbit of the Jarndyce vs. Jarndyce Chancery case can preserve their integrity and realize their expectations; and sometimes they, like Esther, suffer from the ghostly mists of the case.* Yet even within the miasma of a legal action that suffocates all it touches, Dickens continued certain fairy-tale elements from his earlier novels, through the histrionic nature of the characters and through their inability to face responsibility. Skimpole, like Turveydrop, talks about himself as though he were a character performing in a play or novel —*words* make the man, Dickens insisted. Early in the book, Skimpole discourses on principle and states his philosophy (XVIII):

" 'Upon my life I have not the least idea [of principle]! I don't know what it is you call by that name, or where it is, or who possesses it. If you possess it, and find it comfortable, I am quite delighted, and congratulate you heartily. But I know nothing about it, I assure you; for I am a mere child, and I lay no claim to it, and I don't want it.' "

As a Pickwickian, Skimpole could have expressed such sentiments and we might have laughed; now, fifteen years later, the same sentiments take on a tragic tone.

Skimpole's lack of principle, as he wants everyone to believe, is connected to his childishness, a time of life when principle is subservient to self-indulgence. He has recourse to his only possible defense: his inability to cope with an adult world in which work and principle are one test of maturity. Still, Skimpole's standard extends throughout the entire novel, although he is the only character to offer an official excuse. Lack of principle is implicit in the Chancery case itself, in Lady Dedlock, the philanthropic ladies, the Smallweeds, Vholes, Mr. Guppy, Richard Carstone, Mr. Tulkinghorn, Mr. Turveydrop. Carried by the fog, expedience permeates all layers of society and all categories, manners as well as law, government as well as family, industry as well as religion.

* The Chancery case was probably based on an actual trial, the Jennings case, which began in 1798, during the Napoleonic campaign, and continued undecided for more than a hundred years.

Connected as it is to injustice and responsibility, principle or its lack becomes the spine for *Bleak House* and all of Dickens's later fiction. To avow principle is to accept reality, while to deny principle is to try to return to a fairy-tale existence, to deny life in favor of a false Eden.

Not unusually, Skimpole's language here and elsewhere seems inconsistent with that of a "real" person. He is, in actuality, stylized; so that often he seems more like a caricature than a living person. As their names clearly indicate, the same may be said of Miss Flite, Turveydrop, Mrs. Pardiggle, Mrs. Jellyby, and several others. Their fable-like unreality, one might argue, makes them typical "Dickensian creations," remembered more for their eccentricities than as people. However, these so-called caricatures are indeed real people carried to extremes. Through a multitude of details and observed facts, Dickens destroyed the generality of the caricature or the type and pinpointed the particular or the individual. While on the surface Miss Flite appears a flighty fairy-tale creation, her attitude toward the Chancery case is the madness of an age lost in hypocrisy and materialism. Like her birds, she also is perpetually imprisoned. Similarly, Skimpole—although he seems to skim on air—is too carefully presented to be a mere caricature. He is too horribly real for that. His expedience, like the madness of Miss Flite and the selfishness of Mrs. Jellyby and Mrs. Pardiggle, represents the faults of an age: Dickens could never have achieved strong moral comment through caricature, any more than his great predecessor, Hogarth, could have condemned an age simply through satire.

Dickens clearly was writing for adults, and writing with a sense of high moral purpose. With outrage, he perceived the tragic waste beneath the expenditure of energy on worthless causes when so much good work remained to be done. Implicit everywhere is a sense of doom. Even love seems superimposed. As is characteristic of Dickens's later fiction, the orientation toward death or cataclysm remains long after one forgets the partially happy ending. Despite Miss Flite's harmless madness and her strangely imprisoned birds, despite the histrionic quality of the performers, despite the miraculous benevolence of Mr. Jarndyce, despite Esther's discovery of her high birth, despite the romantic story-book ending—despite all these factors, *Bleak House* is brutally realistic, in its way as tough and hard a view of man's condition as Hardy's and Conrad's. In both Dickens's London and Conrad's Africa, the Kurtzes have capitalized on man's savagery and greed.

Furthermore, Dickens's ever-recurring obsession with injustice persists in *Bleak House*. Expanded from the earlier stress on the child's sense of injustice, it here involves all aspects of society except those which are transformed by love. Instead of the small child being wronged in a world of huge, indifferent adults, now everyone is wronged, child and adult alike. Yet the "saving power," as in the romance or fairy tale, is the power of love. Those touched by it are transfigured; a sordid existence becomes tinged with hope. Even as Dickens's fiction changed in emphasis from the individual to society, he retained his belief in the saving grace of love. The real conflict now is between love and greed, between life and materialism, between natural feelings and feelings complicated by pride and vanity, between common sense and sham. Whereas once, as Edgar Johnson has remarked, the individual had to be changed to save the institution (in *Barnaby Rudge, Martin Chuzzlewit, Dombey and Son,* and *David Copperfield*), now the social order itself must be changed to save the individual. This great insight, which had so strong an influence upon George Bernard Shaw and other English Marxists, is revealed also in *Hard Times, Little Dorrit, Great Expectations,* and *Our Mutual Friend,* the latter two perhaps Dickens's greatest novels. It takes Dickens's early optimism full round and provides for the first time in his fiction the inner tensions and conflicts necessary for a tragic sense of life. Yet this insight also led him into a political impasse: How was he to bring about a change in the social order when he opposed radicalism and violence?

Even as late as *David Copperfield* (1849-50), three years before *Bleak House,* Dickens could still be considered a comic writer, for the outcome of his novels was assured: nothing permanently damaging could happen to people who were good, and villainy was certain to be punished. *David Copperfield* itself, with its first-person narrative, acted as a cathartic upon Dickens and became the last of *that* kind of novel. Afterwards, the vision darkened: joy becomes limited, life complicated, happiness qualified, security no longer assured. Cruelty vies with decency and continues even after decency triumphs. All society, as in *Little Dorrit,* lives within the shadow of the Marshalsea, and is, in effect, a prison. Even *Bleak House,* with its proximity to the courts and prison, is not ᶜᵒ bleak as *Little Dorrit, Great Expectations,* and *Our Mutual Friend.* These novels pick up every dark hint from *Pickwick,* but little indeed of the lightness and conviviality. Joviality has disappeared, and gaiety has become a sacrifice to an animal-like struggle for existence. Jingle and Job Trotter become the psychopathic Dolge Orlick and Bradley Headstone; Pickwick's brief stay in debtor's prison is transformed into the permanent frustrations of life in the no-exit Marshalsea; David Copperfield's optimism becomes the frustrations of Pip; the sweet Agnes is transformed into the bitter, sadistic Estella; the amateurish Dodson and Fogg become the professional vultures of *Bleak House* and *Our Mutual Friend,* who swoop down wherever they smell money and good fortune. Society is infested with parasites, and good deeds are almost meaningless except as they aid the individual. All that is left, Dickens suggests, is the tenuous relationship between individuals; the social order itself has veered dangerously out of control.

Dickens's tragic phase opened with *Hard Times* (1854), which extended the themes and tones of *Bleak House* and prepared the ground for the final novels. After *Pickwick,* Dickens realized that the past could not hold back the present, and that his pre-dated narratives (*Pickwick* takes place more in the eighteenth than in the nineteenth century) were little more than masks for evil that had, eventually, to be exposed. Consequently, most of Dickens's later tragic novels seem contemporary in background: *Our Mutual Friend,* for example, is, among other things, much concerned with England's Poor Laws, and *Great Expectations* discusses snobbery from a mid-century view point. Only with a large middle-class reading public could the theme of *Great Expectations* be acceptable, based as it is on a middle-class view of the "gentleman" who gains success through hard work after rejecting the snobbery of the aristocracy. Pip's baptism of fire here is not unlike that of Eugene Wrayburn's in *Our Mutual Friend;* both young men are intended to become "heroes" for the reading public of the 1850's and 60's. Except for *A Tale of Two Cities* (1859), which was hardly a major effort, Dickens had forsaken the historical perspective of the pre-dated story in all of his completed later work.

Part of Dickens's *direct* response to contemporary problems was in no small way the result of Thomas Carlyle's influence. *Hard Times,* we remember, was originally dedicated to Carlyle, and *A Tale of Two Cities* was certainly motivated by *The French Revolution.* Like Ruskin and Shaw, Dickens was captivated by Carlyle's moral earnestness, as well as by his insistence on what later came to be called High Seriousness. Humor, in these terms, was no longer simply comic, but a desperate wit with a double-edged blade that cut through hypocrisy and cant. The irony of *Great Expectations,* for instance, was merely one aspect of Dickens's response to Carlyle's admonition that the "State of England" was decayed at the core. So that its meaning could not be lost, *Hard Times* in construction and prose style is spare and direct. There are fewer humorous vagaries than before, fewer unessential characters, fewer digressions. The very shortened form of the novel (under three hundred pages) places it close to a tract, and the leanness of the plot is a further indication of Dickens's emphasis on its quality as sermon.

Carlyle's influence was far-reaching in the mid-nineteenth century, but surely no one felt it more strongly than Dickens. As early as 1829, in *Signs of the Times,* when Dickens was struggling to perfect his shorthand, Carlyle was already drawing the distinction between the mechanistic and the dynamical elements of society. The latter involved ideals, ideas, values (as later embodied in Sissy Jupe of *Hard Times*), while the former was concerned with facts, statistics, a scientific morality (Gradgrind and Bounderby of *Hard Times*). Carlyle desired a synthesis of the two, for he saw the dangers if either proved too strong, although, like Dickens later, he personally favored the dynamic. While attacking the Millenarians on the Right for opposing reforms and mocking the Benthamites on the Left for extremism, Carlyle feared that industrial change would transform education and religion into material quantities, when they should remain intellectual and spiritual. In his attack upon Macaulay (whom he identified as the chief spokesman for

Mechanism),* Carlyle viewed the historian as a defender of self interest and a profit-and-loss account of events.

Carlyle saw the world, both past and present, in terms of great actions, great ideas, great visions, great men. He envisioned the French Revolution as first an *idea* from which action followed; this historical view approximates his lifelong belief in the conflict between genius (idea, imagination) and mechanical competence (action, the working-out of details, fancy). While institutions are necessary, he claimed, as Dickens also did, that there must be allowances for individual differences. Against empiricism, utilitarianism, and materialism, he offered idealism, mind, and transcendentalism. He believed in a unity of life, a fusion of religious experience and daily event. The Everlasting Yea in *Sartor Resartus* denotes a life of affirmation, duty, and creative energy. The Everlasting No signifies a denial of life, a wasteland of spirit, a sense of despair. Mind—as the German philosophers had taught him—must transform Matter, or else man diminishes. Carlyle believed that society must adjust to suit the needs of an industrial system without destroying the rights of the individual, the basic idea of *Sartor Resartus* as well as all of Dickens's major later novels.

The ideas expressed in *Sartor Resartus* (1833-34) are as important for an understanding of later Dickens as is a knowledge of the eighteenth-century novel for his early work. In the quest of Teufelsdröckh for the Everlasting Yea after the despair of No and the arid Center of Indifference, Carlyle affirmed that the infinite universe should fill man with supernatural awe, that the awareness of the miracle of existence should lead to the active life and creative will, and that society is organic and dynamic, not mechanical. Carlyle rejected the fixed, ordered world of Newton and his scientific followers, positing, instead, an "expanding universe." Failure to accept this ever-growing world makes one an atheist, a materialist who is satisfied with the negations of the Everlasting No. In its broadest sense, religion means an acceptance of life as dynamic and creative. Carlyle tried to replace Benthamism with

* Macaulay's Liberal tendencies increasingly became identified with laissez-faire capitalism, industrialization, commercialism, the cash nexus, the new science—the whole paraphernalia of materialistic progress.

emotion and put feeling into the universe, claiming that neither emotion nor feeling is private and personal but public and available. Man's quest should be not for happiness—one should, after all, reduce the numerator of his desires—but for infinite love and pity and compassion for his brothers. Since life entails duty and social purpose, one's creative energy is fulfilled in meaningful work.

For Carlyle, science is concerned with the limited phenomenal world, with observed data that is not the result of thought. Opposed to this is Kant's noumenal world, nonempirical and observable only through the mind. The latter postulates free will, immortality, a moral God. As soon, however, as man recognizes his moral function, he faces a conflict between duty and desire. Here Carlyle grapples with Kant's Categorical Imperative, which posits that Truth must harmonize all experience into a unity of moral duty. One must function, Carlyle insisted, following Kant, *as if* there is a unity of experience through Truth; the latter is *a priori*, innate, not experiential. Faith, unlike the facts of Science, obviously is not provable. Replacing Kant's respect for man as Spirit is Carlyle's philosophy of Duty, and replacing the German's Categorical Imperative is the Scotsman's insistence on work and inner discipline.

As Dickens himself later demonstrated, work must not be done for self-interest, but for itself, as a kind of duty to one's social conscience. In *Chartism* (1839) and *Past and Present* (1843), Carlyle came to terms with the pressing social, political, and economic problems of contemporary England; and by mid-century, the social novels of Dickens, Elizabeth Gaskell, Disraeli, and, later, Charles Kingsley were also exposing the same abuses. In the first of his tracts for the time, Carlyle attacked the underlying causes that had made Chartism possible and which forced working-class resentment to seek an outlet in agitation. Carlyle looked for general, not particular, reasons and claimed that justice and not merely higher wages was necessary. He attacked the spirit behind the Poor Law (as Dickens was to do in *Our Mutual Friend*), claiming that it suggests that whoever will not work ought to die; and yet work was not always available. Further, Carlyle attacked laissez-faire capitalism (as Dickens was to do in *Hard Times*), while confusing laissez-faire capitalism with democracy, a mistake

Dickens never made. Carlyle inveighed against an age of Imposture, Semblance, un-Truths, dead Faith, False Values (much, again, as did Dickens in *Great Expectations*).

Carlyle—like Disraeli in his "Young England" novels—offered a solution unacceptable to Dickens when he advocated, among other things, a real and responsible aristocracy to administer justice. Aristocracy, Carlyle felt, would provide the discipline that a democracy needs, for he interpreted laissez-faire as a destructive loosening of all values: "let them do," he literally translated it. Furthermore, in attacking the cash nexus of a materialistic society, he left little alternative but a retreat to an earlier age when cash was not the motivating force in human relationships. For Carlyle, medieval times provided precisely the right example of a glorious period when the infamies of industrialization could not corrupt good men. Dickens himself was intermittently taken with the harmonies of the past but more for the purpose of a comic romp than for a serious solution.

Nevertheless, Carlyle's social insights were such that no writer interested in the "State of England" could ignore his strong presence. His recognition that man finds liberation through proper work influenced an entire century of social writers and turns up in Dickens's portraits of Stephen Blackpool, Eugene Wrayburn, and Pip. His attack on the voices of Mammon, even the names themselves (Plugson of Undershot, Sir Jabesh Windbag), was repeated in Dickens's parody of the idle rich and in his burlesque of the snobbish and vain, later to appear, with the names slightly altered, in Shaw's plays. In trying to diagnose ills, both Dickens and Carlyle met on common ground, and in their attack upon the evils of industrialization and its attendant avarice, both were concerned with the same problems that Marx and Engels were to dissect shortly afterward.

The later Carlyle, with his obsessed ranting against democracy in favor of a ruling elite, failed to appeal to Dickens, who was now in the paradoxical situation of agreeing that institutions were evil in their treatment of the individual and yet forced to defend them as a necessary counter to anarchy and chaos.* In the dilemma of

* Even though Dickens ridiculed Utilitarianism for its mechanistic view of man and society, he nevertheless found himself close to John Stuart Mill's

Stephen Blackpool in *Hard Times,* Dickens posed what is, perhaps, the leading question in an industrial society. How can the worker still retain his self-respect and identity, he asked, when only the collective will (Trade Unionism here) gives him the

---

views as they were to appear in *On Liberty* (1859). Mill argued that the sole purpose for which restrictions can be rightfully imposed upon the individual is to prevent harm to others. The individual's own good, whether physical or moral, is not sufficient reason. Mill wrote: "The only freedom which deserves the name, is that of pursuing our own good in our own way, so long as we do not attempt to deprive others of theirs, or impede their efforts to obtain it." Implied in Mill's position is an adherence to laissez-faire capitalism, the results of which Dickens often attacked, but the existence of which he rarely questioned.

Dickens's mockery of Utilitarianism was an attack upon Bentham's and James Mill's brand rather than upon John Stuart Mill's own more complex explanation later set forth in *Utilitarianism* (1863). In that essay, Mill removed Bentham's simplifications and eliminated the seeming selfishness implicit in the latter's stress upon individual happiness. Mill argued, instead, that pleasure is not measurable and is not directly proportional to happiness. Happiness, then, is distinct from pleasure; that is, the common happiness rather than the individual's happiness becomes the basis of Utilitarianism. With the individual good connected to the good of the whole, the entire philosophy is now a social rather than an atomistic one. With this view of Utilitarianism Dickens could hardly quarrel.

The only area of real disagreement occurred in Dickens's and Mill's attitude toward Nature. Dickens was inclined to identify the good in man with the instinctual, believing as he did in the natural goodness of natural man, his heritage from the Romantic Poets and Rousseau. Mill, however, argued quite differently, quite anti-Romantically. Everything, Mill said, indicates that man must amend Nature, not imitate it, must shun instinct and not call it the good. He wrote in *Nature* (conceived 1850-58, published 1873):

> The scheme of Nature regarded in its whole extent, cannot have had, for its sole or even principal object, the good of human or other sentient beings. What good it brings to them, is mostly the result of their own exertions. Whatever, in nature, gives indication of beneficent design, proves this beneficence to be armed only with limited power; and the duty of man is to cooperate with the beneficent powers, not by imitating but by perpetually striving to amend the course of nature— and bringing that part of it over which we can exercise control, more nearly into conformity with a high standard of justice and goodness.

Curiously, in the famous Jamaica case (1865), in which Governor Eyre was attacked for executing 400 Negroes and an innocent Negro member of

power to oppose an even greater tyranny (laissez-faire capitalism)? That Dickens failed to answer the question fully indicates how far the novel fails artistically, but that he was able to derive artistic significance from the theme at all indicates how his later work could incorporate serious social problems in fictional form.

Hard Times began to appear in weekly installments in Dickens's own *Household Words* while he still had completed only half the novel. Perhaps because of its brevity—it is only about a third as long as his regular novels—*Hard Times* possesses a unity and tight organization that make it seem a departure for Dickens. It is, however, less a departure than an abstract or summation of his previous themes. Beginning with *Pickwick,* as we have seen, Dickens had identified industrialization and materialism with the stultification of human responses, and avarice with the lowest debasement of the human spirit. Coketown is symbolic of all industrial towns, in which greed rather than love binds men together. The result is an Inferno in which both victims and masters become dehumanized. In different form, this social analysis of character had appeared in *Nicholas Nickleby,* with Ralph as a distant, more genteel forerunner of Bounderby, and was repeated with Jonas Chuzzlewit, Dombey, and Murdstone (*David Copperfield*).

Hard Times, however, is not an organized social tract but an example of Dickens's feeling that bread alone is not enough; that, as Ibsen and Shaw pointed out, our order, not our disorder, is horrible; that, consequently, we have more to fear from our magnates than from our criminals. *Hard Times* is more than a type of medieval morality play with good and bad characters, the stylized speech of allegorized figures, and the evident didacticism of the socio-religious message. As F. R. Leavis remarked, the beginning with its light and dark imagery—the sunbeam, for example, that starts at Sissy Jupe and ends at Bitzer—illustrates that Dickens was attempting to attach the social theme to an artistic frame.

---

the Colonial Assembly, Dickens sided with Eyre's defenders, while Mill attempted to organize a private prosecution. In fact, the humanists—Dickens, Carlyle, Ruskin, Tennyson—accepted Eyre's inhuman severity in suppressing the revolt, while the scientists and rationalists (empiricists, materialists, Utilitarians)—Mill, Huxley, Herbert Spencer—were outraged by Eyre's transgression of the rules of civilized justice.

At its most obvious, *Hard Times* is concerned with various kinds of evil, evidenced by Bounderby (hypocrisy and avarice), Gradgrind (unfeeling utilitarianism), Coketown (the stultifying, mechanical world), and Stephen Blackpool's wife (hatred and dissolution). Against these manifestations of evil is opposed Sleary's Horse-riding, with its overtones of art and entertainment which appeal directly to the heart. Despite its physical dirtiness and ignorance, Sleary's is wholesome, for it is outside the industrialized, mechanistic life of Coketown. Its world is that of a child's, in which innocence predominates and encourages expressions of feeling. Opposed to Sleary's pleasures are Gradgrind's bloodless system and Bounderby's cant. Dickens always presents Sleary's as innocent, although when necessary its denizens can be hardheaded and shrewd. On the other hand, Gradgrind and Bounderby posit an adult world with no room for childlike qualities—they turn duty into an absence of pleasure and discipline into a failure of joy. In this very area, Dickens parted from Carlyle, believing as he did that pleasure and joy are as vital as moral compliance.

If the need for love is the basic theme of the novel, then all those who reject love as the prime motivating force in human relationships are true villains.* Bounderby's equation of self interest with

---

* Browning's *Paracelsus* (1835) and Bailey's *Festus* (1839) acted as links with Wordwsorth and Blake to continue this theme so basic for the fiction of the entire century: that love and feeling must inform knowledge for the harmonious development of the individual. The theme recurs insistently in every major novel by Dickens, Meredith, and George Eliot.

Aspects of the theme—in itself a trenchant social criticism—turn up in such disparate areas as Ruskin's view of Gothic and Newman's idea of a university, both contemporaneous with *Hard Times*. Ruskin, in "The Nature of Gothic," lauded Gothic because it manifests human imperfections and follows natural laws. It is not dead or passive, but active and vital. Further, Gothic is a reaction against modern industrialism which stifles human impulses by forcing precision and accuracy. By recognizing that man is a fallacious, even a fantastic creature, Gothic allows for qualities like spirit, love, and feeling.

Similarly, in his first set of lectures for "The Idea of a University," Newman argued that it was better for the active intellect to reject the University altogether than to expose itself to drudgery and meaningless routine. That is, fitness for the world—human qualities rather than pure and isolated knowledge—should be the natural end of education.

national welfare is, for Dickens, merely a weak justification for personal greed. He represents, roughly, the laissez-faire attitude of the Manchester School of economics, which advocated a hands-off government attitude, letting supply and demand dictate labor and the market. Consequently, the Manchester School, rightly or wrongly, became associated in the public mind with the severe political opposition to government regulations aimed at relieving the suffering of the laboring class. In sifting several of the ideas of the School through Bounderby, Dickens tried to transcend the level of a tract, at the same time showing the School's heartless materialism, its hypocrisy, and its selfishness. To represent a social issue in individual terms, Dickens turned Bounderby into a canting ignoramus who would deny his own mother in order to demonstrate that self-interest had raised him on the economic scale. Bounderby's values, accordingly, deny every aspect of the human heart. His justification of his system is simply that the mighty should dictate justice.

More important to Dickens than Bounderby is Gradgrind, whose system of education roughly parallels James Mill's training of John Stuart Mill. Gradgrindism is a combination of the free economic policies of the Manchester School and the pleasure principle of the Utilitarians. According to the latter view, the individual by pursuing his own pleasure contributes to the general happiness and welfare. Pleasures themselves remain undistinguished from each other—as Bentham said, pushpin (a children's game) is equal to poetry. In seeking his own pleasure, so the argument runs, one naturally avoids the pain that is the counterbalance of each pleasure. Bentham claimed that since a person would not wish to jeopardize his own happiness, he would also be careful of others', so that society would not interfere with him. And while the laissez-faire school of economics cannot be equated directly with the Utilitarians, both seemed to agree that if the collective good de-

---

These points, obviously, are intended for a commercial age in which individual identity is in perpetual danger of being submerged to the economic machine. It is not chance—even allowing for their vast ideological differences—that Dickens, Ruskin, and Newman should react similarly, with a sense of moral outrage.

pended upon the individual's happiness, then the latter should be promoted without undue restrictions.

Gradgrind's middle-class faith in education is very much like that of Dickens himself, although the form of Gradgrind's school is obviously quite different from what Dickens wanted. Gradgrind believes that the child's human impulses must be limited; that the child must be judged by adult standards; and that feelings do not exist as knowledge and must therefore be ignored, or, better yet, not "felt." Here once again recurs Dickens's major social theme: the injustice of the adult to the child becomes the injustice of society to its individual members, the injustice of government to its subjects, and, finally, the injustice of an economic system to its workers. Within Gradgrind's system, there is no love, no human imagination, no warm heart. His emphasis on facts is unrelenting; like Plato, he is afraid that poetry will debilitate the will, and therefore he exorcizes it from the classroom. Just as Bounderby's industrial system works for profit and gain, and recognizes no other standard, so does Gradgrind's educational system work on a calculus of rugged individualism in which a fact is God, a statistic His Son, and detailed knowledge the stuff of a successful life.

Gradgrind's philosophy, unlike Bounderby's, lacks hypocrisy and is disinterested, for he gains nothing personally from it. Therefore, his downfall when he recognizes that his stultification of human impulses and his frustration of vitality have destroyed his children's lives contains a tragic quality. When Bounderby falls from grace, however, we sense a breath of fresh air, what we feel at Tartuffe's exposure in Molière's play. Bounderby is the schemer found out, but Gradgrind is the well-meaning although misdirected fool whose life's work has come to nought through his lack of perception. With his philosophy reversed, he might have been a Dickensian "hero," sentimental, understanding, and generous, for he clearly loves his children, lacks real meanness, and is unable to be cruel despite his devotion to a system that countenances cruelty. Like Sir Austin Feverel in Meredith's novel (1859), he cannot see beyond his own needs and thus does irreparable harm while attempting to do good. Dickens's warning to politicians and social workers is equally clear.

Ironically, Sissy Jupe's inability to acquire Gradgrind's sense of fact is the very thing that enables her to survive intact. Part of her indefeasible humanity is a subconscious ability to resist what she suspects to be wrong, even though she lacks the power of mind to discover why. Sissy is in the long line of "feeling" girls and women whose resistance to mind makes them heroines in novels of feeling. So far has Dickens moved from Jane Austen, and so far has Dickens's world moved from hers! Following Dickens, D. H. Lawrence's novels consistently feature such heroines, and so too do the novels of E. M. Forster and Virginia Woolf. Such women seem to have been conceived without original sin, trailing clouds of glory; they are born, not made. Despite the onslaughts of villainy, they remain pure and simple. Like Richardson's Pamela and Clarissa, they cannot be seduced: they must be raped, or else they triumph.

That all except Sissy Jupe must suffer is the point of *Hard Times,* for only she has the saving grace of vitality: she lives because she is truly alive. As for the others, once Gradgrind admits that his system has failed—and he is too honest not to see that it has—he is broken in heart and spirit. For her part, Mrs. Gradgrind dies knowing that something is wrong, broken in spirit as she also is as a result of a life of successive frustrations. Tom Gradgrind—who has pursued the letter of the system into selfishness and personal aggrandizement—ends as a clown, a ragged criminal on the run, ostracized by society, finally dying far away, alone and isolated. Louisa, too, is ruined by her father's system. Having no heart to give, she can never respond. As she reminds him, she has been discouraged from enjoying every meaningful aspect of life. She asks him (XII, Book 2):

"How could you give me life, and take from me all the inappreciable things that raise it from the state of conscious death? Where are the graces of my soul? Where are the sentiments of my heart? What have you done, O father, what have you done, with the garden that should have bloomed once, in this great wilderness here [her heart]?"

And the scene between father and daughter—melodramatic but histrionically effective nevertheless—ends with the ironic words: "And . . . [he] saw the pride of his heart and the triumph of his system, lying, an insensible heap, at his feet." Bitzer, the triumph of the system, at the end a more genteel Bounderby, with the ideals of a vulture, ready to perpetuate Gradgrind's ideals and do battle with the Sissy Jupes of the world, later becomes transformed into the vicious Charley Hexam of *Our Mutual Friend*.

Together, then, Bounderby and Gradgrind have ruined all but Sissy Jupe. Fittingly, their victories have been "won" against the background of Coketown, a symbol of all bleak and ugly industrial cities. The very appearance of the town, like Conrad's London in *The Secret Agent* of some 50 years later, is hard, flat, metallic, mechanical, soul-sucking (V, Book 1).

It was a town of red brick, or of brick that would have been red if the smoke and ashes had allowed it; but as matters stood it was a town of unnatural red and black like the painted face of a savage. It was a town of machinery and tall chimneys, out of which interminable serpents of smoke trailed themselves for ever and ever, and never got uncoiled. It had a black canal in it, and a river that ran purple with ill-smelling dye, and vast piles of building full of windows where there was a rattling and a trembling all day long, and where the piston of the steam-engine worked monotonously up and down, like the head of an elephant in a state of melancholy madness.*

In the town Gradgrind lives with his family, including two younger boys named Adam Smith and Malthus, in a home called Stone Lodge. Through obvious names, Dickens indicated things: Gradgrind, M'Choakumchild, Bounderby, Bitzer (suggesting something sharp and rat-like), Sissy Jupe (childish, feminine, frivolously joyful). Coketown itself is eponymic for a town in which prosaic coke is produced, with no nonsense about anything that may fall outside this function. Bounderby and the town have taken on each other's qualities; the one, with his bluster and mediocrity, complements the other, with its sadistic pistons and facelessness. A vast symbol of all that has gone wrong, Coketown in its industrial function precludes human impulses and frustrates normal responses.

* De Toqueville described Manchester—probably Dickens's model for Coketown—as full of "homes of vice and poverty, which surround the huge palaces of industry and clasp them in their hideous folds," where "civilized man is turned back almost into a savage."

Caught in a more desperate situation than Sissy Jupe—who is, after all, so far outside the city that she can successfully evade its false seductions—is Stephen Blackpool, who has little choice but to work within a system that is personally degrading.* In Stephen Blackpool, Dickens centered his own paradoxical belief in institutions which must also be challenged and even denounced. Stephen is cut off not only from his employer but also from his fellow workers, for he refuses to involve himself in what he believes to be unjust. He becomes a martyr (a St. Stephen) to all that is bad in society, although his stubborn resistance to Trade Unionism is not necessarily indicative of Dickens's opposition. Stephen simply wants to be able to choose for himself in a society that discourages choice. Also, having suffered through a drunken wife, Stephen has promised a good woman, Rachel, to remain out of trouble, and his honor is more important than his immediate welfare. Clearly, Dickens intended to ennoble Stephen as a prototype of the efficient and hard-working honorable worker smashed by an economy based on deceit, much as a fundamentally decent Louisa is crushed by a miscalculated educational system.

Dickens, of course, sentimentalized Stephen and made him an evident victim to the coal pit, which had swallowed hundreds. Like the Voreux in Zola's *Germinal,* the pit in *Hard Times* is voracious in its appetites: either Bounderby or Gradgrind can carelessly send men to their doom in the dark. A symbolic figure of all these martyrs to the pit, Stephen joins Tom and Louisa, fellow victims of the "State of England."

The forces of evil, in this parable of right and wrong, are numerous and far-reaching, extending into every aspect of society

* There is, admittedly, a certain loading of the situation on Dickens's part. As conditions exist, Stephen *must* be trapped between the Union and Bounderby. He has few of the choices open to Sissy: if, as she does, he rejects all evil, he starves, or dies a martyr. Likewise, if Sissy were herself in Rachel's place, she could not so easily preserve her freedom of choice. Dickens's thought here reached an obvious impasse: for those not born into the world of imagination and art (the Circus), the choices must always be grim until a utopia is reached. Since Dickens did not strive for such a utopia, Marxist or otherwise, or even think it possible, his desire to "free" the individual from the existing situation, while sincere, had to be ultimately unrealizable.

and infecting particularly the educational system, the one sphere where Dickens had placed hope for rejuvenation. If one does not believe in revolution, or fears anarchy—and Dickens disdained disorder and chaos even if they might lead to better things—then one must, as Dickens did, fall back on a hope of ameliorating society through an evolutionary process of education. This stress on education, as we have seen, had been a persistent theme since *Oliver Twist* and was to continue through *Our Mutual Friend,* twenty-six years later. In one way, then, Dickens was a writer about education in its full, not simply its formal, sense: the education or awakening of a person to the real significance of the world. Sissy Jupe, whose natural goodness is the sole countering force to evil in the novel, is "educated" in the ways of the world through her association with Sleary's Horse-riding. As in the fable or parable, she ventures forth boldly, her dignity and common sense intact, into a world that will try unsuccessfully to bend her to its will.

Seen this way, perhaps Dickens's art is partially lost through exaggeration, but the social indictment remains powerful because it is firmly rooted in the lives of people. In a footnote to "The Roots of Honour" (*Unto this Last*), Ruskin comments that the "essential value and truth of Dickens's writings have been unwisely lost sight of by many thoughtful persons because he presents his truth with some colour of caricature." As was usual, Dickens found more success with his "evil" characters than with his noble ones. Long after we forget Stephen, we remember Bounderby; long after Sissy becomes dim, we recall Bitzer and the intensely colorless Gradgrind. Histrionic, mannered, stylized, the characters of *Hard Times* take the edge off what might have been simply a social tract and make this book an effective jumping-off place for the final triad of great novels.

To go from *David Copperfield* (1849-50) to *Great Expectations* ten years later is to measure Dickens's development not only as a social critic but also as an artist. Primarily, the later novel shows Dickens as an accomplished ironist, with the tone of *Great Expectations* carefully wedded to the theme of social snobbery, and that, in turn, attached to sexual passion. The irony should not be unexpected, for Dickens's letters and incidental asides indicate his dissatisfaction with typical nineteenth-century verisimilitude. On one occasion, he wrote: "It does not seem to me to be enough to say of any description that it is the exact truth. . . . The exact truths should be there; but the merit or art in the narrator is the manner of stating the truth. . . ." He goes on to say that the tendency in his day is "to be frightfully literal and catalogue-like—to make the thing, in short, a sum in reduction that any miserable creature can do in that way. . . ." For Dickens, irony was one way of avoiding unrelieved realism.

In other ways, the close plotting gives *Great Expectations* a unity and coherence foreign to *David Copperfield,* which, with its string of events, is a throwback to the episodic narratives of the earlier fiction. Even the two central characters—both of whose lives are narrated in the first person—show Dickens's advance in character development. Despite the texture and color of *Copperfield,* David himself is inflexible and wooden; despite the presence of adversity, cruelty, even sadism, he never changes. He remains a semi-romantic hero who will overcome setbacks and the meanness of evil people to emerge finally with the usual comfortable living and cozy wife, unmarked by his frightening past. His success is all a matter of time, fortitude, and patience. Throughout his lengthy ordeal, David is rarely tempted from the single path of righteousness; his devotion to truth and goodness never wavers. Pip, conversely, is tempted, succumbs, does change to some extent, and then after misfortune is led back to a clear vision. His unhappiness is more imaginatively realistic than David's; and, as well, his moments of happiness—few though they are—are of greater intensity than David's vague relations with Dora and Agnes provide. The growth from one novel to the other is an indication of Dickens's ability to transform a world of *gemütlichkeit* into one in which moral choice is a matter of personal survival.

The two novels warrant comparison, for both deal in varying ways with Dickens's past. *David Copperfield* is, obviously, a closer account of the author's personal life than the later novel, but each, although in different ways, reveals the shames and guilts of Dickens's past. The long-hidden episode in the blacking warehouse— a secret even to Dickens's wife—is divulged in *Copperfield;* also,

Dickens's parents reappear, with certain changes, as Mr. & Mrs. Micawber; Dora, the child-wife, is a carry-back to Dickens's own wife; further, the development of David's career, with its easy success from literary endeavors, parallels Dickens's own. Although *Great Expectations* is less explicit in presenting details from Dickens's personal life, it carried over anxieties and fears firmly embedded in his mind while avoiding, for the most part, the direct retelling of past events. For this reason and others, *Great Expectations* appears to have been mined from deeper material, and the ore accordingly seems far richer. Moreover, the later novel has a compelling theme which involves Pip at every turn: he can never escape the masochism that comes with sex and snobbery until his attitudes actually change; while *Copperfield* lacks a real theme, based as the novel is on the shifting fortunes of a pleasant but superficial protagonist.

Snobbery, with all its attendant vices, is the theme of *Great Expectations,* snobbery that extends throughout society, beyond Pip even to the nether world inhabited by Magwitch; whomever it touches, it destroys or maims. Snobbery had been Dickens's theme through several novels, and it was to be central to *Our Mutual Friend,* his last completed novel, three years later.* However, in no other Dickens novel does it infuse the entire atmosphere and surround the fortunes of the characters so extensively. As Thackeray had demonstrated in his *Book of Snobs* (1848), snobbery cannot be handled without humor and wit, although these qualities were not to predominate in Dickens's treatment. Instead, humor and wit become transmuted into irony, cousin-german to the comic spirit which Jane Austen and George Meredith used as a

---

* Snobbery is of course connected to dandyism, and once again Dickens had learned from Carlyle (v. *Sartor Resartus,* Chapter 10 of Book III), this time that dandyism can lead only to social disaster. Whenever Dickens created a dandy—whether Pip, Eugene Wrayburn, or Steerforth—he burned out the dandiacal element through illness or death. We remember that in the original version of *Our Mutual Friend* the foppish Eugene was to die, and in the later version he is still badly crippled. For both Carlyle and Dickens the dandy is a man "whose trade, office, or existence consists in the wearing of clothes." As Carlyle says, "he lives to dress." Since for him clothes are all, he lacks being. When one looks at him, one sees only the externals, not the man, only the expectations, not the soul.

moral purge for their vain and snobbish characters. The comic spirit works also as a cathartic for Dickens's characters, leading Pip back to the loyal Joe Gargery and setting right the false values of a snobbish world.

The basic irony underlying a snobbish view of the world—the view Pip acquires with money and gentlemanly status—is that this attitude brings with it profound unhappiness, something quite different from what one expects. Rather than experiencing joy as a result of money and his new social status, Pip finds his position as a "gentleman" demands that he deceitfully hide his past. Thus, if he is to rise, he must live falsely; for as Pip acquires the manners of a gentleman, he becomes increasingly ashamed of his origin and his former friends. His new acquisitions bring fear as well as idleness, need for dissembling as well as loss of perspective.

Furthermore, Pip's love for Estella, attached as it is to the snobbery which makes him miserable, likewise is never a source of joy. His sexual passion for her seems to derive as much from her sadism (her treatment of him as a crude arriviste) as it does from her attractive person. Her treatment of him makes him wretched, and yet even in her frigidity she is irresistible. Pip's feeling for her is akin in several ways to the self-destructive love that Heathcliff and Catherine Linton feel for each other in *Wuthering Heights*. This kind of passion destroys rather than creates. It reduces Pip to a slave rather than fulfilling him. His desire for Estella— coinciding roughly with Dickens's in his own affair with Ellen Lawless Ternan—is as selfish as his desire to be a gentleman. Even love, or what passes for love, is tainted and falsified by Pip's values. Therefore, when he gains his senses, he must *not* marry Estella, even a much chastened Estella; the happy ending which Dickens added at Lytton's suggestion is completely at variance with what precedes. The irony of Pip's "great expectations" is cogent only if he forsakes Estella when sanity returns to him, associated as she is with everything that was previously wrong. Once restored to mental and physical health, he must learn anew how to love, work, and think of others. The two themes of the novel are unified: both material possessions and falsely based love prove to be self-destructive.

For Dickens, an action must confer joy if it is to be worthwhile;

and joy, from *Pickwick* on, has been attached to innocence and real love. Joy is the opposite of greed, and obviously the man who is joyful is anxious to give of himself and to bring happiness to others. This kind of feeling is of course alien to Pip, as it is to most people in an industrialized society, for snobbery brings with it egoism; and, as Meredith and his generation of novelists conclusively showed, egoism by forcing the unnatural precludes genuine joy. Pip's particular kind of snobbery makes him more afraid of Bentley Drummle's opinions than of those of his friends, and the need to hide his dismal past becomes an obsession with him.

Yet even through this mental turmoil, Pip retains enough sense (his moral conscience) to recognize Drummle as an insidious oaf and Joe Gargery as warm-hearted and true, albeit ignorant of the ways of the great world. Even within the *ambience* of his false values, Pip remains considerate, and it is this residual quality which provided Dickens with a jumping-off place for his protagonist's conversion. The conflict in Pip, then, is obvious and far-reaching: he must recognize, despite the inroads of social snobbery, that his past is not so shameful as his false attempt to be someone else. This type of conflict, which treats Pip's complete range of social values, is absent from *David Copperfield,* whose central character must survive not temptations from within but cruelty from without. In Pip, Dickens perhaps for the first time had a protagonist whose inner conflict supersedes the outer one and whose resolution of his problem must be in terms of growth to responsibility and mature judgment, similar in this way to Jane Austen's Emma, Thackeray's Pendennis, and Meredith's Richard Feverel. *Great Expectations,* in this respect, becomes a distinct forerunner of the spate of twentieth-century apprenticeship-to-life novels, in which the protagonist must resolve what *he* wants regardless of outside pressures.

The irony of the snobbery motif becomes increasingly apparent throughout *Great Expectations* when we perceive that the snobbery of both Estella and Pip derives from Magwitch, who, as the father of Estella and the benefactor of Pip, dominates the values of a society which judges him a dangerous criminal. Thus, in *his* snobbery, Magwitch uses Pip as a vicarious means of entering society as a gentleman, exactly as Miss Havisham, in her insane desire for revenge, uses Estella to strike back at all men. Both Magwitch and Miss Havisham are outside society, one a criminal, the other obsessed and mad; and yet both, because of their money, are able to control the fortunes of two innocent individuals. Money gives the insane and the criminal power; their snobbery is strictly a money-value. It is part of the irony that in a greedy world Pip is obviously eager to be a parasite on Miss Havisham but not on Magwitch: the false values implicit in great expectations evidently make madness preferable to criminality.

Here, too, as in many other Dickens novels, snobbery is connected to the theme of injustice: the adult world once again manipulates the child for its own purposes. Pip and Estella are used by forces that they themselves cannot control, and their childhood, like Dickens's own, is destroyed. Once grown, these two must begin anew, creating from the ashes of a burned-out childhood a meaningful adult life. The injustice perpetrated upon children, then, is the sharpest indictment Dickens could make against the false values that snobbery engenders, a point that Dostoyevsky—perhaps echoing Dickens—repeated in the mouth of Ivan Karamazov when he condemns a God who makes innocent children suffer.

The irony of Pip's and Estella's positions is apparent not only when we recognize their source of money, but also when we realize that neither is a gentleman or lady by birth: only money can make them socially acceptable, and the money itself is tainted. Tainted money enters into several parallel themes of the novel, becoming a complementary theme to snobbery and sadism, best exemplified in the business life of Jaggers, the lawyer for Miss Havisham and Magwitch. For Jaggers, business is indeed dirty, for after each transaction he must cleanse himself with soap and water, literally scrub the dirt from his body before he can go forth as a human being. Success in business, Jaggers realizes, means a loss of humanity, just as for Estella and Pip social success in life means a loss of their sensibility. Success of this kind, further, brings a sense of revulsion and disgust: for Jaggers' clerk, Wemmick, it means a double life—one in the business world in the office in Little Britain, the other at home in his miniature medieval castle. To retain any meaning for him, his life must be divided distinctly between business and pleasure; *his* expectations, unlike Pip's, are in the private not public world. Survival for Wemmick entails putting the dirty work behind him every night and literally retreating into a child's dream world, symbolized by the castle, complete with moat, drawbridge, and tiny cannon—the entire paraphernalia of one who regresses into childhood as a defense against incursions of reality into his private life.

The irony involved in snobbery extends further, into the preponderant number of prison images, which are no more fortuitous here than the fog in *Bleak House*. The atmosphere of hulks and convicts finds its parallel in Pip's prison-like heart, full as it is of hidden desires and secret information, as Dickens's own in regard to his childhood experiences. In one way, Pip is as much a prisoner of his past as Magwitch is of his, and Miss Havisham of hers. Restricted by his fixity of purpose to advance himself, while torn by considerations of a basically decent heart, Pip has narrowed his movement to that of an incarcerated criminal. Accordingly, nearly everything that Pip confronts in his quest for status is attached to a prison image, beginning with his initial meeting with Magwitch in the swamps near Joe Gargery's smithy shop. From there, Pip proceeds to Miss Havisham's prison-like home, like its mistress a wasted and abandoned structure. Deserted and gone sour, the brewery imprisons Miss Havisham, as much as she has imprisoned love in her heart. Dickens describes the former brewery (VIII):

> To be sure, it was a deserted place, down to the pigeonhouse in the brewery-yard, which had been blown crooked on its pole by some high wind, and would have made the pigeons think themselves at sea, if there had been any pigeons there to be rocked by it. But, there were no pigeons in the dovecot, no horses in the stable, no pigs in the sty, no malt in the storehouse, no smells of grains and beer in the copper or the vat. All the uses and scents of the brewery might have evaporated with its last reek of smoke. In a by-yard, there was a wilderness of empty casks, which had a certain sour remembrance of better days lingering about them; but it was too sour to be accepted as a sample of the beer that was gone—and in this respect I remember those recluses as being like most others.

Then he turns to Miss Havisham herself (VIII):

> I saw that the bride within the bridal dress had withered like the dress, and like the flowers, and had no brightness left but the brightness of

her sunken eyes. I saw that the dress had been put upon the rounded figure of a young woman, and that the figure upon which it now hung loose, had shrunk to skin and bone. Once, I had been taken to see some ghastly waxwork at the Fair, representing I know not what impossible personage lying in state. Once, I had been taken to one of our old marsh churches to see a skeleton in the ashes of a rich dress, that had been dug out of a vault under the church pavement. Now, waxwork and skeleton seemed to have dark eyes that moved and looked at me. I should have cried out, if I could.

When Miss Havisham commands Pip to "Play!" her order sounds like that of a prison guard, "March!" "Turn!" "Bend!" "Play" is so alien to her that it takes on symbolic importance: it loses all significance of fun for a child and becomes, ironically, part of the disdain an obsessed adult has for a helpless child—all Pip can do is play while Miss Havisham suffers. Even play, in her mouth, is trammeled and reduced, unjustly, to fit her prison-like existence within the ironically named Satis House.

The prison world extends still further: Estella herself is kept a prisoner by Miss Havisham, and her heart is bounded by the latter's desire to gain revenge on all men. In one way, Estella has her freedom removed, as much as Miss Havisham once had hers; the former too is a sacrifice to the adult world which uses her youth and beauty for its own purposes. Her future unhappiness is already foredoomed. In turn, as Miss Havisham has imprisoned Estella for revenge, she imprisons Pip in a hopeless passion—as hopeless as Miss Havisham's for the philanderer Compeyson. Love proves to be a sick and insane obsession in *Great Expectations;* the sole example of normal love is Wemmick's affair, and he lives in a medieval castle.

Midway through the novel, Pip himself remarks ". . . how strange it was that I should be encompassed by all this taint of prison and crime; that, in my childhood out on our lonely marshes on a winter evening I should have first encountered it; that, it should have reappeared on two occasions, starting out like a stain that was faded but not gone; that, it should in this new way pervade my fortune and advancement" (XXXII).

Even the office of Jaggers and Wemmick in Little Britain, overshadowed as it is by the presence of nearby Newgate, that "grim, stone building" around the corner, is itself a prison, with its two staring casts on the shelf that transfix one's eye and unmask one's hidden guilt. Everywhere Pip turns he finds like images both in the real and imaginary world, images that whelm up from within and which can be exorcised only by his conversion to decency and human feeling. As long as he is willing to remain a parasite on another's money—whether Miss Havisham's or Magwitch's—he can never clear his vision.

Pip regains moral freedom only through an illness which purifies him of his false aspirations. If his ideal is to live idly on an unearned income—to become like Bentley Drummle (or perhaps Oliver Twist)—then he must be brought back to reality through the purging quality of a brain fever which "burns out" the former assumptions. His illness takes the form of a restorative quest, which at first weakens him, turning Pip toward death's door before passing him through, as it were, to the other side, toward life. Pip is brought back to vitality by the touch of a good man, the Christly Joe Gargery, who ministers to him throughout his illness. Through Joe, Pip is put in touch with the forces which constitute the sole thing that can save him: he must return to the loving fold of those who have decency and compassion. Only Joe Gargery can warm the heart frozen by contact with Miss Havisham and Estella. When Pip returns to life, reborn, so to speak, after his deathlike illness, no longer the Pip of gentlemanly pretensions, his great expectations also no longer exist, and all those connections with his former life have died or disappeared. Magwitch and Miss Havisham are dead, and Estella is unhappily married to Bentley Drummle. Pip can now be embraced by Joe and Biddy. Moreover, Pip's good deed for Herbert Pocket provides him with the means of economic regeneration through hard work and application. His realization now that his future must be secured solely through his own efforts saves him, and, like Robinson Crusoe, he can himself build his empire.

What Pip expects in the great world is much reduced. Life now means small expectations; miracles, once part of the social fabric, are no more a significant part of his hopes. Not unusually, everyone connected with Pip's former expectations is the ironic victim of his own victimizing. Magwitch dies without knowing that his fortune goes to the government and not to Pip. Miss Havisham burns to death amidst the wasteland of her self-destructive existence. And Estella, according to the original ending, realizes the nature of suffering after a disastrous marriage to Drummle, and only now, much chastened and diminished, lives free of Miss Havisham's sadism.

The tragic workings of the novel demand that Pip lose his social and personal innocence after he understands his infatuation for Estella and what she stands for; and Dickens's realization of this point disallows the revised ending in which Pip and Estella finally come together. In as much as Pip's love has been lacking in joy and selflessness, it has been the love of an incomplete person: selfish love is a contradiction in terms for Dickens. This, however, is the only kind that Pip can feel; it is part of his innocence that he confuses passion with real love. Only with his illness—when he passes through his ordeal of pain and suffering—only then can he mature into a responsible and dutiful human being. Only then can he perceive that his past actions have been foolish, and that his former innocence has indeed been a false guide for life. Everything connected with this state of innocence (the wrong kind) must be left behind, or else the illness has purged nothing and has served no purpose. The illness is for Pip a transition into right experience, and a step toward emotional and intellectual development.

Unlike Huckleberry Finn, who must retain his innocence to survive, Pip must lose his, for it confuses love with passion, respectability with snobbery, the real gentleman with the parvenu, pride with vanity, coarseness with vulgarity. The measure of Pip's innocence is his inability to distinguish between the vulgarity (negative) of Bentley Drummle and the young Estella and the coarseness (positive) of Joe Gargery. He is, at this time, more sensitive to the mockery of Drummle and Estella than to the opinions he respects. Living with shame and fear, he becomes, ironically, a prisoner of his own great expectations. Pip himself recognizes his predicament (XXVII):

My greatest reassurance was that he [Joe] was coming to Barnard's Inn, not to Hammersmith, and consequently would not fall in Bentley Drummle's way. I had little objection to his being seen by Herbert [Pocket] or his father, for both of whom I had a respect; but I had the sharpest sensitiveness as to his being seen by Drummle, whom I held in contempt. So, throughout life, our worst weaknesses and meannesses are usually committed for the sake of the people whom we most despise.

A visible sign of Pip's growing maturity as a result of his personal adversity is his changing attitude toward Magwitch at the very time that the latter is no longer able to help him and has indeed become a burden. Pip's change of feeling toward the renegade criminal is an incisive indication of his growing sympathies and his gradual loss of self-destructive egoism. Pip admits to himself: "I only saw in him a much better man than I had been to Joe." He finds in Magwitch a man who had meant well, and particularly a person who had remained constant throughout the years.

One of the ironies of the novel is that Pip learns about the great world in which his expectations are centered through the lips of Magwitch. From him, he discovers gratitude, pride, fear, revenge, greed, love, and a whole range of feelings of which he had hitherto been ignorant. But not only does he learn about these feelings, he also sees them as they *conflict* with his ideals and preconceptions. For Pip becomes a student of life at the feet of a criminal, and Dickens completes this chapter (XXIX) with the words: "This is the end of the second stage of Pip's expectations."

David Copperfield did not have this conflict because his problems were individual ones, rarely those involving class and status. The theme of class consciousness which entered seriously into *Bleak House* and *Hard Times* as a concomitant of Dickens's development as a tragic novelist extends deep into both *Great Expectations* and *Our Mutual Friend*. By the 1860's, when the latter two novels were published, the middle-class reading public had solidified; as Dickens found the bulk of his audience here, the kind of morality novel typified by *Great Expectations* was obviously directed toward this class. His novels were, in one way, critiques of the middle class by one of themselves. Dickens cautioned humility in a period that valued great achievements; he advised, as had Carlyle, satisfaction with hard work at a time when an unearned income was a young man's ideal, almost his prerogative if he was well favored (Richard Feverel, Pendennis, George Osborne); and he asserted that the decent but low-born individual

was more worthy than the foppish gentleman, all this in an age
when the ideal of the latter still remained from the Regency. At
almost the same time as George Eliot in *Adam Bede* (1859),
Dickens carefully redefined the true gentleman or lady as *any* person who is decent, generous, selfless, and considerate, no matter
what his social status. So far has the center of the novel moved
that Lizzie Hexam (*Our Mutual Friend*), the daughter of a Thames
body-snatcher, is a lady in all but birth. Even more than Richardson in *Pamela,* Dickens passed beyond the middle class into the
lower classes to find his "pure" heroes and heroines.

These developments in the novel, reflecting as they do changes
in the larger world, allowed Dickens the social flexibility of his later
work. As with all great writers, his personal vision symbolized in
miniature the larger social forces which were still protean. For
the twentieth-century reader, the social snobbery implicit in Pip's
great expectations is not so apparent and perhaps not so vicious,
for the quality itself is no longer meaningful in *Pip's* terms. Yet to
the contemporary reader of Dickens, the context and the substance
were familiar: social gradations in Victorian England were much
more fixed than in the pre-Civil War United States, when low birth
could be off-balanced by a quick fortune, with the resultant rise
into all but blue-blooded society. In the United States, the concept
of the gentleman had meaning, but more as a personal standard
than as something embedded in a social context. In England, however, the gentleman, as we readily see in Jane Austen, Meredith,
and Thackeray, is supposed to follow certain standards and certain
procedures, or else he loses both respect and effectiveness. A person of low birth could become a gentleman only after the most
arduous conditioning and provided that, like Pendennis, he had
a certain style or manner that carried all before him. While it was
important that a gentleman be judged by what he was, nevertheless several still called themselves gentlemen merely by reason of
birth and fortune regardless of personal qualities. The novelists
themselves, who except for Thackeray and Dickens came from
middle-class or lower-middle-class backgrounds, naturally cham-
pioned the man who was a gentleman by virtue of his innate worth.
Thackeray himself clearly saw the difference between a Dobbin and
a George Osborne.

In *David Copperfield,* however, Dickens added a further dimension to the qualities of the gentleman in the person of Steerforth, an irresponsible aristocrat who is considerably more than a mere fop. A spirit of anarchy, linking him with Dolge Orlick of *Great Expectations* and the schoolmaster Bradley Headstone of *Our Mutual Friend,* bubbles beneath a seemingly placid surface. Behind the façade of everyday life in several Victorian novels lurked potentially explosive forces ready to burst out into the chaotic and destructive patterns usually associated with the twentieth-century political novel or the late nineteenth-century Russian novel. These forces are perhaps more apparent in the work of Dickens than in any of his contemporaries; for Dickens was, in his secondary characters, close to the Gothic novel of terror, to the nightmarish world in which inexplicable forces surge just below the surface, forces that can indeed disturb a complacent world if protective measures are not taken. These forces have been described and probed in their myriad variations in the novels of Dostoyevsky, Kafka, Camus, Gide, and Conrad, and would indeed seem alien to a mid-nineteenth-century Victorian audience. Yet in several novels of Dickens, such forces move around on the periphery of the main action, ever-present as threats to the stability the main characters hope to attain.

Roaming through David Copperfield's world, the gentlemanly, considerate Steerforth, with every virtue seemingly his, fights a losing battle against his self-destructive tendencies. Dissatisfied, he moves in areas that David cannot of course understand. His is the criminal mind that moves outside society, while David is clearly a potential burger once his personal needs are fulfilled. Steerforth's dissatisfaction, furthermore, is not David's. For the latter, his unhappiness is a temporary condition, and he can, if need be, even come to terms with unhappiness. The terms of his existence, Dickens must have realized, are relatively simple, and therefore the novel somehow needed the complications generated by chaotic forces that remain partially hidden beneath the surface. Steerforth serves precisely this purpose, as later Orlick and Headstone were to do: to suggest another world which moves beyond the gentleman, the worker, and the teacher, a world that is so violent and

uncontrollable that it destroys anyone who approaches it. Steerforth has his counterpart only in Rosa Dartle, whose ability to love
transcends every personal indignity; in their inapproachability,
they recall Emily Brontë's Heathcliff and Catherine Earnshaw.

Similarly, Dolge Orlick of *Great Expectations,* although at the
opposite end of the social scale from Steerforth, has the kind of
discontent that *nothing* can change. Orlick acts as a counter to
Pip, as Steerforth to David. While the two heroes seek a place
within the existing world, the two "villains" with few considerations
for their own safety would destroy the world. Not fortuitously, the
third member of the trio, Headstone, dies while carrying his enemy
to death. It is a mark of Dickens's perception that he saw the
criminal mind as the consequence not only of poor environment
but also of a basic psychological disorientation.

Orlick stands for all those fearful things that remain just outside
society's control. He is the potential revolutionary whom society
cannot understand because it is not attuned to his type. Marginal,
discontented, a trouble-maker, Orlick is the underdog who always
loses and who therefore turns to criminality, where he might at
least gain a temporary victory. Yet his criminality has a certain
justification, and therefore Dickens's ambivalence toward the type.
At one point, Orlick says to Pip: " 'You and her [Miss Havisham]
have pretty well hunted me out of this country, so far as getting a
easy living in it goes. . . .' " In Pip's terms, Orlick must be a villain, for he opposes the kind of society Pip and his friends seek.
Where can Orlick fit in such a world? Where can he fit outside it?
Dickens knew that the answer is Nowhere, and consequently he
can perceive that an Orlick must go underground.

Once underground—that is, outside society's ken—an Orlick,
Steerforth, or Headstone derives his power from his emotions, and
acts in a manner incomprehensible to reason. The author is himself
uncertain in trying to explain the character; he can do no more
than show him in operation. Yet the power and surge of Orlick are
unmistakable, with his malcontent in one way paralleling Pip's
more pallid kind. Both are cut off from what they want, but because
Pip remains rational he can save himself; while Orlick, over-
powered by emotions he cannot begin to explain, is almost destroyed. He runs off into the dark, which claims him.

Such distorted, abnormal individuals qualify one's view of these later novels as fairy tales, although elements of the marvelous are never too distant. Nevertheless, in the conventional fairy tale, Pip would be a popular romantic suitor, and Estella, at first the inaccessible heroine, would finally join the hero in a love union. Pip would be like Eugene Wrayburn (*Our Mutual Friend*), gentlemanly in the established leisurely style of the day, foppish without being effeminate, effete without being decadent or perverse. Eugene is, in actuality, Pip's ideal: a London playboy without serious commitments and with an unearned income, a good education, and a favorable position in respectable society. Yet, Dickens refused to write this kind of novel! Eugene is smashed, literally crushed, and, like Pip, when he recovers he is a new man—serious, responsible, and penitent. A physical wreck, he is now ready for the real world.

In several non-romantic ways, however, fairy-tale elements appear, often offset by countering elements which bring one back to actuality. Dickens does not create a consistent fairy-tale world, for as soon as one *seems* possible, the reality of the social world destroys the image. For example, Pip's expectations depend upon a miracle: he is suddenly the heir of a large fortune which will raise him socially. Then we (and he) learn that the money comes from a criminal who, with all good intentions, is using Pip to gain vicarious respectability. Or, in another way, Pip feels what he thinks is love for the incredibly beautiful and desirable Estella (a Star), but all against a background of sadism, revenge, and a deserted and bleak brewhouse. Ordered to play, he plays, although, as he knows only one game, he is humiliated further by his ignorance even of games. Or again, Wemmick's castle, with its moat and drawbridge, its old knight, and its atmosphere of a former, happier time, is countered by the office in Little Britain, where life must stop when business begins and where the two busts stare down all hope with eyes that debilitate.

The scenes cited above help create both the potential and actual evil that a fairy tale contains, and also convey the closed, oppressive atmosphere peculiar to the genre. The scene of Pip with Magwitch at the very beginning of the novel is indicative of the terror a small boy in a fairy story or a nightmare would feel. This

"evil" atmosphere pervades the novel they are in: the hulks, Magwitch himself, the deserted brewhouse, the office in Little Britain,
Miss Havisham, Compeyson, and Pip's own nightmarish anxieties.
The terror is ever-present: disclosure itself or the imminence of
something to be revealed permeates the novel. Pip's expectations
are rarely free of potential doom. Life takes away from him as
much as it offers, for his goals are false, and his expectations in
excess of what he can rightly demand and still remain a decent
human being. As in the fairy tale, the novel offers temptations
which cannot be refused, or which entail the kind of denial no
character is strong enough to give; and, yet, the temptations contain the destructive element.

Even the escape of Magwitch—patterned as it is on a suspense-
filled device that Dickens learned from Wilkie Collins—is a mixture of the fabulous and the real. The "other world" is indicated
by the unreality of Pip, a would-be gentleman, in the role of whisk-
ing away his benefactor, a wanted criminal. Surely this is the stuff
of a bad dream rather than the real events of life. Yet, involved
with the unreality is the urgency of life and death, and the episode
does end in death, of Compeyson and later of Magwitch. Significantly, the deaths here foreshadow the death of the old Pip and
his rebirth, after illness, into the new one.

Dickens's last two completed books, *Great Expectations* and
Our Mutual Friend—the sole long works he finished in his last ten
years—bring to fruition the social themes that began in rudimentary form almost thirty years before. The emphasis on crime,
violence, death, and disorientation left little room for extended
humor of the kind established in *Pickwick Papers* and his other
early novels. Where it does exist, the humor is nearly always social
in content, less personal, implicit in the irony of *Great Expectations*
and the piquant wryness of *Our Mutual Friend*. No matter what
its form, humor in the later novel is not of paramount significance.
The social nightmare has evidently overwhelmed the comic vision.

Great Expectations, for example, depends for much of its humor
on simple physical description: that of Mrs. Joe Gargery, the Pockets (one of Dickens's typically disorganized families, but presented,
unlike the Jellybys, with affection), Wemmick and the Aged Father
in their miniature castle, Mr. Wopsle's great aunt and her attempt

at education, Uncle Pumblechook and the Christmas party, Mr. Wopsle as a seedy Hamlet.

These descriptions, however, provide little more than vignettes; and although Dickens had not lost his ability to catch a figure or a gesture with a quick stroke, the passages appear in isolation.

My sister, Mrs. Joe, with black hair and eyes, had such a prevailing redness of skin, that I sometimes used to wonder whether it was possible she washed herself with a nutmeg-grater instead of soap. She was tall and bony, and almost always wore a coarse apron, fastened over her figure behind with two loops, and having a square impregnable bib in front, that was stuck full of pins and needles. She made it a powerful merit in herself, and a strong reproach against Joe, that she wore this apron so much. Though I really see no reason why she should have worn it at all; or why, if she did wear it at all, she should not have taken it off every day of her life (II).

"Halloa!" said Wemmick. "Here's Miss Skiffins! Let's have a wedding."

That discreet damsel was attired as usual, except that she was now engaged in substituting for her green kid gloves a pair of white. The Aged was likewise occupied in preparing a similar sacrifice for the altar of Hymen. The old gentleman, however, experienced so much difficulty in getting his gloves on, that Wemmick found it necessary to put him with his back against a pillar, and then to get behind the pillar himself and pull away at them, while I [Pip] for my part held the old gentleman round the waist, that he might present an equal and safe resistance. By dint of this ingenious scheme, his gloves were got on to perfection (LV).

Dickens's comic episodes rarely appeared so peripheral to the thrust of the story, so marginal to the real issues in the novel: a scene here, a character there, a stray passage occasionally. The Christmas celebration itself at the beginning of the novel turns into one of fear for Pip, who momentarily expects his misdeeds to be revealed. Even Pip's attempt to seek entertainment—a performance of Mr. Wopsle's Hamlet—makes him miserable, so amateurish is the production. Pip's own ghostly heritage rarely seemed so seedy and wretched.

Later, in *Our Mutual Friend,* the humor is again relegated to spots, where it takes on a distinctly heavier tone, except in those passages involving the Boffins and Wegg. In describing the Wilfers, Dickens's comic sense had turned to a social function: for beneath Mrs. Wilfer's absurdity lies a sharp sense of social status. She is the typically shabby middle-class girl who marries "beneath" her and then hopes to rise through her daughters' marriages, a Victorian version of Jane Austen's Mrs. Bennet. The theme of the novel is concerned with money—what it means to those who have it, what affect it has upon those who seek it—and in that area Dickens found little source of humor. When juxtaposed to money, even the humorous Wegg loses his curious flavor and becomes drunk with thoughts of potential power, and the soft-hearted Boffins play a game of deception rather than live naturally. So embedded in materialism are the main scenes of the book that the following kind of passage predominates, whereas in the earlier novels the scenes of pure fun had seemed as important as the serious ones.

Tradesmen's books hunger, and Tradesmen's mouths water, for the gold dust of the Golden Dustman [Boffin]. As Mrs. Boffin and Miss Wilfer drive out, or as Mr. Boffin walks out at his jogtrot pace, the fishmonger pulls off his hat with an air of reverence founded on conviction. His men cleanse their fingers on their woollen aprons before presuming to touch their foreheads to Mr. Boffin or Lady. The gaping salmon and the golden mullet lying on the slab seem to turn up their eyes sideways, as they would turn up their hands if they had any in worshipping admiration. The butcher, though a portly and a prosperous man, doesn't know what to do with himself, so anxious is he to express humility when discovered by the passing Boffins taking the air in a mutton grove (XVII).

Money surrounds every transaction; it makes bad marriages possible (the Lammles'); creates a character like Podsnap, the midcentury patriot and materialist; terrorizes poor Betty Higden, whose desire to escape the Poorhouse is her sole aim in life; makes Charley Hexam into a vicious, egocentric Pip, willing to sacrifice his own sister in exchange for respectability; turns Riah, Dickens's attempt at a "good Jew," into a slave to the predatory Fledgeby. The very turn in the novel occurs with Bella Wilfer's decision to surrender unearned money for love, just as *Great Expectations* had pivoted on a similar point, or *Bleak House* on the ability of sane people to reject the false rewards of the Jarndyce case. The fog of that novel joins the Thames of *Our Mutual Friend* and the marshes and hulks of *Great Expectations,* coming together with the destructive mine of *Hard Times* and the ever-present Marshalsea of *Little Dorrit,* to cast a consistent gloom over Dickens's later period. This was truly a dark time for Dickens, when his separation from his wife and the compulsive readings from his own works— particularly the violent scenes—brought hitherto suppressed elements of disorder and disorientation to the surface, all at the expense of his comic vision.

The dark Dickens of the novels after *David Copperfield* heralds a counterthrust to mid-Victorian optimism, a reaction becoming apparent as well in many of Dickens's contemporaries. The early comic novels, which contain some of his finest and freshest writing, caught for Dickens his great audience; and once that was reasonably secured, he proceeded to write the more weighty books upon which his serious reputation must ultimately rest. For these novels go as far beyond his early work as George Eliot's *Middlemarch* moves beyond *Adam Bede,* or Thackeray's *Vanity Fair* beyond *The Fitzboodle Papers,* or Jane Austen's *Mansfield Park* beyond *Northanger Abbey.*

The later Dickens, also, is particularly attractive to the twentieth-century reader who has been nourished in part or full on Conrad, Lawrence, Proust, Mann, Joyce, Kafka, and Dostoyevsky. For in his increasing emphasis on violence, on the dark motives of his characters, on the criminal mind, and on complex psychological phenomena, Dickens was pointing forward, away from his eighteenth-century predecessors who had influenced his early novels, toward the major twentieth-century writers, particularly a novelist like Conrad, whose atmosphere and phrasing is clearly Dickensian in *The Secret Agent* and *Chance.* Also, the later Dickens is an obvious rebuke to those who still claim he was unable to write a tragic novel, for within the terms of nineteenth-century tragedy, *Great Expectations,* at least, has the trappings, as well as the substance, of great tragedy, despite its "happy" ending; and *Bleak House, Little Dorrit,* and *Our Mutual Friend,* although uneven and flawed, contain the seeds of a tragic vision, if not the full flowering.

For the later Dickens, the open road no longer offers the same temptations as it once had, for it has become the railroad; and the Thames, once a source of poetry, is now the den of water thieves. Even the self—which he had once so exalted—seems to be buckling, splitting into fragments, losing most of its potency, barely retaining its shape and its sense of purpose. Still, within a world obviously gone wrong, Dickens argued persuasively for the good man and the loving woman trying to live a normal life. He retained through his personal adversity and deepening gloom a belief in people, and that one quality even now makes Dickens seem consistent, however his style and subject matter may have changed from the jaunty *Pickwick Papers* to the morbid *Our Mutual Friend*.

six

Thackeray's Vanity Fair:
All the World's a Stage

ad Jane Austen been a mid-century Victorian gentleman, she might have written *Vanity Fair;* contrariwise,
had Thackeray been a late eighteenth-century provincial
spinster, he would perhaps have written *Pride and Prejudice* or *Emma,* although not *Mansfield Park.* To relate Thackeray to Jane Austen is to establish continuity in English realism,
after one allows for the change from a provincial to an urban
society. As much as Jane Austen was a rural, though not a
pastoral, novelist, Thackeray was, like Dickens, a city writer. His
characters and situations live through their connection to a live
city, and his particular kind of realism—in several ways closer to
Jane Austen's than to Fielding's, Smollett's, or Hogarth's—rarely
departs from an urban background.

Furthermore, in *Vanity Fair*, Thackeray is concerned with the
reactions of "genteel" characters in a moneyed society, as Jane
Austen was interested in the gentleman in an increasingly industrialized economy. Both are social writers in a special sense: a
"social writer," in modern terms, denotes an author interested in
issues, usually the improvement of the lower classes—he is out
to change things. Thackeray and Jane Austen were social writers
in a quite different way. More dissectors than improvers, they
tried to seek out the best that could prevail in a society heading,
they thought, toward serious decline. In Jane Austen, Thackeray
found a congenial personality: an example of wit, controlled cynicism, and the gentility that could qualify the frankness of Fielding
and Smollett without losing *their* sharpness as social critics.

Both Thackeray and Jane Austen, moreover, began their serious writing careers with burlesques of a kind of fiction that was popular for its wildly romantic excesses. Jane Austen's *Northanger Abbey* was a parody of Gothic romances, and Thackeray's *Catherine* (1839-40) burlesqued the "Newgate Novels" of Bulwer-Lytton (*Eugene Aram,* 1832), William Harrison Ainsworth (*Jack Sheppard,* 1839); Dickens himself in *Oliver Twist* wrote what is partially a Newgate novel. These popular novels of the 1830's,* distortions of the eighteenth-century picaresque, presented crime as the justifiable occupation of great heroes whose aberrations are celebrated as acts of virtue. Their crimes are romanticized, while society itself is revealed as prejudicial and dull. Like another of his favorite authors, Fielding, whose *Joseph Andrews* (and *Shamela*) parodied the sentimentality and false virtue of Richardson's *Pamela,* Thackeray in *Catherine* opposed the heroic tendencies of these Newgate novels, making his murderous heroine a reductio ad absurdum of the genre which refused to see criminals as they really were. Thackeray's interest in realism, which dominated him in *Vanity Fair,* was already manifest, although almost eight years were to pass before his "Pen and Pencil Sketches of English Society" solidified into his one great novel.

Like Dickens, Thackeray found that the realism of Fielding, Defoe, Richardson, and Smollett, as well as Jane Austen, was an adequate counter to the excessive emotionalism in the popular novels of the day. In his series on the *English Humourists of the Eighteenth Century* (1853), proposed as lectures for presentation in England and America, Thackeray revealed his indebtedness.

* Their source was *The Newgate Calendar,* issued in six volumes in 1826, which was itself an enlarged version of *The Newgate Calendar; or Malefactors' Bloody Register* (1774), a series of five volumes describing notorious crimes committed from 1700 to 1774. Also, James Catnach, a printer of popular literature in the 30's, exploited the entire field of highwaymen and public executions, publishing a flysheet devoted to the confessions of criminals and their ignominious ends. This type of novel recurred later in Lytton's career with his *Lucretia, or Children of the Night* (1847), devoted to the exploits of a virtuoso poisoner; *The Haunted and the Haunters* (1859); and *A Strange Story* (1862), which appeared in Dickens's periodical, *All the Year Round.* These books evoked sensations of horror and dread and dealt with the incredible as though it were true. Their sense of mystery and marvel doubtlessly helped lead into Dickens's *Our Mutual Friend* and the unfinished *Edwin Drood.*

Strikingly enough, in his chapter on Fielding, he sees *Tom Jones* as a "picture of manners" and denies that Tom with his flawed reputation can be a hero. We are reminded that *Vanity Fair* is subtitled "A Novel Without a Hero." In his remarks on Hogarth, which, incidentally, manage to ignore the painter's licentious scenes, Thackeray indicates that what Hogarth did for the eighteenth century he would do for the nineteenth:

> . . . they [Hogarth's scenes of "Industry and Idleness"] give us the most complete and truthful picture of the manners, and even the thoughts of the past century. We look, and see pass before us the England of a hundred years ago—the peer in his drawingroom, the lady of fashion in her apartment, foreign singers surrounding her, and the chamber filled with gew-gaws in the mode of that day; the church, with its quaint florid architecture and singing congregation; the parson with his great wig, and the beadle with his cane: all these are represented before us, and we are sure of the truth in the portrait.

The realism of Thackeray purports to show, also, "the truth of the portrait," to give the feel of people and things as observed in their everyday settings. In *Vanity Fair,* as well as in *Pendennis* and *The Newcomes,* one can see what a Victorian is really like, although even his kind of realism has considerable limitations. Thackeray is strongest when he writes about the "typical" Victorian—Major Pendennis, Colonel Newcome, Joseph Sedley, Amelia Sedley, the Osbornes, even Becky Sharp as a Victorian adventuress; but he clearly is unable to limn the sharper or darker edges of character, and this limitation considerably compromises his realism. We feel, with Mario Praz, among other critics, that while Thackeray can catch the world of young men—Clive Newcome, Warrington, Pen, Philip, Henry Esmond, George Osborne—he is unable to vary the kind of young man he chooses to depict. There is a homogeneity to all of these energetic youths; selfishness, vanity, egoism, bravery and loyalty, a certain basic good-heartedness.* Only Warrington differs, but he is a soured sentimentalist simply more aware than they of human limitations.

---

* These young men are often refinements of and variations on the Dandy, a type that Thackeray early satirized in his *Yellowplush* articles (1837-39), which were themselves directed at Bulwer-Lytton's *Pelham* and other fashionable novels. The archetype of the Dandy was George Bryan

The uniformity of these "heroes" results from Thackeray's refusal or inability to handle tragedy in his major novels. In order to suppress excessive romanticism, Thackeray imposed an average or typical behavior on his characters, at the expense of the severe and the marginal, which are also a part of realism. The "average" precludes heroism and insures a safe mediocrity. With Dobbin, for example, Thackeray can remain well within what he knows and feels intimately, but again at the expense of originality and daring. Even with Becky Sharp, Thackeray avoided the full implications of her behavior, for Becky is "explained away" as being like everyone else if only she had had sufficient income or standing. Her motivations, unfortunately, are simplified to her single desire to enter society, while we glimpse in the character all kinds of other interesting possibilities.

Unlike George Eliot, who in her major novels rarely discouraged originality of mind as long as it did not blunt the senses, Thackeray suppressed the originality that goes with genius, heroism, or anti-social behavior. His positive characters at their finest *fit* into a social pattern, and their successful development hinges upon their acquisition of a social character. Thackeray saw an opportunity for happiness, qualified though it may be, as the result of self-realization and hard work. And while it is true he recognized that all ideals must be compromised, all desires only partially satisfied, and all illusions shattered, he is closer to Jane Austen than to Dickens or even George Eliot in his attempt to place and keep people within their natural milieu by offering them reasonable rewards.

Most of Thackeray's early burlesques of sham romance and pseudo-heroics show his rejection of all departures from a norm of behavior. For the same reason that he refused to write romances, he could not write tragedies: as he saw it, tragedy, like romance, was an anomaly usually calling for a hero or heroine. Furthermore, Thackery realized that in his middle-class world, literature, art, religion, even a detailed knowledge of politics, had only a nominal hold, and therefore could be omitted. Once again, the demands of

---

("Beau") Brummell (1778-1840), the Regency fop, whom Thackeray both admired and deplored for his aristocratic exclusiveness, sense of tone, and witty arrogance.

flat realism stripped from Thackeray's novels any real intellectual content. Only in *The Newcomes* is art discussed at any length, and there the standards of the Academy seem unquestionably accepted. When Thackeray did want to introduce politics, he retreated to the late seventeenth century and early eighteenth century of *Henry Esmond* or removed the world of *Vanity Fair* to the final days of Napoleon's reign. Like art and politics, so religion is of small consequence despite the momentous developments in the religious world of Thackeray's time.

All this is to repeat that Thackeray's realism is of a very special sort: it achieves sharpness through the exclusion of much that is also quite real. George Eliot *included* to gain her realism, while Thackeray excluded. There would be no reason to chastise Thackeray for eliminating religion, art, literature, and politics from his novels except that these elements would give him greater claim as a realist. Thackeray, like Jane Austen, is really concerned with relatively simple people in simple situations, and he gains his comic edge through the multiplicity of details he presents as his characters confront their problems.

There is little doubt that Thackeray knew precisely what he was doing when he planned *Vanity Fair*. His letters reveal that he saw life in terms of people rather than of ideas, but that a general view of the world was more important to him than the particularity of a character's idiosyncrasies. In his view, the humble is more representative than the grandiose, the plodder closer to reality than the would-be hero, the dull more secure than the original, the mediocre more acceptable than the bright, virtue more important than intelligence, integrity more enduring than wit, and sympathy more valuable than brilliance. No one is less a cynic than Thackeray; no one has a more sentimental view of the world. He is, as Mario Praz has remarked, interested in goodness, pathos, morality, and nobility. A Thackeray protagonist, it is true, can rise to the occasion when necessary, but he is otherwise dull and mediocre.

Thackeray carried this view to his presentation of the gentleman, whose qualities he wanted to integrate into the middle-class code. In *Vanity Fair,* Dobbin, despite his obvious awkwardness, is the true gentleman, while George Osborne is a Regency man-about-town, more a selfish and vain fool than the gentleman he supposes himself to be. Dobbin's anti-heroism derives in part from Thackeray's detestation of the snobs. We recall that his atomization of the world of snobs ("The Snobs of England") appeared the same year as *Vanity Fair*. For Thackeray, the snob was the traditional gentleman who confused vanity and egoism with real worth; the alternative to the snob is the virtuous gentleman whose birth is of little consequence and whose fortune is small. In attacking the rakish George IV, whose excesses sullied the term *Regency gentleman*, Thackeray offers Dobbin instead. In *The Four Georges*, he writes:

What is it to be a gentleman? Is it to have lofty aims, to lead a pure life, to keep your honor virgin; to have the esteem of your fellow citizens, and the love of your fireside; to bear good fortune meekly; to suffer evil with constancy; and through evil or good to maintain truth always? Show me the happy man whose life exhibits these qualities, and him we will salute as gentleman, whatever his rank may be; show me the prince who possesses them, and he may be sure of our love and loyalty.

The danger of pressing this view is the same danger Dickens had to face: the author salvages a tepid David Copperfield and submerges a far more interesting Steerforth; the dull Amelia and Dobbin, although released from their sentimental illusions, are triumphant, while the witty Becky, who fortunately never had any illusions, is somewhat tarnished. The potentially more interesting character must be besmirched and discarded because he is not a real gentleman or lady or because beneath the surface lurks a rebel. The gentleman or lady indeed remains after all disagreeable elements are purged, with consistency and order retained at the expense of variety and pungency.

Both Thackeray and Jane Austen saw the middle-class merchant threaten the social position of the well-born and the well-placed, and they saw further that there was no stopping this movement; that all one could do was to provide a norm of behavior for the new mobile classes by which to measure and then contain their vulgarity. Thus, the gentleman becomes a necessary counter to the values of the Osbornes, for example, if one grants that gentlemanly behavior is within the range of all, within the range of even a Dobbin. The gentleman will not lack those qualities that really count: sympathy, fidelity, consideration, integrity. In brief, he is a Christian knight—preferably Protestant—although he may lack grace and style. Seemingly awkward, he has true good manners, and seemingly splay-footed, he steps with care amidst his surroundings. He is not, however, a hero, for to be a middle-class gentleman is not a romantic occupation, involved as he is with fools whom he must placate, not antagonize. Since he must demonstrate virtue through example, he can never be very interesting; and therefore Jane Austen's heroes are frequently dull or limned in dim colors, and Thackeray's Dobbin is a gentleman in a novel without a hero, while Pendennis and Clive Newcome are less heroes than erring young romantics.

Amidst the tightening class lines which were to provide barriers to middle-class mobility, snobbery became common as an uneasy and insecurely grounded pride in position. The real gentleman, however, is never a snob. Darcy, we remember, is suspect precisely because his pride seems to be snobbery, while George Osborne is a fool because he is a middle-class snob. More than anyone else, Thackeray helped establish the word "snob" in its modern meaning as a "person with an exaggerated respect for wealth or social position." In "The Snobs of England," later republished as *The Book of Snobs* (1848), the snob is one who "meanly admires mean things." In short, the snob is vain, and he thrives at a vanity fair where he can flaunt his exaggerated values. The *vanitas vanitatum* of Ecclesiastes, as well as the Vanity Fair (a world's fair) of Bunyan, is a world filled with snobs who confuse fashion with virtue.

As a moralist in *Vanity Fair,* Thackeray was anxious to catch the inanity of snobbery and vanity—what Meredith later broadly defined as egoism—and to demonstrate that even the gentleman, society's only counter to vanity, is himself vain, although only relatively so. Writing to a journalist friend, Robert Ball, whose favorable review of *Vanity Fair* nevertheless remarked its "unredeemed wickedness," Thackeray stated his intentions:

If I had put in more fresh air as you call it my object would have been defeated—It is to indicate, in cheerful terms, that we are for the most part an abominably foolish and selfish people "desperately wicked" and all eager after vanities. Everybody is you see in that book, —for instance if I had made Amelia a higher order of woman there would have been no vanity in Dobbins falling in love with her, whereas the impression at present is that he is a fool for his pains that he has married a silly little thing and in fact has found out his error rather a sweet and tender one however, *quia multum amavit* I want to leave everybody dissatisfied and unhappy at the end of the story—we ought all to be with our own and all other stories. (Letter of Sept. 3, 1848, in *Letters,* ed. Ray, II, 423).

If even Dobbin is a fool who misses vanity simply because of dogged sympathy and consideration for others, then no one can escape the hand and eye of the moralist who sees all the world as a vanity fair.

Earlier, in a letter to his mother written while *Vanity Fair* was appearing, Thackeray allowed Dobbin and Amelia humility, if not sense:

Of course you are right about Vanity Fair and Amelia being selfish —it is mentioned in this very number [VII for July, Chapters 23-25]. My object is not to make a perfect character or anything like it. Don't you see how odious all the people are in the book (with exception of Dobbin)—behind whom all there lies a dark moral I hope. What I want is to make a set of people living without God in the world (only that is a cant phrase) greedy pompous mean perfectly self-satisfied for the most part and at ease about their superior value. Dobbin and poor Briggs are the only 2 people with real humility as yet. Amelia's is to come, when her scoundrel of a husband is well dead with a ball in his odious bowels; when she has had sufferings, a child, and a religion— But she has at present a quality above most people whizz: LOVE—by which she shall be saved. Save me, save me too O my God and Father, cleanse my heart and teach me my duty. (Letter of July 2, 1847).

As an extended apologue, *Vanity Fair* demonstrates Thackeray's conservatism and didacticism—to purge the bad, but to retain the good and label it "gentleman."

The original conception of *Vanity Fair* was as unsure and uncertain as Dickens's initial version of *Pickwick Papers,* both beginning as "comic histories" with clear eighteenth-century references. There is good reason to believe that Thackeray conceived of the novel as sketches in vanity connected through character portraits, not unlike the short sketches of *The Book of Snobs.* Lionel Stevenson points out that the modesty of the subtitle, "Pen and Pencil

Sketches," the use of the apparatus of the puppet-master and his show, and the frequent interference of the author disclaiming any responsibility for his characters all indicate a Thackeray unsure where his theme and characters will lead him. Furthermore, his reliance on familiar scenes and situations from his own life, his repetition of characters and even names and references from earlier books, together with his use of real people for his major portraits, all evidence the need for solid support as he unsurely explored his material for a large novel.

Vanity Fair was begun early in 1845, with almost six chapters finished by March and sent off to a number of publishers, who were unimpressed. Thackeray then put the novel aside to catch up on his work for the *Morning Chronicle* and *Punch,* to which he contributed regularly. Nevertheless, by January of the next year, Thackeray submitted and had accepted by Bradbury and Evans a manuscript entitled "The Novel Without a Hero: Pen and Pencil Sketches of English Society," for monthly publication beginning in May. Once again, the novel was put aside and the first number was announced in *Punch* as a "New Work by Michael Angelo Titmarsh / Vanity Fair / by W. M. Thackeray."

The new title summed up for Thackeray his role as teacher and moralist—the Vanity Fair is Bunyan's and Ecclesiastes' as well as Thackeray's. With title and format fixed, Thackeray added several passages to the original manuscript, supplying, as Gordon Ray points out, a moral commentary as the "Manager of the Performance." The small sketches of the original were transformed into the large finished novel, a tour de force which created a panorama of upper-middle-class English society just prior to the accession of Victoria. What Dickens had done on a smaller scale in *Pickwick* for a pre-industrial England, Thackeray would do for the period of the Regency and the early drab years of William the Fourth's reign. *Vanity Fair,* as we know it, appeared from January 1847 to July 1848, at the same time that Dickens was bringing out *Dombey and Son,* Charlotte Brontë *Jane Eyre* and Emily Brontë *Wuthering Heights,* while George Eliot had just recently finished her translation of Strauss's *Leben Jesu* and George Meredith was writing the poems for his first collection that was to be published three years later.

Vanity Fair, as with all great novels, is not only a study of character but also a view of society. Like Dickens in *Great Expectations,* Thackeray stressed that a vain and acquisitive society is not romantic, and that, obviously, its inhabitants are disagreeable in their pretensions and affectations. In several ways, *Vanity Fair* is Thackeray's *Great Expectations.* The epitaph for the Thackeray novel could well fit Dickens's study of snobbery and materialism: "Ah! *Vanitas Vanitatum!* which of us is happy in this world? Which of us has his desire? or, having it, is satisfied?—Come, children, let us shut up the box and the puppets, for our play is played out." As Thackeray's remarks above to his friend and mother indicated, vanity reduces all characters to helpless puppets whose great expectations are mocked by reality.

What, then, are the ingredients of a Vanity Fair, and how does character flourish in a world that lacks substance and morality? Primarily, a Vanity Fair precludes the ability to judge and feel correctly. Transforming right feeling into snobbery and judgment into egoism, it creates confusion between sympathy and sycophancy. Its emphasis upon snobbery stultifies the correct workings of the human heart, as Dickens also showed in *Great Expectations* when Pip rejects Joe Gargery out of shame for his low social position; and the stress upon egoism, the natural result of a crossing of vanity with social and personal pretension, makes a mockery of judgment, as Meredith was to show in the cruel antics of Sir Willoughby Patterne in *The Egoist.*

Thackery intended that each character in his novel, including Dobbin, should transform the greed of a materialistic society into personal terms and become the fool of his own passions. Thus, Becky's calculations are not extraordinary when placed against the society in which she lives, against old Sedley and old Osborne, for example. As predatory as they, she at least has wit and style. Contrariwise, Amelia cannot be excused, for her superficial gentility merely masks her unquestioned acceptance of a society whose comforts she enjoys; so too George Osborne, whose parasitism and snobbery are the Regency gentleman's equivalent of the Victorian wife's silliness; so Joseph Sedley, who carries white supremacy to India and makes a fortune where his activities

can go unquestioned. Even when outside England, he is as predatory as the rest.

In a predatory society, then, expedience is good business, and
false sentiment, as Becky has found out, a sure way to seduce sentimental fools. Like Wickham of *Pride and Prejudice*—whom Becky
resembles in many significant ways—her charming exterior
disguises an expedient nature, and a real sense of wit disarms the
worldly innocent. Becky is of course shrewder than Wickham, but
she too has to make her way cleverly in a world that rejects the
upstart who begins by being sincere and honest. In his own anti-
romantic way that parallels Jane Austen's, Thackeray indicates
that manner often masks an inability to feel and that excessive
charm can denote lack of character. And just as Elizabeth Bennet
must lose her romantic notions of Wickham, whose manner she
confuses with character, so too the reader must reject Becky Sharp
by seeing through her; and so too, in another way, Dobbin must
"see" Amelia as she is at the moment he can finally win her. When
great expectations are based on romantic illusions, the expectation
becomes a vague shadow as the illusion is exorcised. Perhaps
for this reason, Thackeray (at the beginning of Chapter 6) burlesqued the so-called "Silver Fork School" of novelists, who romanticized what he was to treat with irony and satire.*

* "We might have treated this subject in the genteel, or in the romantic, or
in the facetious manner. Suppose we had laid the scene in Grosvenor Square,
with the very same adventures—would not some people have listened? Suppose we had shown how Lord Joseph Sedley fell in love, and the Marquis
of Osborne became attached to Lady Amelia, with the full consent of the
Duke, her noble father. . . ."

The Silver Fork School of novelists (called by Hazlitt the "Dandy
School") flourished in England from about 1825 to 1850. As forerunners
of Thackeray's "Pen and Pencil Sketches," the novels of this school demonstrated a kind of verisimilitude in depicting fashionable life: gaming, danc-
ing, drinking, clubbing, partying. They emphasized social etiquette, dress,
bearing, polite discourse; and their greatest moments came during the London season, when intrigues, questions of status, and maneuvering for position occupied the energies of England's ruling classes. Most of the practi-
tioners of this type of novel are forgotten: Lady Charlotte Bury (*A
Marriage in High Life,* 1828), Mrs. Gore (*Cecil,* or *The Adventures of a
Coxcomb,* 1841), T. H. Lister (*Granby,* 1826; *Arlington,* 1832), although

A Vanity Fair, then, is filled with greed, materialism, false senti-ment, lack of right feeling, coarseness and crassness, as well as snobbery, egoism, and hypocrisy. A vain world is without sub-stance and seriousness; even war, in its terms, is frivolous, a so-cial outing as Thackeray describes it in Chapter 26. The fact that George Osborne is killed is almost marginal, a footnote to history, like one of E. M. Forster's seeming afterthoughts in which a main character is suddenly and inexplicably hit by a train.

George Osborne's desire to believe himself a chivalrous young man who has married a penniless girl for love—and to think him-self a man about town who can plan an assignation with Becky Sharp—can be wiped out in a (personally) meaningless battle that was preceded by a vapid dance. His illusions are so deep that only death can destroy them. Amelia, in her way, must also be-come aware of facts, and it is only fitting that Becky, the very spirit of anti-romanticism, should remove the veil and show Amelia what George was and Dobbin is. Dobbin himself must recognize that his obsession, Amelia, is a silly and frivolous girl, and that his affection has demeaned rather than raised him. Joseph Sed-ley's passion is to be admired and respected, and this goal he never attains, no matter how much money he spends. And Becky herself admires respectability and wants desperately to be middle-class and accepted, but this happy state is never hers. Instead, she must carry the stigma of a high-society prostitute who fluctuates between good and bad days. For Thackeray, the significance of

---

both Disraeli (*Vivian Grey*, 1826) and Bulwer-Lytton (*Pelham, or The Adventures of a Gentleman*, 1828) wrote their first important fiction under the influence of the fashionable novel.

The sources of the School are three: the eighteenth-century novel of manners (Fanny Burney, Maria Edgeworth); the picaresque romance, with the Byronic quest for Wisdom replacing simple adventure; and the German apprenticeship novel, given considerable impetus by Carlyle's translation of Goethe's *Wilhelm Meister's Apprenticeship* in 1824. Bulwer-Lytton's *Pelham* is particularly significant, for here the author substituted an intellectual dandy for the crude picaro of the earlier romance. As it follows the adven-tures of Henry Pelham, the novel becomes a curious mixture of foppery, youthful wisdom, and trenchant social criticism, the English version of Goethe's *Bildungsroman* and a form that, in various guises, was to reappear throughout the century.

a frivolous society is that it debases people and ideals, indeed makes all life meaningless; thus his answer to those who felt he had merely created a world of fools. In their very destructive ability, the qualities of snobbery and frivolity demonstrate their importance.

As we have seen, the irony implicit in the circumstances surrounding George Osborne's death is also manifest in Thackeray's attitude toward his other characters. Like Meredith, he gave to each character a leading passion or "humour" which identified him and shaped his foolishness. Amelia, probably patterned after Thackeray's mother and his wife, as well as his good friend Jane Brookfield, was to act as a contrast to Becky. A typical Victorian girl, she bases the love of her life on a misconception of character, and in order to sustain herself she must continue to believe what the facts themselves belie. Her stupid fidelity to her husband parallels Becky's stupid infidelity to hers. Each is an egoist, and each is tarnished, one by devotion, the other by its lack. In her worship of an ideal, Amelia is denigrated, for she fails to see and understand the real world. Like David Copperfield's Dora, she too is a child-wife, unable either to feel or to think like an adult. Thackeray fully intended her to be this mixture of pathos, helplessness, and foolish idealism, and those who find her merely vapid fail to see that beneath her ready compliance rests a character whose seeming virtue is a compound of petty vices. Thackeray is evidently kind to the girl, even though he cannot have failed to see her weaknesses. Perhaps because Amelia was so close to his own wife—herself mad and helpless when he was writing the book—her foolishness rather than destroying her allows her a modicum of happiness.

Dobbin, perhaps modeled after Thackeray's stepfather Major Carmichael-Smyth, must also worship an ideal. And precisely as Amelia must find out that George Osborne was not worthy of her devotion, so too Dobbin must recognize that Amelia was not worth fifteen years of anxiety. His speech to her in which he chastises his own foolishness as much as her frivolity is a show of naked feeling rare in Thackeray, rare because of its recognition that love itself is not sufficient when reciprocation is impossible, and that misplaced love is no substitute for none at all, a recognition perhaps that real love is unattainable in Vanity Fair. After attacking Amelia's lack of generosity and failure to understand his attachment, Dobbin says:

"No, you are not worthy of the love which I have devoted to you. I knew all along that the prize I had set my life on was not worth the winning; that I was a fool, with fond fancies, too, bartering away my all of truth and ardour against your little feeble remnant of love. I will bargain no more; I withdraw. I find no fault with you. You are very good-natured, and have done your best; but you couldn't—you couldn't reach up to the height of the attachment which I bore you, and which a loftier soul than yours might have been proud to share. Good-bye, Amelia! I have watched your struggle. Let it end; we are both weary of it" (Chapter 66).

As a Christian gentleman who, like Don Quixote, romanticizes reality, Dobbin must of course have an ideal which absorbs his life. And like the Don, he must realize that he has been too lofty for the ideal and that, therefore, *it* could not reach *his* height of devotion. For Dobbin's kind of idealism, reality must always fail. It is ironic that idealism itself, valuing as it does morality, love, duty, obedience, and honor, derives from a seed of egoism that upsets real judgment. If Amelia has restricted her world and constantly misjudged so that she will not *see* George Osborne, so Dobbin has blinded himself so that he will not see her. His very righteousness is the source of his foolishness. In a Vanity Fair, the Christian gentleman is as much an egoist as everyone else, and bases his happiness foolishly on rewards that must also prove tarnished. It is not fortuitous that Dobbin's humility often seems to be priggishness, and his generosity appears a form of self-righteousness. As part of the plan, he too must live dissatisfied.*

As a snob (although with honor), George Osborne does not have the ingratiating qualities of Clive Newcome or the young Pendennis, and, consequently, his egoism often takes on the aspect of vil-

* One may indeed wonder why Dobbin—so common-sensical in other ways —lives by such a vapid ideal. Should he not have seen sooner that Amelia was not worth his attention? To answer affirmatively, however, is to lose Thackeray's point: that even such a basically decent man must be allowed his foolishness, indeed his vanity, in a Vanity Fair. In all matters, old Dobbin is a plodder, or what in horse-racing terminology is called a mudder.

lainy. Young George, however, is less villain than a typical social product of Vanity Fair. He has acquired all the vices of his atmosphere, both pre-Victorian and mid-Victorian. As the spoiled brat of the new English ruling class—the merchant's son turned gentleman—he lacks both the feeling and the manner of a true gentleman. For the merchant class, the gentleman need have only exterior polish, the appearance that can be purchased in one generation. In a Vanity Fair, a price is placed on all goods, and the rank of gentleman, many successful entrepreneurs felt, could be bought for their children. So, old Osborne, the acme of vulgarity, Thackeray's equivalent of Dickens' Podsnap, firmly believes in the rightness of his cause, raising business success to a royal virtue; Thackeray comments, "Always to be right, always to trample forward, and never to doubt—are not these the great qualities with which dullness takes the lead in the world?" (Chapter 35) Because his vulgarity and dullness cannot be diluted in one generation, they are transmitted somewhat modified to young George, just as he in turn passes on his presumptions to his son. The young George at the end of the novel is a copy of his dead father, and both are the true children of old Osborne. The false gentleman is part of the mock-heroic atmosphere of the entire novel, in which all the values of the great world are fitting targets for the darts of the Comic Spirit.

Money itself, Thackeray suggests, is not the sole force for vulgarization, although it complements the egoism and selfishness that seem a necessary part of the merchant's world. Dobbin himself, we remember, is also a merchant's son, but his devotion, while partially the result of selfish desire, can also be directed outward. He has, almost innately, a gentle heart. George, however, can only receive; he is unable to give. Had he instead married Becky Sharp, the carnival of Vanity Fair would have been riotous. Unable to give, George even conceives of honor as a way of satisfying ego rather than as a form of self-effacing duty. And while he is very human in his selfish responses, he is also too materialistic to have true feeling. All his responses are off the top of his emotions. The spur of the moment is his impetus to action, and his behavior marks him as a suitable denizen of Vanity Fair.

Thackeray's anti-romanticism transformed the potentially romantic figure of George—dashing, good-looking, charming—into a somewhat petty young man, the forerunner in a way of Thomas Hardy's suave villains. Thackeray's pronounced anti-romanticism here was an obvious attack upon the very popular Christmas annuals, illustrated gift books full of maudlin sentiment and false emotionalism. These books provided almost the same kind of sham romantic reading fare that Jane Austen had felt obliged to attack in *Sense and Sensibility* nearly a half century before. Thackeray, we remember, had early burlesqued and parodied this kind of reading matter and then, as his vision deepened, came to satirize it in *Vanity Fair*. It was this very common-sensical approach to romance that made critics call him hard-hearted and cynical.

The interrelationships first between George and Dobbin, then George and Amelia, Amelia and Becky, George and Becky, and, finally, Amelia and Dobbin show how frail indeed is the hold one person has upon another. In a world of false sentiment and misdirected love, there are no happy marriages or even fruitful friendships. The lack of fulfilled unions is as much a theme of *Vanity Fair* as it is ostensibly that of *The Newcomes* seven years later. People caught up by Vanity Fair are unable to love, or do so on false premises or for sensation only. Since the novel is built on contrasts and comparisons—the basic foursome whose fortunes cross from first page to last—it is not unusual that Thackeray should derive character itself from the impact of one figure upon another. Thus, George could possibly have been another Clive Newcome or Pendennis had Dobbin not been there as a moral example. Amelia might have been another Laura (*Pendennis*) or Lady Castlewood (*Henry Esmond*) had Becky not set off her vacuity. And even Becky herself might have been another Beatrix (*Henry Esmond*) or Ethel Newcome (*The Newcomes*) were Amelia not there to emphasize her own falseness. The very nature and abundancy of the contrasts lend texture to the narrative and allow Thackeray to demonstrate here more than in any of his other novels the ambiguity of human behavior.

Evidently the ground plan of the novel, as J. Y. T. Greig suggests, was to provide contrasts: Becky, clever and witty but an outsider; Amelia, pretty and dull but inside and relatively secure. As the first girl rises, the second seems to be standing still or in decline; as the first gains her way in the great world, the second seems to lose everything—husband, fortune, even her child. And around these, another pair: George, the counterpart of Becky in his expedience, but less clever, less witty, unattractive in his selfishness; Dobbin, the counterpart of Amelia, although more honest with himself, less silly and frivolous, even somewhat solemn and stodgy. Then from this foursome several combinations of pairings were to take place—all except that of Becky and Dobbin, each of whom immediately recognizes the other as a threat to *his* way.

The novel was to gain texture from the various ironies that could be wrung from this kind of counterpointing. Further subsidiary characters would also provide contrasts and comparisons with the main characters, as well as "fill out" the great world in which all would be ineffectual puppets. Among these minor characters, Thackeray set up a contrast between the two generations: old Sedley and his family, old Osborne and his, old Sir Pitt and his. Further, Thackeray set off George Osborne and Dobbin against Rawdon Crawley, Becky against Lady Southdown (her sister-in-law), Rawdon against Pitt Crawley (his older brother), and so on. All this grouping was evidently part of Thackeray's intention to counterpoint the middle-class world with the aristocracy, to recreate a microscosm of the great world with its multifarious connections and interrelationships, its rhythms of decline and rise, its dull complacency, its blatant vulgarity, its want of substance.

Vanity Fair, then, was to be a novel of inclusion, a social novel in the sense of Balzac's vast *Comédie* and, later, Zola's extensive Rougon-Macquart series. It would include the new merchant class and the aristocracy, represented by the Crawleys and Lord Steyne; the lower classes would be suggested by the upstart Becky, a parvenu much like George Osborne; the gentlemanly ideal by Dobbin. The range would be panoramic, what Gordon Ray has called the novel of real life on the great scale. Yet how much is missing! The great world of society could not have been all there was to life, as Thackeray seemed to have recognized in his Preface to *Pendennis.* There, he complained that no one since Fielding (whom he later chided for being too frank) has "been permitted to depict to his utmost a Man," and therefore the reproduction of real speech and actions is impossible. Nevertheless, even with greater freedom, Thackeray may never have seen the edges and margins of society where so much of significance can occur, for he looked principally for his types in the great world where people are dulled by routine.

All this is to say that Thackeray in *Vanity Fair* and his other ambitious novels was unable to probe behind a sentimental view of life, and that the vision of England which one receives from Dickens's dark novels was of a kind beyond his experience and talent. This criticism is not meant to denigrate Thackeray's large achievement in *Vanity Fair,* but merely to indicate the obvious limitations of his work and to suggest why he wrote no other major novel, despite the many moving passages that exist in his longer fiction. Thackeray lacked a multiplicity of view, and he lacked a tragic sense, although he had an incisive knowledge of what was close to his own experience and a real awareness of human frailty. This awareness, however, is not equivalent to a tragic sense; a sense of inevitability is not the same as tragedy. Thackeray could not have projected Miss Havisham's deserted brewhouse into a sordid image of great expectations smashed, and people destroyed, by ego and vanity; he could not have projected the Thames into a river of death, carrying on its currents the backwash of society, as Dickens did in *Our Mutual Friend;* further, he could not have projected Victorian England as a vast prison, the Marshalsea of *Little Dorrit.*

Thackeray's sentimental and untragic view is apparent in his choice of protagonists who gain moderate success: Dobbin; Major Pendennis, George Warrington, and Pen himself (*Pendennis,* 1850); Henry Esmond (*Henry Esmond,* 1852); Colonel Newcome and Clive (*The Newcomes,* 1855), to mention only those in his major novels. Colonel Newcome, for example, was Thackeray's attempt to present a thoroughly good man whose sole flaw is his failure to understand his limitations, his inability to judge beyond his own frank intentions. A Dobbin grown older, Colonel Newcome is Thackeray's version of Don Quixote (" 'He's an odd man; they call him Don Quixote in India' "). Only this Don is not a "mad" idealist but a middle-class gentleman. Because he is good, the Colonel expects people to be good, and he trails clouds of old-fashioned virtue wherever he follows young Clive. A figure of gentility and righteousness, he attempts to set an example of correct behavior for a "loose" age, a Jesus among the merchants. Yet the Colonel does not reject mid-Victorian values, anxious as he is to make his fortune; but he does attempt to restrict money-making by a code of gentlemanly conduct. While Barnes Newcome is a real "newcome(r)," a typical nouveau riche, the Colonel is a remnant from the eighteenth century, perhaps less Don Quixote than Samuel Pickwick. In his influence on those around him and particularly on his son, he brings out their best, although he comprehends little of the society in which he moves. In standing for traditional values, he holds back the flood of vulgar newcomers and imposes genteel behavior upon the predatory and expedient. This is, for Thackeray, a form of heroism.

The kind of character represented by Colonel Newcome is found in nearly all of Thackeray's novels. He differs from Major Pendennis only in degree, being perhaps more nostalgic than realistic, although the Major himself is concerned also with nostalgia for traditions that are slowly passing. Similarly, Henry Esmond, with his strong sense of honor and chivalry, is indeed an early eighteenth-century figure, recalling a period when a man could be a hero even to his valet. The values of an Esmond are the very values that could redeem mid-Victorian commercialism from uncouthness. Likewise, Thackeray's other historical novel, *The Virginians* (1859), was less a retreat from the present than a moral lesson in behavior. The George Washington of that novel, honorable and chivalrous, is Thackeray's portrait of a gentleman, essentially the Dobbin of *Vanity Fair:* ". . . through evil or good to maintain truth always." Wordsworth's Happy Warrior, "Whose high endeavors are an inward light / That makes the path before him always bright," whose powers manifest a "constant influence, a peculiar grace," is the archetypal figure behind Thackeray's ideal.

With the younger generation, Thackeray sees Pen and Clive as Jane Austen saw Emma: capable of correct feeling and decent behavior once their immature egoism is exorcised. Strikingly, Thackeray is most successful in delineating youths beset by growing pains and awakening to the enjoyable vices the world offers, Scott Fitzgerald young men without their obsessive sadness. In showing their devotion to what is out of their reach (Pen with Miss Fatheringay, Clive with Ethel Newcome, Dobbin with the young Amelia, Warrington with Laura Bell), he demonstrates his skill in catching the youthful mind before it falls into disillusionment, the first step in its maturity. Nevertheless, if we compare one of Thackeray's youths, (say) Pen, with (say) Dickens's Pip, we can see that the former was restricted to a certain world in which disillusion was not final and defeat was only superficial. In *Vanity Fair,* George Osborne is killed by a French bullet, not brought back to act out his comedy. Thus, Thackeray eliminates the one character who could have proven troublesome, the one figure who might have forced him into the deeper view of youth contained in *Great Expectations.* Avoiding this difficulty, he suggests that all his young men, except perhaps Osborne, are capable of being Colonel Newcomes or Major Pendennises when they mature, a view of the world that is, ultimately, complacent, and even false.

This view of life is admirable if one wishes to demonstrate that justice and generosity can still prevail. Translated into the realistic novel, however, these values go only so far. They cannot transcend the ordinary, and they cannot give a sense of real disillusionment or defeat. In brief, such values, full as they are of the nostalgia of a by-gone era, are merely a sentimental way of turning back the clock, a way of repairing the dam rather than trying to build a new one. Such values can only rarely generate a tragic sense, and the realism that Thackeray strives for in *Vanity Fair* is often little more than a longing for the golden age that Samuel Pickwick celebrates.

Where, however, does Becky Sharp fit into this scheme? Is *Vanity Fair* really a comic epic in prose after Fielding, as Kathleen Tillotson has claimed, in which Becky demonstrates the charms of a triumphant villainess in a world of fools and knaves? Can we consider her as a comic freeing force, a breath of wit who disdains stupidity and vanity in others and reveals the sources of hypocrisy in society? Why not consider *Vanity Fair* as simply a comic novel, like Fielding's *Tom Jones,* Jane Austen's *Emma,* Meredith's *The Egoist,* or Dickens's *Pickwick?* Why, in short, seek greater range in what may be an essentially humorous novel?

As a force relieving boredom, Becky provides a welcome

counter to Dobbin, who, like Jane Austen's Knightley, is the conscience and standard of his society. Thus, the major contrast in artistic, not narrative, terms is between Becky and Dobbin. His dull virtue is set off against her attractive vice, and Becky is surely one of the most attractive rogues in English literature. One need only compare her with her eighteenth-century predecessors, both male and female, to see that she exceeds all, including Tom Jones, in intrinsic interest. She is—along with the Brontë heroines—perhaps the first interesting major female character in English fiction, if one agrees that Elizabeth Bennet and Emma are more charming than interesting. In her high spirits and wit, Becky seems in a line from Mary Crawford (*Mansfield Park*), and in her rascality and tenacious grip on life from Defoe's dubious heroines. Yet just as Mary Crawford had to be "destroyed" to make way for Fanny Price, so Becky has to be displaced, finally, to allow Amelia to be triumphant. Both rogues become, if not martyrs, at least pawns to respectability.

Becky's career evidently tells us a great deal about *Vanity Fair* and about Thackeray. As a kind of picaresque heroine, hers is, in one way, a success story that her creator refuses to permit to go unqualified. Becky is not allowed, as Mary Crawford also is not, to be a freeing comic force striking at stuffiness and stodginess, fulfilling the role, as Meredith defined it, of watching over "sentimentalism with a birch rod." This Thackeray does not permit. Becky, again like Mary, is to dissect a dull society and yet, in the end, be herself defeated or at least chastened by it. Thackeray makes sure that her own desires run parallel, not counter, to the society on which she acts as a gadfly. Her wit, then, is not merely a way of exposing a shallow and vain society but also a way of ingratiating herself with this very world. Of course, to us she always appears more calculating and exposed than to the others, and the narrative is, in part, a working out of how they recognize Becky for what she is.

Becky's appeal is structured on a series of paradoxes. We admire her progress in a materialistic world that is reprehensible, and feel that her knavishness is preferable to its foolishness. Yet Becky is little different from it in kind. She is merely more resourceful. As an outsider, she has learned how to survive amidst her enemies. Give her a regular income and position, Thackeray says, and Becky would embrace Vanity Fair; so that while Becky punctures vanity and casts sense upon a gaggle of puppets, she nevertheless is driven not by the freeing force of the comic spirit but by the envy of the jealous have-not. As a poor painter's daughter who had lived on the periphery of a safe world and had feared want even more than lack of position, Becky desires security. In a rare reflective passage (near the end of Chapter 41), she congratulates herself that her wits have removed her from her father's studio to the great world, that she has a gentleman for a husband and an Earl's daughter for a sister-in-law, whereas only a few years ago she was little better than a servant. Yet, amidst her newly-won success, she is economically insecure, and willingly would trade her husband and sister-in-law for a "snug sum in the Three per Cent. Consols." The vanity of human affairs she would exchange for, literally, securities. Thus, while Becky recognizes the world for what it is, she uses it to further her own position. Vanity Fair is her natural habitat.

Becky, then, is a true rogue, willing to trade her wits and virtue for what society can give her. Her very motivations are amoral: that is, she will sacrifice love and personal happiness for external sparkle. Unable to love—love means commitment, and Becky must remain free-wheeling—she comes to believe that her wit is not hypocrisy and her mockery not a form of vanity. Her gospel of common sense, at first so trenchant and refreshing, breaks down as her selfishness becomes itself a form of vanity. When Lady Jane (Pitt Crawley's wife) calls her a "heartless mother, a false wife!," the reader is also ready to concur. Becky's usefulness as a comic force passes now that she is herself a part of Vanity Fair.

That dullness like Lady Jane's and Dobbin's can pass judgment on wit and itself eventually triumph indicates Thackeray's attitude. Becky of course cannot be a heroine, but that she cannot remain even exciting means vivacity must be sacrificed to stability. Through her treatment of her child and Rawdon Crawley, and through her growing hypocrisy—whether for gain or not—Thackeray takes the edge off her sharpness, indeed reduces her style to affectation. Although Becky is most effective when mocking her opposition, Thackeray, to mark her decline, removes her opponents and isolates her. There, she proves unexciting and tiresome, even sluttish. In brief, Becky must be "destroyed" so that Dobbin's disinterested virtue can become the approved standard of behavior.

Thackeray, then, qualified considerably a potentially comic view by having Becky compromise herself. Instead, he accepted Dobbin's somewhat disillusioned, somewhat bourgeois view of society: stable, nostalgic, sentimental, virtuous—with all the qualities that keep life comfortable but lusterless. Moreover, Thackeray clouded the possibility of tragedy by keeping his characters unaware: they rarely have the self-knowledge that can turn a comic figure into a tragic one. The only character who stands for something vital is sacrificed, her early sparkle vitiated by her later tawdriness. It would seem that the only counter to Vanity Fair is safe dullness, unoriginal mediocrity, and humble acceptance of traditional values.

These qualities, it must be added, constitute the strength of *Vanity Fair* as well as its limitations. One must grant that Thackeray's realism is restricted, that his anti-heroism leads, as Mario Praz remarks, to a preference for the picture rather than to the dramatic scene. In mocking romanticism, he lauds respectability. It is obvious that Thackeray, the so-called cynic and man-about-London, could not present real wickedness or unmitigated evil, or even a sustained comic view that would purge silliness and tedium. However, within the area where he felt safe, he successfully filled a world with ordinary people and ordinary events to give a semblance of reality that rings true, true in its way as Tolstoy's people and scenes. Like the Russian writer, Thackeray levels most eccentricities to a common denominator and turns disillusionment into a form of guarded optimism.

Once it is recognized where the author is heading, the reader sees the importance of the sermon qualities of *Vanity Fair*. As mentioned above, the novel is in the form of a morality—the references to Bunyan and Ecclesiastes indicate this—and the author as puppet-master clearly is the preacher leading his flock into righteousness through the temptations of a vain world. This aspect further removes the narrative and characters from the demands of the realistic novel. The characters are not necessarily in the round but, rather, fleshed-out "humours" or "characteristics," and the narrative itself is less "true-to-life" than it is a moral exemplum. Moreover, Thackeray's frequent intrusions, attacked by several critics as a mockery of the "reality" of the novel, fit if the reader allows the frame of the didactic puppet-master. Thackeray's commentary is continuous with the matter, as his letter to Mark Lemon, the editor of *Punch,* indicates:

> What I mean applies to my own case and that of all of us—who set up as Satirical-Moralists—and having such a vast multitude of readers whom we not only amuse but teach. And indeed, a solemn prayer to God Almighty was in my thoughts that we may never forget truth and Justice and kindness as the great ends of our profession. There's something of the same strain in Vanity Fair [see, in particular, the final paragraph of Chapter 8, written for the March, 1847, issue]. A few years ago I should have sneered at the idea of setting up as a teacher at all, and perhaps at this pompous and pious way of talking about a few papers of jokes in Punch—but I have got to believe in the business, and in many other things since then. And our profession seems to me to be as serious as the Parson's own. (Letter of February 24, 1847).

The poet as priest, to which Thackeray refers, has always held an honorable place in western literature, and to castigate Thackeray for interfering in his novel is to assume that fiction is a scientific truth which came into being through spontaneous creation. Every novelist "interferes" as soon as he writes a word. Thackeray's intrusions are few enough, and yet they enabled him to keep in direct touch with his reader, like a conscientious priest with his congregation.

If *Vanity Fair* is sermon, it is also history; it shows, as Gordon Ray has remarked, "how fiction can be used for the comprehensive portrayal of society. . . ." Thackeray was particularly concerned with the unwritten details of history, although in *Henry Esmond* and *The Virginians* he attempted to come to terms with recorded history in, respectively, late seventeenth-century England and eighteenth-century America. In *Vanity Fair,* however, he wrote a social history in which he tried to convey what a middle-class pre-Victorian was actually like. As an historian, Thackeray was interested in continuity, and it is not unusual that his novels contain several binding devices: common images and symbols, recurring characters and situations, even a sameness of style. The quality of his characters as real people Thackeray revealed in a letter to the Duke of Devonshire in which, as historian, he chronicles the later lives of several of his main characters, particularly Becky's affairs, after the novel will have ended. Thackeray furthermore based several of his characters on real people, as Gordon Ray shows in *The Buried Life*. Thus, for him, the line between fiction and history, while real, was indeed thin. He would perhaps have agreed with Joseph Conrad's words that fiction is "history, human history, or it is nothing," and with Henry James's claim that the novelist stands with the historian. The novelist is, as Conrad said, "the preserver, the keeper, the expounder of human experience," words which Thackeray might have rejected even while he accepted the mantle.

As historian, Thackeray, within the limitations suggested above, tried to re-create a pre-Victorian world that would not outrage either the demands of realism or the morality of his middle-class reading public. However, as fictionist, he was unable to see far beyond his own sentimental nostalgia for a purer, perhaps golden, age. *Vanity Fair* reflects this very conflict between historian and author of fiction. As historian, he should have been more inclusive, more objective; as novelist, more personal, closer to his characters and their fates than historical realism demands. The device of the puppet-master was an attempt to reconcile the conflict, to be both the bystander cataloguing human foibles and also the manipulator of the actors in the drama. One role, however, interfered with, not augmented, the other; for Thackeray would have to forgo impersonality as bystander to show preference, as he does for Dobbin, turning social criticism into personal preference. Love and loyalty do indeed hold back the tide of false feeling, but the by-product may be mediocrity. If unattractive virtue *must* prevail over charming vice, no matter what the circumstances, then the claims of the sermon unfortunately pre-empt those of both historian and novelist.

A great deal has been made of Thackeray's sentimentality, particularly by critics who find that it vitiates the advancement of his narrative and the development of his characters. However, much of this criticism has been in the form of carping at a solid tradition in which sexual feeling, unable to be presented directly, was sublimated into sentiment. Thackeray, in fact, avoided much of the worst sentimentality of his day, and we remember that several of his early works published under pseudonyms were satires on the popular reading of the 1830's and 1840's, especially, as has been mentioned, the Christmas annuals which were full of sham sentiment. In *Vanity Fair,* he attempted to avoid excessive sentiment by evading big scenes that would have necessitated wild and tempestuous passion. In the one real chance he had for such a scene (Chapter 53)—when Rawdon Crawley returns from detainment for non-payment of debts and sees Becky and Lord Steyne together—he by-passed any prolonged violence with fewer than a thousand words of comment. Yet the scene does not suffer. Its last words convey all of Becky's defeat and Rawdon's naive displeasure: " 'You might have spared me a hundred pounds, Becky, out of all this; I have always shared with you.' " " 'I am innocent,' said Becky. And he left her without another word." Thackeray's sentimentality rarely upset the neatness of a scene or diluted the essential elements of a situation. When it is directly apparent, it enters not as a way of resolving a scene but as comment, particularly when the emotions of women and children are involved (see Chapter 38, for instance). The sentimentality that is attached to the author's nostalgia is of course another matter, and that, as we saw above, takes the edge from his comedy.

In Thackeray's world, reasonableness is a virtue, while anger is an immature vice. Worldly skepticism replaces violence, while the law of probability supplants the law of accident. As the English critic Geoffrey Tillotson puts it well: Thackeray believed we demonstrate our maturity in "the way we face the remainder of our own lives, not counting on accidents to transform us, but expecting, given our spheres and characters, to continue to exemplify our selves through a course of acts and experiences which in some sort are expected." From Thackeray to George Eliot, we can see, is not a great distance.

Thackeray's achievement in *Vanity Fair* was well recognized by his contemporaries; the novel made him famous and opened up the great world for him. Forster, Dickens' friend and later biographer, and George Henry Lewes, a critic and later George Eliot's common-law husband, praised the work, although both felt that Thackeray had overloaded the novel with "excessive depravity" (Forster) and complained that the "world is not so corrupt as Thackeray would have us believe." In the twentieth century, the critic has to guard against the opposite reaction: that the world is far more corrupt than Thackeray was either willing or able to grant. His "excessive depravity" is small stuff indeed for those accustomed to Dostoyevsky, Kafka, Céline, Faulkner, Gide, and Mann.

Thackeray nevertheless helped develop the English novel; he consolidated it as both a weapon of social criticism and an art form, and in it indicated the temper of his day. By transforming the relatively easy laughter found in the eighteenth-century novel into qualified disillusion, he wrote his own kind of epic for the pre-Darwin years. Those who have compared him with Fielding and found him wanting are themselves too nostalgic to judge Thackeray's achievement. For he, in the long run, realized that a serious author must depict his own age and its philosophy, no matter if he disguises his concern by a removal in time.

SEVEN

George Meredith: An English Ordeal

he work of George Meredith cuts across nearly every aspect of the Victorian novel. However, unlike Thackeray with *Vanity Fair,* or Jane Austen with *Pride and Prejudice,* or George Eliot with *Middlemarch,* or Dickens with *David Copperfield,* he failed to write a novel that attracted a popular audience. Furthermore, Meredith failed even to create characters who caught the popular imagination. He has none of the memorable figures like Dickens's lower-class servants or middle-class hypocrites, no one like Elizabeth Bennet or Becky Sharp or Maggie Tulliver. Chiefly a critic of society, Meredith has suffered the fate of all "social" writers, in that his "philosophy" has reduced the scope of his characters and circumscribed the force of his narratives. Moreover, Meredith avoided the big scene. More concerned with general patterns and overall effects, he shunned the intense dramatic scene of confrontation. When issues had to be resolved, Meredith removed himself and related them at second or third hand. Consequently, the reader of a major Meredith novel rarely experiences the violence of a dramatic scene or the excitement of an open emotional clash. An even greater indictment: except for *The Egoist,* a Meredith novel appears loose, perhaps lacking what Virginia Woolf called "all the usual staircases by which we have learned to climb."

The reasons for Meredith's continuing unpopularity, nevertheless, must go further, for several authors have at one time or another been unpopular only to rise again into fashion. Meredith, however, continues out of favor. Writing in the late 1920's, both E. M. Forster and Virginia Woolf dealt death strokes to his reputation for their generation; her final comment: "This brilliant and uneasy figure has his place with the great eccentrics rather than with the great masters." Forster, while admitting Meredith's ability to contrive a plot, wrote: "His philosophy has not worn well. His heavy attacks on sentimentality—they bore the present generation, which pursues the same quarry but with neater instruments, and is apt to suspect anyone carrying a blunderbuss of being a sentimentalist himself. . . . What is really tragic and enduring in the scenery of England was hidden from him, and so is what is really tragic in life. When he gets serious and noble-minded there is a strident overtone, a bullying that becomes distressing." (*Aspects of the Novel*)

Except for *The Ordeal of Richard Feverel* and *Diana of the Crossways,* perhaps also *The Egoist*—and these read chiefly in the schools—his work is relatively unknown, much as Henry James's work and reputation lay long fallow despite several devotees. Meredith's failure to write one large popular book and to create sympathetic characters is only one among many reasons for his present obscurity. The others, however, are readily apparent when one examines his most popular novel, *Richard Feverel.* Unlike Dickens, Meredith was not a comic-and-tragic writer, but an author who imposed comedy on tragic situations, with no clear demarcation of either. Often misunderstood, he is called obscure and confused. Unlike Thackeray, Meredith was not a satirist, and his wit, compounded as it is of learning and parody, is often dismissed as absurd metaphor. Unlike George Eliot, whose style is both dense and readable, Meredith created one that is dense but difficult, operating simultaneously on a realistic and metaphorical level. Unlike Jane Austen, who had an uncomplicated witty line, Meredith rarely settled for simplicity, and his line is both epigrammatic and diffuse.

In addition, Meredith was, except for George Eliot, perhaps the most intellectualized of major nineteenth-century novelists. Familiar with classical literature as well as with contemporary European fiction and non-fiction, Meredith worked into his novels literary traditions quite outside the grasp of the audience for Jane Austen, Dickens, or Thackeray. Particularly in his use of references and in his metaphysical flights, Meredith displayed the kind of learning bound to discourage all but the most sympathetic readers. Often, his meanings work out on the metaphorical level while remaining unresolved realistically, and this ambiguity—imposed usually for the sake of wit—again discouraged readers. Even George Eliot did not directly impose her great knowledge on the novel but transformed it, except in *Romola,* into fictional terms.

Overall, perhaps because of an individuality that is still confused with eccentricity, Meredith's work has rarely received its due. While *The Ordeal of Richard Feverel* contains several of the flaws common to Meredith's fiction, it nevertheless remains one of the finest apprenticeship novels in the language, a stronger book than either *David Copperfield* or *Pendennis,* although lacking their powerful characterization. Certain remarks Meredith made when discussing the real and the ideal in a letter to the Reverend Jessopp (September 20, 1864) indicate the general trend of his fiction from his first novel, *The Shaving of Shagpat* (1855), through *Richard Feverel* (1859) and his later fiction. Meredith writes:

Between realism and idealism there is no natural conflict. This completes that. Realism is the basis of good composition: it implies study, observation, artistic power, and (on those who can do more) humility. Little writers should be realistic. They would then at least do solid work. They afflict the world because they will attempt what it is given to none but noble workmen to achieve. A great genius must necessarily employ ideal means, for a vast conception cannot be placed bodily before the eye, and remains to be suggested. Idealism is as an atmosphere whose effects of grandeur are wrought out through a series of illusions, that are illusions to the sense within us only when divorced from the groundwork of the real. Need there be exclusion, the one of the other? The artist is incomplete who does this. (*Letters,* I, 157)

He then points out that the writers he most admires, Shakespeare, Goethe, Molière, Cervantes, are all realists, but they understand idealism. "They give us Earth; but it is earth with an atmosphere." Meredith then suggests that he prefers a naturalist ("a plain wall of fact") to a romanticist ("constantly shuffling the clouds and dealing with airy, delicate sentimentalities"). Meredith's work, then, will be a composite of the real and the ideal, of the facts of the naturalist with the fancy of the romantic writer. To a tragicomic vision of the world, he will add a romantic view in which the quixotic hero is naive, innocent, and ripe for an ordeal.

The ordeal of the Feverel family is women; and women are related to egoism, which, in turn, is connected to comedy. The Comic Spirit, as Meredith indicated in *An Essay on Comedy and the Uses of the Comic Spirit* (1877) and in the overture to *The Egoist* (1879), principally seeks out egoism and vanity. Among other things, it drives toward a norm of behavior and action, by which Meredith meant that all departures from sense are fair target for the comic imps, which, like the classical Furies, follow their game waiting for an error in judgment or taste. At the heart of the Comic Spirit is ridicule of a closed society, ridicule directed at every character who cannot reconcile contrasting attitudes. Meredith wrote:

. . . whenever they [men] wax out of proportion, overblown, affected, pretentious, bombastical, hypocritical, pedantic, fantastically delicate; whenever it [the Spirit] sees them self-deceived or hoodwinked, given to run riot in idolatries, drifting into vanities, congregating in absurdities, planning shortsightedly, plotting dementedly; whenever they are at variance with their professions, and violate the unwritten but perceptible laws binding them in consideration one to another; whenever they offend sound reason, fair justice, are false in humility or mined with conceit, individually, or in the bulk; the Spirit overhead will look humanely malign, and cast an oblique light on them, followed by volleys of silvery laughter. That is the Comic Spirit.

In the displacement of "sound reason" and "fair justice" by ego, one finds precisely where high comedy borders on real tragedy in *Richard Feverel* as well as in much of Meredith's other fiction and in *Modern Love,* his long sonnet sequence. Each of Meredith's comic characters responds instinctively with the wrong kind of brain, the mental extension, merely, of what the heart feels. When Meredith insisted on the need for brain, he meant not the simple application of mind to matter, but a separate faculty that generates the type of intelligence implicit in the Comic Spirit. A system or attitude based on wrong reason is self-destructive, demolishing, in turn, Richard Feverel, Sir Willoughby Patterne (*The Egoist*), Nevil Beauchamp (*Beauchamp's Career*), Alvan (*The Tragic Comedians*), Victor Radnor (*One of Our Con-*

querors). It is wrong reason that causes all the incomplete marriages in *Richard Feverel,* and wrong reason, finally, that renders
ineffectual Richard's relationship with every woman who loves
him.

The Comic Spirit, then, becomes a civilizing force, allowing
imagination (both Sir Austin Feverel and Sir Willoughby Patterne
detest and fear poetry) to cut through sham and forcing honesty
without destroying love or romance. Furthermore, the Comic
Spirit attacks the primitive who would destroy all in his struggle to
survive. Both Sir Austin and Sir Willoughby, again, are primitives
—that is, they tyrannize over women and, like Victorian cave
men, conquer to preserve their own sense of security. Comedy,
clearly, forces equality, driving out both platitudes and self-
righteousness, those two qualities which are an integral part of
every would-be dictator. Sir Willoughby utters platitudes because
he fully accepts them and cannot see that not all people also
share them. Further, Sir Austin's Pilgrim's Scrip consists of inverted
platitudes which through false reason reverse the sentimental
ideas of his day, in its own way a kind of conscious mawkishness.
Both men stifle the emotions and use reason incorrectly: to smother
what should be active and contiguous with feeling.

Certain lines that Meredith wrote in an early poem, "The
Woods of Westermain," bear repeating, for they convey in somewhat different form his notion of the Comic Spirit.

> . . . .
> Pleasures that through blood run sane,
> Quickening spirit from the brain.
> Each of each in sequent birth,
> Blood and brain and spirit, three
> (Say the deepest gnomes of Earth),
> Join for true felicity.
> Are they parted, then expect
> Some one sailing will be wrecked:
> Separate hunting are they sped,
> Scan the morsel coveted.
> Earth that Triad is: she hides
> Joy from him who that divides;
> Showers it when the three are one

Glassing her in union.
Earth your haven, Earth your helm,
You command a double realm: . . . .

Meredith's trinity of "blood, brain, and spirit, three"—a naturalist's foreshadowing of the Freudian id, super-ego, and ego—was only viable when blood and brain could function without censoring each other.* When brain (Sir Austin's system) attempts to circumvent blood (Richard's natural feeling, his desire for poetry and nature), then there can be no spiritual synthesis. Spirit is not, of course, an automatic mixture of blood and brain, but is, rather, the result of the individual's power of synthesis, his ability, as the existentialists put it, to create his own essence. The person of spirit—as Vernon Whitford in *The Egoist*—is one who can sustain the darts of the Comic Imps. Spirit can be achieved, however, only through a Wordsworthian communion with Earth, while brain is used not to destroy but to create. We note that Vernon, like Leslie Stephen, who was the model for Meredith's character, is a great walker amid Nature.

The unfortunate person who cannot synthesize brain and blood will desire an egocentric world focusing on his self-righteous ideas of justice, a person, consequently, who is impervious to honest criticism. Moreover, he is usually representative of a certain vulgar element of society, for the ridicule of bourgeois social ideas is at the core of the Comic Spirit. Being closed to criticism and unable to see beyond the propriety of his own narrow views, this character is both tragic and comic, as is a bourgeois society which remains closed to common sense.

Sir Austin's system stifles the workings of the Comic Spirit, for its basis is ego and its apparatus one of restriction. Sir Austin is himself a study in Egoism, with its division between inner and outer selves; its alienation of common sense and right reason from social

* While Meredith's contrast between brain and blood may seem to duplicate Plato's distinction (in the *Phaedrus*) between reason and emotion, or between reason and the appetites, actually it is closer to the symbolic forces of *yin* and *yang*. In that well-known diagram, the lights and darks are intermingled in such a way so as to show their dependence upon each other, recalling in Meredith's case the interdependence of blood and brain which creates the whole person (represented by spirit).

behavior; its separation of body and mind, which precludes the synthesis that provides balance; its denial of Earth; its identification, as Jack Lindsay remarks in his book on Meredith, with bourgeois lies or illusions which are manifest in the Egoist's sentimental and platitudinous reactions. Meredith remarks in the meeting between Lucy and Richard:

> Better than sentiment Laughter opens the breast of Love; opens the whole breast to his full quiver, instead of a corner here and there for a solitary arrow. Hail the occasion Propitious, O ye British young! and laugh, and treat Love as an honest God, and dabble not with the spiritual rouge. These two laughed, and the souls of each cried out to other, "It is I," "It is I."

An egoistic society is a closed one which stifles new ideas and fresh feelings and permits little or no mobility. Because it lacks self-criticism, it emphasizes conventions and conserves traditions. Richard himself, as he develops, is also closed, but with a different atmosphere he might have acquired more resilience and flexibility, the lack of which qualities doom him in Meredith's novelistic lexicon.

Even while devoted to a system that makes feeling subservient to brain, Sir Austin can still admire Richard's energy, his impudence, his spirit; but these qualities, he thinks, are merely boyish and not counter to his own shaping ideas. These qualities, however, are the only ones remaining in a closed system, which cannot recognize individuality (of feeling) and true selflessness. A closed society is, of necessity, tradition-ridden, and it is on just this shoal that Richard's sense of judgment is wrecked.

When an open character—mobile, sensitive, responsive—tries to impose himself upon a closed system, the result can be tragic. But when a closed character—an idealist or a traditionalist—tries to reorder a closed society, the result must be comic: this is, in fact, the area in which the comic spirit shows itself to best advantage. Through the conflicts implicit in the latter situation, Meredith wanted to suggest, as it were, a mode of unpretentious tragedy for the novel. Realizing that Aristotle's definition of tragedy needed amending to suit the peculiar content of the novel—the nineteenth-century novel in particular—Meredith, chiefly following examples from Aristophanes and Molière, tried to relate a tragic framework to situations that otherwise defied Aristotelian principles. Using manners, social status, class structure, and politics as the substance of his novels, he exposed the disparity between the ideal and the real as the basis for his mockery. As a result, in *Richard Feverel, Beauchamp's Career,* and several other novels, the forces of selfish action are arrayed against those of quixotic reaction, and after numerous tragicomic failures, the innocent protagonists have been lost. Meredith propounded that only right reason (the awareness of the Comic Spirit) can overcome bad emotion. By right reason he meant reason that was responsive to the best in man and flexible in its awareness of human possibilities, not the kind of restrictive reason which is man's attempt to control emotion, and which becomes as dictatorial as the unbridled senses.

Caught not only in the coils of Sir Austin's plans but also within the "ordeal" that all Feverels face, Richard is firmly in the line of idealistic "heroes" in Western literature—Don Quixote, Alceste (in Molière's *Le Misanthrope*), Candide; among Meredith's protagonists, he foreshadows Evan Harrington, Harry Richmond, and Nevil Beauchamp. It is clear that the creation of a typical nineteenth-century hero who overcomes his ordeal to gain happiness did not concern Meredith, for Richard is in the high comic rather than the heroic romantic tradition. A part of Richard's idealism is his desire to save people, when, ironically, he is the only one to need saving. But he is unaware of this circumstance, for Sir Austin's system has made him, also, an egoist. Self-deceived, he must "save" Mrs. Mount and his mother, while, significantly, he "loses" his own life. Immersed in the ideal, he loses sight of the real, and chasing an image in a mirror he becomes himself a martyr to a false reflection. This type of "high comic," as Meredith pointed out in the essay on Comedy, has no audible laughter even though the characters are steeped in the comic spirit. "They [characters in *Le Misanthrope* and *Tartuffe*] quicken the mind," he wrote, "through laughter, from coming out of the mind; and the mind accepts them because they are clear interpretations of certain chapters of the Book lying open before us all."

Egoism is most apparent in the relationship between the sexes, and it is, therefore, not fortuitous that Sir Austin's system should be based on the Great Shaddock Dogma: the grapefruit (Shaddock), a sour fruit* rather than Milton's sweet apple, corrupts Adam and Eve. To counter the evil of Eve is the chief purpose of the system; and yet the system is itself obsessed with sensuality. By a curious irony, sensuality pervades a book designed to show the evils of women, and sensuality destroys despite the dogma of the system. Obsession with sensuality obviates the power of choice, and for Meredith responsible choice is tantamount to self-survival.

The Great Shaddock Dogma, as the Pilgrim's Scrip is facetiously called by Adrian Harley the Wise Youth, is a kind of romance that eventually yields to tragedy. When Adam and Eve, the prototypes of the paradisiacal lovers, find their counterparts in Ferdinand and Miranda (Richard and Lucy, in Chapter 18), the romantic elements dissemble the tragedy which underlies the idyl. While Richard believes that his former life is dead and that his new life will be with his Miranda, he little realizes that he dooms himself and Lucy; for the system demands victims.

The egoism implicit in Richard's assumptions is the very egoism that disrupts an equitable relationship between the sexes. Once Lucy has been secured, Richard reverts to masculine superiority; and even after he recognizes the depth of his sin in betraying her with Mrs. Mountfalcon, he returns to her still unpurged of his egoism. He again resorts to masculine primitivism by taking what he considers to be an ideal course—meeting Mountfalcon in a meaningless duel—without regard either for common sense or for Lucy's feelings. Egoism breeds a barbaric inequality, as, conversely, the Comic Spirit forces equality. Women must, according to Meredith's doctrine, *share* in marriage, which is not a retreat from the world (Sir Willoughby Patterne, for example, wants to isolate Clara Middleton once they are married) but a common pursuit. Marriage was to be an expansion, not a contraction. Male egoism precludes expansion, for egoism, like Sir Austin's system, restricts, limits, de-activates. It replaces Earth with Brain, imagination with selfishness.†

* The shaddock is actually a far less agreeable fruit than the grapefruit, for in addition to being sour, its flesh is coarse and dry.

† *Nightmare Abbey* (1818) by Meredith's father-in-law, the facetious

Women are the key to the novel at every turn, and it is, ironically, Richard's glimpse of Sir Austin kissing Lady Blandish's hand that unlocks the mystery of sex in the young man's breast. Tossing in bed, he decides to put his feelings on paper, but remembers his promise to Sir Austin not to write poetry. Bound in by unnatural barriers, Richard's feelings have no outlet. Women, rather than being a natural part of his development, assume the stature of deities. He has, here, lost the power of right judgment.

When Sir Austin warns Richard that "women are not the end, but the means, of life," he of course makes nonsense of his own system, which assumes that women are the end of life and nothing more. Like Sir Austin, Sir Willoughby, later, lets vanity and desire for domination drive away, respectively, Constantia Durham, Clara Middleton, and even Laetitia Dale, whom he gains only under humiliating circumstances; exactly as before Sir Austin has lost Lady Feverel because of his arrogance and indifference, which he disguised to himself as propriety and wisdom. In both instances, women—and how one treats them—become the object of obsessed minds in which inequality, denial of nature, and a failure to laugh destroy balance. The result is a pattern of comedy, with tragedy always in its wake.

The comic role extends beyond Sir Austin to Richard, for Meredith treats his protagonist ironically, as though he were a hero in a conventional romance. Richard meets Lucy in a setting reminiscent of Shakespeare's *The Tempest* under circumstances that recall *Romeo and Juliet,* complete with warring families, secret meetings, and the potential of tragedy. Meredith stresses the idealism of his protagonist by connecting him with Don Quixote and a long line of chivalrous heroes. He even has him try to convert a fallen woman, and later become seriously wounded in a duel. The romantic embellishments exist, however, merely as a comment on

---

Thomas Love Peacock, is concerned with the age-old battle of the sexes in several ways similar to Meredith's treatment in *The Ordeal* and *The Egoist.* Although Peacock is arbitrary and whimsical, his basic insights into egoism are reproduced in Sir Austin, Richard, Sir Willoughby, and Nevil Beauchamp. We remember that in *The Egoist* Mr. Middleton is loosely based on Peacock and Clara on his daughter, indications of the older man's continuing influence upon Meredith.

the system. Sir Austin had wanted to trap and destroy feeling, but instead the system has made the boy into a hopeless romantic. He conceives of himself as both the Red Crosse Knight and St. George, and the dragons he attacks endanger all the insulted and injured whom he hopes to save. Meanwhile, he deserts his wife, while she in turn is pursued by a playboy who sees more worth in her than Richard does. The Comic Spirit stops here and feasts.

We recognize that the system has also been the source of much good in Richard. It has, after all, given him an idealism which would be admirable were it qualified by good sense. It has, also, despite itself, given him a warm heart and a generous disposition. It has, however, confused his mind as to the nature of the good and clouded his heart as to the arrangement of his emotions. The system has made Richard into a romantic in a world in which only the realist survives. As we have seen, Richard conceives of himself as a knight-errant ("His fancy performed miraculous feats.") and as a savior of souls ("By Heaven! if these women [like Mrs. Mountfalcon] are bad, I like them better than a set of hypocritical creatures who are all show, and deceive you in the end [his own mother never enters his mind]."). Finally, he sees himself as a hero striding across society to remake it in his own image ("Wide fly the leisurely-remonstrating hosts: institutions are scattered, they know not wherefore, heads are broken that have not the balm of a reason why."). He plays his foolish role even after Clare's death, a death that foreshadows Lucy's:

"I have killed one [Clare]. She sees me as I am. I cannot go with you [Clare's mother] to my wife, because I am not worthy to touch her hand, and were I to go, I should do *this* to silence my self-contempt. Go you to her, and when she asks of me, say I have a death upon my head that——No! say that I am abroad, seeking for that which shall cleanse me. If I find it I shall come to claim her. If not, God help us all!"

Like the Romantic hero he apes—Richard wants to be Byronic in an age that honors the Great Exhibition and Prince Albert—he wanders through forests in wild storms to purge his guilt (Chapter 46). Like Byron's Manfred, he must obsessively seek himself, and the scene in which contact with Nature purges him of his baser elements has all the trappings of a romantic communion, including the weak symbolism of baptism by rain water. Nevertheless, through communion with Earth, Richard, like the gamekeepers and grooms of D. H. Lawrence, finds harmony and joy, although he still gains little reason. The tiny leveret he carries in his breast makes him aware of gratitude and "the small rough tongue going over and over the palm of his hand" sparks life within him. The lightning flashing down from the sky illumines him with the joy of life. "When he looked out from his trance on the breathing world, the small birds hopped and chirped; warm fresh sunlight was over all the hills. He was on the edge of the forest, entering a plain clothed with ripe corn under a spacious morning sky." The earlier woodland love scene between Richard and Lucy is completed by the forest scene which brings harmony to a less innocent Ferdinand who has deserted his Miranda.

Nevertheless, feelings of joy and the resultant resurrection of spirit have merely vivified Richard: he is still the hero of his own imagination. Lacking judgment, he loses the balance of blood and brain that are necessary to attain stability and to avoid the darts of the Comic Spirit. After his watery resurrection in the forest, he goes to see his languishing bride, only to play the romantic hero who must expiate himself through humility, the role that he feels is required before he can beg forgiveness. And then, still imprisoned by his false ideals, Richard rushes off to fight an unnecessary duel which his faltering judgment tells him is a matter of personal honor.

Like Dickens in *Great Expectations,* Meredith revealed the sham implicit in the romantic novel and made a plea for common-sensical characters, at about the same time that Flaubert was showing what happens to his "romantic heroine," Emma Bovary. Meredith was, in effect, turning the apprenticeship novel upside down. Taking his hero from Stendhal, he then imposed upon Stendhal's satire a semi-tragic viewpoint full of English didacticism. Richard *must* fail, for, not unlike Conrad's Jim, he conceives a role for himself that even a deity might fail to sustain in an age that challenged the wisdom of both gods and kings. Suffering as he does from an excess of imagination, Richard resembles that greatly admired hero of the author, Don Quixote. Meredith calls Richard a hero, and perhaps he sees him as Flaubert saw

Emma Bovary—as of romantic temper and realistic adventures. Richard is clearly in the line of those romantic heroes whose awareness of reality never catches up with the roles they have idealized for themselves.

The several other characters in the novel are presented as various aspects of Richard, as commentators on him in his conflict with Sir Austin's system. Opposed to the romanticism of Richard is the cynicism of Adrian Harley the Wise Youth, whose life is arranged around the reality principle. Against Richard's tempestuous and high spirits is the jaded Sir Austin, now defeated, worn out, in retreat from life, a maker of systems. Significantly, Meredith uses the name Austin for both the defeated Baronet and the undefeated, democratic Wentworth, whose bad marriage has given *him* greater understanding. Even Ripton Thompson provides a counterpoint to Richard. He is allowed to grow up normally, and his feelings, unlike Richard's, are not excessively romantic; he is loyal, true, a good-hearted boy who controls his emotions within suitable bounds.

The women themselves provide a solid comment upon Richard. Clare Doria, his constant admirer, is herself a victim of her mother's system. Led into a senseless marriage, she acquiesces because that is the role of a Victorian woman. Her feelings are dammed up, and rather than embracing the world, she renounces it. Her end is not unlike Richard's; he too has rejected what he should have accepted. Mrs. Doria, while mocking Sir Austin's elaborate plans, falls into a similar trap and tries to reduce her child to an obedient puppet. Obviously fit for each other under normal circumstances, both Richard and Clare succumb to the machinations of their elders, the former broken and defeated, the latter evidently a suicide. Lucy Feverel, in turn, is a variation of Clare. If the Feverel ordeal occurs in its males' relationships with women, then equally so the Feverels are themselves the ordeals of their women. Lucy is a victim of the Feverel pride, precisely as are Clare and Sir Austin's wife. Even Lady Blandish, woman of the world that she is, could have provided the warm and sympathetic influence that Sir Austin's system lacked, and yet she, tragically for all concerned, has no influence on the boy.

Working as an inverted double of Richard is Adrian Harley, a devilish wit whose good sense and awareness of human frailty pro-

vide comic background for Richard's romantic excesses. Opposed
to Richard's dream is Adrian's reality. He thinks and acts as if he
had been perfectly molded by Sir Austin's system, and the irony is
that Adrian more than Richard is Sir Austin's spiritual offspring.
Adrian is cautious yet convivial, fond of good company yet not
dependent upon it, able to see women as they are yet still capable of recognizing worth. Nevertheless, Adrian attains stability
through rejection, and Meredith believed it was better to put on
"the veil of acceptance instead of abnegation." Specifically, Adrian
rejects feeling and disbelieves in human worth. His skepticism provides his point of vantage, but it is also his failing. As much as
Richard is Blood, Adrian is Brain, although in a world in which
Blood alone is folly, Brain is bound to triumph. Adrian is not hurt,
not upset, even though his stability, Meredith suggests, is won at
the expense of his not having lived. Adrian accepts women as flesh
(he carries on a secret affair with one of the maids), not as soul
or spirit. He denies their equality, mocks their needs, and derives
one-sided pleasure from their charms, which he knows he can resist. Adrian is truly wise if one desires to substitute moderation for
adventure. The Wise Youth, then, like Richard, is incomplete, a
half man who cannot hope to attain wholeness. Meredith's mod-
ernity has rarely been more apparent.

In a letter written twenty-seven years after the publication of
Richard Feverel (November 15, 1886), Meredith disclaimed the
cynicism of Adrian and the egoism that cripples his attitude.
"None of my writings can be said to show a want of faith in
humanity, or of sympathy with the weaker, or that I do not read
the right meaning of strength. And it is not only women of the
flesh, but also women in the soul whom I esteem, believe in, and
would aid to development. There has been a confounding of the
tone of irony (or satire in despair) with cynicism." Once again,
Meredith is repeating his injunction: "Set your mind on Earth
and Life, the two perpetually intershuffling." Adrian has, of
course, renounced Earth in order to simplify Life; and while his
fortunes seem stable, his disorder is as great as Richard's. Meredith's next Wise Youth is Vernon Whitford in *The Egoist,* whose
balance is a true synthesis of Blood and Brain. He combines the
good qualities of Adrian and Richard, and, accordingly, he holds

the field as Sir Willoughby, the incomplete man, retreats in humiliation.

Richard Feverel is a very personal book in that it manifests a mode of writing and thinking that was to dominate in the rest of Meredith's novels. It is true that his first novel, *The Shaving of Shagpat* (1855), established the comic method as a "playful" conflict between the ideal and the real. Nevertheless, its plot is too far removed from the recognizable world to assume a central importance, brilliant though the attempt is in several of his aspects, as George Eliot was one of the first to recognize. *Richard Feverel,* moreover, is personal in another way. While not only fixing Meredith's major concerns, it derives certain of its admonitions from Meredith's own life around this time. His marriage to the daughter of the novelist Thomas Love Peacock ended not unlike Sir Austin's, and he was left with a young son to educate and bring up, again a situation similar to that in the novel. The warnings in the novel, then, are for Meredith quite real.

Meredith was to explore further his personal attitude toward women in his long sonnet (stanzas of 16 lines) sequence, *Modern Love,* published three years after *Richard Feverel.* While *Richard Feverel* was concerned with the upbringing of the child, *Modern Love* treated the unhappy marriage which produced the child and maimed the parents. And just as Meredith in the novel accuses Sir Austin of too much Brain, here he accuses women of too much Blood. He claims that "Their sense is with their senses all mixed in, / . . . More brain, O Lord, more brain! or we shall mar / Utterly this fair garden we might win."

The novel and the poem suggest that egoism, vanity, bad judgment, and wrong feeling destroy great expectations for both parents and children, the same theme as in *Vanity Fair* and *Great Expectations* and several of George Eliot's novels. The last sonnet (number 50) of *Modern Love* minimizes pure romance and unrestricted sentimentality and propounds the reality principle:

> Thus piteously Love closed what he begat:
> The union of this ever-diverse pair!
> These two were rapid falcons in a snare,
> Condemned to do the flitting of the bat.

Lovers beneath the singing sky of May,
They wandered once; clear as the dew on flowers:
But they fed not on the advancing hours:
Their hearts held cravings for the buried day.
Then each applied to each that fatal knife,
Deep questioning which probes to endless dole.
Ah, what a dusty answer gets the soul
When hot for certainties in this our life!—
In tragic hints here see what evermore
Moves dark as yonder midnight ocean's force,
Thundering like ramping hosts of warrior horse,
To throw that faint thin line upon the shore!

Unlike Matthew Arnold's lovers who are on a darkling plain "Swept with confused alarms of struggle and flight, / Where ignorant armies clash by night," Meredith's couple is swept by confusion without even the solace of each other, so uncertain is their feeling, so tension-ridden their relationship.

Modern Love goes back, as it were, into an earlier phase of *Richard Feverel* to show another aspect of tragic misunderstanding. Still later, Meredith was to place misunderstanding itself on a more solid social basis, moving from a personal world to the great world. In *Beauchamp's Career* (1875) and *One of Our Conquerors* (1891), for example, the mise en scène includes the political and social world, although the personal qualities demonstrated in *Richard Feverel* remain constant. In all of these novels, however, including *Rhoda Fleming* (1865), *The Adventures of Harry Richmond* (1871), *The Egoist* (1879), *The Tragic Comedians* (1888), and *Diana of the Crossways* (1885), Meredith reiterates his belief that all expectations, great or little, are due to be smashed because of egoism, presumption, and vanity. A romantic view of the world, in each case, is destructive in situations that demand common sense and personal effacement. Romance is suitable if qualified by Brain, and Brain is appropriate when tempered by sentiment. Meredith's novels work on conflicting opposites: when the qualities remain opposite, the character comes to grief; when they are contiguous, the character achieves happiness.

Although fully aware of Carlyle's astringent views, Meredith nevertheless believed in the happiness principle. He was that much of an English utilitarian. He was neither a stoic nor an ascetic—his letters reveal his delight in good food (French cooking) and fine living. Meredith spoke of the "healthy exercise of the senses," by which he meant the individual indulging his appetites with responsible awareness of the consequences. The result would not be a tragic or romantic person but a balanced one.

Notwithstanding, the pull from Carlyle was strong, especially in Meredith's first novel. With its "universal philosophy" based on illusion and reality, on the clothed and the unclothed, with its images of hair that covers the unrevealed and that must be shaved, *The Shaving of Shagpat* is clearly in the line of Carlyle's *Sartor Resartus* (1833-4). Even the latter's heavy Germanisms appealed to Meredith, whose German boyhood was ever with him in his tastes and literary attitudes (among other things, he translated German lyrics for *The Monthly Observer*). This fondness for German culture extended, particularly, to the work of Jean-Paul Richter, a German writer of highly rhetorical prose, a continental counterpart in this respect of both Carlyle and Thomas Love Peacock, with their oblique styles and emotional, nervous prose.

Meredith also knew the work of a school of writers already mentioned as being of influence on the Brontës, the so-called Spasmodic Poets, particularly that of Horne and Bailey, the latter's long epic, *Festus,* being a pretentious and wordy imitation or "extension" of Goethe's *Faust.* Meredith was especially friendly with Richard Henry Horne, to whom he sent some early poems for judgment. Horne's best-known work, *Orion,* is of some interest here, for its theory provides a foreshadowing of certain elements in Meredith. In *Orion,* itself a kind of Hegelian allegory, Horne stressed that love is the happy combination of the mind with the senses (Meredith's Brain and Blood), and that love must be active, even passionate, to take on substance.

As Meredith developed, the influence of Richter, Peacock, and the Spasmodics became dimmer, even though his prose retained some of their rhetorical excesses as late as *One of Our Conquerors* (1891). Carlyle's presence, however, was ever felt, although Meredith interpreted the Scotsman in his own way and refused to become a disciple. Unlike Dickens, who was attracted solely to

Carlyle's moral earnestness, Meredith tried to see the whole man. Writing to his close friend Captain Maxse (in 1865), Meredith remarked:

In reading Carlyle, bear in mind that he is a humourist. The insolence offensive to you is part of his humour. He means what he says. See the difference between him and Emerson, who is on the contrary a philosopher. The humourist, notwithstanding, has much truth to back him. Swim on his pages, take his poetry and fine grisly laughter, his manliness, together with some splendid teaching. It is a good set-off to the doctrines of what is called the 'Empirical School.' I don't agree with Carlyle a bit, but I do enjoy him. (*Letters,* I, 174)

In a later letter to Maxse (in 1869), Meredith explained his former admiration of Tennyson before he recognized that Tennyson lacked philosophy, which is "the palace of thought." He commented further:

Mill [John Stuart] is essentially a critic: it is his heart, not his mind, which sends him feeling ahead. But he really does not touch the soul and springs of the Universe as Carlyle does. Only, when the latter attempts practical dealings he is irritable as a woman, impetuous as a tyrant. He seeks the short road to his ends; and the short road is, we know, a bloody one. He is not wise; Mill is; but Carlyle has most light when he burns calmly. (*Letters,* I, 198-9)

Carlyle, then, meant "fine grisly laughter" as well as instruction. The laughter suggested to Meredith the application of the Comic Spirit combined with an inherent moral doctrine, although, as in Carlyle's early work—particularly *Sartor Resartus*—the presentation was broadly comic. While guarding against too close an identification, one can nevertheless claim that Meredith turned Carlyle's *general attitudes* into fiction. Of course, Meredith's hedonism was as strong as his sense of duty, and his liberal political sympathies never drove him to the same extremes as Carlyle's growing reactionaryism. Both, nevertheless, were concerned with the State of England, even though as a writer of fiction Meredith was less directly involved than Carlyle.

If Meredith found the prophet of Craigenputtock a powerful social and political guide, particularly in novels like *Beauchamp's Career* and *One of Our Conquerors,* he saw in Dickens's work the kind of character creation and humor that were to influence nearly all of his novels from *Richard Feverel* on. In that novel, the most apparent Dickensian creatures are Mrs. Berry and her erring husband, the strong-limbed Berry. The influence, however, stretched further than character portrayal, important as that may have been to Meredith. It extended into a type of sub-humor that runs through Meredith's novels just below the larger comic patterns. Such sub-humor fills in the interstices of the structure, as it were, at the same time that it becomes the verbal equivalent of the fluttery Comic Imps. In *Richard Feverel,* it enters into the description of characters and situations, for example the scene in which Ripton is finally to meet the "Fair Persian," Lucy: "Hero [Richard] and Beauty [Lucy] stood together to receive him. From the bottom of the stairs he had his vivaciously agreeable smile ready for them, and by the time he entered the room his cheeks were painfully stiff, and his eyes strained beyond their exact meaning. Lucy, with one hand anchored to her lover, welcomed him kindly. He relieved her shyness by looking so extremely silly" (p. 312). In *The Egoist,* the identification of Sir Willoughby with his leg and the repetition of the image until it burgeons into a significant symbol is particularly Dickensian.

In the earlier novel, Sir Austin's system itself, surely a reflection of early Victorian educational attitudes (Meredith probably knew Herbert Spencer's essay on education published in the *British Quarterly Review,* April, 1858) seems not unlike Gradgrind's in its essentials; and Lucy in her freshness and warmth and natural gentility is close to Sissy Jupe, of *Hard Times.* The entire theme demonstrating the dangers implicit in stifling the natural instincts is a further indication of Dickens's and Carlyle's presence. Also, Richard's insistence that love is stronger than ambition, perfection, religion, and self-indulgence is in the line of the lesson that Dickens's heroes have learned and foreshadows what Pip has to recognize in *Great Expectation.*

When we return to Meredith's presentation of the Berrys, there is again no denying the prevailing power of Dickens's work. Berry's misuse of words he hardly understands recalls the hilarious errors of Dickens's servants, most obviously Sam Weller, whose talk is far above his class. As a wandering husband, Berry is too comic to take seriously, and as a faulty male he extends the "ordeal" even into the lower classes. Mrs. Berry, who at first mourns her Ulysses and then finds that she neither needs nor wants him, is a warm-hearted creature whose common sense, like Joe Gargery's, cuts through the cant of selfish people. Furthermore, she remains a bastion of sympathy for the children, who are outcasts from their homes, providing love where the parent prescribes duty. In an unjust world, her kind, as Dickens also showed, protects children against foolish parents who would destroy them while molding them to fit pre-conceived images. She supplies the warmth and flexibility from below that Sir Austin is unable to supply from above, and shows the meaninglessness of class distinctions when human beings are at stake.

In an essay written in 1928 to celebrate the centenary of Meredith's birth Virginia Woolf remarked that in *Richard Feverel* Meredith was attempting to destroy the conventional form of the novel, although he succeeded in holding it together "not certainly by the depths and originality of its character drawing but by the vigour of its intellectual power and by its lyrical intensity." By shunning realism—the main ingredient of most major nineteenth-century novels—Meredith was trying to achieve a new form. His ironic use of Wise Youth, Hero, Heroine, Romance, and epical trappings, and his supplementation of the narrative with a journal or diary of quips and comments, are attempts at originality of statement and structure. Endeavoring to escape sentimentality, Meredith avoided, as we have remarked, the big scene. Particularly, at the end, Lady Blandish's letter of narration to Austin Wentworth relating Lucy's death and Richard's despair escapes a potentially melodramatic scene that could have proved embarrassing to the author. This method, however, works two ways: like Conrad, Meredith recognized that the large scene should be sacrificed to the psychological details leading up to it; but at the same time the dramatic scene is also the *natural* outcome of these details, and to avoid it is to plead laziness or incompetence. Earlier in the novel, the potentially dramatic scene between Sir Austin and Lucy, when they meet aware of conflicting motives and past errors, is minimized; and this confrontation scene becomes vapid, losing the energy that should grow out of characters who feel strongly.

One may well argue that the final third of the book, which relates Richard's London adventures with Mrs. Mountfalcon while
Lucy waits anxiously on the Isle of Wight, shows a falling off, a
weakening of the forward thrust of the novel. This decline is perhaps inevitable, for the tightness of the previous narrative is lost
in the episodic nature of the final scenes where the motivation is
weak and tenuous. Character seems to have been sacrificed to
necessities of plot. Moreover, the idea of Richard's conversion of
Mrs. Mountfalcon is suspect, even if one recognizes that Magdalen
bowed before Jesus. And Mountfalcon's attempted seduction of
Lucy while she reads history to him, a throwback to the thousand
and one nights of Scheherazade, is not quite convincing except as a
working out of plot.

The final parts are too concerned with the debilitating effects of
the system and the unraveling of plot structure to retain thickness
and texture. Virginia Woolf perhaps had this very failing in mind
when she said that Meredith's work often lacked the necessary little
touches, that one was always in the presence of "spasmodic hammer-strokes." The latter part of *Richard Feverel* is indeed full of
such hammer-strokes. Everyone is blasted apart by forceful blows.
Anxiety replaces wit, and nerves are substituted for a demonstra-
tion of the Comic Spirit. The change in tone considerably weakens
the tragic possibilities of the novel. Lost is the irony implicit in
Sir Austin's intransigence even when he is faced by obvious failure.

Richard Feverel is a considerable book, nevertheless, once we
recognize that like several of his contemporaries Meredith wrote
novels that fall short of artistic perfection. Only in *The Egoist,* like
Dickens in *Great Expectations,* was Meredith able to achieve a
more nearly perfect novel, and this only by restricting the scope
of the narrative and the mise en scène and by allowing incidents
to spring out of character. The first parts of *Richard Feverel* seem
tight because event derives from character, and the interaction of
the two remains plastic and rhythmic, while the latter parts seem
tenuous because this kind of development thins out amidst fussy
details. Still, *Richard Feverel* retains its power as a lyrical evocation of youth, fond hopes, great expectations. It introduces a new
mode of comedy that displaces old-fashioned romance and sentimentality, at the same time circumventing typical tragedy. Per-

haps as Shakespeare in *Romeo and Juliet* avoided ponderous tragedy though lyrical grace, so Meredith, using similar materials, escaped the heaviness of sentimental tragedy through poetic evocation. The love of Richard and Lucy, like that of Romeo and Juliet, and as well Ferdinand's and Miranda's, transcends the conflicts of their parents or guardians and indicates feelings that remain true even at death. When Richard finally recognizes the worth of Lucy, there is a real marriage of Heaven and Earth.

Sir Willoughby Patterne, that incandescent Victorian gentleman, wants his marriage to take place entirely in Heaven, and when he gains Laetitia Dale at the end of *his* ordeal, he has consummated an arrangement that moves him far closer to Hell. He has won the "woman of intellect," and, consequently, he shall have no more peace of mind.

The first four pages of *The Egoist* (1879)—called the Book of Egoism (like the Pilgrim's Scrip in *Richard Feverel*)—are a manual for the comedy of manners and character that follows, a synopsis of several of Meredith's remarks in *An Essay on Comedy and the Uses of the Comic Spirit* that had appeared two years earlier, and an indication of his fictional method from *Richard Feverel* through his final novels. As we saw above, Meredith transformed the "tragic flaw" of classical tragedy into the "comic flaw" of the social novel and made the flaw one of egoism.* The novel begins: "Comedy is a game played to throw reflections upon social life, and it deals with human nature in the drawing-room of civilized men and women, where we have no dust of the struggling outer world, no mire, no violent crashes, to make the correctness of the representation convincing." For a comic writer to materialize, a cultivated society is necessary. For comedy—the nineteenth-century substitute for tragedy—is obviously a critique of society, of manners, morals, and class. If an audience is to distinguish the comic from the merely humorous, it must have taste. To laugh at

---

* The opening, like that of "The Rape of the Lock," is full of the machinery of the mock-heroic: comic imps (Pope's "light militia"), pretentious passions, affected language, grim warnings. The mock-heroic conveys Meredith's high moral purpose at the same time it comically disguises the serious intent underlying all of his work.

everything is to have no appreciation or understanding of anything. To love comedy, one must know something of the world, more of the world, Meredith suggests, than one needs to appreciate tragedy.

Comedy, furthermore, "is the ultimate civilizer, the polisher, a sweet cook. If . . . she watches over sentimentalism with a birch rod, she is not opposed to romance. You may love, and warmly love, so long as you are honest. Do not offend reason" (p. 3). And one further warning: "The Egoist surely inspires pity. He who would desire to clothe himself at everybody's expense, and is of that desire condemned to strip himself stark naked, he, if pathos ever had a form, might be taken for the actual person." Besides inspiring pity and clothing himself in pathos and sentimentality, Sir Willoughby denies social justice, specifically equality of the sexes. By denying equality, he becomes the butt, instead of the ally, of comedy. His contempt is merely a disguise for egoism and intimations of superiority, which themselves weakly dissemble Folly. The comic is only evoked, Meredith assures us, when "we draw its penetrating attentiveness to some circumstances with which we have been mixing our private interests, or our speculative obfuscation."

Like Jane Austen's irony, Meredith's Comic Spirit is social in nature and works along with common sense. To perceive the form of the Comic Spirit, one must be aware of social norms, and this perception, Meredith suggests, makes one the citizen of a selecter world, for the test of true comedy is to awaken thoughtful laughter. Since comedy is social in nature, one with a strong comic sense cannot take an anti-social position: "Comedy . . . is an interpretation of the general mind." Comedy does not concern itself with peripheral characters or marginal events but with those close to the center of a country's civilization.

In common with all comic writers, Meredith realized that real laughter is of the mind. The laughter of Molière's plays is not audible, although the characters are steeped in the comic spirit. Other kinds of laughter—the kinds not derived from the comic spirit—are, in this view, harsh and dull. The Germans, from whom Meredith had gained much of his literary education, were lacking, he realized, in the one thing that would enable them to grow, a criticism of them that, curiously, Nietzsche was making at about this time. And, similarly, Meredith exhorted the English people to extend their capacity "for delicate choosing in the direction of the matter arousing laughter." He suggested an upper class of those who are aware of comedy. They are, he repeats, the true elite.

The Comic Spirit became for Meredith, as for Jane Austen, a moral force that avoided, and even punctured, sentimentality. Through comedy, Meredith could work well within a social world of real men and events and avoid the retreat into fantasy that the typical romance required. He could also avoid melodrama by falling back upon a comic view of all excesses. In its attack upon excess, comedy provided, in addition, another way of suggesting the synthesis of Blood and Brain into Spirit, another way of mocking immoderation and castigating folly. As we have seen, the Comic Imps that follow the trail of Sir Austin indicate at every turn the nonsense of his egotistical system. Meredith offers as an epitaph for all the Sir Austins and Sir Willoughbys: "Through very love of self himself he slew."

In several ways, *The Egoist* is a better novel than *Richard Feverel* because of its unity and its basically single situation that grows directly from character. It is, furthermore, perhaps Meredith's only novel in which character itself remains substantial, and abstract qualities are fully transformed into concrete phenomena. Since the single situation unfolds amidst repetitions which are merely variations of the central point, the reader achieves new insights into Sir Willoughby as he progressively declines. At the same time, paradoxically, that Sir Willoughby's egoism repulses the reader, the latter becomes sympathetic in his posturing. One soon realizes that Sir Willoughby acts as his society expects him to act, and he is no better or worse than hundreds like him who are the romantic heroes of popular Victorian fiction.

Sir Willoughby's typicality enabled Meredith to attack directly the society that produces and heroizes this kind of character. The single flaw in the novel would seem, then, to be Meredith's relentless persecution of a person more or less vindicated from his author's charge by his inability to be different from his society's norm. To expect better behavior from a Sir Willoughby is to expect a different creature, and yet Meredith inexorably punishes him for a folly he cannot help. For this very reason, Sir Willoughby does not attain tragic stature. As he does not have sufficient independence of judgment, self-recognition can never be his. He indicates, if anything, the tragedy of his society. So constituted, Sir Willoughby gives Meredith a caustic weapon of attack, one such as Carlyle discovered in *Sartor Resartus*. Willoughby uncovered provides a view of naked motives, which are too often clothed in the garments of illusion. The egoism of the age, and Sir Willoughby's in particular, destroys feeling for nature, imagination, and poetry, as well as compassion for other people. While seemingly raising sense to an ideal, it really obstructs sense, and while ostensibly inveighing against folly, it provokes nonsense.

Sir Willoughby's weakness, like Sir Austin's, is manifest in his attitude toward women. His egoism destroys any equitable relationship between the sexes; and marriage, we remember, is to mean expansion for women, not surrender to superior force or contraction of activity. By deifying women, Sir Willoughby denies their human qualities and enervates their active spirit. Thus, because he suffocates first Constantia Durham and then Clara Middleton in an atmosphere of male domination, he frightens them away despite the advantages of the match. His plea to Clara that once married they should isolate themselves is merely another aspect of his desire to create a perfect miniature world in which outside influences can be countered or nullified. In this world, Sir Willoughby would be prime mover and chief organizer, in effect, a god. He wants to possess a wife, not to share marriage. In his world woman is a goddess without rights, an object to be cherished and worshiped as long as she acquiesces in her role, which ultimately denies her very power to love.

Clara Middleton's dilemma is particularly acute because Sir Willoughby *is* accomplished, *does* seem perfect, *is* everything that his society can demand of a man. He is rich, comes from an old and reputable family, is titled, handsome and well-built, athletic, healthy, urbane, generous, a future member of parliament—a man who offers every material advantage to the girl who can catch him. How can Clara explain that such a man repulses her because he is an egoist? What can egoism signify when it is attached to such advantages? Caught between her own feelings and those of her father, attached as he is to Sir Willoughby's wine cellar, she finds her conflict to be one between emotion and duty in a man's world which denies the former and lauds the latter.

"——What could she say? He is an Egoist? The epithet has no meaning in such a scene. *Invent!* shrieked the hundred-voiced instinct of dislike within her, and alone with her father, alone with Willoughby, she could have invented some equivalent, to do her heart justice for the injury it sustained in her being unable to name the true and immense objection; but the pair in presence paralyzed her (Chapter XLI).

Further, while trying to extricate herself, Clara must not hurt Sir Willoughby. She must avoid vulgarity, for he is, of course, particularly sensitive to mention of his desertion by Constantia Durham for Harry Oxford. When Clara suggests that he release her, and he refuses, she mentions running off, but Sir Willoughby's horror touches her sense of shame. Tempted to upset him by admitting that she, a pure maiden, knows that wives run from husbands, and engaged girls from fiances, she resists the urge both because her own sense of propriety will not permit it and because "she could not bear to lower the idea of her sex even in his esteem."

Clara's dilemma is still further complicated by her desire to present herself as the worthwhile object that Sir Willoughby expects her to be, while at the same time removing herself from a situation that is growing increasingly repulsive to her. Clara, then, is isolated by her insight into Sir Willoughby; and she nearly founders on this shoal until she realizes that both Vernon Whitford and Laetitia Dale share her perception into his character. All of them recognize that to desire perfection in an imperfect world is to deny reality and ultimately to destroy those values which can legitimately be gained. Perfection, as Sir Willoughby desires it, is related to egoism and vanity, founded as the latter are on a self that conceives only of a solipsistic world. Such a quest for perfection also precludes tolerance and generosity of spirit. Moreover, it asks for a return to Eden in which woman is the eternal sinner.

In Clara's conflict between duty and emotion—one critic has referred to the situation as Racinian, but Clara has few tragic overtones—Meredith dramatizes the classic situation in which individual feeling finally upsets the order that society wishes to perpetuate.

Dorothea Brooke, in *Middlemarch,* finds herself in similar circumstances when she recognizes she has misidentified a mummified scholar as a genius. However, each woman matures when she realizes that neither Sir Willoughby nor Casaubon is ideal *and* that there is no need for either to be such. Their development as human beings is complete, both Meredith and George Eliot indicate, when they lower their ideals and adjust duty to feeling. We remember that, after some reservations, Meredith called George Eliot "the greatest of woman novelists," and that *Middlemarch* had appeared only a few years earlier, in 1871-72.

Clara Middleton herself is in a direct line of development from Jane Austen's Elizabeth Bennet, particularly in her devotion to common sense and right feeling. As the daughter of a man who lacks judgment, Clara, like Elizabeth, retains the sole right of choice. And precisely as Elizabeth rejects Darcy while she thinks him unduly proud and overbearing (Jane Austen's equivalent for egoism), so Clara refuses Sir Willoughby for similar reasons. Each heroine retains her right to choose, and part of this right entails choosing wrongly as well as rightly. However, free selection also gives her the ability to grow even after she has made mistakes. Both Meredith and Jane Austen realized that the woman's right to choose her own mate is one of her few freedoms in a society that otherwise limited her to a placid role. Meredith's feminism is founded on this very point: that the woman, like the man, selects her mate, and that the "primitive mating call" belongs to the egoist who must be rejected out of hand.

From Sandra Belloni and Rhoda Fleming through Clara Middleton, Diana Warwick, Aminta, and Carinthia Kirby, Meredith stressed that a woman gains her identity through the kind of marriage she makes. Similarly, the men who lose the struggle for balance and sense or who are unable to struggle at all—Richard Feverel, Alvan, Willoughby, Lord Fleetwood, Victor Radnor— suffer disintegration of personality, as Keats's Lamia wilts under the stern eyes of the philosopher Apollonius. They disintegrate because when woman is ranked as inferior, man himself is incomplete and must suffer. By restricting another's freedom of movement and power of choice, he restricts himself.

Meredith's sense of freedom, we see, is particularly relevant in several twentieth-century novelists; Conrad, Lawrence, James, and numerous French existentialists writers immediately come to mind. We know that Lawrence and Hardy were early affected by several aspects of Meredith, and James himself, who at times found severe faults in Meredith's style, was influenced both by Meredith's vision of life and his prose. Isabel Archer's dilemma in *A Portrait of a Lady* comes as much from Meredith as it does from George Eliot, and *The Bostonians* carries on several of the feminist conflicts that Meredith originally suggested.

In *The Egoist,* Meredith made a ritual of courtship and marriage. Recognizing that the nineteenth-century girl was simply a girl and not a woman until she had passed through the "ordeal" of courtship and marriage, Meredith like Jane Austen saw that her decisions during this period were a critical test of what she is and what she will be. All her feelings and common sense must be brought to bear upon this single activity, and upon her decision here rest her chances for happiness. She can prove herself, or fail. Moreover, the "ordeal," like that of the medieval knight, is a trial that must be undergone without help from parent or friend. Thus, Dr. Middleton not only prefers Sir Willoughby as a son-in-law but gives Clara little room indeed in which to maneuver. In *Pride and Prejudice,* similarly, Elizabeth has no help from her parents, one of whom is silly and the other cynical. In *Emma,* Mr. Woodhouse is almost as foolish as Mrs. Bennet, as a parent equally unhelpful. In *Middlemarch,* Dorothea Brooke chooses Casaubon against the wishes of most, and then marries Will Ladislaw in the teeth of even greater opposition.

Clara Middleton "proves" herself more by her rejection of Sir Willoughby than by her acceptance of Vernon Whitford. She gains stature as she comes to terms with her dilemma: how to reject certain unhappiness without injuring Sir Willoughby and outraging her father. As she treads the thin line between propriety and vulgarity—she must herself be careful not to become an egoist —she expands. And as she recognizes that there is nothing essentially wrong in rejecting Sir Willoughby despite their engagement, she passes from a girl to a woman. She has gained the power of choice and has responsibly exercised her will, qualities which in Meredith's lexicon are tantamount to maturity. Her decision is to embrace the world, for marriage with Sir Willoughby would mean a series of renunciations. The life he envisages for them would isolate her like a nun and strip her of her human rights. Instead, she embraces Earth, where her salvation lies. Unlike Renée (*Beauchamp's Career*) and Sir Austin Feverel's wife, she does not let marriage destroy her spirit or negate her will.

Comedy, of course, saves everybody except Sir Willoughby. Clara escapes to life with Vernon, and Laetitia Dale does not forgo her freedom in marrying Sir Willoughby. As her master's slave, Laetitia retains her liberty, even though Sir Willoughby attempts to lead her to sacrificial slaughter. Although he has been weakened by adversity, his ego—an intrinsic element of his character and not simply a changeable part of his personality—nevertheless remains. His dilemma is apparent. Made jealous by Colonel de Craye, evidently held at bay by his fiancée, and pursued by the three Furies, Mrs. Mountstuart, Lady Busche, and Lady Culmer, he must ease out of an impossible situation without seeming to hurt himself. The difference between the egoist and the non-egoist is here comically plain: part of Clara's dilemma is to avoid hurting Sir Willoughby, while his is to avoid seeming hurt.

Sir Willoughby's great midnight interview with Laetitia, which Crossjay Patterne sleepily overhears, brings together all the comic threads of the novel. This scene follows a chapter (39) entitled "In the Heart of the Egoist," in which Sir Willoughby has evolved a plan that will assure him of Laetitia in case Clara Middleton, like Constantia Durham, should flee. To prevent this disaster, he will release her, but first he must officially secure Laetitia, of whose hand he is sure. The Comic Imps are now at their most playful, for Sir Willoughby enters the interview confident of Laetitia's fondness and full of his own generosity in bringing together Clara and Vernon, despite the latter's unfortunate marriage (reminiscent, incidentally, of Rochester's in *Jane Eyre* and Stephen Blackpool's in *Hard Times*). His ego is bared: " 'I am free. Thank heaven! I am free to choose my mate—the woman I have always loved! Freely and unreservedly, as I ask you to give your hand, I offer mine. You are the mistress of Patterne Hall, my wife!' " When she is silent, he repeats, " '. . . I am yours. . . . *Have always loved, I said.*' " He finishes with a lavish flourish, and she rebuffs him.

Lack of reciprocal affection has contracted her heart. She knows that love is an empty dream and marriage a hollow form. Like Louisa Gradgrind, she can no longer feel. Sir Willoughby's system has dried out of her heart, and her contact with Earth has been broken. Then, without comic intention, Sir Willoughby, the cause of her affliction, implores her: " 'I will cure you, my Laetitia [ironically, her name means "happiness"]. Look to me, I am the tonic. It is not common confidence, but conviction. I, my love, I!' "

Later in the scene, as Sir Willoughby's melodramatic utterances reveal him as a victim driven to frenzy by the painful and sadistic darts of the Comic Imps, he charges her with the responsibility of his well-being: " 'Consider this, that it is on your head if my ideal of women is wrecked. It rests with you to restore it. I love you. I discover that you are the only woman I have always loved.' " Sir Willoughby's platitudinous language reveals the depths to which this speech debases him, as Laetitia repeats that she has no ambition and no warmth: " 'My utmost prayer is to float on the stream—a purely physical desire of life. I have no strength to swim. Such a woman is not the wife for you, Sir Willoughby. Good night.' "

If Clara has proven to be "roguish," then Laetitia Dale, the muddy-complexioned but loyal slave, becomes the flaw in Sir Willoughby's neat design of self-protection. She, in effect, becomes transformed from his victim into his chief tormentor. The sacrificial priest who once would have willingly put to the knife Laetitia's great heart now has the edge of her intelligence turned against him, and Sir Willoughby gains a more sober woman than he had bargained for. Like several other Meredithian women who have been disillusioned by men, Laetitia can bring to the marriage only her intelligence, which will give her keen insight into someone who believes in victims. Sir Willoughby's potential triumph has been transformed into the desperate salvaging of his self-respect and his social position.

Mrs. Mountstuart, the female counterpart of Adrian Harley the Wise Youth in *The Ordeal of Richard Feverel,* coins an epithet to describe Clara Middleton, calling her "a dainty rogue in procelain." This eipthet obviously works in contrast to her own about Sir Willoughby, " *'You see he has a leg.'* " Both the rogue in porcelain and the leg recur as motifs throughout the book. In her mordant sense of the comic, Mrs. Mountstuart knows that the dainty rogue will outlast the leg, and that porcelain, although it can be shattered, retains a sheen that the leg of a non-nature-lover soon loses. This description of Clara contains a kind of poetry that disturbs Sir Willoughby because, understandably, he cannot perceive the appropriateness of the phrase or file it away as something inept. When Colonel De Craye's wedding gift of porcelain is smashed en route to Patterne Hall, the engagement, like the vase, is broken, although the rogue remains. Sir Willoughby's leg is insufficient to counter the rogue, for the leg stands for all his merely superficial accomplishments: wealth, title, lineage, outward brilliance, personal beauty. The leg is the English gentleman. If he has a leg, the field is his. The leg, however, only enhances Sir Willoughby's egoism, is, in fact, the basis for his egoism; and the rogue rejects the leg for the walker, Vernon Whitford.

Despite his fine leg, Sir Willoughby dislikes using it, and while Vernon Whitford takes great strides through the woods, Sir Willoughby relaxes in his laboratory. Sir Willoughby's science, however, is merely a disguise for his distaste for poetry and his lack of real culture. Science provides something for him to retreat to, but at no time does he demonstrate any knowledge of or interest in its matter. The laboratory, also, allows him to avoid the label of dilettante. Furthermore, its all-male atmosphere provides relief from women, becoming a kind of safety valve for Sir Willoughby's nervous tension gathered amidst female society. While Vernon expends energy and in his long walks reacts against excessive comforts, Sir Willoughby conserves his strength and rests his leg. The always perfect leg is an evident sign of his inflexibility and his egoistic desire for perfection, both of which destroy any meaningful relationship he might have with a woman. As long as Sir Willoughby values only his leg, he will be a victim of his own illusions.

Nowhere is Sir Willoughby's intractable nature better revealed than in his attitude toward Flitch, the carriage driver. Unable to forgive Flitch for leaving his service, precisely as he was unable to receive Crossjay's father when that hero proved not to be a gentleman, Sir Willoughby treats a contract as inviolable, no matter what human need intervenes. To break a contract, he assumes, whether one of work or marriage, is tantamount to a personal insult. Flitch recurs in the novel as a Comic Fury whose insistent entreaties pursue his master, just as the three women, as a kind of chorus, turn up when least desired. We remember that Flitch is driving the carriage carrying Colonel De Craye's gift of porcelain when it is smashed. Flitch is a social conscience for Sir Willoughby, and it is not fortuitous that he should be present at, even liable for, the symbolic breaking of the engagement.

As a further commentator upon Sir Willoughby, Colonel De Craye is a male counterpart of Mrs. Mountstuart and an evident opposite of the master of Patterne Hall. Opposed to Sir Willoughby's closed nature is his open Irish good humor, his flexible, honest, and ingratiating personality. Although charming, he is, nonetheless, somewhat vapid, and too insubstantial to enter as a serious rival for Clara, even though Sir Willoughby does suspect him and try to maneuver him away. The Colonel is a kind of Wickham with decency: ever ready, a charming companion, and innately well-bred; in short, the easy-going gentleman who can never win the heroine. He is the conventional friend, in one sense like Darcy's Bingley, although with more sense and wit. He lacks both Sir Willoughby's egoism and Vernon's seriousness, and as a comment upon Clara's fiancé, he shows her one possible alternative to life with an egoist.

De Craye is all personality, while Sir Willoughby is a *character,* somewhat akin to the "characters" created by the writers of the early seventeenth century, Joseph Hall, Sir Thomas Overbury, and John Earle, the latter of whom is best known for his *Microcosmographie:* or *A Piece of the World Discovered in Essays and Characters*. These sketches are prose pictures of certain types of persons, based either on temperament or occupation. Often the general type masked an individual model, what we would roughly call a portrait or a profile. Two hundred years earlier, Chaucer had created characters in a similar vein based on the medieval belief in humours or liquids responsible for one's disposition and health: blood, phlegm, choler (yellow bile), and melancholy (black bile).

Meredith dropped the medieval connotations, but retained the generic idea of characteristics by deriving all of Sir Willoughby's actions and thoughts from his basic egoism. In still another way, Meredith's clear-cut motivation for Sir Willoughby derives from the singular characterization of Greek tragic heroes who were identified with one flaw that determined their fate. Thus, Oedipus is rash, Agamemnon vain, Creon proud and presumptuous, Ajax tempestuous, and so on. *The Egoist* retains many other characteristics of Greek tragedy. The classical unity of time is fairly closely maintained once the books gets started, only a few weeks passing while Sir Willoughby suffers his ordeal of women. The unity of place, although not precisely a classical dogma, is nevertheless held to, the action in the main occurring at Patterne Hall. What particularly recommends the classical reference, however, is the strict unity of the plot, with its beginning, middle, and end, its rising and falling action. The plot, furthermore, arises out of character, the incidents all finding their origin in Sir Willoughby's flaw. Moreover, the other main characters gain definition through their reaction to him, as they reject him or fight to free themselves of him.

In addition to these general similarities with Greek tragedy, there is the presence of the Furies and the Chorus, as well as the sense of Fate overhanging all. Further, there is a controlled list of characters, the few peripheral ones being Dr. Middleton, Colonel De Craye, and the three ladies. Except for the Colonel, only Dr. Middleton—modeled loosely on Thomas Love Peacock—retains a distinctive personality, which, curiously, is not unlike Sir Willoughby's in its self-centeredness, its stress on comfort and immediate pleasure, its lack of judgment and its basic folly. If Sir Willoughby is an obsessive egoist, Dr. Middleton is a benevolent one. The peripheral characters themselves form a kind of Chorus around Sir Willoughby. They are the voices of society which he alternately fears and desires to hear, and whose just praise he is anxious to gain.

Nevertheless, despite these trappings of Greek tragedy—which give depth and resonance to the comedy—Sir Willoughby is not, and cannot be, a tragic hero. He has no recognition of what he is, and therefore he remains the comic butt of a predicament he never fully understands. The punch line, as Meredith gives it, is: "But he [Sir W.] had the lady with brains! He had, and he was to learn the nature of that possession in the woman who is our wife." Unaware, he cannot be tragic. Unaware, he remains comic to the end. He is, like Prufrock, "Politic, cautious, and meticulous; / Full of high sentence, but a bit obtuse; / At times, indeed, almost ridiculous— / Almost, at times, the Fool." The protagonist not of tragedy but of a mock-epic, Sir Willoughby will one day awake in Laetitia's arms and drown, again like Prufrock, in the actuality of life. Only then, if ever, will the Comic Imps give him peace.

The Egoist is, in several ways, an extension of aspects of *The Ordeal of Richard Feverel,* beyond the two egoists and their "systems." In both novels, Meredith seemed to reach deeply within personal experience: the early novel a warning to the young father left with his son, the later one a return to his courtship of a girl temperamentally unsuited to him. The creation of Sir Willoughby, furthermore, gave Meredith a weapon with which he could attack Victorian complacency both in its social and political attitudes, as well as in its cultural standards. It was his last major novel, except, perhaps for *One of Our Conquerors,* published in 1891, fourteen years later. Like all significant fiction, *The Egoist* moves rapidly beyond the particular into a general statement about mankind. It expresses again Meredith's insistence upon man's social contract with Earth, upon a realistic approach to social issues, upon the demeaning struggle which may bring success, upon equality and freedom of choice, upon cultural maturity. Moreover, it raises the problems of the dubious rewards of self-alienation, of the cash nexus, of dehumanization, of any philosophy that splits man's body from his spirit, of any system that engenders and lets thrive greed, ego, and vanity. These are, of course, the classic themes of all major fiction, and Meredith, more effectively than many of his contemporaries, came to terms with them.

One of the several victims of provincial criticism of Meredith has been the novel sandwiched between *The Adventures of Harry Richmond* (1871) and *The Egoist: Beauchamp's Career* (1875). Until the last decade or so, it has rarely received fair commendation as a novel (not as a political tract) and one that can compete artistically with the finest of Victorian fiction, ranking just below *Middlemarch, Vanity Fair,* and some of Dickens's novels as a major representation of nineteenth-century ideas. Furthermore, *Beau-*

champ's Career offers an excellent picture of Victorian manners and morals in action, and is full of the wit and verve that the English novel had seen only intermittently since Jane Austen's social satires. It is one of Meredith's least-known novels, but surely one of his most successful.

Beauchamp's Career appeared shortly before Meredith began *The Egoist* and gains its place among his major novels for what may be characterized as its "balance of virtue and vice" among the principal characters, its lack of clear-cut heroes or heroines. Furthermore, the novel demonstrates Meredith's ability to forsake the singleness of purpose which often made some of his other narratives seem somewhat narrow and contrived.

Meredith was, at this time, as in *Richard Feverel* earlier, attempting to separate the novel, and particularly its heroes, from romantic suppositions. Early in *Beauchamp's Career*, he declared that Beauchampism ". . . may be said to stand for nearly everything which is the obverse of Byronism, and rarely woos your sympathy, shuns the statuesque pathetic, or any kind of posturing." Meredith then refined his point: "With every inducement to offer himself [Beauchamp] for a romantic figure, he despises the pomades and curling-irons of modern romance, its shears and labels. . . ." He continued: "It is artless art and monstrous innovation to present so wilful a figure, but were I to create a striking fable for him, and set him off with scenic effects and contrasts, it would be only a momentary tonic to you, to him instant death. He could not live in such an atmosphere" (Chapter IV).

Accordingly, Meredith offers a Beauchamp too full of human frailty to become a hero, and opposite him puts the only villain reality allowed him, an indifferent and complacent England. The conflict in the novel, then, is between an imperfect Nevil Beauchamp and an imperfect England, both impervious to reason or criticism. It is, apparently, Meredith's point that the inflexibility of each should prove self-destructive: the unalterable Nevil drowns to save a lower-class child, while the star of England will likewise sink as long as her social assumptions continue unyielding and rigid. Dr. Shrapnel and Everard Romfrey, who, roughly, divide the two Englands between them, remain intransigent at the end of the novel—only Nevil's memory can even momentarily bind them—

for neither, with characteristic stringency, will dare submit to the other.

In the course of the novel, each major character suffers through an ordeal: Nevil, the loss of the election and the near fatal illness that saps his energy and reduces him to a shade; Dr. Shrapnel, the whipping by Everard Romfrey which almost kills the old radical; Romfrey himself, the loss of his infant son—his last chance for a direct heir; Cecilia Halkett, the gaining of Nevil's marriage proposal too late to save her from a loveless union with Blackburn Tuckham; Rosamund Culling, the indignities she bears in trying to redeem herself in Nevil's eyes, all of which result in her self-sacrificing marriage to Romfrey. Accordingly, as Lionel Stevenson has remarked, the book is filled with loveless marriages: Nevil's own to Jenny Denham, Cecilia's to Tuckham, Romfrey's to Rosamund Culling, Renée's to an aged Frenchman. Not a single relationship in the novel is based on reciprocated love, and each marriage is expedient or cruel in its avoidance of romance. Personal feelings are masked, outward manners are maintained even when enmity is present, headlong action replaces reasonable behavior, self-interest supplants charity. The very foundations of society are rooted in deceit. This situation is England's ordeal, and nowhere else in the Victorian novel does one receive such an uncompromising view, unrelieved by any all-saving romanticism. Meredith's so-called optimism was never less evident.

Beauchamp's Career is structured on a series of disappointments and gains its unity from the way these events mount in intensity until Nevil's death shatters the hopes of both Dr. Shrapnel and Romfrey. Meredith's intentions in the novel gain clarity if one briefly compares *Beauchamp's Career* with George Eliot's *Felix Holt* (1866), political novels which superficially resemble each other. Nevil is paired with Felix, Cecilia Halkett with Esther Lyon, and the issue of an election in which radical politics plays a significant part is of moment in both narratives. In George Eliot's novel, however, idealism proves stronger than desire for personal advancement, as Esther chooses to renounce her inheritance and cast her lot with the poor Felix. Meanwhile, Harold Transome, the rich and landed radical, graciously loses both Esther and the election. No one is seriously hurt. The rich remain rich, and the poor find love and integrity. In short, Felix is a romantic figure, a type of proletarian hero who maintains his nobility; and Esther Lyon, once she forsakes her simpering egoism, is able to attain nobility and love with Felix. She, in turn, becomes a kind of proletarian heroine, who, although above the lower classes in manner and education, is willing to share their future. Meredith, however, who surely knew George Eliot's novel, turned away from this type of easy romanticism, with its popular resolution of problems.* More politically farsighted than George Eliot, he foresaw the impossibility of a "happy" resolution among the diverse elements of society, and he therefore made no attempt to present either of the classes as faultless.

Consequently, Meredith's characters are not one-sided. Even as Romfrey gains in stature, despite his deplorable whipping of Dr. Shrapnel, Nevil begins to decline, to whimper, and, finally, to become expedient and something of a bully. Transformed into a zealous martyr to his ideas, Nevil seriously compromises his integrity, while Romfrey remains loyal to his own vision of a Whig-Tory England. Meredith suitably honors the intentions of each. Similarly, Cecilia Halkett, the daughter of a wealthy Tory, is able to rise above her inheritance and understand the noble sacrifice that Nevil is making, while Jenny Denham, the ward of Dr. Shrapnel and sympathetic to his ideas, is unwilling to marry Nevil without love and is dismayed by his intimidation of her into the union. In each instance, Meredith honors the honesty of the people involved without regard for their or his political sympathies. For this reason, the narrative of *Beauchamp's Career,* weighted as it is by successive disappointments and mounting frustrations for each character, attains a tragic stature unique among Meredith's novel. For even though Nevil dies in a heroic action, he is, by now, broken and dispirited, and the reader is already disenchanted by his expediency. Thus, Nevil's decline is complete, his death dramatically necessary for the narrative, and his fate the final step, Meredith suggests, in any attempt at unthinking idealism. Meredith's vision

* At approximately this time, about 1700 landowners owned two-fifths of the land; income from real estate went as high as a million dollars a year; and the aristocracy and landed gentry, with few exceptions, controlled the great government offices. See *The Age of Equipoise* by W. L. Burn, 1964.

of the Victorian social compromise is unyielding, and his untainted realism provides a faithful, albeit gloomy, view of the class structure.

The first in the series of disappointments that form the spine of the novel is concerned with the Venice idyl between Renée de Croisnel and Nevil, in which young love is darkened by the girl's coming marriage to the dissolute Marquis de Rouaillout. Nevil's reaction to Renée's situation foreshadows his reaction to nearly every succeeding episode in his short career. Inspired and strengthened by his messianic role, he wants more to save her than to love her. Nevil's egoism is such that he must sacrifice himself, and his ardor is fanned by her position as a pawn, with her family's approbation, in a loveless marriage. Later in the novel, when she throws herself at Nevil, thinking that he has remained unchanged in his love, she now finds that, almost alone, he must save England, and that he thinks only of his candidacy in the coming election. Thus, even love, however self-centered, becomes spoiled and a matter of expediency in Nevil's struggle to rescue England from complacency. This rigidly inflexible attitude is further revealed in his relationships with Rosamund Culling, Cecilia Halkett, and Jenny Denham, all of whom find themselves caught in an unyielding trap of idealism and brought close to nervous exhaustion.

Accordingly, as the novel develops, it unfolds increasing examples of wasted energy and vexing frustrations. Even Romfrey, certainly the opposite of Nevil, is brought by his nephew to the brink of unhappiness and dissatisfaction, weathered and experienced as the "crochety unintelligible Whig" is. Nevil's idealism, like that of Dostoyevsky's Idiot, seems to spark the conscience of each character, not to action but to dissatisfaction, not to thought but to self-defense. This "ability," ironically, provides his sole career in an indifferent society where the honest have become deceitful, consciously or not, and the just self-righteous. Though Meredith champions Nevil, he recognizes that his reforming spirit— given the form it takes and given the nature of the force to be overcome—is futile. When Jack Lindsay, whose partisan study of Meredith contains many valuable insights, talks of Nevil's recognition of the class struggle and of Meredith's realization that England must be remade from the bottom up, he simplifies the author's thoughts, as would any critic who treats Meredith from a single point of view. Meredith sees, with far-ranging foresight, that by its very nature Nevil's attack upon Whig and Tory principles contains the seeds of its own destruction, for Nevil's plans are based on a quixotic dream rather than reality. Though strong words seem suitable in the mouth of Dr. Shrapnel (for he is old and mature enough to understand the nature of his attacks), in the mouth of a self-righteous and inexperienced Nevil these verbal assaults on government seizure of private farms, on middle-class desire for comfort and property, and on the sell-out to Mammon and the priest, become presumptuous and silly. His principles, however just, seem to stem from the same thoughtless and immature youth who, at a very young age, was going to uphold England's honor by defying the entire French Guard and was persuaded by Mrs. Culling to challenge only the colonels of the Imperial Guard.

By developing in full relief the opponents of Nevil's "serious foolishness," Meredith was able to realize characters of very different political opinions who are neither villainous nor entirely sympathetic. Romfrey, for example, although far from lovable, is within his rights when he ridicules his nephew's priggishness and refuses to take him seriously. The same attitude is maintained by the other characters on the "wrong" side of the political fence: Tuckham, Colonel Halkett, Seymour Austin (a senior politician), all of whom treat Nevil with some respect for his idealism but with little regard for the quality of his ideas. Of course, they expect Nevil to come to his senses eventually, and they look upon his apostasy as an inexperienced youth's temporary madness.

Nevil, consequently, is unable to convince one mature person of his principles, with the possible exception of Cecilia Halkett, and her motives are mixed with an admiration close to love. Nevertheless, she is, perhaps, the only "antagonistic" person in the book to recognize the grandness and integrity of his youthful idealism, and this recognition, in turn, gives her dramatic standing. In one scene in particular, her presence is illuminating while Nevil's is vague and pale: Cecilia, despite the obvious pressures upon her, now realizes that Nevil's ideas contain a great deal of truth, though she recognizes that his manner of conveying them is detrimental to their success. Notwithstanding, she is ready to accept an offer from him. Her warm feelings have enabled her to rise from the strict Toryism of her birth, and she can feel sympathy even for Dr. Shrapnel. In her growth to a greater sympathy of ideas, she is not unlike many of George Eliot's heroines, especially Esther Lyon of *Felix Holt*. In this passage, Nevil is trying to gain an apology from Romfrey for the whipping of Dr. Shrapnel. As he talks to Cecilia, he endeavors to have her father, Colonel Halkett, intervene with Romfrey. When Cecilia suggests her cousin Cecil as instigator, Nevil answers:

"Then point that out to your father," said he, perceiving a chance of winning her to his views through a concrete object of her dislike, and cooling toward the woman who betrayed a vulgar characteristic of her sex; who was merely a woman, unable sternly to recognize the doing of a foul wrong because of her antipathy, until another antipathy enlightened her.

He wanted in fact a ready-made heroine, and did not give her credit for the absence of fire in her blood, as well as for the unexercised imagination which excludes young women from the power to realize unwonted circumstances.

At this crucial point, Meredith begins the reversal of fortunes. Cecilia becomes increasingly warm and understanding, while Nevil declines in energy and honesty. After this scene, his feeling for the girl is obviously connected with her large fortune, which would enable him to buy good writers for *Dawn,* a radical journal he plans to publish. Meredith astutely plots the novel so that when Nevil finally proposes to Cecilia and she rejects him (she has already accepted Tuckham as her only alternative), the reader has also rejected Nevil, so far has Cecilia risen in stature. Nevil's idealism has taken the form of an all-consuming passion, and he is, paradoxically, too far tainted by principles to remain in normal equilibrium.

Meredith's qualified meliorism (his critics have often tended to characterize him as a bounding idealist, at one with joyful nature and the seasons) has rarely been more apparent. As Nevil succumbs to self-corrupting egoism, he declines physically and mentally. Then, when his terrible illness breaks his body, we see that he has been almost completely enervated. His impulses have slowed, he is less headstrong, more hesitant, in effect, defeated and rendered impotent, not wiser. His hasty marriage to Jenny Den-ham against her will is only a single instance of his debilitation. As formerly his ideas seemed out of proportion to his youth, so now his actions become entirely politic. Unfortunately, he no longer has even the charm of a brash idealist tilting at windmills. When we look for Meredith's social and political values, we must find them in the structure of the novel itself, not in the phrases of the various characters. The culture at stake is mirrored not by Dr. Shrapnel's diatribe—in itself of some historic interest—but in what happened to a Dr. Shrapnel and to a young aristocrat who decides to follow him. The action of the novel, in short, defines the values in question. When we see Nevil shift his ground, become tainted and expedient, when we see Romfrey unmoved by his gross in-justice to Dr. Shrapnel, when we hear the latter's verbal attacks on society as merely a faint voice in the wilderness, and when we see woman after woman sacrificed to expedient and loveless mar-riages, then we realize that Meredith by the very arrangement of the novel has critically appraised certain aspects of the later Victo-rian Age. By frustrating Nevil's attempts to assume a heroic role, Meredith, through his narrative, directly attacks Victorian bour-geois standards that prevent the valiant from becoming illustrious and indirectly suggests that all forms of idealism and potential greatness must be smothered by this or any complacent society.

The reversal of fortunes, suggested above in regard to Nevil and Cecilia, applies to everyone committed to a course of action. As hopes are defeated, frustrations increase, and the chance of equi-table termination of an ugly situation lessens. If we keep this point in mind, Nevil's seemingly fortuitous drowning takes on added sig-nificance; for he has already thrown away his life—though Mere-dith in a letter he wrote at the completion of the MS of *Beau-champ's Career* to Moncure Conway, an American editor and lecturer, shows that he thought Nevil's frustrating experiences not quite wasted.

It [*Beauchamp's Career*] is philosophical-political, with no powerful stream of adventure: an attempt to show the forces around a young man of the present day, in England, who would move them, and finds them unutterably solid, though it is seen in the end that he does not altogether fail, has not lived quite in vain . . . A certain drama of self-conquest is gone through, for the hero is not perfect. He is born of the upper class, and is scarcely believed in by any class, except when he vexes his own, and it is then to be hated. At the same time the mild spirit of a prosperous middle class, that is not extremely alarmed, is shown to be above persecuting; so that the unfortunate young man is in danger of being thought dull save by those who can enter into his idea of the advancement of Humanity and his passion for it. . . . I think his History a picture of the time—taking its mental action, and material ease and indifference, to be a necessary element of the picture (Quoted by Lionel Stevenson, *The Ordeal of George Meredith*, pp. 195-196).

Once Nevil tries to move this type of society, his physical drowning is merely the inevitable dénouement of a series of failures. The drowning of course kills Nevil, but the several failures have already morally weakened him and, along the way, changed him into a selfish young man. Such is the ability of entrenched power to corrupt the innocent who let excessive idealism blind them to the difference between what they want and what they can obtain in a closed society. When Meredith claims that Nevil had not lived wholly in vain, he recognizes that his young idealist has possibly touched the minds and spirits of others, but also that his original quest, from the point of view of all classes, was futile. After his illness, Nevil can do nothing but die—the end is not merely convenient for the novel but necessary for the hero. Those critics who have argued that Nevil's drowning is absurd should perhaps be concerned more by the manner of death than by the death itself, which is dramatically important and inevitable. Like many of Meredith's other egoists who perish physically or spiritually, Nevil, his ideals smashed and lacking direction, must also die. Deficient in wisdom, which would have counseled moderation, Nevil becomes a sacrifice to his generation.

Meredith had originally planned to call the novel by the preposterous title of "Sir Henry Firebrace of the Beacon, Knight Errant of the Nineteenth Century," with his friend Maxse the hero of that novel, just as Maxse became later the basis for Nevil. The original title firmly places Nevil—as before, Richard Feverel— in the line of idealistic protagonists in western literature—Don Quixote, Alceste, Candide—and, in English fiction, suggests *Beau-*

champ's Career as an almost direct descendant of the novels of Sterne, Smollett, and Fielding. As we have seen, creating a typical nineteenth-century hero did not concern Meredith, for Beauchamp, much as his predecessor Richard Feverel and his descendant Sir Willoughby Patterne, is a comic rather than a romantic figure.

Since the essay on comedy came between *Beauchamp's Career* and *The Egoist,* possibly Meredith's two most carefully wrought novels, we should expect the ideas permeating the essay to find root in his own practice. We can, in fact, see that Nevil is closely akin to that comic idealist Alceste, who desires an egocentric world which will revolve around his self-righteous ideas of justice, and who is impervious even to honest criticism. Once *Beauchamp's Career* is identified as a high comic novel, the insights gained illuminate several aspects of Meredith's technique and also suggest how the comic spirit works to make Nevil's decline inevitable.

The ridicule of bourgeois society, which is central to the comic spirit, abounds in *Beauchamp's Career* and extends to every character with the exception of Seymour Austin, the experienced elder statesman whose balance and sense of reality can be likened to the same qualities in Célimène of *Le Misanthrope.* The comic spirit flourishes healthily in a society which openly recognizes irreconcilables, but destroys savagely in one which is solemn and inflexible.

Under these conditions, Nevil himself becomes preposterous. Full of idolatry and pretensions, while mined with conceit, he is fair game for the darts of the comic spirit. Dr. Shrapnel, in turn, is a repository of good intentions, but bombastical, vain in his messianic principles, at times a figure of absurdity with his great height, his noisy virtue, his overbearing purity of soul. His dogmatism is on a par with that of Romfrey, and if extremes ever do meet, these two would have more in common than we should at first grant them. Even Cecilia Halkett, in her role as a warm and sympathetic character, is put into an absurdly comic situation when she gravitates toward Nevil at almost the very moment he —blind to her personal virtues—is considering marriage for her money. In addition, Rosamund Culling, whom we first meet as a person of independence and distinction, once pursued by Nevil's

revengeful spirit turns into a highly neurotic woman whose sole
quest is to recover her dignity after maligning Dr. Shrapnel.
Only Renée escapes being made ludicrous by the comic spirit; because her development occurs outside Nevil's sphere of influence,
she can become her own person without falling a victim to his
idealism.

It was Nevil's misfortune to be born into what Bergson called
a closed society, one that tends to stifle revolutionary ideas and
permits relatively little to occur outside the set rules of acceptable
behavior. Nevil himself, as he develops, is also closed. With a different atmosphere, he might have acquired more resiliency and
flexibility, but the lack of these qualities dooms him. However,
Nevil's part of Tory (even Whig!) England lived untroubled by
dreams or intuitions, or even ideals; and these qualities—not mind
—are all that Nevil can offer. Unresponsive not only to delicacies
but also to large ideas, Nevil's society is, nevertheless, surprisingly
good-natured about his absurd apostasy from aristocratic principles. Romfrey, once one recognizes his intransigence, is kind to
Nevil throughout the latter's ordeal, although the old Earl is not
above his jokes at his nephew's expense. Even though he detests
Nevil's ideas and refuses to take him or them seriously, Romfrey
admires his energy, his impudence, his spirit. These qualities, however, are perhaps the only ones remaining to a closed society,
which cannot recognize individuality (of principle) and true selflessness.*

In *Beauchamp's Career,* even the most selfless of characters,
Dr. Shrapnel, is unable to present basically sound ideas in a reasonable rather than in an emotion-ridden language. Only Seymour

---

* Several years earlier in "The Function[s] of Criticism at the Present Time"
(1864), Matthew Arnold had also written about a closed society, in his case
one closed to ideas. But he warned that a fresh idea alone was not enough,
for it could be lost if before maturity it was forced into the antagonistic
market place. "Let us think of quietly enlarging our stock of true and fresh
ideas, and not, as soon as we get an idea or half an idea, be running out
with it into the street, and trying to make it rule there. Our ideas will, in
the end, shape the world all the better for maturing a little." *Essays in Criticism,* first series (London, 1896), p. 36. Nevil's comic-tragedy—surely the
comic-tragedy of all idealists—is his inability to recognize this point.

Austin, the "wise man" in the book, can differentiate Shrapnel's sense from his nonsense, and he does it too late. Any system or attitude based on selfish reason (ego) is destructive, demolishing Richard Feverel, Sir Willoughby Patterne, Victor Radnor, and Alvan, among others. It is selfish reason that causes all the loveless marriages in *Beauchamp's Career,* and selfish reason, finally, that renders ineffectual Nevil's relationship with every woman in the novel who loves him.

Integral to Meredith's idea of right and selfish reason, as we saw above, is his attitude toward the evils of women's dependent role in society. For selfish reason, in its various guises, humiliates Renée, Rosamund, Cecilia, and Jenny, and shows Nevil to be here as bourgeois as his Tory foes. This point is clearly illustrated when Renée runs away from her husband to throw herself at Nevil—the unhappy girl willing to deny her own independence by this act of subservience. But Nevil pays only the barest of lip service to this one of Dr. Shrapnel's principles and cannot prevail against his feelings which demand her dependence. While her recognition of his dilemma identifies her with the comic spirit, his attitude sinks him ever deeper into an all-consuming egoism. Similarly, when Rosamund Culling has deceived Romfrey about Dr. Shrapnel, Nevil loses all respect for her dignity and sees her only as a traditionally weak woman. Lost completely upon Nevil is her growth to emotional maturity with her confession to Romfrey. In addition, he refuses, or is unable, to recognize any change in Cecilia Halkett, who can overcome the prejudices of her background sufficiently to sympathize with Dr. Shrapnel's principles. Furthermore, Nevil never sees that Jenny Denham does not want to marry him and does so only to please her guardian—to this too he is blinded by egoism, by selfish reason.

Perhaps here we can perceive most clearly the terrible irony in Meredith's attack upon certain aspects of Victorian society and culture. For Meredith says that the idealist must be an equivocally motivated egoist before he can protest, that his schemes must derive from emotion and not from reason, and that all bourgeois society must be closed to right reason, closed as it is to the freeing power of the comic spirit. The demons that in an open society would have been purged by comedy are only partially expelled by Nevil's death, for in a society closed to equality, the comic spirit cannot adequately flourish. Every age, perhaps, needs its Aristophanes, its Molière, indeed, its Meredith.

Beauchamp's Career is a mixture of ironic comedy, wasted energies, lost hopes, smashed ideals, crushed sensibilities—the whole paraphernalia of Meredith's heritage from Carlyle that countered the excessive optimism of Browning and the hesitating but triumphant faith of Tennyson. Unlike Trollope, who in his political novels justified his upper-class hero and demonstrated his own hopeful social conservatism, Meredith remained critical of all positions, refusing to glorify Nevil even while basically agreeing with his ideals. In describing England's ordeal, Meredith is suggesting that her finest sons must be sacrificed to expedience, untested principles, and false premises. Just as Conrad's Kurtz ("Heart of Darkness") was to go to the Congo a bounding idealist only to lose all principles in questing for ivory, so Nevil under pressure first becomes desperate, then loses his innocence through illness, and, finally, dies immolated in the swirl of exhausted ideals. And over the muddy boy whom he saved from drowning Romfrey and Dr. Shrapnel can only stare at each other, dumb in the knowledge of what has happened, "This is what we have in exchange for Beauchamp!" Meredith presages the new race, but will it, he asks, ever produce a Nevil Beauchamp? Romfrey and Dr. Shrapnel perhaps finally recognize the worth of that tragicomic martyr to their principles.

At one time, it was fashionable to mock Meredith, particularly in the trough of his decline in the 1920's and 1930's. His philosophy was considered shallow and his expression judged overblown and sentimental. Such was also the fate of two Meredithians, Thomas Hardy and D. H. Lawrence, and yet all three speak authentically to us in the twentieth century. Meredith's insistence on unity and fullness of feeling cannot now be easily dismissed, and his obsession with a return to Earth no longer seems extravagant to an age disenchanted by material accomplishment. Meredith had his own religion, secular in its expression but transcendental in its scope. As he wrote in one of his letters:

Does not all science (the mammoth balloon, to wit) tell us that when we forsake earth, we reach up to a frosty, inimical Inane? For my part I love and cling to earth as the one piece of God's handiwork which we possess. I admit that we can refashion; but of earth must be the material (To the Reverend Augustus Jessopp, September 20, 1864).

EIGHT

George Eliot: The Sacred Nature of Duty

uring her lifetime, George Eliot was admired and respected as a worthy successor to Dickens and Thackeray. The latter two themselves, as well as Meredith, paid tribute to her work, Dickens in particular writing enthusiastically to her about *Scenes of Clerical Life,* her first attempt at fiction. After her death, however, George Eliot sank in critical esteem. Charged with having too much mind and too little art, she was called too ponderous and knowledgeable to be creative. Even Henry James, in his sympathetic review of John Cross's biography of George Eliot (in *Partial Portraits*), found her less responsive to her art than to her moral obligations, claiming further that her characters and situations "are not *seen,* in the irresponsible plastic way." His charge that reflection and deep study triumphed at the expense of observation and perception was repeated by generations of readers who transformed the artist into a scholar. Like Meredith and many other Victorian novelists, George Eliot came increasingly under attack by twentieth-century critics anxious to defend the modern and discredit the "old fashioned."

George Eliot's early work had originally created her great popularity, but after the temporary decline of her reputation, it was *Middlemarch,* once considered ponderous, elaborate, and forbidding, which came to be praised. Virginia Woolf, while missing George Eliot's satire ("The movement of her mind was too slow and cumbersome to lend itself to comedy"), found her power at its highest in *Middlemarch,* "the magnificent book which with all its imperfections is one of the few English novels written for

grown-up people." That was written in 1925. Today, George
Eliot's reputation is no longer in eclipse, and the entire body of
her work is taken seriously. Once again, she ranks with Dickens and
Thackeray, while F. R. Leavis places her above both in the line
of the greatest English novelists, which he declares to consist of
Jane Austen, Henry James, Joseph Conrad, D. H. Lawrence,
and her.

In *Adam Bede* (1859), George Eliot's first novel and second
work of fiction, the style and emphasis differ considerably from the
methods of her immediate contemporaries, returning despite apparent dissimilarities to certain facets of Jane Austen's novels.
George Henry Lewes, George Eliot's common-law husband whose
fondness for Jane Austen's fiction we saw in his letters to Charlotte
Brontë, was obviously a strong influence in suggesting this model
for George Eliot. In *Scenes of Clerical Life* (1858), written at
Lewes' recommendation, the influence of Jane Austen's world is
even stronger than in *Adam Bede,* although these long stories are
relatively slight and tentative.

The time of the first of the stories, "The Sad Fortunes of the
Reverend Amos Barton," is moved back to the 1830's, specifically
to the year *Pickwick Papers* was published, 1837, still a pre-industrial England just before its face was to darken. George Eliot's
England here, as in *Adam Bede* and most of her later novels, is
pastoral, strongly reminiscent of the England of Wordsworth and
his followers. *Adam Bede* itself is dated prior to the turn of the
nineteenth century, before the railroads and factories had taken
hold. Already, George Eliot's kind of realism is manifest in the
mixture of sentimentality and provincial life that constitute her
clerical scenes, filled as they are with discussions of duty and religion, in particular of Methodism.

Halfway through "Amos Barton" (Chapter 5), George Eliot
answers the reader who thinks her characters uninteresting and
prosaic, an answer, incidentally, in keeping with Wordsworth's
remarks in his Preface to the second edition of the Lyrical Ballads.
In claiming that the majority of Englishmen are uninteresting, her
remarks—like Fanny Burney's in her Preface to *Evelina*—strike
the death blow to the romantic novel:

At least eighty out of a hundred of your adult male fellow-Britons returned in the last census are neither extraordinarily silly, nor extraordinarily wicked, nor extraordinarily wise; their eyes are neither deep and liquid with sentiment, nor sparkling with suppressed witticisms; they have probably had no hairbreadth escapes or thrilling adventures; their brains are certainly not pregnant with genius, and their passions have not manifested themselves at all after the fashion of a volcano. They are simply men of complexions more or less muddy, whose conversation is more or less bald and disjointed. Yet these commonplace people—many of them—bear a conscience, and have felt the sublime prompting to do the painful right; they have their unspoken sorrows, and their sacred joys; their hearts have perhaps gone out towards their first-born, and they have mourned over the irreclaimable dead. Nay, is there not a pathos in their very insignificance—in our comparison of their dim and narrow existence with the glorious possibilities of that human nature which they share?

This is not the great commercial world of Thackeray, or the titled gentlemanly world of Meredith, or the "exaggerated" realistic world of Dickens, and certainly not the romantic world of the Brontës. It is, instead, the provincial world of Jane Austen with some of the shine and polish removed, with an added element of tragic consequence. Removed indeed is the happy ending implicit in Jane Austen's narratives. George Eliot's subject is more prosaic —poor incomes, early deaths, unhappy husbands and wives, frustrated and unrelieved desires; in short, a kind of French realism censored for English consumption. The difference between the two is one of temperament and of the changing times. Jane Austen wrote about provincial England when the country was still provincial, while George Eliot's England, only fifty years later, had faced changes which naturally transformed the tone and content of fiction. Thus, her provincial society contains not only the everyday lives of ordinary people but also a sense of imminent tragedy. While overtones principally of Jane Austen, but also of Goldsmith, Fielding, and Richardson, are apparent in her early fiction, George Eliot was responding to her own more desperate times and modulating her fiction accordingly.

Scenes of Clerical Life is further significant as illustrative of the author's early religious sympathies, feelings that are developed in *Adam Bede* and then later modified into humanitarianism. "Janet's Repentance," the third of the scenes, begins with a discussion of Methodism and its emphasis upon faith, not works. Evangelical Methodism, George Eliot held at this time, raised the believer to a sense of duty beyond the mere satisfaction of self, "which is to the moral life what the addition of a great central ganglion is to animal life." As soon as a man has faith, he rises to a higher order of experience through the self-mastery (itself a duty) of impressions, desires, and impulses. As Mr. Tryson, the dying Methodist minister tells the troubled Janet, we need to drown ourselves in God. As long as we rebel against God's will, we stifle ourselves in a room full of poisoned air. Outside of the room is the sweet pure air of heaven, that, to complete the analogy, is the spirit of God to which we must submit.

The kind of Methodism which informed George Eliot's early years was calm and based on love, not bigoted or wild as it often was among Wesley's followers. Aware of man's need for salvation, of the revelation of God's grace in Christ, of the necessity of spiritual renovation, and of the experience of redemption through faith, the Methodist was generally prone to become emotional, led on as he often was by itinerant and semi-literate preachers whose sole knowledge consisted of the Bible and whose professed morality was strict and inflexible. Precisely this quality of emotionalism, in Wesley's teachings as well as in his nature poetry, helped foster the romantic movement in English poetry. The Methodist revelation of God's work—Wesley's "The whole creation appeared to me in a new light"—is comparable to the new conceptions of Nature in Cowper, Blake, and Wordsworth. Opposed to Calvin's determinism, Wesley's perception of spiritual realities gained through faith restated the Arminian doctrine of God's interest in *every* man, and His ceaseless endeavors to generate love in every soul. As that ultra-romantic imitation of *Faust,* Bailey's *Festus,* demonstrated, universal redemption was possible through the individual's faith. It is not far to go from this belief to the sense of democracy implicit in George Eliot's early fiction.

We can see that *Adam Bede* is all of one piece: for George Eliot's belief in the morality implicit in Methodism was here transformed into the moral function of art. She wrote in the *Westminster Review,* the influential journal of which she was sub-editor from 1855 to 1857, that ". . . a picture of human life such as a great artist can give surprises even the trivial and selfish into that attention to what is apart from themselves, which may be called the raw material of moral sentiment." Exactly as Methodism was supposed to overcome one's destructive absorption with self, so too art was to make one relate to other objects. George Eliot demonstrates through all her heroines that one must live for others; a life devoted to self, as that of Hetty Sorel, Rosamond Vincy, and Gwendolen Harleth, is a life that is limited and, finally, wasted or destructive.

Furthermore, Methodism emphasized the commonplaces of life, and *Adam Bede* is itself an illustration of this attitude. George Eliot's remarks in *Adam Bede* agree with Wordsworth's in his Preface to the *Lyrical Ballads* that the principal object in his poems was "to choose incidents and situations from common life, and to relate or describe them throughout, as far as was possible, in a selection of language really used by men, and, at the same time, to throw over them a certain coloring of imagination, whereby ordinary things should be presented to the mind in an unusual aspect, and further, and above all, to make these incidents and situations interesting by tracing in them, truly though not ostentatiously, the primary laws of our nature: chiefly, as far as regards the manner in which we associate ideas in a state of excitement." Wordsworth then goes on to explain why he chose to represent rustic life and why he used simple language and elementary feelings. In *Adam Bede,* George Eliot writes:

Therefore let Art always remind us of them [common coarse people]; therefore let us always have men ready to give the loving pains of a life to the faithful representing of commonplace things— men who see beauty in these commonplace things and delight in showing how kindly the light of heaven falls on them. There are few prophets in the world; few sublimely beautiful women; few heroes. (Chapter 17)

She writes further that to give love to such rarities as beautiful women and heroes is to withhold it from the great multitude with whom one must live: ". . . more needful that my heart should swell with loving admiration at some trait of gentle goodness in the faulty people who sit at the same hearth with me . . . than at the deeds of heroes whom I shall never know except by hearsay. . . ." *

It is difficult to determine precisely how far George Eliot was influenced by Lewes's essay on "The Lady Novelists" in the *Westminster Review* (July 1852), in which he remarked that fiction should be based on real experience and that its function is to enlarge the reader's sympathies to the plight of common humanity. In a later essay, "Realism in Art" (*Westminster Review,* October 1858), written while *Adam Bede* was still in preparation—and several years after George Eliot had become his "wife"—Lewes claimed that realism is not a counter to idealism but to what he called "falsism." True art, he said, intensifies details and is not a distortion or falsification of the real. In this respect, the common appearances of daily life are sufficient for the artist who can dramatize and heighten.

What Lewes was saying about literature, Ruskin was writing about painting; and in her "Art and Belles Lettres" section of the April 1856 *Westminster Review,* George Eliot devoted several pages to Ruskin's third volume of *Modern Painters.* In one passage, again reminiscent of Wordsworth, she wrote: "The truth of infinite value that he [Ruskin] teaches is *realism*—that doctrine that all truth and beauty are to be attained by a humble and faithful study

---

* In her way, George Eliot was to write an epic of small things. Certainly, the type of detail we find was suitable for a time in which new discoveries in biology and evolution had introduced a sense of minutiae. Even prior to Darwin's *Origin of Species,* the techniques (not necessarily the content) of the Pre-Raphaelite Brotherhood showed a concern with detail that was characteristic of a commercial, scientific, and relatively closed society. Writing in 1868, Dante Gabriel Rossetti stated that it was the "qualities of realism, emotional but extremely minute, which marked the style."

It is ironic, incidentally, that in the Fleshly School Controversy (in 1871) Rossetti was accused by Robert Buchanan (in his *The Fleshly School of Poetry*) of voluptuousness, sensuality, and decadence; for we remember that Rossetti gave impetus to the Pre-Raphaelite Brotherhood in 1848 when the common aim of Hunt, Millais, and his own work was strict attention to realistic detail.

of nature, and not by substituting vague forms, bred by imagination on the mists of feeling, in place of definite, substantial reality." For vagueness, she offered form; for excess of emotion, definite states of feeling; and for unrestricted imagination, the toughness of a trained mind that would, like Dante's and Shakespeare's, combine detail with great conceptions.

Nevertheless, George Eliot's preoccupation with common life did not deceive her, as it did many later realists, that faithful representation of what she observed was itself sufficient for good art. In her journal for November 30, 1858, for example, she mentions that she refused to tell the story of *Adam Bede* previously because ". . . I would not have it judged apart from my *treatment,* which alone determines the moral quality of art. . . ." In a letter almost five years earlier (February 1, 1853), long before she had thought of writing fiction, George Eliot felt that Mrs. Gaskell's *Ruth* (1853) would not be an enduring piece of fiction because she ". . . seems to me to be constantly misled by a love of sharp contrasts—of 'dramatic' effects. She is not contented with the subdued colouring—the half tints of real life. Hence she agitates one for the moment, but she does not secure one's lasting sympathy; her scenes and characters do not become typical."

In writing her novels, George Eliot tried to hold a number of elements in suspension. While recognizing that art has a moral quality which must not be subverted, she also perceived that art should not solely teach, that it must be more than sermon. Further, while recognizing that fiction must be representative of common life and common feelings, she also realized that it must embrace the particular by showing small distinctions between things, the "half tints of life." Thus, fiction is to be both particular and typical, both original and representative, both moral and yet not an apologue. As she suggests in several letters and essays in the 1850's, art must be the result of a combination of character with circumstances, not merely characters presented from a singular viewpoint by an author bent upon a didactic purpose. In George Eliot's terms, to restrict the presentation of character to one point of view would be immoral. Adam Bede himself is by no means the "perfect hero" that many at first took him to be. Similarly, the seemingly unattractive Tom Tulliver (*The Mill on the Floss*) and Casaubon

(*Middlemarch*), as George Eliot emphasized, are painted with sympathy, and the two novels are not conceived solely from the points of view of Maggie and Dorothea Brooke, respectively.

George Eliot took exception to much of the didacticism in the Victorian novel which, she thought, simplified the psychology of people and reduced them to types without sufficient individualization, or, conversely, emphasized individuality at the expense of the type. While holding Dickens in high esteem, for example, she felt that he idealized people and thus created stereotypes. In her essay "False Testimonials" (in the collection *The Impressions of Theophrastus Such*), she cited Dante, ". . . who is at once the most prosaic and homely in his reproduction of actual objects, and the most soaringly at large in his imaginative combinations." As George Eliot developed her ability to integrate large ideas into the patterns of her novels, she increasingly showed that precise representation of real things could be combined effectively with a soaring imagination. As she became accustomed to the novel form, which she had come to relatively late (like Joseph Conrad, she was almost forty before she began to publish fiction), she applied ideas to life and enlarged upon her early beliefs without forgoing their basic tenets. *Romola* (1863), *Middlemarch* (1871-2), and *Daniel Deronda* (1876), although not equally successful, are, nevertheless, valiant efforts to give sweep and scope in the grand style to the English novel.

Adam Bede, however, is far simpler than *Middlemarch,* holding a position relative to that novel which George Eliot's early uncomplicated beliefs hold to the intellectuality of her later years. As her first long work of fiction, *Adam Bede* returns to a period in the author's life when certain restrictive aspects of Calvinism and Methodism still held meaning, and when the realistic representation of simple, ordinary life meant more to her than the infusion of ideas into the novel. To go from *Adam Bede* to *Middlemarch* is to experience the development of a great creative sensibility, although the early novel in itself immediately established George Eliot as a serious and effective novelist, success that was not only critical but also financial.

The milieu of George Eliot's first novel is one that Jane Austen's Emma Woodhouse clearly considered vulgar, the world of farmers and artisans rather than bourgeois gentlemen. George Eliot's artisan-protagonist is a kind of Robert Martin now come to the fore as the "hero" of the novel.* Adam is of the respectable working class, innately genteel and sympathetic and interested in education in order to better himself. Nevertheless, he is far from the gentlemanly Darcy and Mr. Knightley of Jane Austen's novels; far from Charlotte Brontë's Rochester, Meredith's Richard Feverel, Thackeray's George Osborne, Pendennis, Henry Esmond, Dobbin himself; quite far indeed from Dickens's typical heroes, and even from Pip in *Great Expectations,* which nevertheless indicates the new direction. The break in the "aristocratic" hierarchy is almost complete; a new kind of realism is imminent.

Now, we have the honest worker as protagonist, the man of common sense and inbred dignity, Adam or Caleb Garth of *Middlemarch,* or Felix Holt. With this type, however, one also finds bourgeois values, mediocre tastes, little culture. The middle-class reading public has successfully forced the democratization of the novel. The revolution in reading taste begun in the eighteenth century has come full turn. Mrs. Poyser as the voice of small culture and large common sense informs us that henceforth intellectual truth must coincide with the truth of feeling and that class distinctions are no longer meaningful in an age when taste, or what passes for it, is within the reach of all.

* George Eliot perhaps took her text from that influential poem, Wordsworth's "Character of the Happy Warrior," especially lines 33-42, 57-60:

> He labours good on good to fix, and owes
> To virtue every triumph that he knows:
> —Who, if he rise to station of command,
> Rises by open means; and there will stand
> On Honourable terms, or else retire,
> And in himself possess his own desire;
> Who comprehends his trust and to the same
> Keeps faithful with a singleness of aim;
> And therefore does not stoop, nor lie in wait
> For wealth, or honours, or for worldly state . . .
>
> —He who, though thus endued as with a sense
> And faculty for storm and turbulence,
> Is yet a Soul whose master-bias leans
> To homefelt pleasures and to gentle scenes . . .

As George Eliot's journal for November 30, 1858, reveals, *Adam Bede* was based on an anecdote related to her by her Methodist Aunt Samuel almost twenty years previously, a tale that told of an ignorant girl who had murdered her child and refused to confess. The aunt stayed with the girl throughout the night before her execution, praying as Dinah Morris does with Hetty Sorel, and the girl finally confesses her crime. She then accompanied the repentant girl to the place of execution, offering God's comfort until the end. This story George Eliot repeated to Lewes, who saw in it fictional possibilities. Subsequently, George Eliot thought of combining her aunt's recollection with some elements in her father's early life and character. She found, she said, that the chief difficulty of construction was to connect the unfortunate girl with the hero. The novel, originally called "My Aunt's Story," was begun on October 22, 1857, with the character of Dinah Morris only loosely modeled on her recollections of her aunt, and with Adam himself no more than generally representative of her father.

When she began the novel, George Eliot writes, the only elements she had determined on "besides the character of Dinah were the character of Adam, his relation to Arthur Donnithorne and their mutual relation to Hetty . . . the scene in the prison being of course the climax toward which . . . [she] worked." Lewes himself suggested the relationship of Dinah to Adam, convinced as he was that the reader's interest would focus on her. George Eliot accepted the idea that Dinah should be a significant character and from the end of the third chapter worked with the connection between the two principals. This original piecemeal conception of *Adam Bede* recalls that in *Middlemarch* also Lydgate, Dorothea Brooke, and Casaubon only come together after the novel has been developing for some chapters.

Lewes suggested the only part of *Adam Bede* that does not ring true, the final union between Dinah and Adam. Here, the novel fails to live up to original premises: to show beauty in small things, to demonstrate the dignity of lives in which purpose and duty predominate, and to suggest that each person has the initiative, even the obligation, to work out his own moral and religious destiny provided he does not transgress another's rights. The marriage between Adam and Dinah comes as a concession to the popular romantic novel, and it is curious that Lewes, who in theory deplored the falsely sentimental, should have suggested this element. The union is by no means inevitable, and its evident softening effect on the inflexible purpose of Dinah foreshadows George Eliot's own changing philosophy: that human happiness should be salvaged even when it conflicts with duty. Despite the faults of the ending, however, its weakness is not to be compared with that of Dickens's revised ending of *Great Expectations,* whose falseness is more destructive of what appeared earlier.

The conclusion notwithstanding, the symmetry of *Adam Bede* is apparent, containing the pattern that would appear in all of George Eliot's novels except *Daniel Deronda:* an individual tragedy surrounded by community life, and the resultant conflict between the individual and the group. A George Eliot novel is dense and richly textured not only because of the ethical and psychological commentary but also because of the pressure of many lives which crowd the pages and give substance to the chief characters. Therefore, despite many quiet and subdued pages of analysis, her novels are in *movement,* containing rhythms that are peculiarly her own. *Adam Bede* begins, characteristically, in the workroom where the protagonist and his brother, Seth, work as carpenters. There, the slow clumsy rhythms of their speech and minor disputes reveal the pace of the novel. This First Book, with its workaday and religious scenes, joins with the birthday feast of the Third Book and the harvest supper celebration of Book Six to fix the travail of Hetty Sorel, the shame of Arthur Donnithorne, the purity of Dinah Morris, and the inner conflicts of Adam Bede. Balance and rhythm are gained through the realistic representation of the ordinary event heightened and selected to create drama.

As we first see him, Adam disproves the claims of those who have found him to be a conventional hero. Like Oedipus', his evident flaw is a certain hastiness of temper that displays his lack of sympathy, forgiveness, or even humor. He is evidently gifted above his class, or, as George Eliot suggests, he is representative of a class that should not be underestimated. Despite his rough manner and immaturity of judgment, he has a gentle heart that is, after suffering, flexible and amenable to changing situations. Under adversity, he matures, and after forgiving Arthur Donni-

thorne, he is, as it were, a man ready to claim Dinah. His hastiness and bad judgment, both the result of an egoism that must be
exorcised, are part of the realistic characterization that George
Eliot intended as a counter to the romantic novel. In addition, as
Adam develops under the strain of conflict, he himself gives
movement to the narrative: he must awaken from self-deception,
as later Romola, Dorothea Brooke, and Gwendolen Harleth also
must. His growth under adversity illustrates his human qualities.
He recognizes, with Mr. Irwine's counsel, that to judge another is
much more delicate than he had once granted, full as he was of an
inflexible morality that left little room for human warmth and
sympathy.

The opening up of Adam's spirit is analogous to what occurred
in George Eliot when she renounced her early religious beliefs
with their strict doctrines of morality and came to embrace a
more flexible view of human failings. This growth of sympathy did
not, of course, preclude an adherence to duty and discipline or
condone moral laxity. One is reminded of the oft-quoted passage in
a conversation (in 1873) between F. W. H. Myers and George
Eliot; as Myers recollected it:

> I remember how, at Cambridge, I walked with her once in the Fel-
> lows' Garden of Trinity, on an evening of rainy May; and she, stirred
> somewhat beyond her wont, and taking as her text the three words
> which have been used so often as the inspiring trumpet-calls of men,—
> the words *God, Immortality, Duty,*—pronounced, with terrible earn-
> estness, how inconceivable was the *first,* how unbelievable the *second,*
> and how peremptory and absolute the *third* (*Essays—Modern,* pp. 268-
> 9).

Duty, however, as Dinah Morris demonstrates and Mr. Irwine
preaches, should not disallow Christian forgiveness and afford an
excuse for hardness of heart. Here is George Eliot's early Calvinism, with its stress on man's sinful state, already being superseded
by her ever-growing humanitarianism. Dinah Morris's Methodism
is soft and tender, an evident rebuttal to Calvinistic and High
Church rigidity, a religion acceptable to the "liberated" George
Eliot who could embrace all but God and Immortality. Adam
himself first says to Arthur: " 'There's a sort of damage, sir, that

can't be made up for.' " Then softens: " '. . . I'm hard—it's in my nature. I was too hard with my father, for doing wrong. I've been a bit hard t' everybody but *her* [Hetty]. . . . But feeling overmuch about her has perhaps made me unfair to you. . . . I've no right to be hard towards them as have done wrong and repent' " (Chapter 48).

Through the growing understanding of others' pain, Adam transforms vindictiveness into sympathy and his desire for punishment into a recognition of human frailty. After Hetty's tragedy, he himself feels great sorrow, and the nature of his ordeal opens him to true love, first through sympathy which enlarges his spirit and then through a sense of connection with all those who suffer adversity. Presently, Adam can distinguish between the young love he felt for Hetty, much of it based on his own egoism as well as on her superficial attractiveness, and the mature love he feels for Dinah, the result of his recognition of duty and her substantial qualities as a human being.

George Eliot, here and elsewhere, is careful to differentiate between the kind of love or feeling that derives from an immature mind and leads to a false attachment (Adam and Hetty, Dorothea and Casaubon, Romola and Tito Melema, Gwendolen and Grandcourt, Maggie Tulliver and Stephen) and the kind of love that is based on mutual understanding (Adam and Dinah, Dorothea and Will Ladislaw, Gwendolen and Daniel Deronda, Deronda and Mirah, Maggie and Philip Wakem, Esther Lyon and Felix Holt). The latter attachments take account of essentials—how deeply people feel, how they stand adversity, how far their sympathies extend—in contrast to the former, which usually involve selfishness or simply physical attraction. In *Adam Bede,* the shifting scale of love first shows Adam's passionate feeling for Hetty, which she does not return, opposed to Arthur Donnithorne's superficial infatuation with the pretty girl; then Adam's feeling for Hetty is itself contrasted with his growing love for Dinah, which surpasses his love for Hetty as much as that love exceeded Arthur Donnithorne's. Also running through the novel is Seth's feeling for Dinah, a foreshadowing of how Adam is later to feel and a sober counter to his passion for Hetty.

George Eliot conceived of love as a mixture of feeling and duty.

It was for her a momentous and terrible thing, for to love completely meant the total commitment of the entire person. One held nothing back. Although George Eliot cannot be considered a tragic writer—her view of life, as we shall see later, is ultimately anti-tragic—nevertheless we do know from her letters how aware she was of the tragedy implicit in making wrong decisions. If a person is to gain happiness in a world which always demands duty and discipline, then every attempt at happiness—to love, for example—is fraught with danger. Only the mature mind can conceive of love—George Eliot herself ran away with Lewes at thirty-five. The immature mind, however, confuses love with personal desire, a form of egoism that is self-destructive.

Adam Bede is based on the exposure of human folly in a social setting, the great theme that runs through the nineteenth-century novel from Jane Austen through Thomas Hardy, the substance of all the major fiction of Dickens, Thackeray, and Meredith. Later, with Conrad, human folly is transformed into human sin, and earlier, with Fielding and the other eighteenth-century novelists, folly was more individualized than social. In *Adam Bede,* folly is exorcised by suffering and penance, and maturity is the product of smashed hopes and unrealized great expectations.

For Adam himself, his expectation of Hetty's affection is cruelly circumscribed when she prefers Arthur. For Arthur, the social esteem he expected to win as a good master is changed to ostracism. His desire to be a romantic hero, a Don Juan as well as a benevolent master, is mocked by his actual experience after he seduces Hetty. Hetty in turn suffers for her crime, first through her agonizing trip to find Arthur and then through her agony to find herself. All three sufferers contain an excess of foolish pride which must be drawn off before they can function as adults. Pride, or egoism, as Dinah teaches, and as George Eliot demonstrates in nearly all of her major novels, is destructive of life, for it supposes a society in which our sins do not hurt anyone else. George Eliot in *Adam Bede* is concerned with showing that an individual's sins hurt not only himself but others as well, and that the mature person must place himself above personal desire. Dinah warns the revengeful Adam that: "There is no sort of wrong deed of which a man can bear the punishment alone; you can't isolate yourself and say that the evil which is in you shall not spread. . . . An act of vengeance on your part against Arthur would simply be another evil added to those we are suffering under. . . ." Since Dinah Morris herself is outside personal ambition, she can avert tragedy. She is involved in the tragedy of others, but her own life brings happiness. For, as Carlyle once counseled, she has lowered the denominator of her desires. Her moral progress, further, is assured by the degree of her sympathy with individual suffering and individual joy. In a letter two years before *Adam Bede* was published, George Eliot considered just this compassion the sole basis for moral stature and personal happiness.

The structural pattern of *Adam Bede* results from the symmetrical interweaving of the four main characters, just as *Middlemarch* later was to attain symmetry through the connection between the stories of Dorothea Brooke and Lydgate. In *Adam Bede,* the major contrasts occur between Adam and Arthur and then between Dinah and Hetty, with the latter as the link between the two men. Had Dinah known Arthur, the symmetry would have been complete, for exactly as Hetty early in the novel is the tie between Adam and Arthur, so later Dinah is the link between Adam and Hetty. The rest of the characters—Seth, Mrs. Bede, the Poysers, Mr. Irwine, among others—move around the main figures as a kind of community which provides continuity for the protagonists. The latter gain their very social substance from immersion in a real community in which life continues despite personal folly. On this ground, George Eliot gained her strength; and when she forsook it, her work, as in *Romola* or *Daniel Deronda,* became artificial.

Very often in *Adam Bede,* the minor figures in the community —particularly Mrs. Bede, the Poysers, and Mr. Irwine—seem more vital and human than the main characters. George Eliot has been compared to Shakespeare for her richness of texture, the result of her ability to create rounded minor characters like those mentioned above, the Dodsons and Gleggs of *The Mill on the Floss,* the Garths, Vincys, Farebrothers, and Bulstrodes of *Middlemarch,* the Transomes of *Felix Holt.* Unlike Dickens's minor characters who often seem to have a function rather than a full life, George Eliot's always appear solidly in the setting from which they draw their sustenance. Thus, Mrs. Bede is a well-meaning but nagging mother whose grumbling and discomfort are less selfishness than the unhappiness of a dissatisfied woman. And Adam's peevishness with her—which he recognizes as wrong, though uncontrollable—is also a natural outcome of his parents' unsuccessful marriage.

The Poysers, even more than the Garths of *Middlemarch,* demonstrate how relevant provincial life was to George Eliot's genius. With her warm-hearted irritability, her keen sense of position, and her common sense about false pride, Mrs. Poyser shows a vitality missing in the more prosaic Adam. Her crochets make her human, as do those of the Dodsons and Gleggs in *The Mill on the Floss.* Like George Eliot, she recognizes with her old-fashioned sense of integrity that duty and discipline are necessary safety valves for the individual will; and that disorder and chaos can result from a failure to realize traditional values. That these values should be suggested by a rustic like Mrs. Poyser indicates George Eliot's sympathies and signifies her belief that such people themselves constitute England's solidity.

In her presentation of her minor characters, George Eliot's place in the pastoral tradition is apparent. Her "good" people gain strength from the land, even though they may be tenants and not owners. Learning, culture, urban cosmopolitanism are all superseded by the kind of mettle that Mrs. Poyser demonstrates and which extends also to Adam and Seth. Hetty and Arthur, however, deny the integrity and sincerity involved in a life close to the earth (Arthur administers his property rather than living close to it), and accordingly they must suffer. George Eliot's commitment to the land is obvious in the natural descriptions in *Adam Bede* as well as in her diary notations in the spring of 1856. There she evokes the vitality, as it were, the muscularity, of flowers and earth in a way that curiously foreshadows D. H. Lawrence's sinewy descriptions sixty years later. She and Lewes would avidly hike over the countryside near Ilfracombe on what she called geological expeditions "alternated with delicious walks." She writes (between May 8 and June 26, 1856):

I never saw it [the golden furze] in such adundance as here; over some hills the air is laden with its scent and the gorgeous masses of blossom perpetually invited me to gather them as the largest possible specimens. It was almost like the fading away of the evening red when the furze blossoms died off from the hills, and the only contrast left was that of the marly soil with the green crops and woods. The primroses were the contemporaries of the furze and sprinkled the sides of the hills with their pale stars almost as plentifully as daisies or buttercups elsewhere. (*Letters,* ed. Haight, II, 244)

Like Wordsworth with the leech gatherer in "Resolution and Independence," George Eliot found renewal in "encountering" the land. It was the kind of confrontation which indicated—as Wordsworth's "Michael" also demonstrated—that sincerity, integrity, and duty were still possible in a complex world. George Eliot never forsook her belief that hard work on the land was a discipline imposed by one's better self. Whether or not God Himself existed, the individual could generate his own God by drawing upon the self that transcends ego and vanity.

George Eliot's obvious antipathy to Hetty Sorel—her cat-like descriptions of the girl show her real dislike—stems from Hetty's basically parasitical nature. Like Rosamond Vincy and Gwendolen Harleth, whom she roughly foreshadows, the vain Hetty hopes to transform personal beauty almost effortlessly into more enduring qualities. George Eliot's first description of her sets the standard: she calls hers a "springtime beauty" that is as insubstantial as a lovely season. Hetty must, as Gwendolen must, suffer the consequences of her self-indulgence and through severe punishment become purified.*

* Hetty Sorel, in several ways, recalls Scott's Effie Deans (*Heart of Midlothian,* 1818) and Mrs. Gaskell's Mary Barton (*Mary Barton,* 1848) and is a dim throwback to Jane Austen's Emma. In a great many ways, however, *Adam Bede* as a whole most recalls Hawthorne's *The Scarlet Letter* (1850): the one's Methodistic sense of duty and the other's Calvinistic sense of sin and doom; the presence of Hetty Sorel and Hester Prynne as common sinners; the use of Arthur Donnithorne and Arthur Dimmesdale as common traducers of female sanctity. The obvious similarity of proper names makes the connection seem more than fortuitous. In a note to George Eliot's letter to Sara Hennell of 24 March 1857, Gordon Haight indicates that George Eliot and George Henry Lewes began reading *The Scarlet Let-*

Much has been made of the fact that George Eliot, admittedly not physically attractive, struck down the beautiful Hettys, Rosamonds, and Gwendolens for reasons of revenge. By nullifying their physical attractions, so the specious argument runs, she gained her own triumph of mind and spirit. Whether any part of this rings true is impossible to determine, but one can argue cogently that George Eliot reacted to her heroines ethically: that they shocked her moral sensibility by their assumption of superiority and their lack of responsibility. Silly and fatuous, even absurd, they lack earnestness. Dinah Morris, Maggie Tulliver, Dorothea Brooke, Romola, and Mirah Lapidoth, on the contrary, are earnest and selfless, aware of their function in a world which must punish parasites. For George Eliot, as for Ruskin and William Morris, beauty must also be functional.

Several of George Eliot's male characters—Fred Vincy, Tito Melema, Grandcourt, Arthur Donnithorne, Tom Tulliver—demonstrate the same failings as do her weak women. When the weakness is merely the result of circumstances rather than a substantial part of the character, then salvation is possible. Neither Fred Vincy, Arthur, nor Tom Tulliver falls into real vice, although each lacks certain qualities of judgment and balance. Arthur Donnithorne is, roughly, an upper-class counterpart of Hetty, as Grandcourt is later of Gwendolen Harleth. Because Arthur is unable to square passion with duty and allows passion to dominate, his ruin is assured. George Eliot's publisher, John Blackwood, felt that Arthur "is the least satisfactory character," but, his opinion notwithstanding, the portrait of Arthur's immature vanity *is* satisfactory even if his character as a whole may not be. His desire to be admired and respected, like Lydgate's futile attempts (in *Middlemarch*) to be a famous researcher, is based less on reality than on personal presumption. Since he himself has never felt hatred or contempt, when his actions have called up these strong emotions in others, he is temporarily unable to understand what is expected of him or even to comprehend that these emotions are valid. In all

---

ter at this time. She started to write *Adam Bede* in October of the same year.

innocence, Arthur is condescending to Adam; he wants to be manly without the will to be a full man, and his penance requires the realization of all his former failings, the recognition that one can make his own tragedy.

Similarly, Adam himself must soften his hardness of heart so that he can be touched by the suffering of others. With the growth of pity and compassion in him, slow as if may be, he too grows. George Eliot's preachment—that suffering is both good and necessary to achieve common sense and balance—contains, however, a basic optimism. Unlike the tragic hero, George Eliot's hero or heroine can re-enter normal society once he or she has been purged through suffering. The forgiveness implicit in her philosophy, a carry-over of her belief that all potentially can experience grace, is here not unlike Jane Austen's, however different they may otherwise be in intention and artistry. The test for a good person George Eliot stated explicitly in the Epilogue to *Romola:*

> There are so many things wrong and difficult in the world that no man can be great—he can hardly keep himself from wickedness—unless he gives up thinking much about pleasures or rewards and gets strength to endure what is hard and painful. . . . I believe, when I first knew him [Tito], he never thought of doing anything cruel or base. But because he tried to slip away from every thing that was unpleasant, and cared for nothing else so much as his own safety, he came at last to commit some of the basest deeds. . . .

Adam, who is of course no Tito Melema, must nevertheless learn what Mr. Irwine and Dinah Morris already know. Like Mr. Farebrother of *Middlemarch,* Mr. Irwine is more indulgent than strict, more aware of the spirit than the letter of his religious calling, and thus flexible and moderate in his expectations. Recognizing man's imperfections because he shares them himself, Mr. Irwine is as compassionate as Dinah, although her compassion proceeds from a flawless character. Her perfection, however, results in an excess of virtue, what might border on self-righteousness. As one recent critic has remarked, there ". . . is a distasteful over-carefulness about Dinah's idiom." She is too conscious of virtue, too anal in her desire to be right, too self-effacing for the realism of character and event that George Eliot professes to desire. Outside all earthly cares, she moves like a ministering angel, and, consequently, she is disembodied, unwomanly, a spirit of pure goodness amidst contaminated matter. At times, she is anti-life in her constant concern with sorrow, not joy:—". . . trouble is appointed for us all here below, and there comes a time when we need more comfort and help than the things of this life can give," she tells Hetty. Too often, she seems to have a direct pipeline to infinity.

Under no personal pressures herself, Dinah exists to purify others, and her role therefore is suspect. We are never aware that she has known temptation, except the somewhat dubious temptation to marry Adam. With all her goodness and selflessness, Dinah appears priggish, even frigid. As if realizing this, George Eliot did not create her type again. In *Mill on the Floss,* Maggie Tulliver, a secular relative of Dinah, is tempted, does succumb, and suffers real pain and anguish, and so on through Dorothea Brooke. Only Romola harks back to Dinah, especially the Romola who moves among the sick like the Christian Mother, but her very perfection weakens the novel. The spirit of pure virtue cannot help appearing incongruous in novels that are realistic in their other elements. By *Middlemarch,* however, George Eliot saw the foolishness and immaturity in Dorothea's desire to be saintly, her wish to sacrifice herself on the altar of scholarship, and she made her heroine realize that altruism is not the sole ingredient of virtue. To live is also important.

Nevertheless, *Adam Bede* retains its power and solidity of purpose and execution. Perhaps after *Middlemarch,* it is George Eliot's most successful novel. With *Mill on the Floss,* it evokes with both force and grace the English countryside as a source of strength in the English character. And although *Adam Bede* lacks the tragic sense of the later pastoral novels of Thomas Hardy, it strongly demonstrates a side of English fiction almost totally neglected since Jane Austen's concern with provincial life. The apprentice novelist in *Adam Bede* was able to handle even human mediocrity and platitudes with compassion. By showing that excellence of character was in itself no longer a standard of virtue, she struck a new note in English fiction.

The grandness of *Middlemarch* (1871-2) when completed was far in excess of what George Eliot had originally expected, for while working on the first parts, she lamented that she did "not feel very confident that . . . [she could] make anything satisfactory out of *Middlemarch*." Her remarks recall Conrad's anxieties when he was working on *Nostromo*, his fear that the idea of the novel was greater than his powers of execution. Subtitled "A Study of Provincial Life," *Middlemarch* does not depart radically from the style of *Adam Bede* and *The Mill on the Floss*, although its length, breadth, and more ambitious intentions carry it considerably further than the two earlier novels. The artificiality of *Romola* (1863) was put behind as George Eliot returned to what she knew best. So full was her knowledge and so vast her sympathies that she could write to Blackwood:

I don't see how I can leave anything out, because I hope there is nothing that will be seen to be irrelevant to my design, which is to show the gradual action of ordinary causes rather than the exceptional, and to show this in some directions which have not been from time immemorial the beaten path—the Cremorne walks and shows of fiction (Cross, III, 117).

This statement harks back to the remarks on realism in *Adam Bede*, the kind of realism that moved George Eliot to write about things she knew intimately. But the author has so developed since the early novels that those books seem little more than initial preparations for the big work to follow. In variety of characterization, intricacy of plot design, and breadth of human concern, George Eliot had matured into a major novelist. The large strides in intellectual development that she made in the 1840's and 1850's under the respective influence of rationalists like Charles Bray and Charles Hennell, London literary life itself, and then George Henry Lewes seemed to culminate in the late 1860's and early '70's with the planning and execution of *Middlemarch*.

The largeness of mind that George Eliot demonstrates in her one great novel was a further development from the younger brilliant but restricted girl still partially under the influence of Evangelical Methodism, with its sacrifice of Man's needs to God's.

When George Eliot recognized that individual welfare should supersede self-sacrifice, that duty and discipline do not in themselves bring happiness, and that God must, at times, be sacrificed to Man, she traveled one of the main roads that led from early Victorian faith to late-Victorian disbelief.* In her intellectual at-

* William Hale White in *The Autobiography of Mark Rutherford* (1881), like Samuel Butler in *The Way of All Flesh* (1872-84) and Mrs. Humphry Ward in *Robert Elsmere* (1888), described the growing dissent of his protagonist from the accepted beliefs of the community. Unlike George Eliot, however, White's protagonist does not have the resources to resolve his doubts intellectually and accept an agnostic position.

The quest for religious faith created a whole new genre of fiction devoted to the anguish and tribulations of those who found unbelief while seeking belief. While not concerned with loss of faith per se, Newman's *Loss and Gain* (1848) nevertheless chronicles with personal anguish the slow, torturous passage of his autobiographical protagonist toward Rome, who achieves a goal of the sort usually reserved for one who finds himself drifting altogether from belief. More characteristic of the type is J. A. Froude's *The Nemesis of Faith* (1849), which in epistolary fashion relates the growing doubts of its clergyman protagonist and his heroic battle to preserve his integrity in the face of unsolvable questions. Despite his fearful struggle, his inability to square his conscience with his situation leads to his downfall. Froude's novel, like most others of the type, is religious to the core despite the unbelief of his hero, who is neither rebellious nor disaffected.

Perhaps the greatest of all novels of doubt is *Robert Elsmere*. Mrs. Ward here took a well-placed, seemingly secure clergyman and made him undergo the fire of unbelief until he finds himself in despair. Elsmere's own doubts are further reinforced by a published attack on orthodoxy, *The Idols of the Market Place*, and he comes to think of Jesus as a symbol of spirit devoid of his supernatural trappings. With his faith gone, he plunges into social work, in a kind of reversal of Kingsley's Christian Socialism.

Pater's *Marius the Epicurean* (1885), although seemingly different in content and tone, is also a novel of belief and unbelief, a prose epic, in a way, defining the demarcation between Christianity and paganism. Unlike the above heroes, who start with belief and through doubt move relentlessly toward unbelief, Pater's Marius goes from his early acceptance of Cyrenaic doctrine to his devotion to Christian ideals. Marius apprentices himself to a doctrine that will attract the whole man, while his former Epicureanism merely satisfied his sensual appetites. Perhaps Joyce's *A Portrait of the Artist as a Young Man,* with Stephen's titanic spiritual struggle and his final resolution in a career devoted to art, is a fitting culmination of the entire genre.

Obviously, religious novels assumed many forms in the nineteenth century. The road that George Eliot herself took is surely typical of all these

titude toward faith and good works, and their place in the individual's happiness, she was at the center of religious controversy, as later she was to be at the center of all the serious literary and philosophical developments of her time.

Her developing attitudes are of fundamental importance for an adequate understanding of *Middlemarch,* especially as her intellectual history indicates how she transformed theological concepts into human concerns. There is the famous and oft-quoted letter to her father in which she claims that her conscience will no longer permit her attendance at church even if her refusal means separation from him and their home. She writes: ". . . I could not without vile hypocrisy and a miserable truckling to the smile of the world for the sake of my supposed interests, profess to join in worship which I wholly disapprove" (February 28, 1842). The young girl must, like Dorothea Brooke and Daniel Deronda, seek her own identity.

Under the influence of her schoolmistress, Miss Lewis, George Eliot had been a strong Calvinist, although strongly tempted by the arguments of the Oxford Movement.* Oscillating between the

---

protagonists as well as the hundreds more who filled the best-sellers of their day, which charted men's spiritual prowess as relentlessly as popular modern novels chart their protagonist's sexual achievements.

* The Oxford Movement at first grew out of Lord Grey's assertion of state control over the English Church, a move denounced by Keble in a sermon in 1833. The Movement—led by John Henry Newman—was an attempt to strike down Liberal tendencies within the Anglican Church. The *Tracts for the Times,* 29 written by Newman, tried to show that the Apostolic Succession—that is, the line from the early apostles to the later clergy —had been passed on to the Anglican Clergy of the nineteenth century in some mysterious transmission of divine power. This order of priesthood, so Newman argued, formed a Church beyond the power of the state, and any attempt to suppress or control it was sacrilegious. As the Tracts continued, Newman's researches eventually led him from the Anglican Church toward Rome, culminating in the famous Tract 90, which demonstrated that nothing in the Thirty-Nine Articles of Anglicanism was contrary to Roman Catholic dogma. With this, the Anglican authorities came down on the Tractarians as heretics who were contaminating English youth. The Bishop of Oxford halted the publication of the Tracts, and Newman himself joined the Roman Catholic Church in 1845.

The final outcome of the Oxford Movement was a split between High and

question of scriptural authority for Episcopalianism, which the Oxonians had raised, and the doctrinal question of justification by faith, raised by the Calvinists, she felt that, in either case, the repression of earthly desires was necessary to enjoy eternal bliss. "I find," she wrote Miss Lewis, "as Dr. Johnson said respecting his wine, total abstinence much easier than moderation. . . . Oh that we could live only for eternity! that we could realize its nearness!" Part of George Eliot's maturation involved her recognition that suppression of earthly feeling is not equivalent to virtue, and repression of desire no sure road to salvation, or happiness.

As *Adam Bede* itself demonstrated, this break from strict religious doctrine did not occur suddenly, but was the result of much soul-searching and a great deal of reading. Before meeting the Brays and Hennell, whose influence was final, she followed very closely the arguments of the Oxford controversy, particularly those of Isaac Taylor, whose *Ancient Christianity and the Oxford Tracts* questioned three fundamental points in her own early re-

---

Broad Churchmen, with the triumph of the latter and the opening up of Oxford and Cambridge Universities to Dissenters and even to non-believers. In spiritual terms, the Movement awakened both clergy and flock to a new sense of tradition, reverence, and devotion that was to keep religious belief in the forefront of Victorian concerns. Tennyson's "In Memoriam," which catches the religious hopes and doubts of a "typical" Victorian, was itself started during the peak of the Oxford controversy.

With the advent of the German Higher Criticism of the Bible, English clergymen revived questions set into motion by the researches of the Tractarians. In particular, the publication in 1860 of *Essays and Reviews* set off an extensive controversy. Jowett's contribution, *On the Interpretation of Scripture*, asked why strict rules of criticism could not be applied to Biblical texts without loss of religious belief. The popularity of *Essays and Reviews* led the Church to try to convict two clergymen in church court, a sentence that was eventually reversed. At about the same time, Bishop Colenso of Natal questioned the historicity of the Pentateuch, concluding that the Mosaical books were based on legend. In the furor that followed, Colenso was excommunicated.

In a countering move, William Hurrell Mallock's *The New Republic* (1877) satirized this broadening movement in the Church as well as the scientific method of rationalists like Huxley and Tyndall. Even this late, then, when higher criticism, Darwinian evolution, and common sense seemed to call for a more liberal Church movement, there were serious attempts to hold the line of orthodoxy and tradition.

ligious beliefs: (1) her extreme asceticism, (2) her application of common sense to religious beliefs, and (3) her attempt to discover the relevance of church origin to belief. While the Oxford Tractarians examined the early Church to seek "Pure Christianity" before Rome became ascendant over the Church, Taylor tried to show that "pure Christianity" did not exist even before Roman control and must instead be sought in the Gospels, which, he said, were originally the basis for the Reformation. As one critic writes: "Thus Newman, examining Antiquity, finds it wanting and consequently becomes a Roman Catholic. At the same time Isaac Taylor looks at Antiquity, finds it wanting and adheres to Evangelical Protestantism." George Eliot herself, under Taylor's and Hennell's influence, was to abandon all theological dogma and, with Taylor, to question her previous exaltation of celibacy and the ascetic life. Self-suppression, which the young Dorothea Brooke considered a kind of exalted martyrdom, she found was not a good in itself, although she still accepted some personal prohibition if it served the welfare of others.

George Eiot's reading of Charles Hennell's *Inquiry Concerning the Origin of Christianity* (1838) helped her to replace God with duty and Christ with moral justice. Hennell's religious naturalism and his suggestion that many of the finer thoughts and feelings of mankind find their expression in fiction and poetry were intoxicating ideas to the young Evangelical, although Taylor had already started her on the road to rationalism and humanitarianism. The fact that all notions of miraculous revelation have disappeared, Hennell wrote, and that all hopes of Heaven have been reduced to mere speculation indicates that the individual now must strengthen his moral character through adversity and earthly duties. She read further in Hennell that one must discover "in the Universe itself a Son which tells us of a Father, and in all the natural beauty and moral excellence which meet us in the world in ever-present Logos, which reveals the grace and truth of its invisible grace." With that, she had fully emerged from the cocoon of provincialism that her early home life had imposed upon her.

As Gordon Haight points out, the influence of the Brays' radicalism also moved her from her father's Toryism and introduced her to the great social and political questions that had followed the

Reform Bill of 1832: Trades Unionism, Free Trade, Anti-Corn Law agitation, the growth of Chartism, the development of Cooperatives, the Young England movement, Catholic Emancipation, Socialism in England (Robert Owen's) and on the continent (Louis Blanc's). At the same time she knew the Brays, she was deep in her translation into English of David Strauss's *Leben Jesu,* one of the turning points in nineteenth-century religious thought. The mere fact that George Eliot, at twenty-four, would undertake the laborious translation of this example of German Higher Criticism suggests the extent of her independence from traditional orthodoxy.

In brief, Strauss rejected traditional religious belief as untenable in a scientific age and tried, instead, to find a viable "working" religion. Discarding both supernatural interpretation of Scripture and rationalist criticism which regarded Scripture as history, Strauss, like Hennell, sought a "natural" explanation for miracles and mysteries. He asserted that a belief in miracles is based in human nature rather than in the actual truth of the existence of miracles. Thus, because they are eternal human truths, miracles cannot be subjected to scientific analysis.* As Strauss wrote, in George Eliot's

* This very conflict—between human truth or intuition and scientific analysis or empiricism—was at the heart of the meetings of the Metaphysical Society, founded in 1869 and lasting until 1880. A loose outgrowth from the Cambridge Apostles in the 1820's, the Society became a distinguished forum for this most insistent of Victorian problems. Its membership included leading rationalists and scientists like Frederic Harrison, Sir James Stephen, John Morley, Thomas Henry Huxley, Leslie Stephen, John Tyndall; theists and churchmen like Cardinal Manning, James Martineau, Dean Stanley, W. G. Ward, F. D. Maurice, Gladstone, R. W. Church; critics, poets, and philosophers like Ruskin, Bagehot, Froude, Tennyson, Knowles. Browning, Mill, Newman, and Spencer were asked to join, but refused.

At the first meeting, Tennyson read his "Higher Pantheism," a poem that deduces a first cause from natural phenomena; that is, through nature, one sees the garment of God. At the third meeting, Huxley denied the immortality of the soul, revelation, and the whole vocabulary of spiritualism. These countering statements indicated the two opposite poles—the very points which Tennyson had set forth in *In Memoriam* (1850) and which became intensified in the decade after the publication of Darwin's *Origin of Species* (1859).

Darwin's book and its successor in 1871, *The Descent of Man,* intensified the soul-searching occasioned earlier on a smaller scale by Lyell's *Principles*

translation, "The supernatural birth of Christ, his miracles, his resurrection and ascension, remain eternal truths, whatever doubts may be cast on their reality as historical facts." These miracles exist as ideas, as if they were true, and mythical though they be, they are true ideas, true myths which stand not for matters of fact but for states of feeling. Christianity becomes, under these conditions, a product of the mind rather than a piece of history.

As we shall see, these ideas, only barely disguised, work themselves out in *Middlemarch*. Later, in the 1850's, when George Eliot translated Feuerbach's *Wesen des Christentums,* her intellectual horizons had broadened considerably through her position as sub-editor—virtually *the* editor—of the *Westminster Review*. Through this important journal, she met her future husband George Henry Lewes, as well as Carlyle, Dickens, Spencer, Cobden, and several other intellectual leaders, and came into intimate contact with the most exciting ideas of the century. The translation of Feuerbach fitted almost exactly into her own rapidly developing ideas, particularly the German critic's emphasis upon the divine being as nothing else than the human being, "or rather the human nature purified, freed from the limits of the individual man, made objective. . . ." As Basil Willey writes, with George Eliot distinctly in mind:

Feuerbach's work belongs to that powerful stream of tendency, flowing from Hegel to Marx, which was driving men deeper and deeper in upon themselves, and teaching them to discover in their own needs and longings as individuals, but above all as members of human society, the source and indeed the whole reality of the ideal worlds of thought and faith. Religion is simply a mirage, reflecting in shadow-pictures the real

---

of Geology (1831) and Chambers' *Vestiges of Creation* (1844). Darwin's findings were as revolutionary in their potential for the nineteenth century as Copernicus' discoveries in the sixteenth. The linkage of man to the animal species, as well as the determinism and mechanism implied in natural selection, created a sense of cosmic pessimism among Darwin's serious readers. More than merely upsetting traditional religious beliefs, *The Origin of Species* upset man's centrality and made him a minute (and therefore more democratic) figure in the vast passage of time. Along with commercialism, industrialization, and other similar forces, evolutionary biology now seemed to reduce man's grandeur and enclose him amidst forces he was powerless to resist.

tensions and discontents of earthly life . . . (*Nineteenth Century Studies*, p. 231).

As man replaces God—God literally *does* become Man in the incarnation, Feuerbach claims—so does love "transcend the difference between the divine and human personality." Further, Feuerbach felt that "if we do not sacrifice God to love, we sacrifice love to God." Thus, with Man, not God, as central in the universe, love between people becomes of paramount importance.

George Eliot's developing humanitarianism appears obvious. She had come to realize, to her own satisfaction, that to deny man is to deny religion and that to deny love—to suppress it or to consider it immoral—is to deny the God that is in man. One step further: love, therefore, not the priestly blessing, determines a marriage. Marriage must be, as Feuerbach writes, "spontaneously concluded, spontaneously willed, self-sufficing," or else it is not a true marriage or even a moral marriage. As she translated these lines in 1854, how important these ideas must have been to George Eliot who, at thirty-five, took the momentous decision to go to Germany with George Henry Lewes, now separated from his wife and children.

Perhaps no less momentous was Dorothea Brooke's decision to marry Will Ladislaw, because love dictated it, in the face of considerable opposition. The pattern of George Eliot's development through the 1840's and '50's did not fully work its way out in any of her novels until *Middlemarch*. Although Dinah Morris contains much of the early fervor, and Maggie Tulliver, as well as Romola, much of the early asceticism, only Dorothea Brooke has sufficient room to develop from an idealistic provincial more than willing to sacrifice herself into an experienced woman striving for personal happiness. At first eager to be sacrificed—Mario Praz has shrewdly compared many of George Eliot's heroines to the Blessed Virgin—Dorothea perceives that reality is not always arranged as a young and immature woman wishes it. Her ordeal, then, is to make intellectual truth agree with the truth of feeling. Her husband, after Casaubon, must suit both.

Considerably more of the effectiveness of *Middlemarch* depends upon the credibility of Dorothea's development than several critics have been willing to grant. Many have rightly praised the novel for its great density and variety, while deploring George Eliot's lack of success with her heroine. Yet, Dorothea, although not perhaps caught with the same delicate touch as (say) Gwendolen Harleth, is nevertheless strong enough to bear her share of a long novel. From the first page, when she is described "as being remarkably clever, but with the addition that her sister Celia had more common sense," and as having a mind that "was theoretic, and yearned by its nature after some lofty conception of the world," she is placed in the long line of romantic heroes and heroines whose awareness of reality rarely catches up with the roles they have idealized for themselves.

Before discussing Dorothea's character in detail, however, we should keep in mind that the story of Dorothea and the story of Lydgate, the unfortunate doctor whose vague passions and careless indifference nullify his intelligence, were conceived at different times and were to be published separately.* Originally, Lydgate was to be the center of *Middlemarch,* while Dorothea was the subject of a separate tale, called "Miss Brooke," unconnected to Lydgate or the novel. When, on August 5, 1869, George Eliot wrote the first chapter of *Middlemarch,* it was not the present first chapter concerning Dorothea; three days before, she noted that she had begun the Vincy and Featherstone parts. Not until sixteen months later is Dorothea mentioned in George Eliot's diary (December 2, 1870), still unrelated to the novel:

> I am experimenting in a story ["Miss Brooke"], which I began without any serious intention of carrying it out lengthily. It is a subject which has been recorded among my possible themes ever since I began to write fiction, but will probably take new shapes in the development. I am today at p. 44 (*Letters,* ed. Haight, V, 124).

Exactly what George Eliot meant by "experimenting" and by "new shapes" is difficult to determine, but speculation would suggest that "Miss Brooke" was to be a great advancement over her previous heroines, Dinah Morris, Maggie Tulliver, Romola, and

---

* An extended analysis of the development of *Middlemarch* can be found in Jerome Beaty's *Middlemarch from Notebook to Novel: A Study of George Eliot's Creative Method* (1960).

Esther Lyon. None of the four is really satisfying, for their limited habits of mind and their "virtuous" reactions to circumstances are obviously restrictive. "Miss Brooke," George Eliot's remarks would indicate, was to move in larger circles, perhaps to make mistakes like the others, but nevertheless to have sufficient ground on which to maneuver.

Dorothea's avid willingness to sublimate love for duty is a manifestation of ego, analogous to Meredith's Sir Willoughby Patterne's desire to redeem his social role at the expense of his self-respect. Indiscriminate self-denial can create as much vexation as egoism. Dorothea's ego, which makes her "enamoured of intensity and greatness, and rash in embracing whatever seemed to her to have those aspects; likely to seek martyrdom. . . .", frustrates the freeing power of the comic spirit. When she is barely out of her teens, her heroes are ascetics like Pascal, St. Augustine, and Milton, whom she would have married "when his blindness had come on." Ironically, she confuses Casaubon, who has weak eyes, with Milton and offers to learn classical languages in order to read to him. Her altruism is a kind of reverse egoism, for it forces her into moral judgments that in their harshness become anti-life. Very often she sounds like the priggish young Mary Ann (Marian) Evans who wrote that moderation was impossible, that only complete abstinence was tolerable. Her high moral judgment strangles honest feeling and vitiates common sense. Her need for principles stultifies necessary emotions and, as her correspondence with Casaubon shows, confuses the consecration of self with love.*

The quixotic Dorothea sets out, like the great Don, to tame the

---

* Speculation about George Eliot's source for Casaubon has fallen on several of her contemporaries. Mark Pattison (1813-84), Rector of Lincoln, Oxford, as well as biographer of Isaac Casaubon (1875), has often been cited. His wife has also been mentioned as a primary source of Dorothea, although George Eliot herself wrote: "She [Dorothea] is more like her creator than any one else and more so than any of her creations" (*Letters*, ed. Haight, V, 308, September 10, 1872). Gordon Haight (in *George Eliot and John Chapman, With Chapman's Diaries*, 1940) suggests Dr. R. H. Brabant —Hennell's father-in-law and a somewhat pretentious scholar—as a more likely original for the portrait. Probably, Casaubon combined the fussy characteristics of several of the scholars, critics, and teachers George Eliot encountered in literary and theological circles.

foolish and the frivolous, and to bring enlightenment to the Philistines while martyring herself to duty. Her romanticization of reality, like Marianne's in *Sense and Sensibility,* is the triumph of sensibility over sense. Dorothea, however, is more complicated than any of Jane Austen's heroines, whether deluded or not: compare, for example, Emma, whose path to maturity is strewn with relatively minor difficulties. On the other hand, Dorothea will submit only to what she respects, although this willingness is itself a display of pride; she desires to help other people, although this altruism itself does not make her happy; she despises self-indulgence, although she indulges her own self-righteousness and exalts the harshness of her moral principles; she is full of social sympathy, although she finally comes to see that realization of self is the mark of maturity; she at first desires a fatherly husband, one whose knowledge will immerse her in a serious world of great scholarship and literature, although she eventually must find happiness with a young man who, as a kind of fawn-like, comic imp, seems somehow much younger than she; she grasps after loftiness and intensity and confuses it with love, although she herself is unable to love when she marries Casaubon; she judges herself severely when she falls beneath her self-imposed standards, although, later, she repudiates many of her earlier standards and still judges herself severely; finally, she attempts to exorcise ego through good works, although each endeavor becomes itself a mark of ego. However, no matter what her illusions or delusions, Dorothea can recover from adversity through pain and suffering. As long as nothing comes easily, she can see her way clear to happiness.

George Eliot evidently never forsook her belief in the power of pain to drive out foolishness. Her somewhat pretentious remarks on the painful but moral effect of the Franco-Prussian War are particularly relevant to her attitude toward Dorothea. She wrote to Mme. Eugène Bodichon, an Englishwoman married to a French army surgeon:

I am very sorry for the sufferings of the French nation, but I think these sufferings are better for the moral welfare of the people than victory would have been. . . . in a great proportion of the French people there has been nourished a wicked glorification of selfish pride, which like all other conceit is a sort of stupidity, excluding any true conception of what lies outside their own vain wishes (*Letters*, ed. Haight, V, 113, August 25, 1870).

The heroine of her own romance, Dorothea is perhaps the first complex Victorian heroine, whose situation is further complicated because she has neither tradition nor parents to fall back upon. In commenting upon Jane Eyre, we remarked that while she was tortured by certain feelings of rebellion, her decision not to run away with Rochester was somewhat eased by her reliance on tradition: a decent girl does not violate the conventions of her society. These same conventions also apply to Jane Austen's heroines, with their slight divergence from convention providing the margin of her irony. In Dickens, the "heroine"—now necessarily in quotes—is so far caught by a conventional role that she becomes factitious and false. In Thackeray, Becky Sharp diverges far from convention because while within it she cannot obtain what she wants, but her easily-resolved moral promiscuity places her outside the area of serious conflict.

In her isolation from props that could support her, Dorothea Brooke, then, would seem to have no major predecessors in Victorian fiction. Watched over by a foolish uncle, whose wandering and tiresome remarks remind us of Mr. Woodhouse (*Emma*), she must make her own decisions and suffer through the consequences of her acts. Nowhere else in the Victorian novel are we made so aware that the main character must commit each act as though it were his final one. Nowhere else do we find a complex morality so closely connected to the power of immediate choice. Only George Meredith was to treat a similar theme, in *The Egoist*, published five years later. There Clara Middleton, also with a foolish father, must come to terms with herself, but her conflict is somewhat eased by the obvious truth of her own feelings. As far as *feelings* are concerned, she need not mature; her problem is to extract herself from a situation that she well recognizes is intolerable. She suffers little of the pain that Dorothea undergoes. As Clara's name indicates, she has clarity of purpose.

We can only speculate about how much of Dorothea's intricate problem George Eliot foresaw in "Miss Brooke." Perhaps these intricacies were to be the main ingredient of the experimentation she called attention to above. Perhaps, also, she had vaguely in mind the notion of interweaving Dorothea's story with Lydgate's, even though they were conceived separately and at first glance would seem to have little relevance to each other. Only a superficial reading, however, would fail to perceive that the two stories first parallel and then overlap each other, each darkening the potential tragedy of the other.

As with many other Victorian characters, marriage becomes the focal point of conflict. The decision here, particularly for a woman, is the chief decision she will make. With her mobility restricted and a career as such proscribed, a woman only gained her freedom in a liberating match. Although the male had greater maneuverability, marriage for him too, if he was to remain respectable, determined both the course of his success and the extent of his happiness. Lydgate is a male double of Dorothea: with his great hopes of personal success, he complements her desire for personal sacrifice. He too romanticizes his talents and forsakes the present for a goodlier future. Ironically, his ideals, like Dorothea's, and, incidentally, like Rosamond Vincy's, are in excess of his power and ability to realize them; and therefore disappointment, not inner success, is to be the chief mark of his career.

As Dorothea, lacking judgment, marries for mind alone, so, too, Lydgate, lacking judgment, marries for feeling alone. The two themes—conceived at different times and as separate stories—work effectively in counterpoint. In Book IV, titled "Three Love Problems," the three main lines of development become clear: Dorothea and Casaubon (also Dorothea and Will); Rosamond Vincy and Lydgate; and Mary Garth and Fred Vincy. Meanwhile other counterpointing elements are also in full operation: the hard-working Garths and the parvenu Vincys; the pseudo-respectable, hypocritical Bulstrode and the specter from his past, Raffles; the individualistic Will and a society which confuses individuality with eccentricity; the candidate Mr. Brooke and the Middlemarch voters; and, finally, the development of these lives against the background of the Middlemarch world itself, George Eliot's creation of a town-world which provides the setting, public opinion, and attitudes of the larger outer world.

Within the microcosm of Middlemarch, the connections among

the several characters help give the novel thickness, exactly as the connections between characters and town convey that sense of "rhythmic solidity" which constituted George Eliot's genius. One critic, Joan Bennett (*George Eliot: Her Mind and Her Art*), has demonstrated what now seems obvious: that in all of George Eliot's novels, except *Daniel Deronda,* the relationship between the individual and his background gives the narratives size and dimension. So too, the interrelationships among the principal characters convey the sense of intricate detail and motivated action and connect them in common sympathy or antipathy. Early in the novel, Casaubon reveals himself to be jealous of Dorothea and Will, and later this attitude recurs, in different form, when Lydgate is piqued by Rosamond and Will, and recurs still again, in another form, when Dorothea becomes jealous of Rosamond and Will.

Weakened by wrong marriages and frustrated by nagging memories of self-doubt and insufficiency, both Dorothea and Lydgate have begun to fall into apathy and moral stupidity. More than merely unhappy or dissatisfied with their choices, they are suffocated: Dorothea "felt with a stifling depression, that the large vistas and wide fresh air which she had dreamed of finding in her husband's mind were replaced by anterooms and winding passages. . . ." Similarly, Lydgate felt "there was constantly pressing not a simple weight of sorrow, but the biting presence of a petty degrading care, such as casts the blight of irony over all higher effort." He finds that marriage, rather than extending the possibilities of his ambition, has restricted not only success but also joy. Having screened marriage through his own ego, he, like Dorothea, entered it with closed eyes. And if Rosamond with her petty affectations makes a farce of his efforts, so Lydgate mocks his own pretensions by succumbing to her childish tears and blond curls. Driven by a false ideal—he carelessly assumed that a pretty skin covers a warm soul—Lydgate ventures into a trap from which there is no escape. As a final irony, he writes a treatise on gout; the great researcher has become a martyr to the middle class!

The presence of Will Ladislaw among this group—and perhaps the choice of his name was not fortuitous—in various ways sets them astir. As an outsider to Middlemarch society, Will is as

suspect to the townspeople as he is to the reader for being a romantic cliché: an altruistic idealist. If even the reader's sympathies,
abetted by George Eliot's partisanship, cannot make Will credible,
then it is understandable that he causes concern for Casaubon,
Dorothea, Rosamond, and Lydgate. Will is perhaps unbelievable
because he is created outside society, and George Eliot was only
able to create character *and* personality within a social milieu. If
we look ahead to a type suggested by Will, Daniel Deronda, we
see, again, a character who is removed from his natural atmosphere, and therefore a character who remains incomplete despite
the author's painstaking analysis of his motives and ambitions.

More interesting as an idea than as a person, Will is deracinated
(his foreign name), and seemingly indifferent (his mobility) and
frivolous (his lack of solid substance). As a contrast to the desic-
cated Casaubon, he appears the perpetual "young man"; as a
contrast, in Rosamond's eyes, to the unromantic Lydgate, he ful-
fills her dreams of a traditional Don Juan. To Dorothea herself,
he seems, for a time, to be all that she fears, a profligate who lacks
the high seriousness necessary for her friendship. Almost to the
very end of the novel, Will does seem to lack seriousness, to be too
much an outsider, to be too mobile and witty for the unlaughing
and somewhat stolid Dorothea. When, in Book IV, Dorothea reveals her benevolent humanitarianism, claiming that one must desire what is good even when it is unrecognizable, and by so doing
become "part of the divine power against evil," Will answers that
his religion is to "love what is good and beautiful when he sees it."
He refuses to be bound to what he does not like. Unlike Dorothea,
even in her liberation, he can remain outside of any fixed system.
Thus, although Will does recall George Henry Lewes—whose
common-law marriage to George Eliot seemed to have been made
in heaven—he does not suit Dorothea as much as Lydgate would
have.

Here, however, we recognize George Eliot's anti-romanticism,
for in failing to bring Dorothea and Lydgate together as a potentially marriageable couple, she emphasizes the nature of Lydgate's
tragedy and Dorothea's awakening. The romantic lines of the narrative would have demanded a conventional ending: a marriage of
Lydgate and Dorothea after considerable adversity, his high ser-

iousness matching her moral principles. With such an ending, the main thrust of Dorothea's narrative would not have been substantially changed. The first marriage would stand as an ordeal which matured her, as Lydgate's marriage to Rosamond, now disposed of in some way (perhaps death in childbirth), would have matured him.

Like Thackeray, and unlike Dickens, George Eliot did not believe in miracles. When Dobbin and Amelia Sedley finally marry in *Vanity Fair,* all joy is dead, the marriage being the natural outcome of a sequence of events rather than the continued affection of a couple mutually attached. Thackeray's anti-romanticism is evident, just as the realism of *Middlemarch* was never more apparent than in Lydgate's unhappiness. But if George Eliot gained realism by depicting the tragedy of Lydgate's situation, she also struck a false, not an ideal, note when she resolved the attachment of Dorothea and Will, based as the relationship appears to be on seemingly unsuitable characters. In these terms, Will is more a savior of Dorothea than a lover, a young Lochinvar who will lead her from duty to happiness; and George Eliot knew that saviors are mythical, not realistic. Will, in any case, amply serves his function as a counter-force—he brings joy to Dorothea and exemplifies George Eliot's own moral liberation, her will to happiness despite temporary adversity.

Inevitably, someone had to be punished or the novel would pass into pure romance. Perhaps because Lydgate's choice of Rosamond is more devastating than Dorothea's of Casaubon, he must be smothered while she recovers. Perhaps the indictment of Lydgate's loss of will is stronger because Rosamond is such a simpering and affected fool, while Casaubon, despite his wizened spirit, attains some tragic standing. Inflated with desires beyond her means to command, Rosamond is all ego. Brought up above her merchant-class birth, she romanticizes Lydgate, admiring not the man but his gentlemanly manner and origin, just as Dorothea romanticizes Casaubon into a balding eagle instead of recognizing him as a rachitic sparrow.

As a more respectable descendant of Hetty Sorel, Rosamond has the confidence of the ignorant and the frivolity of the pampered. Her judgment is based upon selfishness and her "love" upon personal ambition. Less attractive than Hetty (because, unlike the dairy girl, she is not artless), Rosamond receives the brunt of George Eliot's attack upon provincial vanity and nouveau-riche affectation. Her influence upon Lydgate, not unlike Arabella's upon Jude in Hardy's novel, enervates his ambition and debilitates his powers of concentration, although his original choice of her reveals *his* weakness.

Even though Lydgate and Dorothea are often close in temperament and attitude, their tastes in marriage could not be more different, the former for passion, the latter for ennoblement. Casaubon's note of proposal, with its offer of an unsullied mind, is bereft of love, bereft even of any sign of affection, based as it is on the terms of a marriage of convenience. Casaubon's scrupulosity, his pride, his discipline all seem aspects of a great ego as grasping as Sir Willoughby's, until George Eliot did what Meredith was unable to do: gain favor for the egoist while showing the pitiful empty shell of the man. Casaubon, literally, has nothing to give, and yet he has the sensitivity of a man fully alive to every nuance of a potentially ridiculous situation. *He* knows, even if Dorothea does not, that an old man and a young girl are the source of mockery, or at least whispers; that only discipline can maintain the control prerequisite for dignity. Yet, he must provide some further mark of respect for his young bride, and here his great project is to do what the man cannot. Nevertheless, even to him, the great scheme recedes as the categories and details accumulate. His key to all mythologies is the product of a small mind, for Casaubon sees only minutiae, not philosophical ideas. The project is, in reality, mock-heroic. The pretentious topic itself sufficiently ridicules Dorothea's presumption in marrying a would-be Milton.

Here, with all the ingredients of a cruel tale, George Eliot demonstrates how sympathy and compassion can be transformed into art. For even as Dorothea recognizes Casaubon's frailty, as she recognizes her tremendous error in judgment and recognizes that her character has been her fate, she softens in her attitude toward him. Her early criticism of him—criticism that no amount of tenderness or submission could have disguised—is qualified by her realization of his weakness and her recognition of her own strength. Thus, Dorothea *grows* in understanding as the result of a foolish marriage. Through pity and loyalty, both of which develop into real human concern, she loses her early romanticism and begins to see the world as it is. As much as Lydgate is reduced by his marriage, so Dorothea matures through hers. The cross-currents of these conflicts result in a particularly effective doubling and paralleling of character and scene. The recurrence at different intervals of various aspects of the same situation, be it a foolish marriage or a strained relationship, sets up its own rhythms, establishes its own pace, ultimately dictates its own rules.

As we have seen, George Eliot was able to create characters against their background with a success perhaps unequaled by any Victorian novelist except the Thackeray of *Vanity Fair*. Even Dickens seems least successful with characters who stay inside their expected social roles. Through exaggeration and adroit use of chiaroscuro, he partially disguised the essentials of realism that George Eliot hoped to retain through selectivity. Nevertheless, hers is not the naturalist's method of accumulating massive detail, but the realist's way of including only what is necessary, physically and psychologically, to give the feeling of life. One is reminded of her remark that her *treatment* is the difference. Unlike Dickens, she rarely lost sight of the total vision while she pursued details, frequently achieving a tightness and unity that Dickens gained only in his somewhat shorter novels like *Great Expectations*. Dickens often simplified or distorted social types to gain a particular emphasis, while George Eliot emphasized everything that would *not* simplify a social type, that would convey both the type and the individual—what we mean when we say she foreran the contemporary psychological novel.

Only Thackeray in *Vanity Fair* was able to transform the singleness of personal desires into the multiplicity of a social event, until both seem united as cause and effect, as personality and situation. In Thackeray, as in George Eliot, the particular becomes a mode of definition. In *Middlemarch* itself, the precision of details enhances the reality of character and situation. Real people live in a real town. Perhaps the very concreteness of this and George Eliot's other novels caused Virginia Woolf to mistake solidity for stolidity when she remarked that George Eliot's mind was too cumbersome for satire. Nevertheless, detail builds up background and minor characters. We are always brought back to the fact that *Middlemarch* is a study of provincial life, the history of a town which gives sustenance to its inhabitants.*

Within *Middlemarch,* George Eliot catches a cross-section of the social types who inhabit a provincial town. The Vincys, with their pretensions to gentility and breeding, exemplify the pre-Victorian family on the rise from merchant class to middle-class respectability. Each member of the family, Mr. Vincy, his wife, and his well-meaning but dissolute son Fred, indicates perfectly the style of his class, yet remains individualized; and when Rosamond is developed, she too retains the broad attitudes of her class as well as the features which distinguish her. Similarly, the Garths, related to the Vincys by family connection but not by attitude, represent those who remain fixed in their integrity, those who refuse to substitute presumption for sincerity. From this background, Mary Garth comes forth, honest, practical, natural, and perceptive. In her awareness of duty and discipline, she knows she must seek her own type of happiness, perceiving that romance is the affectation of a flaccid mind unable to focus on reality.

While the Garths resist social hypocrisy and the Vincys assume hypocritical attitudes to advance their position, Bulstrode is hypocritical about his unsavory past. His is of course the more insidious posture, for he dons a religious mask to disguise a basically corrupt self. Perhaps Bulstrode is sincere in his religious beliefs, but nevertheless his self-righteousness is the defense of a man lacking compassion or understanding. His former sins are not so immense that George Eliot would have denied him forgiveness had he relieved his conscience and sincerely repented. But Bulstrode's hypocrisy—here like Featherstone's monomania and the Vincys' desire

---

* In *North and South* (1855), Mrs. Gaskell foreshadowed in miniature many of George Eliot's devices in *Middlemarch,* particularly in her use of a northern English manufacturing town as background for her characters. Also, Mrs. Gaskell's Margaret Hale—as Jane Austen's Emma before her and Dorothea Brooke after—must mature to an understanding of her own self before she can emerge as a full human being. The reader's admiration for George Eliot grows when he compares *Middlemarch* to a solid workmanlike novel like *North and South* and sees how her grasp of character and situation, her ability to interweave people and place, transcended Mrs. Gaskell's own mature achievement.

for respectability—is indicative of an ego full of the selfishness that destroys equitable social life.

In the intricacies of town life, egoism is treacherous because it spreads and engulfs even the idealistic and innocent. Thus, Lydgate is sucked into Bulstrode's plans and becomes suspected as an accomplice in the death of Raffles. As "Bulstrode's man," his ideals are compromised and his hopes become expedient gestures. The great expectations of nearly all are smashed. The town itself forces a kind of stabilizing effect on those who would digress from certain invisible norms; not only individuals but the entire community circumscribes both expansion and foolishness, and democratically imposes a kind of dull mediocrity. When a person has his roots planted solidly in society, he must develop the way society permits him: the lay of the land often determines the slant of growth.

In these terms, Dorothea must exchange her romantic sense of duty for personal happiness only by flouting society as well as all her previous beliefs; Lydgate must compromise his great plans to find success ultimately as an expert on the gout; Bulstrode finds all his philanthropy and righteousness defeated by gossip that never allows him to escape his past; Rosamond must have her confidence shattered by the criticism of others before she can re-establish her equilibrium; Fred Vincy must be severely chastised by disappointment before he can gain Mary Garth; Casaubon must recognize that his great work will not be completed and that his young bride no longer idealizes him; even Mr. Brooke—a Victorian Mr. Woodhouse—must lose his election and become a figure of mockery. Of the major characters, only Will Ladislaw escapes the crushing of his expectations, but he is isolated from the life of Middlemarch. His removal from town life is his way of escaping its influence, but also the reason for his insubstantiality.

Lest, however, *Middlemarch* seem more tragic than the facts warrant, we should remember George Eliot's words just before Book IV was published: "I need not tell you [Alexander Main, a friend] that my book will not present my own feeling about human life if it produces on readers whose minds are really receptive the impression of blank melancholy and despair" (March 29, 1872). An expression of outright despair, George Eliot felt, would overbalance one aspect of life at the expense of broad realism. It would also entail a kind of preaching that undermines artistic attainment. Several years before she started *Middlemarch,* she said that artistic teaching is the highest of all teaching, because it deals with life in its highest complexity. But if it "ceases to be purely aesthetic—if it lapses anywhere from the picture to the diagram—it becomes the most offensive of all teaching."

The "diagram" for George Eliot would be the presentation of sheer, unrelieved despair or melancholy. The "picture," as we receive it in her best novels, retains the solidity of a balanced view of life, or as balanced as her powers could achieve. That George Eliot is not with the supreme creators—Dante, Tolstoy, Sophocles, Shakespeare, Dostoyevsky, or even Dickens—is obvious; for despite the thick texture of her realistic "picture," she lacked their vision and variety. Nevertheless, she stands as a giant among nineteenth-century English novelists for her ability to probe into human motivation, and to derive from cause and effect not the restrictive tones of the naturalist but the richer comment of the comic-tragedian in whom compromise, smashed hopes, and a possibly limited happiness are the stuff of lives filled with adversity and duty.

NINE

Thomas Hardy's "Mayor"
and the Changing Novel

nless a novelist can raise drabness to metaphysical torment or the ordinary to cosmic hilarity, he is doomed to
mediocrity. In *The Mayor of Casterbridge,* as well as in
Jude the Obscure, Tess of the D'Urbervilles, and *The
Return of the Native,* Thomas Hardy was able to transform insignificant details into cosmic importance, so that trivialities expand
into great moments. Even though Hardy's prose rarely sparkles,
part of his success lies, curiously, in his use of language. Its di-
rectness and sincerity, its sense of unwavering truth, its refusal to
compromise with the vision it conveys all make it suggest more
than at first seems possible. Hardy constructed a world in which
universal unhappiness and despair appear to be the natural consequence of having been born.

If the above description seems to fit Kafka more than Hardy,
that is the result of the latter's peculiar kind of realism. As he
noted in 1880: "Romanticism will exist in human nature as long
as human nature itself exists. The point is (in imaginative literature) to adopt that form of romanticism which is the mood of the
age." Hardy's romanticism was not that of Stevenson or early
Conrad, no more than his realism was that of Zola or Gissing. Although Hardy's roots, like Meredith's and George Eliot's, were
solidly within a nineteenth-century intellectual framework—a
pre-Freudian world of Darwin, Spencer, and Huxley—nevertheless, his characters and plots obviously move in a sphere unknown
to his contemporaries, an area of personal anxiety and neurosis
that no other Victorian, excepting Dickens in some aspects, had
attempted to define. Hardy's mixture of romantic realism is pe-

culiarly close to that of Flaubert in France; while both eschewed
the strict realism of the naturalist, each skirted a sentimental or
romantic conception of character and plot. What they cultivated
instead was a kind of symbolic realism in which the actual fact
exists prosaically but can nevertheless be projected far beyond the
immediate historical situation.

When Hardy wrote in 1886 that his "art is to intensify the expression of things . . . so that the heart and inner meaning is
made vividly visible," * he foreshadowed Conrad's famous definition of realism: "by the power of the written word to make you
hear, to make you feel—it is, before all, to make you *see*." This
kind of realism entails, among other things, a new type of protagonist and a new way of developing scenes: one finds, for example, characters and scenes that relate to the narrative on both
a nonrealistic and realistic basis, in the same way that some of
the seemingly nonfunctional passages work in Conrad's major
novels and in Lawrence's *The Rainbow* and *Women in Love*. To
define Hardy's realism, particularly that of *The Mayer of Casterbridge,* is to reveal a major turning point in the development of the
English novel: the novel is no longer solely an important social
document but has become as well a significant psychological history.

Hardy once remarked that "Coleridge says, aim at *illusion* in
audience or readers—*i.e.,* the mental state when dreaming, inter-
mediate between complete *delusion* (which the French mistakenly
aim at) and a clear perception of falsity." † In this "suspension of

---

* Quoted in Florence Hardy, *The Early Life of Thomas Hardy, 1840-1891,*
pp. 231-232.
† *Ibid.,* p. 197. Five years before *The Mayor of Casterbridge,* Hardy set
down some notes on fiction, apparently for an article never written, which
reveal a good deal about the planning that went into *The Mayor.* "The real,
if unavowed, purpose of fiction is to give pleasure by gratifying the love of
the uncommon in human experience, mental or corporeal. . . . The writer's
problem is, how to strike the balance between the uncommon and the ordinary so as on the one hand to give interest, on the other to give reality. In
working out this problem, human nature must never be made abnormal,
which is introducing incredulity. The uncommonness must be in the events,
not in the characters; and the writer's art lies in shaping that uncommon-

disbelief," Hardy found a way both of raising the implausible to a philosophic system and demonstrating that art is a "disproportioning" of reality. As aware as George Eliot that the realism of the naturalist is not art, Hardy used chance as a way of infusing "imaginative realism" into his narratives, for chance not only suggested something supernatural, but it also fitted the terms of his own beliefs.

In *The Mayor of Casterbridge,* as well as in his other major novels, chance becomes a universal symbol of Hardy's personal philosophy; what he calls chance is everything over which man has no control. Although man's will is not nullified by chance, neither can will itself overcome chance; the latter is, in its functioning, the will of the universe, what Hardy, in his long narrative poem, *The Dynasts,* later called the Immanent Will. This force operates in the world without conscious design; even though it is not a controlling force, in that it does not direct man, it frequently seems to evoke more malignity than benevolence. Hardy's view evidently derived directly or indirectly from Schopenhauer's definition of will as ethically evil, the force that causes and sustains pain. For Schopenhauer as well as Hardy, life is made to seem futile, a period full of mere glimpses of happiness in an expanse of pain. There is no escape except through nullification of the will, for unfulfilled wishes cause pain, while attainment of desire brings disgust.

Hardy claimed, notwithstanding, that chance is not a sinister intelligence, that it can work either for good or evil. With Michael Henchard, chance seems more apparently sinister because he lacks proportion and balance, is himself *sinister* in the original sense of the word. That Henchard—and also Jude, Clym Yeobright, Tess, and Eustacia Vye—happens to be constituted *this* way is, however, of no consequence to the principle of chance. Each may have been completely different, Hardy suggests, but, except for Tess, each would still have become a victim, because each is obsessed by inexplicable forces that waste his energies. As

---

ness while disguising its unlikelihood, if it be unlikely" (Florence Hardy, p. 193).

D. H. Lawrence, with some disappointment, noted, Hardy "used" chance as a way of punishing his social deviates, while at the same time claiming that chance is an indifferent force.

Lawrence, however, was really arguing for his own brand of rebellion and aggressiveness. Hardy's point is different, perhaps more complex, and certainly more consistent. His emphasis on chance and the Immanent Will places his characters in curiously existential situations that ring true on several levels. One of the results of a chance-filled universe is the creation of anxiety-ridden individuals who, futilely or not, must each seek his own identity in a maze of possibilities. *Identity* is the key word in *The Mayor:* who is the father? who is the daughter? what is the allegiance of each? who can rely on what forces? Closely connected to the theme of identity in the novel is the pervasive theme of deception. Even if one intends good will (or *bonne foi,* as Sartre called it), it can easily be dissipated in a universe in which deception is a condition of existence. Under such circumstances, the will is made indifferent or neutral, even nullified.

In *The Mayor* nearly all human relationships are based on precisely such deceptions. Henchard is not Elizabeth-Jane's father, yet leads her to believe he is. Elizabeth-Jane is not his daughter, but thinks she is. Susan, although she knows differently, allows Henchard to believe that Elizabeth-Jane is his daughter. Lucetta deceives Farfrae about her past, as she deceives Henchard about her marriage. Henchard has deceived the townspeople about *his* past, as much as later he deceives Lucetta about his former relationship to Susan. In such relationships, the character's true identity cannot be clear to the reader, is often unclear to himself. Only Farfrae (his name implies his distance from the fray) is far from this deception, but even he is deceived by Lucetta. Only the fact that he does not think or probe too deeply saves him.

The possibility that something new may indifferently turn up to unbalance a seemingly stable situation is close to the absurd universe that the existentialists posit. The prime tenet of such a universe is that one may count on little, often on nothing. Anything is possible, plausible, probable. All those given, accepted facts one usually takes for granted are removed, or else become hostile in unfamiliar contexts. Each situation requires a new posture, a new response.

Thus, a good deal of Henchard's seemingly placid acceptance of his lot—strikingly close in this respect to the attitude of Camus' Meursault—is the consequence of the absurdity of his situation. If the existential absurd is broadly analogous to the Freudian unconscious, then we can see that Henchard can never consciously find or fix his bearings. If he seems to acquiesce too easily to his worsening situation, we remember that he is reacting to something absurd that drags him under, as if it were a pull from his unconscious. In a way, the absurd is both within and without; it is found in the Immanent Will of the universe and in the recessive depths of the individual.

As we shall see, the duplication of characters and situations that occurs so frequently complements the deceptive actions of the main characters. Deception of course entails a dual situation—the ostensible one and the underlying one; similarly, duplication entails a multiple play of action. In *The Mayor* the character-duplications are evident: Henchard's "two daughters," Elizabeth-Jane's "two fathers," Susan's "two husbands," Lucetta's "two lovers," Farfrae's "two wives," Henchard's double past and his double life. The duplication of scenes is also ever-present: Henchard meets Lucetta where he met Susan, in the vast amphitheatre; he leaves Casterbridge as a trusser, as poor as he entered it; he arrives in Weydon-Priors twice; he faces the furmity woman twice, and each time is destructive to his fortunes. The possibilities for duplication are seemingly endless, as though Hardy were working with musical motifs which must reappear at the introduction of each theme. However, it becomes clear that the doubling elements are less musical than philosophical: that Hardy has used duplication, as before deception, as a whole mode of being for modern man. People reappear, situations recur, ideas duplicate themselves as a way of forcing the power of circumstance upon man. If as Hardy claimed character is fate, then man must reassert himself, events must recur, situations must be repeated. Man is never free of his past; the contemporary Fury is the individual's unconscious.

Thus, Hardy's "philosophy of chance"—if carried to this extent—evokes several modern responses. While its form is still Victorian, its point cuts deeply into post-Freudian ideas, and it shares many points in common with modern existential beliefs. While certainly neither original nor consistent, it did allow Hardy to move from the realistic-romantic nineteenth-century mold into his unique expression of changing values. Like any valid psychological or existential insight, it allows the formulation of a universal truth. Many of Hardy's readers are put off by his chance-filled universe; but on the contrary, it appears that a reliance on chance is a reliance on all those factors which the conscious self cannot control. Certainly now, seventy-five years after the publication of *The Mayor,* it is impossible to doubt Hardy's premise: that unseen, inexplicable forces operate which counter or obviate what the will commands. If Hardy learned anything from the classic Greek dramatists, he learned this.

In *The Mayor of Casterbridge,* the unreality, even the absurdity, of a chance-filled world is at once indicated in the fable-like beginning, with its simple evocation of distance and timelessness. Hardy writes:

One evening of late summer, before the nineteenth century had reached one-third of its span, a young man and woman, the latter carrying a child, were approaching the large village of Weydon-Priors, in Upper Wessex, on foot. They were plainly but not ill clad, though the thick hoar of dust which had accumulated on their shoes and garments from an obviously long journey lent a disadvantageous shabbiness to their appearance just now.

The straightforward, matter-of-fact style conveys both the immediate setting and the potential doom awaiting the couple. They walk along the road together, yet alone, and their isolation here foreshadows their inability to connect personally, even though later they do remarry. The fact is, Henchard must always be alone and isolated ("his taciturnity was unbroken, and the woman [Susan] enjoyed no society whatever from his presence"). She and he walk to the fair-grounds unknown and unknowingly, only to be separated even further there by his perverse act of selling her and the child. Later, the still isolated Henchard enters Casterbridge, painfully builds up a business alone, tries unsuccessfully to win a friend in Farfrae, unsuccessfully woos Lucetta, then remarries Susan, who is dutiful but unloving, tries unsuccessfully to win Elizabeth-Jane as his daughter, and gradually loses each in turn, leaving Casterbridge as alone, stripped, and alienated as when he entered.

Henchard's rashness of temperament and lack of moderation, leading to bursts of anti-social behavior while he is drunk, do not by themselves adequately explain his character. In his bull-like strength (Hardy emphasizes his physical strength in the fight with Farfrae), in his inability to love (he offers marriage, but never love), in his need to humilate himself (among other things, his marriage with Susan lowers him in public opinion), in his antiheroic tendencies (he rises in stature as, paradoxically, he demeans himself)—in all of these Henchard is more an inexplicable force than a frail human. Like Conrad's Lord Jim, he seems himself to choose the terms of his victimizing, and yet he is unable to help himself—the kinds of forces that will destroy him are, Freud indicated, too deep in the unconscious to manifest themselves in easily recognizable form. Henchard's quest is to pursue a course of action that will satisfy both his destructive drives and the overt desires of his social life. He is, Hardy suggests, a man obsessed by a single passion and, therefore, a man doomed in a world that rewards flexibility. Chance will always victimize him.

Farfrae's balance and flexibility are suggested not only by his name but by his musical ability; he is truly in harmony with the world and can make it bow to his tune. It is not fortuitous that at his first appearance in the Three Mariners he wins over the guests, who judge him a good fellow, albeit a foreigner. His songs indicate that he is the correct mixture of romanticism and realism: when necessary he can turn each on and off. While Henchard as it were sulks in his tent, Farfrae sings and dances. In his flexibility Farfrae is in tune with the music of the spheres, while in his alienation Henchard must remain discordant and gruff. Perhaps part of our distaste for Farfrae (which Hardy perhaps would not share) is based on his graceful ease in attuning himself to the tones of the world, whereas Henchard in his bear-like massiveness stumbles and flounders at every turn.

By moving at the extremes of behavior which he himself cannot understand, Henchard recalls in part, among Hardy's earlier contemporaries, Dickens's Steerforth (*David Copperfield*) and Bradley Headstone (*Our Mutual Friend*) and foreshadows Conrad's Lord Jim, Gide's Lafcadio and Michel, Camus' Meursault, and several of Mann's artists, each of whom is obsessed by demons that they fail to recognize, although all perceive that there is something within they must control. When control, nevertheless, becomes impossible, they commit acts which directly or indirectly injure others and which also lay the groundwork for their own destruction. Only Dickens among other major nineteenth-century English novelists was aware of the self-destructive demons nourished within an otherwise respectable and controlled individual, although he, like Hardy after him, was unable to account for them.

Hardy's other immediate predecessors and contemporaries, Thackeray, George Eliot, and Meredith, were so far committed to a "normal" world that they avoided all extremes of social behavior; but Hardy, like Dickens in his later novels, attempted to create a society in which the extremist, what Dostoyevsky considered the criminal or underground man and later French novelists the rebel, clashed with the social norm. Hardy differed from Dickens, however, by concerning himself *primarily* with what happened to the radical who is the potential criminal and rebel: Henchard, Jude, Clym, Eustacia, and all those who are destroyed by their intransigence and/or their obsession with a single mode of behavior. Moreover, since they are unable to help themselves, Hardy's world seems excessively cruel, even antagonistic to individual needs, a world in which chance becomes a malevolent rather than an indifferent force. Yet the savagery of Hardy's world—in which continued cruelty, pain, and suffering become the norm for his heroes and heroines—is merely a reflection of man's insignificance when he attempts to exert more force than he has or tries to function without self-understanding. Hardy's protagonist usually means well and is, like Henchard, basically decent. But as Albert Guerard has pointed out, his obsessions are clearly uncontrollable—like Gide's and Malraux's protagonists, as well as Conrad's Jim and Kurtz, he must defy the restrictions placed upon him, and in his defiance lies the stuff of his self-destruction.

Henchard's fixed, linear behavior further strengthens the fable or fairy-tale atmosphere that surrounds the narrative, with its seeming simplification of character development, and also becomes the substance of Hardy's "symbolic realism." The Fair scene itself, with its readers of Fate, its games of chance, its auctions of animals, its waxworks and peep shows and conning medical men, with its hag-like furmity woman, who, like a *Macbeth* witch, stirs her large pot, is a timeless symbol of man's irrational quest for pleasure in a grim world of expedience. Moreover, at a Fair, anything goes; normal behavior is no longer adhered to, and eccentricity can itself become the norm. In Freudian terms, the id can here triumph over (or force out) the censorship of the superego, and man's ego, his ultimate behavior, is deflected into cruel acts both to his loved ones and to himself. Thus, the relatively simple act of auctioning horses at the Fair becomes an unambiguous foreshadowing of Henchard's sale of Susan, and the swallow circling through the tent trying to escape is an obvious reference to Henchard's desire to escape a marriage that he claims has bound him in penury. The Fair, then, assumes its traditional significance: a place where people are liberated from personal cares and freed from their daily burdens. Like the quickly curving swallow, Henchard is to fly from the tent alone.

Escape itself becomes, ironically, a form of isolation that Henchard can never avoid; and the sordid business at the Fair becomes the terms both of his freedom and his thralldom. When he sells Susan, that act is the only one in which *he* throws off another human being; the rest of the novel finds him "being sold" and thrown off. Hardy remarks: "Henchard's wife was dissevered from him by death; his friend and helper Farfrae by estrangement; Elizabeth-Jane by ignorance." Moreover, Lucetta leaves him for marriage with Farfrae; the sailor Newson returns to claim Elizabeth-Jane; the town itself casts him out as Mayor. Further, one part of Henchard is dissociated from the other, so that his personality is split, a split manifest on the surface as the sober part and the drunken part, but of course the division goes far deeper. Hardy evidently lacked the psychological equipment to analyze the double role that grips Henchard, although his artistic suggestion of the type is psychologically true. Conrad, in *Lord Jim,* likewise lacked the analytical knowledge, but he was able to create a "true" type: in Jim, the split occurs between his romantic ideals and his realistic situations, and his tragedy is his inability to reconcile the two. Henchard's tragedy, similarly, is his inability to reconcile drunkenness (romance) and sobriety (realism). The self-destructive Henchard cannot perceive that the latter preserves while the former destroys.

Henchard's isolation from himself is given nearly exact definition in Hardy's use of several overlapping scenes that both indicate his alienation and emphasize the element of fable. Man is split and isolated, first, by his juxtaposition to surroundings that dwarf his stature and diminish his spirit. In Chapter 19, for example, Henchard gazes at the cliffs outside Casterbridge and his eyes alight on a square mass of buildings cut into the sky. Hardy describes the bulky monument as a pedestal missing its statue, the missing element significantly being a corpse; for the buildings were once the county jail, their base forming the gallows where crowds would gather to watch executions. This passage occurs soon after Henchard has read Susan's letter telling him that Elizabeth-Jane is not his daughter, Henchard having recently tried to convince the girl that she is his. Then, after Henchard learns the facts, Newson's daughter comes to him and says that she does accept him as her father. We recognize that the missing corpse is the doomed Henchard, trapped between uncontrollable forces, one part trying to gain love and life, the other, unable to effect an attachment, caught by death. Like the Captain in Strindberg's *The Father* (1887)—another man also snared in the tightening coils of wife and daughter—Henchard has to discover exactly what he is and what is his: who is the father? who is the daughter? His family unsettled, the Captain dies in madness, while Henchard expires abandoned to his masochism.

This powerful scene in which the split Henchard foresees his own doom recurs in a different context when, after the cruel mummery, the despondent and suicidal outcast thinks of drowning in the river as a solution to his misery. The sight, however, of his straw effigy floating in the water—the same effigy that had horrified Lucetta and caused her fit—suggests his own death, acts out, as it were, a substitute death, and dissuades him. "Not a man somewhat resembling him, but one in all respects his counterpart, his actual double, was floating as if dead in Ten Hatches Hole." The supernatural aspect of the sight impresses Henchard, and, ironically, the effigy, which in another way has helped destroy him, here saves his life. "That performance of theirs killed her [Lucetta], but kept me alive."

"Supernatural" aspects of the fable further appear when man is enclosed in a historical setting that indicates his fate. The Roman amphitheatre at Casterbridge serves the purpose of a meeting-ground and at the same time frames the puny dimensions of puppet-like man against a mighty historical past. Henchard, who has been heroic amidst the townspeople, is now diminished by the immensity of the amphitheatre where he meets Susan; and their immediate problems, when viewed against the melancholy background, seem petty indeed.

This kind of scene recurs in various forms: it appears, as we saw, when Henchard gazes at the Franciscan priory with its gallows and missing corpse; it reappears with intended irony near the end of the novel in the form of the pre-historic fort, Mai-Dun, where Henchard hides, telescope in hand, to spy on Farfrae and Elizabeth-Jane. The fort is described as "of huge dimensions and many ramparts, within or upon whose enclosures a human being, as seen from the road, was but an insignificant speck." Here, Henchard, already in decline because of his personal losses, squanders even his physical dimensions, dwarfed as he is by the fort and made to seem still smaller by the meanness of his objective— to scan the Roman *Via* for the two lovers. Then the amphitheatre itself recurs as a meeting-place for Henchard and Lucetta, the successor to Susan; within the huge enclosure, her pathetic figure revives in his soul "the memory of another ill-used woman who had stood there . . . [so that] he was unmanned." As they meet, the sun rests on the hill "like a drop of blood on an eyelid," a half-closed eyelid which sees reality only absently, masked as the latter is by personal ambition and willful revenge. His strength drained, the once heroic Henchard finds his revengeful feeling for the woman turning to pity and disdain amidst the hugeness of their overwhelming enclosure.

Not only is man insignificant and absurdly pathetic in relation to natural surroundings, Hardy suggests, but also in his contacts with uncontrollable human forces. The reappearance of the furmity woman, that Fate who reveals the iniquity of Henchard's past, indicates how limited his career can be once he has offended the order of the universe. He bends to his burden, and like Oedipus, he expands spiritually as he declines physically. Further, his reliance on the weather-prophet, a person deep within superstition, exemplifies Henchard's growing insecurity and also puts him at the mercy of a human interpretation of the uncertain elements. That Henchard should rely on a fabulous prophet, who, mysteriously, seems to be expecting him, demonstrates his recurring fears now that Farfrae opposes him. The "hero" can no longer rely on his own devices and by taking counsel from a false prophet wills a destiny that crushes him. The furmity woman and the weather-prophet "destroy" Henchard on the fable level as much as Farfrae, Lucetta, Elizabeth-Jane, Susan, and the town itself nullify him on the realistic level. Split by the two forces, Henchard is indeed trapped.

Hardy had the poetic ability, as Lawrence did after him, to suggest the whole in every part, to bring into each scene a miniature of the entire work. This is particularly evident in *The Mayor of Casterbridge,* where the structure is tight, the plot limited to essentials, and the main characters few. One recognizes the novel's stylization in the anti-realism of implausible events, in the evident symbolic patterns, and in the poetic evocation of characters and events. Albert Guerard has commented that at the poetic and imaginative level Hardy is capable of tragedy, although when he thinks philosophically he seems commonplace and his limitations become obvious. His finest scenes, frequently, are those in which "pure thought" does not dominate, scenes which remain close to a fable tradition and can be suggested poetically rather than realistically.

Unlike George Eliot and Thackeray, whose obvious forte was

realism, Hardy, like Conrad and Lawrence, was more at home when he could avoid a head-on realistic scene and, instead, evoke the conflict obliquely. He could, so to speak, be true to human feeling but not to human truth. Lacking the philosophical orderliness of George Eliot and Thackeray's uniformity of viewpoint, as well as the sheer vivacity of Dickens and Meredith, Hardy retreated to the oddities of life which determine man's frail existence. Thus, as we suggested above, his reliance on cosmic irony and the chance occurrences of implausible events bolstered his way of working; for a dependence on chance enabled him to touch his subject, as it were, from the side and gave philosophical substance to his oblique attacks upon complacency, deviation, and immoderation. Chance, in effect, was his weapon to strike through surface reality to areas where the poetry of men offers resistance to the drab starkness of a malevolent universe.

We can see, then, that certain short but powerful scenes fulfill Hardy's genius, although they may well seem peripheral or fanciful to the unsympathetic reader. In Chapter 29, for example, Lucetta and Elizabeth-Jane encounter a rambling bull, whose uncertainty seems to be theirs as well as Henchard's. The bull proves to be dangerous, an old cranky one, and uncontrollable except by an experienced hand. It begins to pursue the two women, the air from its nostrils blowing fear over them, until Henchard runs up, seizes the stick attached to the nose-ring, and subdues the frustrated animal. How ironical the scene becomes! for Henchard is recognizably the bull, or at least suggestive of the bull first in its brazen fierceness and then in its flinching half-paralysis once a stronger force masters it. Henchard is himself literally imprisoned by a nose-ring of events, and the two women whom he saves are, ironically, the Furies who will not give him rest.

This kind of intense scene, otherwise ordinary, joins with several others of the same type to comment indirectly upon the main characters and to create an atmosphere of lost opportunities and muddled human relationships. Earlier, upon recognizing that Lucetta and Farfrae are lovers, Henchard is offered an apple by the nervous Lucetta, which he rejects just as she has rejected his proposal: both offers are based on deceit and both are to bring unhappiness. Then, late in the novel, the dead body of the goldfinch in Henchard's gift to the Farfraes is a sentimentalized but effective symbol of the isolated Henchard, his life snuffed-out, forgotten, and alone in the darkness. The selling-scene itself, which runs like a leitmotif through the novel—for it becomes the basis both of Henchard's potential salvation and his real destruction—contains the grotesqueness and expediency that are essential to a world that pays only lip service to the amenities of life.

According to Ruth Firor (in *Folkways in Thomas Hardy* (1931), wife-selling was common in rural England in the nineteenth century. No doubt such practices were the consequence of the tremendous changes occurring in rural areas, for agricultural England was beginning to be caught in the squeeze between the growing industrial urban centers and the decaying farm economy, particularly in the years preceding the repeal of the Corn Laws. Nevertheless, Hardy treats the episode less as a commonplace than as a sacramental crime. Like the Mariner's murder of the Albatross in Coleridge's poem, or Cain's murder of Abel, Henchard's sale of Susan is a universal crime from which there is no deliverance. The Mariner must eternally confess his crime, and Henchard must as well admit his. Since this stain on his past can never be effaced, such being the nature of the crime, he must reveal to the court the truth of the furmity woman's accusation.

Wife-selling is a sacramental crime even in a pagan society because it nullifies the choice and will of another being and it destroys the stability of what must be everlasting, no matter how unstable: the family. While it is true that Susan nominally agrees to the sale, she nonetheless does so only because Henchard is temporarily insane from drink. Further, the crime is universal because it derives not from reason, but from passion, the great motivator of all great crimes. Thus, when passions rule, man has damned himself and become a creature of insanity. For twenty-one years Henchard practices control and enjoys success, but a universal crime cannot be wiped away by repentance; like Oedipus, another criminal acting out of passion, Henchard must pay (with his entire being) for a sacramental crime. Confession does not lead to absolution; it leads only to further pressures, which must themselves be relieved by the destruction of the whole person. From that can be reborn something: a new being, perhaps; in some sense, an awareness, a feeling of humility, or simply an acceptance of one's frailty.

If Henchard's crime is indeed "sacramental" then Henchard could be seen to be a "wounded" king, a cousin of Jessie Weston's Fisher King. Henchard's "wound" is of course his irrational act committed while drunk; the wound is psychological: an act, a memory, a past. As long as the wound is hidden beneath other deeds, the King functions brilliantly. But the poisoned wound is ever there, ready to suppurate and fester. Only by squeezing out the pus, by bringing it to the surface, can the system be cleansed.

Such a wounded King chooses what Dostoyevsky called "exalted suffering" over cheap happiness. In some inexplicable way, like a shaman he takes upon himself the salvation of his people; his suffering, in fact, becomes a focal point for all their ills. That some wrong he has once committed is the reason for their bad fortune (drought, plague, flood) does not diminish the fact that it is only through him, their scapegoat, that balance can be reachieved. In contemporary fiction, such a scapegoat is the underground man, the isolato, the hopelessly alienated enemy, possibly the "schlemihl." He suffers so that other people can enjoy life or be oblivious to its pain. There is for all but the "schlemihl" no such thing as cheap happiness; the only joy offered him is the sense of power he has achieved in rejecting life, the very power which will cause him exalted pain. He is above the mass, for he has a Nietzschean strength of will. He measures his will, often, by the amount of pain and torment he can bear. Pain in itself becomes a good, not an evil, in this formulation, for pain elicts further strength of will. In one place Nietzsche indicates that he hopes that life will become more evil and more full of suffering, for then man's will may be further tested. At precisely this point of tension, the ruler experiences exalted suffering. Can anything equal the exquisite exultation Oedipus feels at the moment he gouges out his eyes?

Similar grotesque suffering recurs in Henchard's fight with Farfrae; the declining Mayor realizes that he cannot destroy his rival, for at the moment of triumph he is struck by the sadness of his inhuman act in the past, and to think of killing Farfrae is to relive his former shame at the Fair.

This scene is itself duplicated by one shortly after. As Farfrae is defeated by Henchard at the height of his good fortune (as, conversely, the Scotsman had triumphed over the Mayor), so too Lucetta, at her peak of assurance, is trapped by the satirical mummery, which causes her death. Everyone closely associated with Henchard's past is tainted by his misfortune. Only Farfrae and Elizabeth-Jane can escape because they are outside Henchard's range and remain flexible: they can move *with* chance and defy the Fates, although Farfrae escapes death or serious injury only because Henchard is guilt-ridden. The tragedy of Lucetta, on the other hand, is the tragedy of any Hardy woman who seeks a clear path to happiness without the perceptive awareness of potential evil, and who tries to defy the precepts of a malevolent universe that demands obedience to its strict terms of behavior.

Henchard himself, confused by the pressures of the outside world, declines rapidly once he forgoes his twenty-one-year penance and returns to drink, his position in the town having been exploded by the furmity woman. He celebrates the breaking of his oath, appropriately, with the recitation of verses from the 109th Psalm, to the effect that a wicked man shall lose his family, his riches, even all semblance of dignity; and, his name despised, he will be swiftly destroyed. Hardy evidently conceived of Henchard as an enduring Job, an inarticulate sufferer of destiny's wager, but one without the possibility of salvation through faith. Henchard, like Job, is caught amidst forces he cannot understand, caught among forces, however, created by the terms of his own character rather than those strictly imposed upon him. Therefore, Henchard's tragedy is potentially greater than Job's (he is closer to the Greeks than he is to the Hebrews), for his only salvation would be to transcend himself, an impossibility for one who is condemned to be destroyed.

All of Henchard's acts reveal a fatalism, as if he must drive himself until he falls. Thus, his seeming impetuosity in ignoring all advice is more than mere rashness or ill temper. It is the chief constituent of an innate need to debase himself, to act out a role that will ultimately diminish him. Nowhere more than in the scene when the obsessed ex-Mayor kneels to welcome the Royal Personage passing through Casterbridge is his growing insignificance stressed.

Fortified by drink and carrying a small Union Jack, Henchard, wearing a brilliant rosette over his weatherbeaten journeyman garments, tries to regain some of his former glory without disguising his present misery. Advancing to the Personage, Henchard waves the flag and attempts to shake his hand, until, seized by Farfrae, he is removed forcibly. From the large-sized individual who struggled against powers he could not understand, Henchard here dwindles into the court fool, whose pathetic figure, however, causes not comedy but vexation and annoyance. Reduced from his former self and diminished by the blows of chance, Henchard allows his former employee to sweep him aside as a foolish meddler.

Nevertheless, Hardy's Henchard, although dwarfed by his natural surroundings, isolated by his townsmen, and made absurd by his grotesque acts, is still of heroic stature, evidently a nineteenth-century counterpart of an Aeschylean or Euripidean protagonist. Hardy had early recognized that Aristotle's definition of classical tragedy needed to be transformed or amended to suit present-day realities and wrote his own definition shortly after completing *The Mayor of Casterbridge:* "Tragedy. It may be put there in brief: a tragedy exhibits a state of things in the life of an individual which unavoidably causes some natural aim or desire of his to end in catastrophe when carried out." * Thus defined, Henchard, as well as Clym, Jude, and several others of low birth, is a tragic hero, frustrated and hindered by the very things he hopes to attain and blinded by the obsessive nature of his quest. Clearly, Henchard's flaw is, as we suggested, more than a rash temper; his whole character, Hardy is careful to indicate in his definition, is his fate.

His character, like Lear's, is of heroic proportions, although so molded that the vast energies are dissipated in foolish acts of pride and vanity. As an outcast, Henchard gains identification with a whole host of alienated figures, Ishmael, Oedipus, the Ancient Mariner, Lear himself, but, most of all, with the Cain of the Bible, whom Hardy saw as the obvious prototype of all outcasts. Once fallen from his eminence, Henchard, now no different from the "naked" man who had entered Casterbridge nearly a quarter of a century before, leaves the town: " 'I—Cain—go alone as I deserve—an outcast and a vagabond. But my punishment is *not* greater than I

* Florence Hardy, p. 230.

can bear.' " Henchard's ordeal—all part of the universe's unconscious design—is a peculiarly nineteenth-century one even though Hardy carefully drew attention to its Greek and Biblical counterparts. True, Henchard is caught within the workings of a destiny he cannot understand, but he has committed the unnatural act of ridding himself of a family burden, and this while frenzied (drunk). Further, while his free will can work successfully within a certain sphere—only by sheer energy and drive has he become a leader, for he is a man of small ability—it nevertheless is restricted to a line of action in which the whole person is not engaged. Still further, while the novel is subtitled "A Story of a Man of Character," indicating that the emphasis is to be on man and on character, the definitive acts in the novel clearly derive from an area outside Henchard's control. A split individual, an absurd universe, a misdirected will —all these elements help to define a new type of nineteenth-century man.

Henchard's display of will in the face of adversity, his pride that amounts to arrogance, his exhibition of physical strength— all these qualities place him close to Nietzsche's Noble Man. The Noble Man is an aristocrat of the spirit, one who refuses the normal weaknesses of the human race. The Noble Man does not give in to what Nietzsche considered to be Christian weaknesses. He tries to bend all to his will, which is the sole thing he can count upon. Essentially, his will is a will to power, although his struggle for power was to take many different forms in late nineteenth- and twentieth-century literature. Implied in this struggle, whether misdirected or not, is a monstrous ego, the ego of the rebel, the stranger, the alienated fool. Dostoyevsky's Underground Man is first an egoist before he becomes a saint.

If we compare Henchard with George Eliot's Adam Bede, we can distinguish sharply between two kinds of lower-class protagonists and show further how Hardy was moving from the traditional matter of the novel. Adam is in the line of somewhat prosaic young men whose aims are restricted to what they can possibly attain. Imperfect in certain ways, these characters do not set goals that are outside their reach, and they display relative equanimity in their quests. Adam himself is by no means perfect, but his imperfections are of a kind that will provide only disappointment, not nullification. Moreover, the terms of his desires are themselves small and always bounded by the explicable. There is little in the world that Adam could not understand, George Eliot leads us to believe, provided he was mature and intelligent enough to extend himself. What is true of Adam is also true of Dickens's protagonists, Thackeray's middle-class gentlemen, Jane Austen's genteel provincials, and Meredith's romantic heroes: the world holds few secrets from those who would banish ego and vanity in favor of common sense. Henchard's world is obviously quite different. While a simple frettish woman disappoints Adam, a whole series of reappearing women seem to doom Henchard, and each time he fails it is almost always over a woman or related to one. Moreover, while imperfections of character are merely a sign of immaturity in Adam, they *constitute* the character of Henchard. While Adam has to go through an emotional ordeal in order to purge himself of his temper and gain insight into real love, the ordeal of Henchard is not a matter of development but of life and death, the ordeal of the tragic hero set back by phenomena outside his control.

In addition, while Adam has to understand only visible things, Henchard must master invisible forces and obviously he cannot succeed, for he himself engenders several of the forces which help destroy him. Furthermore, Adam is the lower-class "hero" who is *like* everyone else despite low birth, while Henchard is *unlike* anyone else—he is marked, like Cain, almost from the beginning, and marked he goes through the novel, a grotesque figure of wasted energies and misdirected will. Adam was not intended to be, and cannot be, a tragic hero, while Henchard could not be the center of a conventional love story or the protagonist in a dramatic narrative lacking tragedy.

George Eliot was interested in presenting the detailed grandeur of passions that Wordsworth considered "incorporated with the beautiful and permanent forms of nature." Hardy, also, was interested in the "permanent forms of nature," though not as something necessarily ennobling; rather, as a background for human tragedy and as a silent force supposedly indifferent both to man and to its own powers. Nature, like society, gives Henchard something from which to be isolated and helps define the terms of his alienation, while in George Eliot it brings about attachment and purification. This distinction is important, for Hardy turned the Victorian lower-class "hero" into an unreasonable, guilt-stricken, and alienated figure who is denied even the saving powers of nature.

The seeming simplicity of Henchard's actions should not obscure Hardy's not-so-simple conception of his character. The grotesqueness and obsessiveness of Henchard's position—in several ways he is not unlike a muscular version of Kafka's K.—become more meaningful when we see that his tragedy, like K.'s, is played out against a relatively calm and imperturbable background. The townspeople themselves are under no pall of tragedy; even Farfrae is untouched by the deeper aspects of Henchard's position, as is Elizabeth-Jane, whose relative insubstantiality precludes her suffering too much. Susan, likewise, is too simple and flexible to suffer little more than shame at her position, and her early removal from Henchard would seem more a source of happiness than misery. Perhaps Lucetta suffers for a short time on a scale comparable to that of Henchard, but she, like Elizabeth-Jane and Susan, is not solid enough to transform suffering into tragic feeling. Only Henchard is tragic, only Henchard really suffers, and this emphasis helps convey his monumental anguish. His profile dominates Casterbridge, and even in decline he has size and scope.

Although Henchard is diminished by juxtaposition with the amphitheatre, as well as with the Roman road and the Chapel on the Cliff, he nevertheless gains identity from their massive impressiveness at the same time he is dwarfed by their grandeur. One is reminded here of that great scene in *Tess of the D'Urbervilles* in which Tess lies immolated on the stone slab of Stonehenge, the pretty dairy girl identified with a vast history of martyrs and victims. So, too, Henchard gains in massiveness and substance through identification with his surroundings. Like many other Hardy heroes, Henchard cannot be separated from the earth, which denotes both defeat and life. The spirit of place remains close to him: he works in the earth before coming to Casterbridge and dies close to the earth after leaving. He places his trust in the earth, and when it, like everything else, fails him, he willingly forsakes life.

The outline of *The Mayor of Casterbridge,* as befitting a tragedy, is quite simple, despite the several new incidents occurring in each chapter. Hardy himself was afraid that the demands of weekly publication, with the need to force an incident into each installment, would strain the credulity of the reader of the novel as a whole; but while the play of intercrossing incidents—especially those concerning the returned sailor Newson—does seem overworked at times, the main profile is clear. Perhaps the very simplicity of the novel caused Henry James to call the author, "the good little T——— H———," a remark that caused Hardy considerable discomfort.

The important elements, however, do stand out boldly, so boldly that Joseph Warren Beach thought the spareness was more suitable to a motion-picture scenario than to a novel. Yet fullness of development could not have been Hardy's intention, certainly not the fullness of *Tess of the D'Urbervilles* or *The Return of the Native,* both of which are longer novels with fewer single incidents. What Hardy evidently intended was a Greek tragedy appropriate for his own time. Certainly the formal elements of the novel (although these elements are not necessarily its virtues) attempt the simple line of Greek tragedy, with the apparent rise and fall of incident leading to the hero's recognition of his situation. Even the moral alienation of Henchard, which places him close to a twentieth-century "hero," finds its source in the isolation of Aeschylus' and Euripides' protagonists. Consider, also, the leitmotif of the furmity woman, together with the recurrence of themes of isolation, the reappearance of key people, the use of the weather prophet, the prevalence of classical architecture, the starkness of the landscape, the morbidity of Henchard's "sickness," the victimizing of the hero by women, the use of folk customs like the skimmity ride, the presence of the townspeople as a chorus, the aura of fatalism cast over the main character because of events lying outside his control, the inability of the main character to find happiness as long as there is a taint on his conscience—all these are throwbacks to the chief elements of Greek tragedy now reproduced and brought to bear upon the novel, elements, moreover, that have become the common staple of the novel after Hardy.

Henchard is an Oedipus who instead of marrying his mother after twenty years remarries Susan after a similar lapse of time; in another way, he is an Orestes whose revenge is against himself, not his mother, for having killed a part of his own being. Henchard can never be free from himself, just as he can never be free from society. Often, the conflict in a Hardy protagonist is between social convention, which restricts, and the individual need to be free, which can never be fulfilled in the terms the individual expects. This conflict can take several forms, although rarely does Hardy shape it along the simple line of duty versus passion. Frequently, he complicates the terms of the inner conflict by showing that duty itself can be and often is degrading, while passion can as frequently lead to fear and insecurity as it does to personal happiness. Doubtless, Hardy changed the terms of the traditional conflict (especially strong in the Victorian novel) because they would, under certain conditions, lead to a qualified happiness and "heroization," both of which he felt falsified a tragic sense of life.

As several critics have remarked, criticism of Hardy during his novel-writing days was directed more toward his pessimism than toward the sexuality of his themes. Perhaps Hardy's readers would have more readily accepted Lucetta's happiness (after sufficient penance) than the cruel death that she must suffer. D. H. Lawrence, for instance, was outraged that Hardy killed off his "living" characters and let the prosaic ones escape, and Lawrence's opinion was not far from the general public's dismay at Hardy's lack of optimism. Hardy himself wrote in 1886: "These venerable philosophers seem to start wrong; they cannot get away from a prepossession that the world must somehow have been made to be a comfortable place for man." * Hardy suggests his own prepossession in the last line of *The Mayor:* "that happiness was but the occasional episode in a general drama of pain."

A frequent criticism of Hardy is that as a counter to mid-Victorian optimism (or what passed for it) he would not allow anyone to be happy who could feel deeply or think broadly. There is some truth to this stricture, for Hardy had been strongly influenced by Darwin's work during his maturing years prior to his first published novel in 1871. The battle between man and nature, manifest in

* Florence Hardy, p. 234.

the mysterious and even malevolent power that determines the process of natural selection, becomes translated into a cosmic pessimism in which man is countered at every turn by antagonistic forces. Because man can never be sure of himself—like the Greek hero, he can be struck down at the peak of his success— Hardy's novels seem cruel. Henchard undergoes rebuffs that seem in excess of what his original crime demands, and his punishment appears more than what a basically decent man deserves. That Hardy will not give him the chance to recover after penance, a kind of resurrection traditional in the nineteenth-century novel, is evident in his relationship with Elizabeth-Jane. During his decline, Henchard has hopes of living closer to the girl: "In truth, a great change had come over him with regard to her, and he was developing the dream of a future lit by her filial presence, as though that way alone could happiness lie." This passage is measured against a later one in which the girl, now married, rebuffs his attempt at reconciliation: " 'Oh how can I love, or do anything more for, a man who has served us like this [deceived her about her real father].' " Thus, one of Henchard's few real acts of demonstrable affection is rejected out of hand, and rejected, moreover, by a girl now secure with a husband and a father. The cruelty here is unbearable for the reason that Henchard has been discarded by one who is solidly part of society, while, previously, his rejections had at least been at the hands of people equally insecure. Now, Elizabeth-Jane, respectable, cared-for, loved, confident, and youthful, strikes at Henchard's last vestige of dignity: he indeed becomes the dead goldfinch forgotten in the dark cage.

The cruelty of the main lines of the novel does help prevent a potentially sentimental tale from becoming mawkish. Like Conrad, Lawrence, Joyce, and Virginia Woolf after him, Hardy was clearly reacting to Victorian sentimentality, although he did not evade it on several occasions when he was sure his audience desired tears. However, by imposing the starkness of Greek classical tragedy on a late 1820's rural English setting, and intermixing that with a Darwinian cosmos, Hardy tried to avoid an excess of direct feeling. Nevertheless, he failed to recognize that Greek tragedy is not necessarily bleak and pessimistic but merely the working out of man's conflicts with himself or with his state and gods. He did recognize, though, that to approximate such tragedy he would have to manipulate many things artificially in order to make his philosophy—one necessarily alien to the surrounding culture—work out consistently. The Greek tragedian could write with his entire culture behind him, while Hardy was generally isolated from the practices of his literary contemporaries and certainly from the beliefs of a dominant part of his audience. Therefore, we sense the strain, the need to impose consistency even at the expense of art.

The cruelty of Hardy's pursuit of Henchard is mitigated, if only partially, by the latter's stubborn resistance to forces that would soon have defeated a man of lesser stature. The mere array of circumstances aligned against Henchard—in this sense comparable to Job's ordeal—makes his struggle seem epical. Henchard's opposition to the onslaughts of chance incidents, each of which might demolish him, exemplifies his power of defiant endurance. When he declares scornfully, " 'But my punishment is *not* greater than I can bear,' " he seems, in his Promethean strength, to become as large as the forces which are attempting to nullify him. The fact that Henchard *is* tragic—that despite several excessive circumstances, Hardy is still able to convey a tragic sense—gives him a power beyond that of a mere mortal, who would appear pathetic, not Promethean. When Henchard has been defeated, one has witnessed the conflict of a powerful will with an implacable force, and his dying wishes give him the unearthly power of a maddened Lear, whose defiant cry of "Ere they shall make us weep, we'll see 'em starved first" should be the epitaph for Casterbridge's former Mayor. Significantly, Hardy wrote in his diary just two days after finishing *The Mayor* his own epitaph for Henchard: "The business of the poet and novelist is to show the sorriness underlying the grandest things, and the grandeur underlying the sorriest things."

Henchard, we should remember, is a decent man whose early sins are not those of a cruel or ill-intentioned character, but rather the mistakes of a man carried away by a frenzy he finds impossible to control. In his dealings in Casterbridge, he is particularly fair and honest. He willingly destroys himself by admitting the furmity woman's accusation in court, and his action in remarrying Susan is an attempt to do what is right even though no love is involved.

Although Henchard is a primitive in his inarticulateness, he recognizes the need for a softer side at the same time he is unable to summon these feelings. He agrees, out of duty, to take care of Susan, Elizabeth-Jane, Farfrae, and Lucetta, while feeling intimately only about Farfrae, who returns mere decency for the Mayor's compulsive need for companionship. Henchard, however, so dominates all relationships that he forbids any opposition; lacking love, which itself forces flexibility, he loses all hold upon humanity, including at times his own. His inability to love is equated to his self-destructive tendencies, and it is difficult to distinguish where each begins or ends. Consequently, Henchard often seems harsher than his character warrants simply because he smashes certain moral bonds by acting from duty rather than love. Moreover, Hardy appears to nullify him exactly as he, in turn, nullifies others by refusing them the deeper feelings that he himself is unable to summon. The disparity between Henchard's abortive attempts to be decent and the ill results of his efforts is the extent to which Hardy's philosophy precluded uncontested happiness.

The quality of one's happiness is determined by his flexibility and aims; if he can, like Farfrae and Elizabeth-Jane, remain outside any dominating obsession and live more by common sense than force of will, he will not be destroyed or even seriously injured. Hardy indicates that if one is an idealist—that is, one who tries to impose his will upon an antagonistic or indifferent world —then his exertions create a Promethean conflict leading to his destruction; if, however, one is a realist and does not attempt to change himself or the world, his chances of destruction are minimized. This pattern is not of course always true for Hardy's characters—Tess is an evident exception—but it does define the major figures of *The Mayor*.

Nevertheless, even to suggest that the other characters in the novel have individual lives is to see how far Henchard overshadows them and how much of *The Mayor* is his novel alone. To a much greater extent than either George Eliot, Thackeray, or Meredith, or the later Dickens, Hardy used a single character to dominate his narratives. Even Becky Sharp fails to predominate in *Vanity Fair* to the degree that Henchard controls Hardy's novel, and we must return to *Wuthering Heights* to find a comparable figure,

that of the domineering Heathcliff. We recognize that for Hardy
the dominance of the central character, even though he be an
anti-hero, was another carry-over from Greek tragedy, the nature
of whose protagonist determined the nature of the drama. If the
novel is, as Hardy believed, an outgrowth of events from a particular character who shapes them (except those things which chance
controls), then the novel must be directed in its details by this
single force. Thus, the events that help nullify Henchard are those
that develop from his own character: he makes the world that
first envelops and then squeezes him to death. The subtitle, we
note again, is "A Story of a Man of Character."

Hardy's use of the town, similar to George Eliot's presentation
of *Middlemarch* as a comment upon the main characters, creates
a chorus that is as malevolent in its gossip as it is a form of social
commentary. Hardy took the Greek chorus as both a representation of public opinion and a force for warning the protagonist of
excesses and remolded it into an interfering group of townspeople
who directly influence the protagonist's fortunes. Accordingly, the
town is both public opinion and participant in the drama: its opinion is more than mere warning, it can force its way. George Eliot
and Hardy realized that the town's opinion in a democratic age
would entail more than mere commentary; with class mobility less
restricted, the individual's business was no longer his sole concern:
the individual now belonged to everyone. In *Middlemarch,* town
gossip cuts through Bulstrode's hypocrisy and ruins his reputation,
while in *The Mayor* the skimmity ride destroys Lucetta's hopes
for happiness. In each, the town becomes a force for reliving the
past, whose unwelcome recurrence is the basis for gossip and hearsay.

Both George Eliot and Hardy show a sharp awareness of social
structure, recognizing that the mighty (Bulstrode) and the outsider (Lucetta and Henchard) can each be destroyed by a demon-
stration of majority opinion, whether it be justified or not. Further,
both use country customs, implicit in the chorus, as a way of trapping the urbanized characters, and by so doing remove the country from mere picturesqueness and take the romance from the
pastoral. This is not to claim that George Eliot and Hardy forsake
the picturesque quality of rural life—one need think only of the

Poysons in *Adam Bede* or of the dairy workers in *Tess*—but it is to suggest that in their later work they discount the pictorial quality in favor of a more individualized comment. The farmer and his wife are no longer merely decorative; they now have sentiments that must be heeded and values that can upset those whom they oppose. Thus, the chorus of townspeople and farmers has come full turn; in a democratic age, it loses its aloofness and sense of cosmic justice. Now, it too is involved, and no one can escape its approval, condemnation, or interference in his personal life. The chorus, as Kafka's K. was to learn, can impose its will regardless of the individual's rights, more often than not sending the alienated protagonist into exile. Hardy's Henchard, then, is in some ways the English prototype of the twentieth-century's isolated hero, the dominating figure in a world suddenly inexplicable to human reason.

Hardy is important, therefore, not only intrinsically but also historically. If we compare him again with Jane Austen, Thackeray, Dickens, Meredith, and George Eliot, and then with the nearest pivotal English novelist after him, Joseph Conrad, we can see how he has changed the nineteenth-century novel, although change in itself is of course no criterion of quality. The century that began with Jane Austen's well-balanced heroines of strong mind, who literally "will" themselves into normal behavior, rushes toward its end with the willful self-destructiveness of Hardy's heroines and heroes, who "will" themselves not into normality but into an obsession with guilt and penance. From the suave, unquestioned "inner-direction" of Darcy and Mr. Knightley, who live within an intensely realistic world of everyday fact, to the "inner-direction" of Henchard, whose compulsive life is played out in an absurd puppet show that passes for the real world, is a far cry.

Granted, obviously, that Hardy's major predecessors and contemporaries had each brought individual genius to the novel, it is nevertheless in "the good little T——— H——" that we find the first sustained attempt to examine new aspects of late Victorian reality and to probe into areas barely suggested before in English fiction. In Hardy, almost for the first time, we have an author who is counter to the central tendencies of his age, the enemy personified; (we can only marginally claim this for Dickens and Meredith). Hardy recognized that idealism is a component of egoism, and that the true idealistic hero is not one who conquers or triumphs as Christ did, but one who can destroy himself in muddle and noncomprehension. Hardy was primarily concerned with the stranger whose attempts to get inside society are self-destructive. Already, we recognize a world that is somewhat subversive and antisocial; Greek tragedy serves modern sensibilities, and its external determinism is now internalized and seen as of man's own making. The stranger is indeed Promethean in his quest for a particular kind of truth, but the mere fact that he is a stranger is sufficient to doom him. In his perception of the great grotesque depths lying beneath conventional morality, Hardy in *The Mayor of Casterbridge* and his other major novels wrote a parable for our times. The lesson is that life itself destroys even when man is basically good. On this note, an age of fiction turns into a a living nightmare.

1 Benjamin Disraeli: *The Politics of Necessity*

There has recently been increased interest in Disraeli's three mid-career novels, with strong attempts being made to demonstrate their artistic worth as well as acknowledge their political acumen. These novels—*Coningsby, or The New Generation* (1844), *Sybil, or The Two Nations* (1845), and *Tancred, or The New Crusade* (1847), the so-called "Young England" novels—were written principally to set forth Disraeli's political aims, and only incidentally for any aesthetic or literary pleasure they might convey. This intention in itself would not preclude the possibility of their giving another dimension of enjoyment, but, as we shall see, Disraeli is so indifferent a literary artist that we are left with little more than the political goal.

Unlike his Dandy Fiction of the 1820's and 30's (*Vivian Grey,* 1826; *The Young Duke,* 1830; even *Contarini Fleming,* 1832), which fitted into the conventions of the Silver Fork School mocked by Thackeray in *Vanity Fair,* these three novels are serious, didactic, almost Evangelical in their call to a new kind of faith. Specifically, as his spokesman Sidonia states, Disraeli favored an alliance between the working classes and the land-owning aristocrats as a way of restraining the growing power of the rising merchant class. Inevitably, this alliance would put more power into the hands of the Crown, the Established Church, and the titled landowners, a return, in form and spirit, to the political hierarchy of the Middle Ages, all reminiscent of Carlyle's *Past and Present* (1843). As the leader of the Young England movement designed to wrest power from complacent Tories like Sir Robert Peel (himself the son of a manufacturer), Disraeli attempted to create rapport between the "two nations," the working classes who must work and the aristocrats who must learn to lead.

These novels were written during the time when Chartist agitation was at its height, and the potential violence of the movement was obvious. Like Carlyle, Ruskin, and several other Victorian prophets, Disraeli favored reform while fearing democracy. His program of alliance to hold back the merchants and placate the working class demonstrates a desire to return to medieval traditions rather than to find a program to ameliorate the obvious political inadequacies of the government. Disraeli remained consistent, for even his support of the 1867 Reform Bill was more an act of expedience to defeat Gladstone than a sincere wish to advance the growth of democratic procedures.

In *Sybil,* for example, Disraeli's confused politics vitiate the force of the book, even though this is perhaps the most successful of the three novels. The two halves of the novel are shared by Egremont, Disraeli's benevolent, sympathetic aristocrat, an extension in several ways of Sidonia, himself taken from Carlyle's remote "great man"; and Gerard, the noble spokesman for the rights of the working class. As Egremont argues, so does Disraeli:

> The new generation of the aristocracy of England are not tyrants, not oppressors, Sybil [Gerard's daughter], as you persist in believing. Their intelligence, better than that, their hearts, are open to the responsibility of their position. . . . They are the natural leaders of the People, Sybil; believe me they are the only ones (Book IV, Chapter 15).

As an agitator, Gerard believes exactly the opposite: that leadership can come only from the People, as his daughter, Sybil, indicates. Thus far, Disraeli has suggested a meaningful conflict, although he weakens it by making Gerard so handsome and honorable and Egremont so noble and forebearing. Then, Disraeli introduces a further fact, that Gerard himself descends from an ancient aristocratic family, and this fact explains his noble manner. This revelation completely upsets the balance, for Gerard is now no more a working man by blood and spirit (things that count for Disraeli) than is the author himself.

Involved is Disraeli's instinctive and intellectual distrust of working-class aims and those who represent the working class, a distrust that invalidates a good deal of his political program. Further, the House of Lords—made up of the traditional aristocracy he supported—opposed every measure that might have helped the working man and only relented when faced by violence and by a possible packing of the House. Traditional landowners had fought every progressive program from the Reform Bill of 1832, through the repeal of the Corn Laws, on to the 1867 Reform Bill. There is little to indicate that Disraeli's "Young Englanders" were ready for the kind of cooperation he advocated. On the contrary, the historical evidence demonstrates that except for a small band, the aristocracy was unwilling to give in to anything less than coercion. As for Disraeli's desire for renewed strength in the Crown, the example of the later years of George III, the Regency (1810-20) and the monarchy (1820-30) of George IV, as well as the rule of William IV (1830-37) should have indicated that the Crown was itself hardly open to progress. In fact, even though Victoria brought respectability to the throne after the disreputable rule of the previous twenty-five years, her own views revealed an unwillingness or inability to understand the changes taking place and the need for reform. The young queen in the 1840's was not ready to provide rallying ground for an alliance between workers and established aristocrats. Her sympathies were indeed all with the latter, her comprehension of the life of the former almost non-existent.

The element in the novels that weakens Disraeli's views even more than does his political confusion was his inability to make meaningful the characters who espouse his various views. Egremont is an allegorical figure, as is Sybil, Disraeli's version of a romantic heroine. Gerard, and Marney, Egremont's reactionary brother, and the leader of the Hellcats, Bishop Hatton, are likewise stock figures. As a consequence, the political ideas—inconsistent as they were to begin with—seem simply grafted on to appropriate lay figures without regard for human consequences.

For this and other reasons, Disraeli's novels can hardly be called political novels in the same sense as we would apply the term to Dostoyevsky's *The Possessed,* or James's *The Princess Casamassima,* or Conrad's *The Secret Agent,* or Greene's *The Power and the Glory*. To this list, we might add several of Dickens's novels, perhaps even Thackeray's *Vanity Fair,* certainly Meredith's *Beauchamp's Career.* In these books, the political ideas are part of the people involved, and we believe in the people before we believe in their politics. In Disraeli's fiction, we are expected to approve political ideas divorced from any credible holder of them. We have, in fact, a mixture of *Realpolitik* with romantic ideas straight out of Scott and Byron. The two elements hardly go together, for the effective political novel features few heroes, or else cuts down would-be heroes, while the romantic novel assumes that heroes are possible and even necessary. In this area, Scott himself ran into difficulty, and every subsequent novelist influenced by his work similarly floundered unless he modified it by an honest assessment of social reality.

Disraeli himself seemed to realize the futility of his views when he turned to *Tancred*. Earlier, his young Coningsby had set out to make his mark in politics, to be honest, moral, righteous, and to demonstrate the stuff of which Young Englanders were made. He had refused to compromise himself by running against Millbank, the enlightened manufacturer. He was willing to lose his rights to Lord Monmouth's great fortune by holding to his personal views that the Tories as constituted were a dead party. Coningsby is idealistic, hopeful of effecting real change, and he goes forth to set the world aright. Only three years later, in *Tancred,* Disraeli's young apprentice has given up the political quest, and now quests for his religious identity. Politics and social issues are no longer sufficient; man needs spirituality. Accordingly, Tancred seeks his real homeland, the Near East, the source of meaningful religious ideas. At the end of the novel, the Christian Tancred and a Jewish girl, Eva, link themselves in a symbolic joining of the two religions. Obviously, Disraeli's point is that religious rejuvenation is necessary; man must grow in spirit before he can come to terms with political and social issues.

All this is of course close to Charles Kingsley's Christian Socialist Movement, founded in 1848, the year after *Tancred* was published. In Kingsley's view, only the Church and the individual's religious identity could be forces for curing social ills. His two novels, *Yeast* (1848, in *Fraser's Magazine*) and *Alton Locke* (1850) attempted to show how disastrous can be the effects of social ideas (like the Chartist beliefs) without a religious foundation. It is curious that Disraeli should find himself moving into Kingsley's camp, for the two men otherwise have little in common. In fact, Disraeli's approach to Christian Socialism demonstrates the short-comings of his earlier views in *Coningsby* and *Sybil,* where the idea of Christian Socialism or its equivalent never enters.

One receives the impression that Disraeli was striking around to find some ground on which to justify his fear of Chartism and his desire to hold back the floodtide of democratic thought. His actual program, based as much of it was on expedience, was inadequate to the problems it tried to alleviate and eliminate. Like Kingsley, whom he resembled in some ways, he fought a holding action, while many men with less vociferous ideals worked quietly toward real reform. Some even wrote more effective novels.

2   *The Way of All Flesh,* by Samuel Butler

Had Butler published *The Way of All Flesh* at the time he finished it, in 1884, instead of letting it appear posthumously, in 1903, it would have indeed created an explosion. As it was, by 1903, the intervening nineteen years had already seen the major fiction of Hardy and the early work of Conrad, among others, and Butler's ideas were themselves becoming assimilated into the general revolt against Victorian social complacency. Even in 1872, however, when he began it, and in the twelve years Butler took to finish it, *The Way of All Flesh* was only carrying to conclusion certain ideas already contained in Dickens, Thackeray, and George Eliot. Dickens, after all, had severely questioned parent-child relationships; Thackeray, in *Vanity Fair,* had had some harsh things to say about romantic love; and George Eliot, even before *Middlemarch* (1871-72), had upset many Victorian sacred cows.

Nevertheless, it remained to Butler to reject all fathers. In many ways, the Victorian era appears to be one of fathers, of ever-present parents and their ever-present repressed children. It is not fortuitous that Freud's emphasis upon parent-children relationships should appear as a summation and an analysis of certain nine-teenth-century tendencies. Butler's novel heralds a new century by dramatizing the break from the old: the rejection of parents allows the flowering of the child, a clean beginning, perhaps even a return to innocence.

Ernest's rejection of fathers, however, went further than Butler's ridicule of the Pontifexes. Like Joyce's Stephen Dedalus shortly after, Ernest turns upon all forms of domination—Church, God, family, tradition—in order to find his Self. How different this now becomes from Dickens, who questioned the family, but argued in several novels that one should seek his true center in family life! Butler looks ahead to Joyce and Lawrence, while Dickens, despite his dissent, was concerned with moderate reaction and behavior.

Ernest's ideal—once it is defined—is not, however, very exalted, even though like Joyce he argues for the autonomy of the individual and like Stephen Dedalus turns to writing. But writing for him comes too easily. Unlike Stephen, he does not reject one type of pain in order to embrace a new kind of torture. Butler and Ernest both believe that happiness is a reward that awaits one who finally makes the right decisions. In this sense, *The Way of All Flesh* fits into the mold of the traditional apprenticeship novel, that of *Great Expectations, Tom Jones, Pendennis*. Ernest clearly does not continue his revolt; once he has attained maturity, he inherits a huge fortune and settles in to a bourgeois existence. Butler rejects continual struggle, as in Joyce and Lawrence, and even heroic defiance, as in Ibsen and Hardy. Ernest finally makes the correct choices and finds his place, and that is the full extent of his ideals.

We can see that *The Way of All Flesh* bridges two distinct points of view, although it does not convince us as a novel, for Butler fails to accept the consequences of Ernest's actions. In brief, Butler never entirely divested himself of the very beliefs he eagerly attacked. His fierce fight for the individual's autonomy was a rejection of Darwinian mechanism and an acceptance of Lamarck's (and Erasmus Darwin's) emphasis upon Will. Yet Butler based his position on inherited wealth: Ernest is constantly being "bailed out" by Overton (sometimes literally), and of course his future is assured by money his aunt leaves him. Consequently, it seems as if free will is a fine thing when one is protected against too much freedom. Butler would have us believe that Ernest achieves full maturity, but he actually attains it by stumbling into the path of righteousness because someone is there to assure his future.

There is much that is dishonest in Butler's view, the kind of dishonesty that is his heritage from an Age which asked most of the right questions but then supplied few valid answers. The difference between Stephen Dedalus and Ernest Pontifex is the difference between honest revolt and dishonest wishful thinking. For despite all of Butler's outrage at hypocrisy and vanity, he presents a mixed Ernest-Overton who is, in many ways, appalling. Overton, in particular, is insufferable, and yet one recognizes that he cannot be separated from Butler himself, and that his views are eventually the ones Ernest accepts and which we are expected to sympathize with.

The central point of Overton's gospel is hardly arguable: the need of the individual to live in dignity. The details, however, are unsettling and unacceptable: stress on manual labor—a stress that is pure romanticism; emphasis upon faith and emotion over intellect—an emphasis that in context is false, for Butler never shows anyone who demonstrates true intellectual power; denunciation of marriage as unworkable and inevitably destructive for the man—a denunciation that is suspect coming from Overton, who seems, like his creator, rather like a somewhat fastidious homosexual; attack upon those who seek truth, with support for those who live by emotion and faith—again a purely romantic viewpoint; use of Towneley, the perfect university man, as a kind of ideal— when Towneley, like Butler's own Pauli, should be a figure of fun. All of these elements seriously compromise Ernest's dash toward freedom; when we leave him, we wonder if he is really as good as Butler would have us think. The former prig and naive creature has disappeared, but in his stead we find a smug young man. Butler's point (as Meredith's with Nevil Beauchamp) might have been that idealism destroys even when we think it saves, but then Ernest's end could not have been so complacent and self-satisfied.

Clearly, what still counts in the novel, as Arnold Kettle and several other critics have observed, is the criticism of Victorian morality in the first two-thirds of the book. What is of lesser importance is Butler's positive stance, based as it is on insufferable ideas and people. In the first parts, however, Butler brilliantly dissects that bastion of Victorian morality: the family life of a clergyman. It was a brilliant stroke on Butler's part to focus on the home life of a clergyman. A businessman would be expected to have a compromised morality, as would an army or navy man; the same could be said for a barrister or a surgeon—all of these would be professional men with a stake in dishonest proceedings. But a clergyman of the Established Church was supposedly on the side of the angels: he could walk on water, the average Victorian was led to believe.

With Theobald Pontifex (the surname itself, with its connection to a high priestly function, even a Pope, indicates presumption, while *Theobald,* the Christian name, ironically means *bold for the people*) Butler does not present a particularly wicked or vicious man. Not unlike Tolstoy's Ivan Ilych, Theobald is hardly malicious; on the contrary, he does what he believes is right, and often merely threatens to do worse; his growl is frequently worse than his behavior. He is no more sadistic or unfair than other fathers in dozens of Victorian novels. Theobald is an average man, disciplining his children in the sole way he knows how and giving them what he thinks is excellent advice for getting along in the world. Butler's point, however, is that such parents completely destroy their offspring; and here he provides a solid psychological insight. A truly malicious or evil father would evoke immediate antagonism: through rebellion, the offspring could save himself or else be shattered. In either case, there would be a clear course of action. But a Theobald is more gruesome, for he supplies no apparent substance to rebel against. Criticism of his behavior simply rolls off and away. He is innocent of any tangible wrong-doing, and that is Butler's very point: that innocent and unthinking parents do the real harm. Parents who assume god-like poses inevitably fail to see the consequences of their actions, and they fail because of their inability to judge themselves clearly. They cannot judge beyond the needs of their own ego. Consequently, Theobald has no understanding of Ernest, makes no allowance for individual behavior, provides no leeway for what Ernest is: he treats him merely as a father treats a child, any child.

When we see Butler's criticism on this level, and not simply as cruel satire of Theobald and his aspirations, we feel a tragic tone underlying his attack upon Victorian morality. In this sense, Ernest's survival depends upon his rejection of his father, no matter what he himself turns out to be. Believing as he did in Vitalism, Butler tried to merge Spirit with Matter, and since Theobald represented only Matter, he could not possibly suffice. For the great middle class, Victorian spiritual life was based upon Matter, upon Protestant capitalism in which money and property are sacramental. Even for Butler, as we saw, money is necessary to provide the good life and to enable Ernest to pursue what his intuition tells him is correct. Yet Butler's criticism holds regardless of his own inability to reject the very forces he was attacking.

The novel succeeds in creating a sense of frustration, in enclosing us in a stifling atmosphere. Only Dickens, Thackeray, and George Eliot were capable of giving us this feel of daily life in an ordinary Victorian household, and often Dickens's descriptions were heightened for comic effect. Butler's version of "Life with Father" comes without adornment. When Butler comments on youth in the following passage, his remarks come as the deepest indictment one can make against a society: that it forbids happiness even to those who are innocent.

To me it seems that youth is like spring, an overpraised season— delightful if it happens to be a favoured one, but in practice very rarely favoured and more remarkable, as a general rule, for biting east winds than genial breezes. Autumn is the mellower season, and what we lose in flowers we more than gain in fruits. Fontenelle at the age of ninety, being asked what was the happiest time of his life, said he did not know that he had ever been much happier than he then was, but that perhaps his best years had been those when he was between fifty-five and seventy-five, and Dr. Johnson placed the pleasures of old age far higher than those of youth. True, in old age we live under the shadow of Death, which, like a sword of Damocles may descend at any moment, but we have so long found life to be an affair of being rather frightened than hurt that we have become like the people who live under Vesuvius and chance it without much misgiving (VI).

In rejecting his father and grandfather, Ernest Pontifex rejects his immediate heredity, as Butler felt one could will himself into being something else if he desired it sufficiently. Through an act of will, he becomes like his great-grandfather, John Pontifex, who loved music, built his own organ, and kept his own counsel. John Pontifex was his own man, and when he fell back upon himself, there was something there for support. These acquired characteristics of John were passed on to Ernest, who in turn passes them on to his own children. *The Way of All Flesh* becomes "proof" of Butler's Lamarckian ideas, a rejection of Darwin's emphasis on chance and an acceptance of habit, a rejection of determinism and a stress upon will.

The ridicule of the Home leads of course to the rejection of the School as well. Like Rousseau and most nineteenth-century novelists, Butler assumed that man was basically a good creature who was corrupted by the demands society made upon him. Even more than most of his contemporaries, Butler tried to follow the idea through and condemned all things except basically good people. There is of course a difficulty in this argument—for example, that good creatures, like Ernest's Aunt Alethea (Truth herself!), can be born to insufferable people like George Pontifex—but this aspect did not trouble Butler. A man like Dr. Skinner, again not in any sense evil or vicious, nevertheless perpetuated through his school an institution which made "the worse appear the better reason" in the eyes of those too young to find out for themselves.

Dr. Skinner becomes simply another version of Father, institutions, hypocrisy, drudgery, intellectual nonsense, religion and church, family, Darwin, Victorian morality, all those aspects of life which Salinger's contemporary Ernest, Holden Caulfield, also rebels against. Any one institution for Butler—whether the home, church, or school—was a microcosm of the larger cancer. When Ernest decides to go along with the burning of Theobald in effigy —surely one of the most cold-blooded scenes in Victorian fiction— he is present at a ceremonial fire: the destruction of the body and values of an entire age. When Theobald ("a poor thing enough, made of paper, calico, and straw") goes up, while his son watches, all fathers go up, and the past is burned out.

All of these aspects of the novel tend to make it seem better than it is. The apparatus is stringy and often supernumerary. Overton, the narrator, seems a spokesman for Butler, while Ernest seems also to be a spokesman, so that there are actually three overlapping forces operating in the novel. Yet Overton is rarely fleshed out; and we are expected to accept his values when they appear very questionable. Further, the latter third of the novel is sketchy. Ernest's attitude toward his children seems high-handed and unpersuasive, at least when measured against the earlier scenes of parent-children relationships. Also, Butler's gospel of manual labor—Ernest as a seller of used clothes—seems misplaced when Ernest later adjusts so readily to a leisurely life on an unearned income. All of these elements—and several more, including the unreality of Aunt Alethea—weaken the novel as fiction and make one see it as sermon. Only in the first sections does Butler present the material with sufficient weight and cogency, but these passages are sufficient to justify the novel, debilitated as it became when he lost direct touch with the sources of his hatred.

3 *Alton Locke: Tailor and Poet, An Autobiography,* by Charles Kingsley

Kingsley's *Alton Locke* (1850) is the kind of minor novel that remains with us less for its intrinsic worth than for its exposure of certain conditions which continue to make us feel guilty. In this century, Orwell's *1984,* a much different type of book in virtually every way, will one hundred years from now be read with the same kind of galling curiosity. Kingsley's theme is the familiar one that bread is not sufficient. But here the theme is set forth not by a conservative anxious to avoid the questions raised by the Chartists and Luddites, but by a man sympathetic to the working-man's cause. Through the fortunes and misfortunes of Alton Locke, Kingsley claims that political and social freedom for the worker—including the vote and better working conditions—must never be separated from religious feeling.

It is not surprising that Thomas Carlyle was instrumental in getting *Alton Locke* published, for Carlyle's spirit hangs heavily over the book, as it would later over Dickens's *Hard Times* (1854), a novel curiously close to Kingsley's in many ways. Both are concerned with the condition of the working-man, both are compassionate toward his lot, and both see the decent worker—not the aristocrat or the Crown—as the backbone of English life. Both writers fear rebellion and chaos, and therefore both opposed political movements that lost sight of spiritual goals. When Locke attempts to gain freedom through Chartism alone, he must come to grief, Kingsley argues, just as Stephen Blackpool—acting here as Dickens's spokesman—opposes the Trades Union because it submerges the individual spirit in group activity.

In his "Address to the Working Men of Great Britain," written in 1854, Kingsley argued the kind of democracy that shows an instinctive distrust of the lower classes, in Kingsley's terms a fear of their potential violence. Like many other Victorians, he favored reform while panicking before the idea of democracy. He writes that democracy means a government ". . . by men accustomed to live in Demoi, or corporate bodies, and accustomed, therefore, to the self-control, obedience to law, and self-sacrificing public spirit, without which a corporate body cannot exist: but that a 'democracy' of mere numbers is no democracy, but a mere brute 'arithmocracy,' which is certain to degenerate into an 'ochlocracy,' or government by the mob, in which numbers have no real share: an oligarchy of the fiercest, the noisiest, the rashest, and the most shameless. . . ." He notes further that when the working classes are fit to take their share in government, no power on earth can keep them from taking it; "and that, till then, happy is the man who does the duty which lies nearest him, who educates his family, raises his class, performs his daily work as to God and to his country, not merely to his employer and himself; for it is only he that is faithful over a few things who will be made, or will be happy in being made, ruler over many things."

Ultimately, this is the message that Alton Locke must learn. It is at the root of Kingsley's Christian Socialist Movement, which he formed in 1848, with the help of Thomas Hughes, J. M. Ludlow, and F. D. Maurice. As long as Locke isolates his social and political beliefs from their religious roots, he will find himself in trouble. Furthermore, religious ideas like Locke's early Calvinistic Baptism are inadequate, for such belief squeezes out all joy and insidiously makes the workman accept his lot as God's will. On the contrary, Kingsley's Christianity is a muscular one which frees rather than imprisons, which makes joy a condition of life, and which historically connects contemporary man to the liberating power of Jesus Christ. In the novel, his view is set forth by Lady Ellerton, who preaches the union of Christ and Socialism. Through her, Locke is convinced that the Chartist Movement as it stands is insufficient and that he must now work for the coming of the new order. Near the end of the book after his long struggles as an apprentice tailor, after the expiration of his unjust prison sentence (he spent years in prison for social agitation), after his disillusionment in love, Locke says:

If by a Chartist you mean one who fancies that a change in mere political circumstances will bring about a millennium, I am no longer one. That dream is gone—with others. But if to be a Chartist is to love my brothers with every faculty of my soul—to wish to live and die struggling for their rights, endeavouring to make them, not electors merely, but fit to be electors, senators, kings, and priests to God and to His Christ—if that be the Chartism of the future, then am I sevenfold a Chartist. . . . (XL)

Kingsley, like Dickens, was striving to change men's hearts, a struggle that recurs throughout the century and was to culminate in the work of D. H. Lawrence. Lawrence, in effect, accepted Kingsley's (and Dickens's) argument that the whole man must be activated and not simply the body, but replaced their Christianity with his own notion of "blood consciousness." In the broadest sense, these arguments for the whole man are obviously truisms. We see clearly—as did several Victorians—that no problem is ever alleviated simply by granting higher wages, better working conditions, or better housing, however necessary and moral such elements of welfare may be as stopgap measures. So far, Kingsley is obviously correct. But his argument also takes on the hollow rhetoric of those who, fearing radicalism, caution slowness. It follows that the nineteenth-century working-man must wait until *others* feel he is ready for equality, and then he can assume it. Such advice removes the decision from him, for the assumption is that the *others* are somehow superior in wisdom as well as just and that they will, like Disraeli's "Young Englanders," give way when they recognize readiness.

This is by no means a cogent argument, and therefore the flabby intellectual spine of the novel. While weak here, Kingsley is effective when he shows Locke struggling to raise himself and when he catches his protagonist's envy at those who possess easily what he must strive diligently to obtain. In many ways, the novel foreshadows Gissing's *New Grub Street,* for some of the best scenes show Locke trying to make his way as a writer and gradually compromising his principles in so doing. There are excellent scenes of the poverty-stricken, particularly of the drunken Downes and his dead, starved wife and children, scenes which indicate Kingsley's clear sympathies with the down-trodden and oppressed as long as they do not attempt to think, or act. When Kingsley makes his characters think—Sandy MacKaye, for example, the skeptical Scotsman based on Carlyle—then they become platitudinous or intellectually shallow.

Kingsley himself reveals his romantic, "safe" view of England when Locke visits his wealthy cousin at Cambridge, where he is ashamed of his lower-class appearance. Nevertheless, Kingsley uses the occasion to have Locke admire "fine young Englishmen" rowing and boat-racing on the river, a patriotic outburst that destroys the reader's belief in his views. It is typical Podsnappery: "The true English stuff came out there; I felt that, in spite of all my prejudices—the stuff which has held Gibralter and conquered at Waterloo—which has created a Birmingham and a Manchester, and colonized every quarter of the globe—that grim, earnest, stubborn energy, which since the days of the old Romans, the English possess alone of all the nations of the earth. . . . for I, too, was a man, and an Englishman." It is a mark of Dickens's intellectual superiority that he mocked precisely such views; Kingsley's exalted Manchester is Dickens's Coketown, the "town of unnatural red and black, like the painted face of a savage" that squeezes out blood and spirit.

Despite his sympathy for the poverty-stricken and the desolate, Kingsley has not worn well, but less for the old-fashioned nature of his narrative than for the intellectual assumptions behind the novel. He thought laxly and loosely. Much more lucid and compelling is Meredith's Nevil Beauchamp, who, like Locke, tilts at windmills, only to find himself beaten by internal and external forces he cannot possibly understand. Locke comes out of the fray perhaps a wiser man, certainly a more religious one, but Nevil Beauchamp has probed into the very complex heart of evil and been partially destroyed by it.

4   Anthony Trollope's *Barset*

In the course of his long and, on the whole, favorable essay on Anthony Trollope, Henry James remarks: "There are two kinds of taste in the appreciation of imaginative literature: the taste for emotions of surprise and the taste for emotions of recognition. It is the latter that Trollope gratifies, and he gratifies it the more that the medium of his own mind, through which we see what he shows us, gives a confident direction to our sympathy."

The limitations of Trollope, as well as his strengths, are evident in James's placement of him in the second of the two categories, among those having the ability to provide gratification of the taste for emotions of recognition. Clearly, all great writers gratify both tastes; in fact, their work demonstrates a merging of the two categories, so that no artifical distinction is possible. Trollope is surely not in this company, and among Victorian novelists perhaps only Dickens and George Eliot can be so placed. Yet these qualifications—as Henry James generously indicates—are not to cheapen Trollope's reputation or minimize his considerable accomplishments. There is no question that, standing as he does just below the first rank of nineteenth-century English novelists, he is a fine creator of recognizable people and considerable satire, a writer who envisioned a province, Barset, and peopled it, much as Hardy later filled Wessex and Faulkner, Yoknapatawpha County.

What principally bothers us in Trollope is what also disturbed Henry James. James was incredulous at Trollope's "little slaps at credulity," those frequent intrusions which destroy the fiction of fiction:

. . . but they are even more inexplicable; for they are deliberately inartistic, even judged from the point of view of that rather vague consideration of form which is the only canon we have a right to impose upon Trollope. It is impossible to imagine what a novelist takes himself to be unless he regard himself as an historian and his narrative as a history. It is only as an historian that he has the smallest *locus standi*. As a narrator of fictitious events he is nowhere; to insert into his attempt a back-bone of logic, he must relate events that are assumed to be real.

James cites Balzac as a writer who could no more have thought of admitting that his fiction was fictitious than Garrick would of removing his makeup in the middle of a performance.

If our own age has insisted on any one point, it has demanded that the novelist, poet, and playwright maintain distance from their audience. Twentieth-century art, which is often so obscenely personal, nevertheless must be cast in an impersonal form: the particular anxiety must become the universal wound. Trollope has suffered from his extreme healthy-mindedness; for the very kind of realism which entered into all aspects of his work resulted as well in the personal intrusions. When James paid tribute to him as a meritorious novelist of the usual, he was acknowledging Trollope's common-sensical, balanced, reasonable approach to man and society: a writer who caters to the taste for emotions of recognition. Yet within such reasonableness, fiction is fiction; it is not history, and the novelist is not an historian.

There is one other point which has militated against a wider acceptance of Trollope's gifts. There is an undeniable element of effeminacy in his point of view, particularly in his early work (which has remained more popular than his later, bolder, more astringent fiction). Yet even though somewhat feminine, he is less strong than George Eliot, less ironic than Jane Austen, less forceful than the Brontës. In many passages, he reads like an emasculated Thackeray, which was perhaps an inevitable consequence of his writing so often about clergymen. Even his masculine men seem devoid of their sex; their manner is antiseptic, their touch without feeling, their look cool and innocent. Unlike Richardson, he could not create a Lovelace.

For either reason, or perhaps for both, Trollope's real gifts have often been easily dismissed in serious critical circles. Nevertheless, the life that he evokes in *The Warden* (1855) and *Barchester*

Towers (1857), as well as in the later Barset novels (*Doctor Thorne,* 1858; *Framley Parsonage,* 1860-61; *The Small House at Allington,* 1862-64; *The Last Chronicle of Barset,* 1866-67), is the significant world of the nineteenth-century organization man, with fine black cloth and shovel hats in the place of twentieth-century gray flannel. His archdeacon, Dr. Grantly, is a perfect man of business: efficient, rational, and sincere, particularly when sincerity will not result in foolishness. He is a man of sufficient integrity to pass as a man of integrity. His faith is of course secondary to his social and political role in church affairs, a common enough occurrence in a secular society.

What novelist has caught the secularity of Victorian society more exactly than Trollope, even leaving out of account his savage indictment of greed and materialism in *The Way We Live Now* (1874-75)? Only Dickens before him and Lawrence after were as indignant and vehement. Of course, Trollope was always careful of his audience, and therefore revealed only part of his disdain, or else masked it. We remember that he conceived of his readers as consisting primarily of women; this assumption would also explain his frequent interruptions, many of which seem pointed at female readers interested principally in the romantic elements of the narrative.* Nevertheless, Trollope had a view of society which went considerably beyond the somewhat gentle surfaces of his narratives in which violence, serious injury, and lasting hurts do not exist.

Revealed in his first Barset novels—to take the two which have remained most popular—is an ironic anti-romantic point of view that would have surprised readers who came to his books, so they thought, for romance. One need only compare Scott's romantic rebellious Scotsmen with Trollope's self-seeking, indulgent clergy-

---

* "I [*Trollope*] would not for the value of this chapter have it believed by a single reader that my Eleanor could bring herself to marry Mr. Slope, or that she should be sacrificed to a Bertie Stanhope. But among the good folk of Barchester many believed both the one and the other" (*Barchester Towers,* XV). Or later: "How easily would she [Eleanor] have forgiven and forgotten the archdeacon's suspicions had she but heard the whole truth from Mr. Arabin. But then where would have been my novel? She did not cry, and Mr. Arabin did not melt" (XXX).

men to see how far Victorian England has moved toward accepting what the Romantics had castigated. We recognize that Trollope's clergymen move in the same world and hold the same assumptions as Theobald Pontifex in *The Way of All Flesh*. And what Butler does with Theobald is not far removed from what Trollope does with Dr. Grantly, Mr. Slope, and, inadvertently, even with Mr. Arabin.

Trollope realized that a nineteenth-century clergyman more than anyone moved in a realistic, non-romantic world, depending as he did entirely upon outside monies—benefices, wills, interest—for his living. This situation had of course always been true, but now with the growth of a middle class his income became of greater moment: his class consciousness demanded a standard of living often beyond his immediate reach. Clearly, he cannot work with his own hands to make his way. He must depend only upon his ability to compromise the other world in order to feed his body in this one. Trollope's point is that few people can resist such temptation, and therefore it is absurd to expect the clergyman to be different. ("If we look to our clergymen to be more than men, we shall probably teach ourselves to think that they are less, and can hardly hope to raise the character of the pastor by denying to him the right to entertain the aspirations of a man." [*Barchester Towers,* I). This view seems to have been shared by the great majority of Victorian novelists.

Further, the clergyman by the very nature of his calling moves in an anti-romantic world, for his black-clad figure forbids excesses, looks askance at sexual indulgence, even at romance, outside marriage, denies, in theory at least, the things of this world. His is a closed, rigid world which allows only for the kind of conduct approved by clergymen, as opposed to an open, more adventure-filled, romantic world in which man's actions are optional and he is allowed mobility and freedom of choice. Certainly, Dr. Grantly and even the kindly Mr. Harding are complacent and self-satisfied within their tight island of conduct. The latter reveals his smugness and worldliness when he learns that Eleanor is to marry Mr. Arabin—he approves because the latter is a clergyman, belongs to the same social set as he, and acts with suitable sobriety. Thus, this little world perpetuates itself.

Mr. Arabin himself—described sympathetically by Trollope—allows for no divergence from certain "acceptable" standards of conduct. In his way, he is a denier—of life, of laughter, of independent thought and action. His is the very voice of propriety and righteousness, much tighter and more rigid than Elizabeth Bennet's Darcy, whom he superficially recalls (just as Eleanor Bold superficially recalls Elizabeth). His satirical asides at any deviation from right conduct contain smugness and complacency, unhappy and bitter though he is. In his way, he conveys the sense of a closed society even more than do Jane Austen's characters; after all, they still retain laughter, while Mr. Arabin rarely seeks mirth.

Trollope presents all these clergymen sympathetically. Even Dr. Grantly—despite the author's sly jibes at his materialism and self-righteousness—is basically a decent man within this kind of world. He is, in effect, a norm, in certain ways the best one can expect from human beings. Mr. Harding is also the best one can hope for: gentle, kind, generous, and willing to accept a disproportionately large living as long as he is unaware of the impropriety. It is in this area that Trollope most reveals himself, for the side effects of his presentation are often more than he bargained for. Unintentionally, in his presentation of Mr. Arabin he indicates a man he approves of as the best in this society, and yet Mr. Arabin, except for his notions of integrity, is virtually a mockery of an acceptable human being. In nearly every respect, as we have seen, he is not only anti-license, he is anti-life, the kind of fellow D. H. Lawrence would have made into a cuckold or killed off in a snowstorm.

In a society in which Mr. Arabin is admired and a Mr. Slope makes his way, a Madame Neroni is almost welcome despite her transparent airs, her false dignity, and her languid artiness. In her fashion, she too, like Thackeray's Becky, is of course anti-romantic, for her view of love, marriage, and romance is cynical and mocking. Madame Neroni toys with those who are falsely romantic and those who approach love with the assumptions of egoists. Give Trollope a bit more freedom and his Madame Neroni could be a comic freeing force. However, within a closed, rigid society, she must, like Mary Crawford in *Mansfield Park,* be contained so that her real powers of temptation have no further repercussions. Accordingly, despite her wonderful sense of comedy, Madame Neroni is presented as vulgar and coarse; she would, clearly, emasculate any man who wooed, no less married, her.

In any closed society, the energetic, rebellious ones must always be castigated. Since they fail to play according to the established rules, their motives must be discredited. This is obviously society's way of restraining them to protect its own established interests. Trollope assumes that this attitude is necessary, as did Jane Austen and Thackeray before him. Yet for the time Madame Neroni is on stage, all others fall before her. When she outstares the Countess De Courcy, when she reduces Squire Thorne to virtual tears at her unhappy plight, when she dangles Mr. Slope at the end of her languid finger, she upsets all pre-conceived notions and threatens to topple their worlds. Like Meredith's comic imps, she rushes in wherever man's egoism provides an opening.

All this is to say that Trollope is excellent in catching people, but weak in inventing situations. His eye caught details of appearance and behavior that only the comic eye can find, but his basic assumptions—his acceptance of the very things he gently satirized— made it impossible for him to progress from the stereotyped situations he presented. He had little of Dickens's range, little of George Eliot's power of interpretation. Without these elements, it was inevitable that he should fail to project his characters into meaningful dramatic situations. Even in books like *Orley Farm* (1861-62) and *The Eustace Diamonds* (1871-73), and the political novels (*Phineas Finn,* 1867-69; *Phineas Redux,* 1873-74; *The Prime Minister,* 1875-76), Trollope wrote about unusual situations but failed either to dramatize them or exploit their possibilities.

In John Bold, for example, Trollope had a man who potentially was capable of a broad range of interests, who had money and mobility, who had views that cut across the accepted attitudes of his day. John Bold is a "new man," that is, a crusader who rejects the platitudes received as gospel by Dr. Grantly and Mr. Harding; the age of the gentleman was passing into the age of the reformer and the bold man who relies upon public outrage to gain his ends. In Bold, Trollope had a character quite out of the ordinary in his early fiction, and yet he does little with the man, before conveniently killing him off between *The Warden* and *Barchester Towers.*

We see too little of Bold in action, and when his audacious moves might have really led him into new areas he is gently eliminated from contention, to make way for the more solid Arabin.

Thus, in these novels, and later, Trollope was on the trail of many significant things even when he failed to follow fully the direction of his thought. However, compared as he inevitably is with Dickens, Thackeray, and, later, George Eliot, his considerable talents appear to suffer. Never a full critic of rank and social classes, rarely an incisive commentator on a wide range of human foibles, only sporadically a creator of interesting situations, Trollope nevertheless meaningfully caught important aspects of Victorian life. Even the people upon whom we look askance, and whom Trollope obviously supports, gain fullness from his cynicism and frank realism. Like Jane Austen, he was indeed a hero of the usual and the trivial.

5　*New Grub Street,* by George Gissing

Gissing's views in most of his major novels—*The Unclassed* (1884), *Demos* (1886), *The Nether World* (1889) *Born in Exile* (1891), and *New Grub Street* (1892)—pretend to far less than Hardy's sense of metaphysical torment. Like Biffin in *New Grub Street,* he aimed at a merciless realism which would not allow him to accept Hardy's sense of heightened tragedy. To make the novel tragic, Biffen claims, is to borrow from the drama, not to work within the limitations of the novel. Gissing's drabness, however, is not so much the result of his rejection of man's potential heroism, as it is his dislike for those he wrote about. Hardy was able to give the dimension of tragedy even to "small" people because he felt sufficient sympathy for them and could see their lives as tragic events. The same is true of Dickens, perhaps the chief literary influence upon Gissing. Comedy may derive from disdain of humanity, but tragedy or a tragic view must be based on sympathy and identification with the victim.

Further, Gissing seems to have turned to a drab view of the world because of his own depression rather than because of any identification with the hopes and needs of those who live drably. In this sense, Gissing creates little life outside of his own sense of misery; and since valid characters cannot be created within this limitation, they inevitably appear a homogeneous group, often merely duplicated from one book to another. In *Demos,* for example, although Gissing's material calls for a sympathetic treatment of the poor, he seems actually disdainful: poverty becomes equivalent to sin. The alternative is not of course to find poverty ennobling, or to romanticize it, but merely to identify with those for whom trivial incidents and fateful circumstances are tragic. Poverty was itself so immense an experience in Gissing's own life that, unlike Dickens, he could not begin to look upon it reasonably, or get even a little beyond it to see it objectively. It remained a nightmare perhaps because he turned in distaste from its uncleanliness, its lack of dignity, its inescapable noisomeness. For Gissing, there was little dignity in adapting to one's condition when it could not be changed.

Gissing's beliefs are briefly suggested in *The Unclassed* when Waymark contrasts Christ and Prometheus, or Pessimism and Optimism. Christ advocates abnegation of self, denial of the very will to live. Prometheus, on the contrary, defies limitations: his theft of fire indicates man's acquisition of a conscious will or soul. "But Prometheus is saved in a different way from Adam; not by renunciation, but by the prowess of Hercules, that is to say, the triumphant aspiration of Humanity. Man triumphs by asserting his right to do so. Self-consciousness he claims as a good thing, and embraces the world as his birthright. Here, you see, there is no room for the crushing sense of sin. Sin, if anything, is weakness." Like several other *fin de siècle* writers—in particular the poet John Davidson—Gissing was concerned with the human will, its powers, its energies, its ultimate direction. He rebelled against acquiescence; he revolted against denial and negation. In this view, poverty circumscribed the assertion of will, forcing an inaction and inertia that deny man's Promethean drive toward self-consciousness. Like a form of sin, poverty negates man's will to achieve his birthright: freedom of choice and the pursuit of personal happiness, the twin points of frustration in virtually every Gissing character.

As Biffen remarks in *New Grub Street,* the life he wishes to portray, the "sphere of the ignobly decent," "ordinary vulgar life," is "unutterably tedious." Thus, Biffen tries to catch the sense of monotony in poverty. He comments further that if he presented life as anything else it would be untrue, perhaps melodramatic, as in Dickens's work. One cannot even laugh, he claims, for laughter is an imposition upon life, and his guide is "Let us copy life." The realistic-naturalistic novel as he conceived it is to go beyond Zola, who created deliberate tragedies by heroizing even his villains.

Biffen's outline for his own novel is fairly close to what Gissing himself did in his representative novels. *New Grub Street* is a partial exception, perhaps, to this deadening doctrine, and that is why Gissing here was able to transcend his other work. Even so, *New Grub Street* is rarely a novel of Life. It is more a fiction of ideas, and even those are small and circumscribed ones. It gains its distinction from Gissing's inside knowledge of London literary life rather than from anything the novelist has created. London's literary world is presented like one of Zola's well-researched and documented slices of life, whether in a laundry or a mine or a bar, but without Zola's selection of events and circumstances that convey the feel and arrangement we expect from literature. Gissing offers the matter straight: literature is simply an attractively packaged commodity. Not one disinterested writer passes through Gissing's book; all are frauds, materialists, expedient. Even his suffering protagonist, Edwin Reardon, comes to heel and forsakes the serious, psychological novel to attempt a popular pot-boiler, which, incidentally, he cannot do well.

Gissing's point, taken over from naturalism, is that once circumstances have conjoined to make Reardon hit the skids, his disintegration is complete. He must fail, not as a heroic writer trying to do his best, but as a hack who cannot even do hack-work well. His marriage itself must come apart, for Reardon has married above his class, and as soon as he cannot maintain his standard of living his mate will not linger to share his misfortunes. Thus, on every side Reardon is frustrated: Gissing's view of what happens to a man who attempts to rise beyond his role and who encounters circumstances which inevitably limit him severely.

Reardon is, of course, an honest man, and honesty in the London literary world leads to disaster. Since literature is merely a commodity and has no other significance, it provides neither pleasure nor a sense of achievement for the creator; it is simply a means to wealth and power. Reardon, however, believes in certain ideals, one of which is that literature has a moral and social function. In his early novels, which never caught on, he insisted on serious literature, perhaps the kind of fiction which Gissing himself wrote in *Workers in the Dawn* (1880), *The Unclassed, Demos, Isabel Clarendon* (1886), *Thyrza* (1887), and *The Nether World* (1889). Unlike the numerous literary hangers-on, who feed upon literature, Reardon went directly to the heart of the problem: to create fiction which others could write about. He aimed high, and he fell low.

As against Reardon, in an obvious diagrammatic opposition, is Jasper Milvain, who seeks success in the literary world by giving his editors and audience precisely what they want: trivial essays, insignificant sketches, literary gossip for those who want to be "inside" but who do not wish to read seriously. With a vast reading-public awaiting him, Jasper finds it foolish to disappoint its expectations. And in providing fuel for the fire, he achieves proportionately as much success as Reardon receives disappointment. A Milvain rises only as a Reardon falls.

Surrounding these two opposing forces is a small army of literary plodders, those who make a living from literature without possessing any particular talent. They are little more than Literary Machines. Marian Yule, whose father is himself such a second-rater, is tied to meaningless research in the British Museum to provide fodder for Mr. Yule's articles. She recognizes the complete futility of her work and those who work like her: "When already there was more good literature in the world than any mortal could cope with in his lifetime, here was she exhausting herself in the manufacturing of printed stuff which no one even pretended to be more than a commodity for the day's market." She thinks of her father, who lacks real talent and writes only about other writing, who makes new books out of those already existing, all in a "trackless desert of print." She thinks of a Literary Machine that would efficiently turn out books and articles and relieve her of the thankless chore.

In such areas, where relatively untalented people are attempting to hang on, Gissing is effective, for this kind of material is quite suitable for his brand of hopeless realism. But when he moves into the larger areas where a novel either takes on substance or drifts into inconsequence, then he reveals the limitations of his pre-cut plan. As part of the fate of every unlucky man is a woman who fails to understand the canker eating at his soul. Marriage based on a mild passion raised to the temporary frenzy we call love can only be destructive. As Jasper Milvain argues, a true marriage is based less on love than on money, position, mutual agreement on what passes for the good life. Marriage to a poor woman as the consequence of a strong attachment is suicidal, as Reardon and a whole host of Gissing protagonists discover. Once again, this arrangement is too fixed, too diagrammatic, tending to make most Gissing women arbitrarily into bitches and their men into fools.

What is perhaps of most interest in a Gissing novel—more important than what the novel says—is what it suggests about his world. The chief element for Gissing, as later for Orwell, is disgust. His is a fiction of dissatisfaction in which almost no human connection brings happy results unless it is initially based on cynical material assumptions. Only a Jasper Milvain can be happy, and yet Gissing obviously hates the egoistic young man and his vapid aspirations. Thus, no matter which way Gissing was to turn— whether toward his sincere poverty-stricken writers or toward his superficial and compromised gossip-mongers—he found little to embrace. The former he disdained for their futility, the latter for their expedience. In between there is no joy, no sense of creativity, no regard for values, nothing to sustain the human spirit. Gissing does not even have the optimism to go along with the art-for-art's-sake group, which rejected what he rejected, only to embrace what he found unsatisfactory. Further, he clearly did not share the sympathies of the realists and naturalists with their subject matter. As we have seen, he found poverty and poor people revolting, dangerous, a threat to civilized values.

What remains of significance, then, is Gissing's sense of nausea, the kind we usually associate with later twentieth-century existential writers. In actuality, however, Gissing's fiction is not isolated; it is bordered on one side by Hardy's and on the other by early Conrad's. While Gissing does not have their sense of moral outrage, he nevertheless does indicate their tone of bafflement and hopelessness. He is perhaps even more baffled and hopeless than they because he rejected their implied heroism: for example, that of the Mayor of Casterbridge or of Conrad's Kurtz and Jim. Gissing's men of stature are on a much smaller scale, almost approximately those in Biffen's novel "Mr. Bailey, Grocer." Gissing leads into authors like James T. Farrell and George Orwell, but he is possibly more aware of tedium, more burdened by the deadening weight of existence itself.

Gissing's work remains as a blob of pain, a tortured outcry that could not lead to any solution or even to any definition of the problem. Much of it was surely an outgrowth of his own sensibility, of his absurdly bad marriages and relationships with women, of internal forces operating that precluded the possibility of happiness or contentment for him. Nevertheless, at his best, in *New Grub Street,* his personal anguish reaches a somewhat more general level, and at these moments his blob of pain stains the entire world.

An Age of Fiction—Selected Criticism and Scholarship

Allen, Walter. *The English Novel*, 1958.

Altick, Richard. *The English Common Reader, 1800-1900*, 1957.

Baker, Joseph E., ed. *The Reinterpretation of Victorian Literature*, 1950.

Booth, Wayne. *The Rhetoric of Fiction*, 1962.

Briggs, Asa. *Victorian Cities*, 1963.

————. *Victorian People*, 1954.

Brown, Alan. *The Metaphysical Society, Victorian Minds in Crisis, 1869-1880*, 1947.

Buckley, Jerome Hamilton. *The Victorian Temper: A Study in Literary Culture*, 1951.

Burn, W. L. *The Age of Equipoise*, 1964.

Cecil, Lord David. *Early Victorian Novelists: Essays in Revaluation*, 1935.

Cook, Albert. *The Meaning of Fiction*, 1960.

Coveney, Peter. *Poor Monkey: The Child in Literature*, 1957.

Cruse, Amy. *The Victorians and Their Books*, 1935.

Dalziel, Margaret. *Popular Fiction 100 Years Ago*, 1957.

Decker, Clarence R. *The Victorian Conscience*, 1952.

Engels, Friedrich. *The Condition of the Working Class in England in 1844*, 1952.

Forster, E. M. *Aspects of the Novel*, 1927.

Hollingsworth, Keith. *The Newgate Novel, 1830-1847*, 1963.

Holloway, John. *The Victorian Sage: Studies in Argument*, 1953.

Hough, Graham. *The Last Romantics*, 1949.

Howe, Susanne. *Novels of Empire,* 1949.

———. *Wilhelm Meister and His English Kinsman,* 1930.

James, Louis. *Fiction for the Working Man, 1830-1850,* 1963.

Karl, Frederick R. and Magalaner, Marvin. *A Reader's Guide to Great Twentieth-Century English Novels* (the Introduction), 1959.

Kettle, Arnold. *An Introduction to the English Novel,* 2 vols., 1960.

Leavis, F. R. *The Great Tradition,* 1954.

Leavis, Q. D. *Fiction and the Reading Public,* 1932.

Lubbock, Percy. *The Craft of Fiction,* 1926.

Maison, Margaret. *Search Your Soul, Eustace: A Survey of the Religious Novel in the Victorian Age,* 1961.

Miller, J. Hillis. *The Disappearance of God,* 1963.

Moers, Ellen. *The Dandy: Brummell to Beerbohm,* 1960.

Neff, Emery. *Carlyle and Mill: An Introduction to Victorian Thought,* 1924.

Parrott, Thomas Marc and Martin, Robert Bernard. *A Companion to Victorian Literature,* 1955.

Peckham, Morse. *Beyond the Tragic Vision,* 1962.

Praz, Mario. *The Hero in Eclipse in Victorian Fiction,* trans. by Angus Davidson, 1956.

———. *The Romantic Agony,* trans. by Angus Davidson, 1933.

Pritchett, V. S. *The Living Novel,* 1946.

Rosa, Matthew W. *The Silver-Fork School,* 1936.

Routh, H. V. *Towards the Twentieth Century,* 1937.

Sadleir, Michael. *XIX Century Fiction: A Bibliographical Record Based on His Own Collection,* 2 vols., 1951.

Schilling, Bernard. *Human Dignity and the Great Victorians,* 1946.

Stang, Richard. *The Theory of the Novel in England, 1850-1870,* 1959.

Stevenson, Lionel. *Darwin Among the Poets,* 1932.

———. *The English Novel,* 1960.

Summers, Montague. *The Gothic Quest,* 1938.

Thomson, David. *England in the Nineteenth Century (1815-1914),* 1950.

Thomas, Patricia. *The Victorian Heroine,* 1956.

Tillotson, Kathleen. *Novels of the Eighteen-Forties,* 1954.

Tomkins, J. M. S. *The Popular Novel in England, 1770-1800,* 1932.

Trevelyan, G. M. *History of England,* vol. III, 1952.

Turner, E. S. *Boys Will Be Boys,* 1948.

Van Ghent, Dorothy. *The English Novel: Form and Function,* 1953.

Varma, Devendra. *The Gothic Flame,* 1957.

Watt, Ian. *The Rise of the Novel,* 1957.

Willey, Basil. *Nineteenth Century Studies*, 1949.
Williams, Raymond. *Culture and Society, 1780-1950*, 1958.
Wright, Austin, ed. *Victorian Literature: Modern Essays in Criticism*, 1961.
Young, G. M. *Victorian England: Portrait of an Age*, 1953.

Jane Austen—Works

NOVELS

Sense and Sensibility, 1811 (first known as *Elinor and Marianne*).
Pride and Prejudice, 1813 (first known as *First Impressions*).
Mansfield Park, 1814.
Emma, 1816.
Northanger Abbey, 1818 (first known as *Susan*).
Persuasion, 1818.

JUVENILIA

Love and Friendship, 1790; Fragments—*Lady Susan*, ca. 1794; *The Watsons*, begun in 1803 or 1804.
Letters to her Sister Cassandra, ed. R. W. Chapman, 1932, 1952.
Letters, 1796-1817, ed. R. W. Chapman, 1955.

SELECTED CRITICISM AND SCHOLARSHIP

Austen-Leigh, J. E. *Memoir of Jane Austen*, 1926.
————. W. & R. A. *Jane Austen, Her Life and Letters*, 1913.
Babb, Howard S. *Jane Austen's Novels: The Fabric of Dialogue*, 1962.
Chapman, R. A. *A Critical Bibliography*, 1953.
————. *Jane Austen—Facts and Problems*, 1950.
Jenkins, Elizabeth. *Jane Austen*, 1949.
Lascelles, Mary. *Jane Austen and Her Art*, 1939.
Mudrick, Marvin. *Jane Austen: Irony as Defense and Discovery*, 1952.
Wright, Andrew. *Jane Austen's Novels: A Study in Structure*, 1954.

Jane Austen: A Collection of Critical Essays, edited by Ian Watt, 1963.
"Pride and Prejudice": Text, Backgrounds, Criticism, edited by Bradford A. Booth, 1963.

Sir Walter Scott—Works

NOVELS

Waverley, 1814.
Guy Mannering, 1815.
The Antiquary, 1816.
Tales of My Landlord (*The Black Dwarf* and *Old Mortality*), 1817.
Rob Roy, 1817.
Tales of My Landlord, second series (*The Heart of Midlothian*), 1818.
Tales of My Landlord, third series (*The Bride of Lammermoor* and *A Legend of Montrose*), 1819.
Ivanhoe, 1820.
The Monastery, 1820.
The Abbot, 1820.
Kenilworth, 1821.
The Pirate, 1822.
The Fortunes of Nigel, 1822.
Peveril of the Peak, 1822.
Quentin Durward, 1823.
St. Ronan's Well, 1824.
Redgauntlet, 1824.
Tales of the Crusaders (*The Betrothed* and *The Talisman*), 1825.
Woodstock, 1826.
Chronicles of the Canongate (*The Highland Widow, The Two Drovers,* and *The Surgeon's Daughter*), 1827.
Chronicles of the Canongate, second series (*The Fair Maid of Perth*), 1828.
Anne of Geierstein, 1829.
Tales of My Landlord, fourth series (*Count Robert of Paris* and *Castle Dangerous*), 1832.

POETRY

The Lay of the Last Minstrel, 1805; *Marmion*, 1808; *The Lady of the Lake*, 1810; *The Vision of Don Roderick*, 1811; *Rokeby*, 1813; *The Bridal of Triermain*, 1813; *The Lord of the Isles*, 1815; *Harold the Dauntless*, 1817.

EDITIONS

The Minstrelsy of the Scottish Border, 1802-03; *The Border Antiquities of England and Scotland*, 1814-17; *Provincial Antiquities of Scotland*, 1819-26; *Lives of the Novelists*, 1821-24; *Life of Napoleon Buonaparte*, 1827; *Tales of a Grandfather*, 1828-31; *History of Scotland*, 1829-30; *The Works of Dryden*, 1808; *The Works of Swift*, 1814.

TRANSLATIONS

Bürger's *Lenore*, 1795; Goethe's *Goetz*, 1799.
Journal (1825-32), 1890.
The Letters of Sir Walter Scott, 12 vols., edited by H. J. C. Grierson, 1932-37.

Selected Criticism and Scholarship

Corson, James Clarkson. *A Bibliography of Sir Walter Scott*, 1943.
Davie, Donald. *The Heyday of Sir Walter Scott*, 1961.
Fiske, C. F. *Epic Suggestions in the Imagery of the Waverley Novels*, 1940.
Grierson, H. J. C. *Sir Walter Scott, Bart.*, 1938.
Hillhouse, J. T. *The Waverley Novels and Their Critics*, 1936.
Lockhart, J. G. *The Life of Sir Walter Scott*, 8 vols., 1837-38.
———. *Life of Scott*, in 1 vol., Everyman ed., 1906.
Pearson, Hesketh. *Walter Scott: His Life and Personality*, 1954.
Pope-Hennessy, Una. *Sir Walter Scott*, 1948.
Ruskin, John. *Fors Clavigera*, Letter No. 31, July 1, 1873.
Welsh, Alexander. *The Hero of the Waverley Novels*, 1963.

Daiches, David. "Scott's Achievement as a Novelist," *Literary Essays*, 1956.
Hazlitt, William. "Sir Walter Scott," *The Spirit of the Age*, 1825.

The Brontës—Works

NOVELS

Anne Brontë: *Agnes Grey*, 1847; *The Tenant of Wildfell Hall*, 1848.
Charlotte Brontë: *Jane Eyre*, 1847; *Shirley*, 1849; *Villette*, 1853; *The Professor*, 1857.
Emily Brontë: *Wuthering Heights*, 1847.

Selected Criticism and Scholarship

Bentley, Phyllis. *The Brontës*, 1947.
Crandall, Norma. *Emily Brontë: A Psychological Portrait*, 1957.
Gaskell, Elizabeth. *Life of Charlotte Brontë*, 2 vols., 1857.
Hanson, Laurence & E. M. *The Four Brontës*, 1949.
Hinkley, Laura. *The Brontës: Charlotte and Emily*, 1945.
Hopkins, A. B. *The Father of the Brontës*, 1958.
Paden, W. *An Investigation of Gondal*, 1958.
Ratchford, Fannie E. *The Brontës' Web of Childhood*, 1941
Shorter, Clement. *The Brontës and Their Circle*, 1917.
————. *The Brontës: Life and Letters*, 2 vols., 1908.
Stanford, Derek and Muriel Spark. *Anne Brontë*, 1959.
Visick, Mary. *The Genesis of Wuthering Heights*, 1958.

Chase, Richard. "The Brontës, or, Myth Domesticated," *Kenyon Review*, 1947.
Schorer, Mark. "Fiction and the Analogical Matrix," *Kenyon Review*, 1949.

Charles Dickens—Works

NOVELS, STORIES, TRAVEL NOTES, AND HISTORY

Sketches by Boz, 1833-36.
The Pickwick Papers, 1836-37.
Oliver Twist, 1837-38.
Nicholas Nickleby, 1838-39.
The Old Curiosity Shop, 1840-41.
Barnaby Rudge, 1841.
American Notes, 1842.
Martin Chuzzlewit, 1843-44.
Christmas Books, 1843-48.
Pictures from Italy, 1846.
Dombey and Son, 1847-48.
David Copperfield, 1849-50.
Bleak House, 1852-53.
A Child's History of England, 1852-54.
Hard Times, 1854.

Little Dorrit, 1857-58.
A Tale of Two Cities, 1859.
Great Expectations, 1860-61.
Our Mutual Friend, 1864.
The Mystery of Edwin Drood (unfinished), 1870.

Letters of Charles Dickens, 3 vols., edited by Walter Dexter, 1938. A greatly expanded edition of the complete letters will be published in the near future.
Charles Dickens and Maria Beadnell: A Private Correspondence, edited by George P. Baker, 1908.
Letters of Charles Dickens to Wilkie Collins, edited by Lawrence Hutton, 1892.
Letters of Charles Dickens to the Baroness Burdett-Coutts, edited by Charles C. Osborne, 1931.
The Heart of Charles Dickens, as Revealed in His Letters to Angela Burdett-Coutts, edited by Edgar Johnson, 1952.
Selected Letters, edited by F. W. Dupee, 1960.

Selected Criticism and Scholarship

Adrian, Arthur A. *Georgina Hogarth and the Dickens Circle*, 1957.
Butt, John and Tillotson, Kathleen. *Dickens at Work*, 1957.
Chesterton, Gilbert Keith. *Charles Dickens: A Critical Study*, 1913.
Cockshut, A. O. J. *The Imagination of Charles Dickens*, 1961.
Ford, George H. *Dickens and His Readers: Aspects of Novel-Criticism Since 1836*, 1955.
Ford, George H. and Lane, Lauriat, Jr. *The Dickens Critics*, 1961.
Forster, John. *Life of Charles Dickens*, edited by J. W. T. Ley, 1928.
Gissing, George. *The Immortal Dickens*, 1898.
House, Humphry. *The Dickens World*, 1941.
————. *All in Due Time* (Part III), 1955.
Johnson, Edgar. *Charles Dickens: His Tragedy and Triumph*, 2 vols., 1952.
Lindsay, Jack. *Charles Dickens: A Biographical and Critical Study*, 1950.
Pearson, Hesketh. *Dickens: His Character, Comedy, and Career*, 1949.

Orwell, George, in *Dickens, Dali, & Others*, 1940.
Wilson, Edmund, in *The Wound and the Bow*, 1941.

William Makepeace Thackeray—Works

NOVELS, SATIRES, AND ESSAYS

Catherine, 1839-40.
A Shabby-Genteel Story, 1840.
The Paris Sketch-Book, 1840.
The History of Samuel Titmarsh and the Great Hoggarty Diamond,
    1841.
The Fitz-Boodle Papers and Men's Wives, 1842-43.
The Irish Sketch-Book, 1843.
The Luck of Barry Lyndon, 1844.
The History of the Next French Revolution (in *Punch*), 1844.
Jeames's Diary (in *Punch*), 1845-46.
The Snobs of England, by One of Themselves (in *Punch*): *The Book
    of Snobs*, 1848.
Christmas Books, 1847-57.
Vanity Fair, 1847-48.
The History of Pendennis, 1848-50.
The History of Henry Esmond, 1852.
The English Humourists of the Eighteenth-Century, 1853.
The Newcomes, 1853-55.
The Virginians, 1857-59.
Lovel the Widower, 1860.
The Four Georges, 1860.
The Adventures of Philip, 1861-62.
Denis Duval (unfinished), 1864.

The Letters and Private Papers of William Makepeace Thackeray,
    edited by Gordon Ray, 4 vols., 1945-46.

Selected Criticism and Scholarship

Dodds, John W. *Thackeray: A Critical Portrait*, 1941.
Greig, John Y. T. *Thackeray: A Reconsideration*, 1950.
Mudge, Isadore G. and Sears, Earl H., eds. *A Thackeray Dictionary*,
    1910.
Ray, Gordon. *The Buried Life*, 1952.
———. *Thackeray: The Uses of Adversity*, 1955; *The Age of Wisdom*,
    1958.

Stevenson, Lionel. *The Showman of Vanity Fair*, 1947.
Tillotson, Geoffrey. *Thackeray the Novelist*, 1954.

George Meredith—Works

NOVELS

The Shaving of Shagpat, 1856.
Farina, 1857.
The Ordeal of Richard Feverel, 1859.
Evan Harrington, 1861.
Emilia in England (Sandra Belloni), 1864.
Rhoda Fleming, 1865.
Vittoria, 1867.
The Adventures of Harry Richmond, 1871.
Beauchamp's Career, 1876.
On the Idea of Comedy and the Uses of the Comic Spirit, 1877.
The House on the Beach (short stories), 1877.
The Egoist, 1877.
The Tragic Comedians, 1880.
Diana of the Crossways, 1885.
One of Our Conquerors, 1891.
Lord Ormont and His Aminta, 1894.
The Amazing Marriage, 1895.
Celt and Saxon (published posthumously and incompletely).

POETRY

Modern Love, 1862; *Poems and Lyrics of the Joy of Earth*, 1863; *Ballads and Poems of Tragic Life*, 1887; *A Reading of Earth*, 1888; *A Reading of Life*, 1901; *Last Poems*, 1909.

Letters of George Meredith to Alice Meynell, 1923.
The Collected Letters of George Meredith, edited by C. L. Cline, 3 vols., 1968.

Selected Criticism and Scholarship

Beach, Joseph Warren. *The Comic Spirit in Meredith*, 1911.

Forman, Maurice Buxton. *A Bibliography of the Writings in Prose and Verse of George Meredith*, 1922.

————. ed. *George Meredith: Some Early Appreciations*, 1909.

Kelvin, Norman. *A Troubled Eden: Nature and Society in the Works of George Meredith*, 1961.

Lindsay, Jack. *George Meredith: His Life and Work*, 1956.

Priestley, J. B. *George Meredith*, 1926.

Stevenson, Lionel. *The Ordeal of George Meredith*, 1953.

Wright, Walter. *Art and Substance in George Meredith*, 1953.

George Eliot—Works

NOVELS

Scenes of Clerical Life (1857-58).
Adam Bede, 1859.
The Mill on the Floss, 1860.
Silas Marner, 1861.
Romola, 1863.
Felix Holt the Radical, 1866.
Middlemarch, 1871-72.
Daniel Deronda, 1876.

SHORT STORIES

"The Lifted Veil," 1859; "Brother Jacob," 1864.

POETRY

The Spanish Gypsy, 1868; *The Legend of Jubal and Other Poems*, 1874.

ESSAYS

The Impressions of Theophrastus Such, 1879; *Early Essays*, 1919; *Essays of George Eliot*, ed. by Thomas Pinney, 1963.

TRANSLATIONS

The Life of Jesus by D. F. Strauss, 1846; *The Essence of Christianity* by L. Feuerbach, 1854.

The George Eliot Letters, 7 vols., ed. by Gordon Haight, 1954-56.

Selected Criticism and Scholarship

Beaty, Jerome. *Middlemarch: from Notebook to Novel: A Study of George Eliot's Creative Method*, 1960.
Bennett, Joan. *George Eliot: Her Mind and Her Art*, 1948.
Cross, J. W. *George Eliot's Life as Related in Her Letters and Journals*, 1884.
Haight, Gordon. *George Eliot and John Chapman, with Chapman's Diaries*, 1940.
Hanson, Laurence & E. M. *Marian Evans and George Eliot*, 1952.
Hardy, Barbara. *The Novels of George Eliot: A Study in Form*, 1959.
Harvey, William John. *The Art of George Eliot*, 1961.
Stang, Richard, ed. *Discussions of George Eliot*, 1960.
Stump, Reva. *Moment and Vision in George Eliot's Novels*, 1959.

Thomas Hardy—Works

NOVELS

Desperate Remedies, 1871.
Under the Greenwood Tree, 1872.
A Pair of Blue Eyes, 1873.
Far from the Madding Crowd, 1874.
The Hand of Ethelberta, 1876.
The Return of the Native, 1878.
The Trumpet-Major, 1880.
A Laodicean, 1881.
Two on a Tower, 1882.
The Mayor of Casterbridge, 1886.
The Woodlanders, 1887.
Tess of the D'Urbervilles, 1891.
The Well-Beloved, 1892.
Jude the Obscure, 1896.

POETRY

Wessex Poems, 1898; *Poems of the Past and Present*, 1902; *The Dynasts* (Part I, 1904; II, 1906; III, 1908); *Time's Laughing-Stocks*, 1909; *Satires of Circumstance*, 1914; *Moments of Vision*, 1917.

Letters, edited by Carl J. Weber, 1954.

Selected Criticism and Scholarship

Beach, Joseph Warren. *The Technique of Thomas Hardy*, 1922.
Brennecke, Ernest, Jr. *Thomas Hardy's Universe*, 1926.
———, ed. *Life and Art by Thomas Hardy*, 1925.
Cecil, Lord David. *Hardy, the Novelist*, 1943.
Chase, Mary Ellen. *Thomas Hardy, from Serial to Novel*, 1927.
Firor, Ruth. *Folkways in Thomas Hardy*, 1931.
Guerard, Albert. *Thomas Hardy: the Novels and Stories*, 1949.
Hardy, Evelyn. *Thomas Hardy: A Critical Biography*, 1954.
Hardy, Florence. *The Life of Thomas Hardy, 1840-1928* (combines *The Early Life* and *The Later Years*), 1962.
Hynes, Samuel Lynn. *The Pattern of Hardy's Poetry*, 1961.
Lawrence, D. H. *Thomas Hardy* (in *Phoenix*), 1936.
Purdy, Richard Little. *Thomas Hardy: A Bibliographical Study*, 1954.
Southworth, James Granville. *The Poetry of Thomas Hardy*, 1947.
Rutland, William. *Thomas Hardy: A Study of His Writings and Their Background*, 1938.
Weber, Carl J. *Hardy of Wessex*, 1940.
Webster, Harvey. *On a Darkling Plain: the Art and Thought of Thomas Hardy*, 1947.
Hardy: A Collection of Critical Essays, edited by Albert Guerard, 1963.
Modern Fiction Studies: Hardy Number, VI, 3 (Autumn, 1960).
The Southern Review: Thomas Hardy Centennial Issue, VI (Summer, 1940).

Five Victorian Novelists—
Selected Criticism and Scholarship

BENJAMIN DISRAELI

Masefield, Muriel. *Peacocks and Primroses: A Study of Disraeli's Novels,* 1953.
Monypenny, W. F. and Buckle, G. E. *The Life of Benjamin Disraeli, Earl of Beaconsfield,* rev. ed., 2 vols., 1929.

SAMUEL BUTLER

Cole, G. D. H. *Samuel Butler and The Way of All Flesh,* 1947.
Jones, H. F. *Samuel Butler: A Memoir,* 2 vols., 1919.
Muggeridge, Malcolm. *The Earnest Atheist: A Study of Samuel Butler,* 1936.

CHARLES KINGSLEY

Kingsley, F. E., ed. *Charles Kingsley: His Letters and Memories of His Life,* 2 vols., 1877.
Pope-Hennessy, Una. *Canon Charles Kingsley,* 1948.

ANTHONY TROLLOPE

Booth, Bradford A. *Anthony Trollope: Aspects of His Life and Art,* 1958.
————, ed. *The Letters of Anthony Trollope,* 1951.
Cockshut, A. O. J. *Anthony Trollope: A Critical Study,* 1955.
Sadleir, Michael. *Trollope: A Commentary,* 1945.

GEORGE GISSING

Donnelly, Mabel Collins. *George Gissing: Grave Comedian,* 1954.
Gissing, Algernon and Ellen, eds. *Letters of George Gissing to Members of His Family,* 1927.
Gapp, S. V. *George Gissing, Classicist,* 1936.
Korg, Jacob. *George Gissing: A Critical Biography,* 1963.

Character Index

Index